Film posters for Robert Siodmak's *The Dark Mirror* (*Variety*, October 16, 1946).

The Dark Mirror

German Cinema between
Hitler and Hollywood

LUTZ KOEPNICK

University of California Press

BERKELEY   LOS ANGELES   LONDON

University of California Press
Berkeley and Los Angeles, California

University of California Press, Ltd.
London, England

Portions of the following have been significantly reconceptualized and rewritten and are
used by permission: "Unsettling America: German Westerns and Modernity,"
Modernism/Modernity 2, no. 3 (1995): 1–22; "Siegfried Rides Again: Westerns,
Technology, and the Third Reich," *Cultural Studies* 11, no. 3 (October 1997): 418–442;
"En-Gendering Mass Culture: The Case of Zarah Leander," in *Gender and Germanness:
Cultural Productions of Nation,* ed. Patricia Herminghouse and Magda Mueller
(Providence: Berghahn Books, 1997), 161–175; "Screening Fascism's Underground:
Kurt Bernhardt's *The Tunnel,*" *New German Critique* 74 (spring/summer 1998): 151–
178; and "Sirk and the Culture Industry: *Zu neuen Ufern* and *The First Legion,*" *Film
Criticism* 23, nos. 2–3 (winter/spring 1999): 94–121.

Library of Congress Cataloging-in-Publication Data

Koepnick, Lutz P. (Lutz Peter)
  The dark mirror : German cinema between Hitler and Hollywood / Lutz Koepnick.
    p.   cm.   (Weimar and now ; 32)
Includes bibliographical references and index.
  ISBN 0-520-23310-7 (alk. paper) — ISBN 0-520-23311-5 (pbk. : alk. paper)
    1. Motion pictures—Germany—History.   2. Motion picture producers and directors—
Germany—Biography.   3. Germans—California—Los Angeles.   I. Title.   II. Series.
PN1993.5.G3 K645   2002
791.43'0943—dc21   2001007068

Manufactured in the United States of America

11   10   09   08   07   06   05   04   03   02

10 9 8 7 6 5 4 3 2 1

The paper used in this publication meets the minimum requirements of ANSI/NISO Z39.48–
1992 (R 1997) (*Permanence of Paper*). ⊗

Contents

Illustrations

Acknowledgments

This book argues that we must understand the course of German cinema between the early 1930s and the mid-1950s as one of enduring ruptures, enforced displacements, and imaginative detours. It is impossible, I suggest, to reconstruct the history of German cinema during this period as linear or unified. Nor can we explain its developments as the outcome of unambiguous intentions or transparent causes. Although written under very different historical conditions, the story of this book itself in some sense mirrors the fractured logic that I trace in the following pages. *The Dark Mirror* was conceived as a book from the beginning, yet it experienced many turns, trials, and diversions before it arrived at its final destination. Special thanks go to Eric Rentschler for having urged me not to lose my focus, patience, and direction. Many other colleagues and friends were invaluable in helping me to sharpen arguments, revise immature interpretations, gain new insights, and circumvent potential embarrassments, especially Nora Alter, Antje Ascheid, David Bathrick, Russell Berman, John Davidson, Karen Fiss, Gerd Gemünden, Sabine Hake, Miriam Hansen, Tony Kaes, Karen Kenkel, Alice Kuzniar, Dick Langston, Johannes von Moltke, David Pan, Patrice Petro, and Lawrence Rainey. The manuscript benefited greatly from the two anonymous readers who evaluated it for the University of California Press. Finally, I am particularly thankful to Hester Baer, who not only helped me out with a good deal of archival research but proved to be an incisive reader and critic of various drafts of this book.

I was extremely fortunate to have Eric Smoodin as my editor at the University of California Press. Without his steadfast enthusiasm and open-minded guidance this book would never have gotten off the ground. Many thanks to Joe Abbott, who did a great job copyediting the book for publication. Washington University provided me with many of the resources needed to conduct research and carry out the writing. I owe particular gratitude to Edward Macias, dean of Arts and Sciences at Washington University, for offering financial support to illustrate this volume. Peter Latta of the Filmmuseum Berlin—Deutsche Kinemathek assisted in gathering most of the illustrations for this volume. Unless noted otherwise, all stills and images appear with the permission of the Filmmuseum Berlin—Deutsche Kinemathek.

I am grateful for having had the opportunity to test some of the ideas and interpretations put forward in this book in lectures and conference papers before. Drafts of certain chapters were presented at Dartmouth College, Duke University, Stanford University, and Washington University, as well as at the annual meetings of the Modern Language Association, the Society for Cinema Studies, and the German Studies Association. Preliminary versions of some portions of this book have also previously appeared as articles. In all cases, however, earlier readings underwent significant rewriting and reconceptualization. For their kind permissions to make selected use of earlier materials, I would nevertheless like to thank the publications in which they appeared (for specific acknowledgments of permissions please see the copyright page).

This book would not have been even remotely possible without the tireless support and encouragement of Christa Johnson. She has accompanied me on many of the journeys that have led to its completion, whether it meant embarking on research trips to Berlin or Los Angeles, watching yet another (painful) Nazi feature or (perversely pleasurable) film noir, or sitting together in front of the computer screen and fixing my Germanic syntax. Our two daughters, Nicola and Kirstin, were both born during the years I spent researching and writing *The Dark Mirror*. In more than one way Christa, Nicola, and Kirstin have made this study's voyage between different times, cultures, and locations meaningful for me. And it is to them that I dedicate this book.

Introduction: The Dark Mirror

This book traces the origin of what I understand—with full awareness of the term's evocative and ambiguous history—as the *Sonderweg* (special path) of German popular cinema. In a series of typological readings, *The Dark Mirror* first investigates how Nazi entertainment features during the 1930s aspired to bring Hollywood to the Third Reich and then how Hitler refugees attuned German cultural material after 1939 to the demands of the Hollywood studio system. Throughout the following pages my principal interest is in the ways that German film practitioners, whether in Berlin or Hollywood, negotiated different cultural codes and encouraged their audiences to identify themselves as others. In all eight case studies we witness German directors, film stars, and film composers inviting their viewers to cross spatial and cultural boundaries. Yet rather than leveling crucial differences between Nazi film culture and the exiles' Hollywood, this study argues that German cinema during the Hitler era split into incompatible and nonsynchronous parts. To put it simply, whereas in Nazi society cinematic pleasures served the purpose of domination and hierarchical segregation, the exile filmmakers of this book hoped to sustain notions of modern culture as a source of emancipation and multiplicity. Poised between Hitler and Hollywood, the golden age of German cinema, I suggest, owed its existence to a process of division, displacement, and doubling that cannot be reintegrated into any kind of unified national narrative.

By investigating the course of German film from the 1930s to the 1950s, this book contributes to current debates about the role of national cinemas as sites of cultural difference and particularity. Until very recently, to write about national cinemas meant to support semi- or noncommercial film practice, to commend the critique or subversion of mainstream conventions, to privilege auteurism over popular filmmaking. German cinema always played a prominent role in this kind of writing. Primarily focusing on the 1920s and 1970s, critics celebrated expressionist film and New German Cinema as beacons of oppositional meaning and cultural experimentation, as a national cinema whose insistence on product differentiation warranted cultural diversity and self-critique. The cultural turn of film studies since the late 1980s has led to a far-reaching demise of such normative conceptions of national cinema. Rather than tracking the careers of international art house directors, culturalist film history has drawn our awareness to how popular cinemas other than Hollywood may have produced local meanings or instilled Hollywood-like conventions with particular styles or accents.[1] In the perspectives of this newer scholarship European cinemas are no longer defined solely in terms of their art film productions. Instead, they are seen as cinemas that have always been quite familiar with categories of genre and stardom, as national cinemas that were and still are by no means embarrassed about their popular films or audiences or preferences.

The Dark Mirror wants to contribute to film studies' reconsideration of the national and the popular. It builds on recent work in German film scholarship that has emphasized the extent to which German cinema has been from its very inception a cinema of cultural transfers and transcultural fusions, of border crossings and transgressive identifications.[2] Unlike a great deal of postwar scholarship, which simply disparaged European genre cinemas as bad objects, *The Dark Mirror* is intended to develop a nuanced vocabulary able to assess the narrative energies and stylistic shapes of German popular filmmaking. The point of this book, however, is neither to join those who, by stressing the continuities of popular traditions and domestic affiliations, hope to normalize the course of German national cinema[3] nor simply to recite the culturalist view of the popular as a site of individual empowerment and difference. Nazi entertainment cinema, I will argue, deserves special attention in today's debate because it charged the act of going to the movies with eminently political functions. Employing highly rationalized modes of industrial production and distribution, Nazi cinema appealed to both the national and the popular in order to break Hollywood's hegemony in Europe. It capitalized on populist notions of linguistic, cultural, and racial belonging to integrate the viewer as a consumer into the imagined community of the nation. Whether or not it really succeeded with these objectives, Nazi cinema raises fundamental questions about the interaction between state and Fordist mass culture, between politics and modern distraction, between institutional contexts and individual acts of reception. As perhaps the single most successful European alternative to Hollywood ever, Nazi cinema urges cultural studies neither to reduce all relevant questions of power and domination to cultural matters nor to heroize contradictions between ideological designs and consumer practices as expressions of subversive difference and aesthetic resistance.

Contrary to the nationalist and revolutionary rhetoric of the Nazi movement, the German cinema of the Third Reich, according to Karsten Witte, "had little to call its own."[4] Nazi feature films borrowed freely from Hollywood models and from older domestic traditions. They transported fantasy to places far beyond the order of the day, and they were eager to please German and foreign audiences alike. Nazi cinema may have pursued the idea of synchronizing sights and sounds into peculiar German expressions, but we can neither consider its modes of spectatorial address intrinsically fascistic nor assume that its self-proclaimed Germanness only worked with and on the German viewers' imagination. What complicates the picture even further is the fact that the history of German film during the Nazi period entails not only the narrative of Hollywood in Berlin but also the exile of hundreds of mostly Jewish-German film practitioners to the Hollywood studio system—Berlin in Hollywood. The professional survival of Hitler refugees in Southern California rested largely on their competence to adapt to the studios' production modes. As important, however, it often depended on their willingness to mimic the very past they tried to leave behind. Studios hired refugee actors to play Nazi soldiers, immigrant composers to bring German musical traditions to Hollywood screens, émigré directors to imitate the expressionist language of Weimar cinema or to reference exoticized notions of European history and high culture. It is the historical irony of Nazi cinema that, in its very attempt to refix German identity and bring Hollywood home to Berlin, it triggered the rise of a German cinema of exile that not only outlasted Hitler's rule but in which "Germany" reemerged as specter and simulacrum, a performative "Germany" replete with slippages, masquerades, and displacements. Situated between Hitler and Hollywood, German popular cinema after 1933 developed along incompatible spatial and temporal axes. There is no way to recuperate its history of doubling and enforced displacement as simple or normal.

This book maps the positions of German film between the 1930s and 1950s, between the inauguration of the Nazi culture industry on the one hand and the disintegration of the Hollywood studio system and the concomitant demise of a number of paradigmatic exile careers on the other. My aim is to approach the locations of German film during this era by examining what might be seen as eccentric moments and atypical figures. It is the extreme and extraordinary, I suggest, that best illuminates the continuities within the discontinuities and the discontinuities within the continuities of

German film, Nazi or Hollywood. The first part of this book inquires into the extent to which Nazi entertainment features of the prewar era were readable in terms of Hollywood cinema. It reconstructs the bearing of Hollywood on Nazi film culture during the 1930s and probes the ambivalent ways that Nazi genre films transformed America into a fantastic playground of the imagination. Ever since the turn of the century, the topos of America had provided a site at which Germans debated the rapid rise of modern industrial culture, articulated social utopias and anxieties, and struggled over the relationship between high art and the popular. Nazi cinema, in its mission to create its own Hollywood in Berlin, reckoned with this Americanist imaginary. It invited audiences to identify themselves temporarily as American others, yet it did so not in order to liquefy but rather to redefine cultural differences in terms of radical alterity. It domesticated the "complex signifier"[5] of Americanism so as to remake the viewer's fantasy, fortify the boundaries between self and other, and thus erase the possibility of recognizing other cultures as potential sources of self-critique and enlightenment.

The second part of *The Dark Mirror* turns the tables and focuses on what, from the Nazi regime's point of view, would have seemed a monstrous return of the repressed: the ways in which exile film practitioners after 1939 adjusted German cultural materials and experiences to the commercial expectations of the Hollywood studio system. The influx of European talents to Hollywood after the outbreak of World War II coincided with fundamental transformations of the classical studio system, which in some respects anticipated the system's disintegration during the 1950s. The chapters of part 2 are devoted to the work of Hollywood exiles after 1939 who not only understood how to convert institutional changes into sources of individual success and creative experimentation but who also, at some point in the course of the 1950s, tried to return to West Germany and offer their talents to the reemerging film industry of the Federal Republic. It is in their jagged biographies and films that some of the paradoxes of exile become the clearest. Often torn by the challenges of professional and cultural assimilation, these film practitioners indexed German materials in order to make Hollywood products more self-reflexive, respectable, diverse, or simply glamorous. Whether imagined or authentic, German cultural traditions were meant to mirror studio operations or to align them with the changing demands of American wartime and postwar leisure. The figure of "Germany" thus became an important player in the transformation of studio filmmaking. It helped diversify the products of Fordist mass culture during the 1940s as much as it helped shape Hollywood's response in the 1950s to middle-class calls for more participatory forms of recreation. Rather than reify cultural boundaries, the exiles' spectral "Germany" acted as a catalyst of accommodation and renewal. It bridged seemingly incompatible codes, complicated generic formulas and spectatorial identifications, and thereby decentered modern industrial culture from within.

It has become a commonplace among historians of German culture to point out the modernity not only of Nazi society but of Nazi entertainment cinema as well. Feature films of the Third Reich, far from breaking with the modern, relied on the templates of a modern consumer society. They appealed to fantasies of social and geographical mobility, showcased the latest fads and fashions, and endorsed the achievements of technological progress. *The Dark Mirror* probes what is modern about the course of German film after 1933 — and what is not. Suffice it to say at this point that this study operates with a differential concept of modernity. Modern societies entail various strands of modernization (social, political, economic, technological, aesthetic, and religious), strands that compete with and at times, in fact, displace each other. Modernity unfetters individuals from the restrictions of mythic or traditional lifeworlds, yet whenever modern societies prioritize certain tracks of modernization over others, they may just as well produce new myths and reinscribe unquestionable traditions. In the specific context of this study German film after 1933 must be seen as modern not only because it alluded to the signifiers of social or technological modernity but also because the doubling of German popular cinema resulted in a transatlantic scenario in which different meanings, norms, and institutional practices competed with each other. The modernity of German film between Hitler and Hollywood, in this sense, was often curiously circumstantial and inadvertent. Both in Berlin and Hollywood it rested on numerous film practitioners who had a peculiarly modern sense of provisionalness and contingency forced on them and who in their films either worked through or disavowed the fleetingness of meaning in the modern age. At their best their works practiced forms of popular modernism that explored cinematic representation as a realm of shifting constructions of agency and individual autonomy. At their worst their films incorporated selected aspects of modern civilization in order to recast history as nature, erase the values and constitutional achievements of political modernity, and dispense with any utopian sense of culture as emancipation.

Having thus established some of the central concerns and perspectives of this study, I will in the remainder of this introduction explain the signposts according to which *The Dark Mirror* follows the paths of Nazi and exile cinema from the early 1930s to the mid-1950s. I will first sketch the theoretical stakes of this study; second, delineate why the role of film sound will be of great importance for my examination; and third, explain the historiographic model that informs the itinerary of this book.

HITLER AND HOLLYWOOD

In juxtaposing Nazi entertainment cinema and the work of Hollywood exiles, this study confronts one of the most enduring tropes of German thought throughout the postwar era: the identification of Nazi manipulation and Hollywood mass culture. In Hans Jürgen Syberberg's 1977 *Hitler, ein Film aus Deutschland* (Our Hitler), this figure has found its most emblematic formulation within postwar German cinema.[6] Presenting Hitler as a would-be Cecil B. DeMille, Syberberg's six-hour opus proposed that twentieth-century show business and fascism were virtually identical. According to Syberberg both Hitler and Hollywood obliterated the autonomy of art and used aesthetic experience for the purpose of mass manipulation. In doing so they compromised the utopian power embedded in myth, in Richard Wagner's music, and in preindustrial forms of popular culture. Syberberg's film advocated a rigid antinomy between, on the one hand, fascism and Hollywood and, on the other, Syberberg's own art cinema, "which engages in a heroic struggle with commercial cinema over the right to inherit nineteenth-century popular culture, with its romantic myths, its kitsch objects, its sentimentality and peasant piety, as well as its wit, sarcasm and peasant slyness."[7] According to Syberberg both Hollywood and Hitler degraded the mythic by transforming politics and culture into spellbinding movie sets. Both exemplified a cynical triumph of instrumental reason over the irrational substratum of what Syberberg understands as authentic culture. In the unyielding perspective of *Our Hitler* Hollywood in fact turns out to be even more fascist than fascism itself. For thanks to their hegemonic position during the postwar era, Hollywood feature films exploited the Germans' need to mourn their past and thus extended Hitler's strategies of mass deception beyond the Nazis' historical demise. Syberberg's film, by way of contrast, wants to recuperate what could make German culture authentic again. His Wagnerian exercise pits Wagner's romantic longings for redemption against their own legacy in Hollywood and Nazi Germany. It intends to emancipate the irrational from the grasp of instrumental reason so as to help Germans overcome the fact that after Hitler they have lived "in a country without homeland [Heimat]."[8]

A widespread view within contemporary criticism suggests that Syberberg's critique of American industrial culture basically repeated the identification of Hollywood and Hitler Germany in Max Horkheimer and

Theodor W. Adorno's *Dialectic of Enlightenment* (1944/1947). Similar to Syberberg, Horkheimer and Adorno indeed saw industrial mass culture as a tool of domination that stripped reason down to pure forms of instrumental rationality. The classical Hollywood studio system, in Horkheimer and Adorno's understanding, applied Fordist principles of production to the realm of cultural expression. Driven by the pressures of monopoly capitalism, Hollywood mass culture negated autonomous art and its peculiar power to establish noncoercive, mimetic relationships between nonidentical particulars. Horkheimer and Adorno in fact saw no principal difference between the makeup of studio films and that of commercial advertising, because both media employ modern technology to engineer desire and organize conformity: "In both cases the insistent demand for effectiveness makes technology into psycho-technology, into a procedure of manipulating men. In both cases the standards are striking yet familiar, the easy yet catchy, the skillful yet simple; the object is to overpower the customer, who is conceived as absent-minded or resistant." [9] Similar to the coordination of cultural life in German fascism, the studio system streamlined products and homogenized audiences. Assembly-line entertainment films imprinted the stamp of absolute sameness on their recipients. In both the Hollywood culture industry and Nazi Germany the modern formalization of rationality resulted in nothing other than a terrorist regime of identity. Everyone was effectively provided for with one and the same product. Every possible response was preordained by the film itself.

In recent Anglo-American debates about popular culture Horkheimer and Adorno's notion of the culture industry has "received less than favorable treatment." [10] The following three arguments strike me as today's most substantial charges against the disapproval of Hollywood in *Dialectic of Enlightenment*.[11] First, Horkheimer and Adorno, in their hyperbolic critique of mass culture, underestimated the rationality of Hollywood's consumers—their ability to form qualified judgments and to develop unforeseen strategies of reception. Horkheimer and Adorno overlooked crucial differences between the function of films as streamlined commodities and their status as symbolic texts whose meanings and pleasures are established in the discriminating appropriation of the recipient. The culture industry thesis thus not only ignored the productivity of consumption but also failed to elucidate the many ways films can enter their viewers' imaginations and resonate with consumers' everyday experiences. Second, as they directly correlated the dynamic of modern rationalization with the politics of culture, Horkheimer and Adorno failed to distinguish between different and nationally specific versions of industrial mass culture. Although we should clearly be very careful not to isolate the political from the economic, we must take into consideration the fact that from their very inception some formations of industrial culture—unlike the American model, whose emergence corresponded to the consolidation of organized capitalism—were shot through with variegated political or administrative agendas. Contrary to Horkheimer and Adorno's view, the political effects of modern mass culture depended not only on the rationalization of cultural production itself but on how it interacted with specific social, economic, and constitutional contexts. And third, critics have argued that Horkheimer and Adorno's animosity toward empirical analysis led them to exaggerate the homogeneity of Hollywood's production methods. Although indeed aspiring to a Fordist and Taylorist organization of labor, studio filmmaking was less a process of seamless collaboration "than of negotiation and struggle— occasionally approaching armed conflict." [12] Responding to ever-increasing pressures for product differentiation, the classical studio system rested on its ability to maintain unstable equilibriums. Far less unified than Horkheimer and Adorno assumed, studio filmmaking could not do without games of internal and external tug of war.

Most critics today seem to agree that the culture industry thesis—and, hence, the identification of Hollywood with Hitler—was motivated in large measure by Adorno's elitist rejection of the popular, which makes this aspect of Adorno's work unsuitable for the agendas of contemporary cultural studies. If *The Dark Mirror* nevertheless draws on (and modifies) the theoretical model of the culture industry, it does so not only because Adorno himself participated in the drama of displacement at stake in these pages but also because—on a conceptual level—Adorno's critique of modern mass culture was much less Manichean than many critics today want us to believe. Adorno read industrial mass culture as a negative utopia, "as the fulfillment, under conditions of domination, of legitimate human needs for plenty, inclusion, play, and happiness." [13] Industrial culture reified what autonomous art no longer dared to say except in the cryptic language of determined negation—the promise of a better life. Rather than situate modern mass culture and twentieth-century modernism as radical opposites, however, Adorno claimed that both owed their existence to the existence of its respective other. Modern art was born as a reaction to the gradual commodification of cultural material during the second half of the nineteenth century. Modern mass culture, on the other hand, emerged out of high art's compromises with public taste and commercial interests. Adorno may have opted for aesthetic modernism as a last repository of authentic meaning under the sign of organized capitalism. Unlike the elitist Syberberg, however, Adorno remained keenly aware of the fact that the practice of high art in modern culture in some sense at once presupposed and reinscribed mass culture. No overarching cultural reform or spiritual redemption could be expected from art anymore. Its glimpses of truth were borrowed from the ruptures of the age itself.

This book is guided by the assumption that even though we clearly need to move beyond the equation of German National Socialism and American mass culture, Adorno's dialectical understanding of modern culture can help us to evaluate the political dimensions of industrial mass culture between roughly the 1920s and the late 1950s. As we will see, the culture industry thesis provides a valuable benchmark against which we can measure different versions of modern culture and their methods of coping with older aesthetic traditions and utopian desires. Moreover, what makes Adorno important for a nuanced study of German-American film relations during the peak decades of Fordist modernity is that his work presses us to triangulate Hollywood mass culture and Nazi Germany with a third and, as it turns out, highly instructive variable: the legacy of Richard Wagner. According to Adorno's seminal *Versuch über Wagner* (written in 1937/38),[14] Wagner's music dramas foreshadowed the twentieth-century culture industry in embryonic form. Wagner's orchestration favored sonic effects over structural coherence so as to assimilate high culture to popular taste. At the same time, however, Wagner's music dramas contained elements of modernist negation. The weakness of Wagner's subjects was "not only a symptom of decadence but also a move toward overcoming alienation."[15] It is Wagner's curious ambivalence between regressive reconciliation and utopian nonidentity that—as I argue in this study—elucidates the competing positions of German cinema between Hitler and Hollywood. As it probes different appropriations of Wagner's aesthetic program, *The Dark Mirror* submits not that Hollywood was more fascist than fascism but, on the contrary, that fascism—following the definitions of *Dialectic of Enlightenment*—was more Hollywood than Hollywood. Whereas the Wagnerian film ideologues of Nazi cinema, to put it schematically, endorsed film sound as a means of engineering coercive forms of sameness, German exile cinema was at its best whenever it explored possible tensions between the aural and the visual and thereby actualized Wagnerian utopias of nonidentity. Syberberg's desire to mobilize Wagner's music against Hitler and Hollywood, I suggest, answers the wrong question. As the dissimilar narratives of Hollywood in Berlin and Berlin in Hollywood in this book reveal, the point is not to ask "Wagner or modernity?" but rather "Whose Wagner?" and "What kind of modernity?"

THE SOUNDS OF MODERNITY

Adorno's work on Wagner informs one of the principal propositions of this book: that we cannot speak about German cinema after 1933 without speaking about how it used synchronized sound to manage the viewer's attention. Throughout this book I argue that the legacy of German national cinema was by no means only visual. In contrast to those who have canonized the canted angles of expressionist film art or the muted designs of the New German Cinema as *the* dominant language of German filmmaking, this book emphasizes that German cinema since the early 1930s was bound up with sound and film music. To be sure, as my title already suggests, *The Dark Mirror* is not meant solely to chronicle the uses of sound in Nazi or exile cinema. International film culture after 1930 was decisively audiovisual. Any attempt to reduce it to one of its components would eliminate the possibility of nuanced analysis and evaluation. Yet this book repeatedly stresses the sonic dimension of German cinema because it is in the different treatment of film sound that some of the most striking differences between Nazi feature productions and the work of Hollywood exiles emerge. Whether they worked in Berlin or Hollywood, German film practitioners embraced synchronized sound as a means to reinforce, modernize, or reject the prominent role of the acoustical in conventional constructions of German identity. By examining the relationship between sounds and images we can best understand how German cinema negotiated the tensions between romanticism and twentieth-century modernism, between autonomous art and the popular. It is by listening to their sound tracks that we can tax how German filmmakers tackled the Wagnerian legacy of modern industrial culture.

The sound of music and of the German language had played a significant role in the symbolism of the German nation long before the Nazi takeover and the coming of the sound film. In the face of the division of Germany into many disparate political entities and regional groups, German intellectuals since around 1800 had conceived of musical and linguistic dispositions as the nation's most palpable common ground. Romantic philosophers such as Johann Gottfried Herder and Johann Gottlieb Fichte had laid the groundwork for the view of language as the primary predicate of German identity. Although often divided about how to reconcile the abundance of regional dialects with the idea of the linguistic nation,[16] a myriad of nineteenth-century writers and literary critics were quick to follow Herder's and Fichte's lead. They endorsed the German language, not as a catalyst to but a sign and essence of German national identity. Likewise, in the absence of political unity nineteenth-century composers and conductors had been eager to elevate music to the principal component of what it meant to be German. "The idea of a German nation-state had to overcome a long history of political fragmentation and regional differences, but music represented a mode of artistic expression in which all Germans could share."[17]

Nazi film practitioners, in their efforts to remake Hollywood in Berlin, reckoned with the sonic construction of German nationhood during the nineteenth century. After seeing the first talkie shown in German theaters, Lloyd Bacon's *The Singing Fool* (1928), future Minister of Propaganda and Popular Enlightenment Dr. Joseph Goebbels noted in his diary in September 1929: "I was surprised about the already far advanced technology of sound film. Here is the future, and we are wrong to reject all this as American bunk. . . . The content was dreadful, New-York-style, sentimental kitsch. But nonetheless: what we have to recognize here is the future and coming opportunities."[18] Less than four years later Goebbels set out to convert opportunity into practice. As I will show in the four chapters of part 1, Nazi film practitioners embraced sound film to orchestrate collective fantasy and capture the national imagination. Reorganized under Goebbels's direction, German cinema aspired to offer audiovisual spaces in which the sounds of German voices and musical traditions could integrate the viewer into the national community. In many respects Nazi sound films revived early cinema's preference for self-contained attractions. They packaged German sounds into cinematic spectacles in the hope of folding individual viewers into the Wagnerian *Gesamtkunstwerk* of the German nation.

Like many other facets of Nazi society, however, Nazi cinema was characterized by striking discrepancies between ideological intentions and institutional practices. Feature films of the Third Reich might have been designed to broadcast German linguistic and musical properties, but some of the most notable aspects of Nazi cinema must be seen in how it more broadly employed cinematic audiovision to regulate desire, discipline affect, and shatter unwanted forms of solidarity. Eager to please popular demand for cosmopolitan pleasures as much as to conquer foreign markets, Nazi feature films used synchronized sound to transport viewers to imaginary elsewheres and elsewhens without challenging the fixity of cultural boundaries. The addition of sound helped amplify pleasurable fantasies about the self as other, yet at the same time sound was used to restructure sense perception, contain spontaneity, and recast cultural difference as incompatible alterity. Nazi cinema subjected sound to a curious dialectic of rationalization. Rather than bridge the gap between self and other, synchronized sound played an important role in separating one from the other. Whether or not it featured purely German sounds, Nazi cinema transformed linguistic and musical expressions into ideology. What was communicated seemed to matter less than the very act of vocalization and intonation, the magic ritual of speaking, singing, and hearing. As it incorporated word and music into the operations of mechanical reproduction, Nazi cinema demythologized spoken and musical language, but by depleting communicative reason and supplanting concrete experience, Nazi feature films also remythologized the world.

In the totalizing perspective of Horkheimer and Adorno's *Dialectic of Enlightenment* the sound designs of the American culture industry were every bit as totalitarian as the Nazis' domestication of language and music. Whatever fascist domination did to language in Nazi Germany was similarly effected by advertising and diversion in organized capitalism. Both Hitler and Hollywood, according to Horkheimer and Adorno, stripped language from everything that did not serve the purpose of producing conformity. Both fascism and American capitalism favored the formula, the set phrase, the unequivocal sign over semantic ambivalence and communicative substance:

> Instead of making the object experiential, the purified word treats it as an abstract instance, and everything else (now excluded by the demand for ruthless clarity from expression—itself now banished) fades away in reality. A left-half at football, a black-shirt, a member of the Hitler Youth, and so on, are no more than names. If before its rationalization the word had given rise to lies as well as to longing, now, after its rationalization, it is a straightjacket for longing more even than for lies.[19]

As I will demonstrate in part 2 of this study, the work of Hitler refugees in Hollywood urges us to correct Horkheimer and Adorno's account of sonic rationalization and manipulation. In all four chapters of the second part I discuss how German exiles explored possible tensions between the acoustical and the visual in order to speak out against the leveling effects of modern rationalization and mass culture. Contrary to Horkheimer and Adorno's assumption, I show how the work of some German Hollywood exiles traversed different cultural codes, bridged gaps between self and other, and reclaimed the possibility of communicative reason. Instead of fastening the straightjacket around longing, the exiles of this study took recourse to linguistic and musical materials in order to complicate dominant viewing positions and puncture the screens of sameness. Whereas part 1 of *The Dark Mirror* traces how Nazi cinema redefined modern life as nature, part 2 documents the extent to which exile audiovisions were able not only to express a peculiarly modern sense of multiplicity and contingency but also to encode the promise of a different and better life in modernity.

REFRAMING/REFRACTING THE PAST

This study borrows its title from a 1946 thriller by Robert Siodmak that—like many films shot by Hitler refugees during the 1940s—engages the viewer in a mystifying splitting and multiplication of identity. Siodmak's *The Dark Mirror* features Olivia de Havilland playing two identical twins, Terry and Ruth Collins, who are charged with the murder of a man but refuse to reveal who actually committed the crime. Dr. Scott Elliott (Lew Ayres), a young psychologist, analyzes both sisters in order to uncover different personality traits and thus identify the perpetrator. During the therapy Dr. Elliott falls in love with one of the sisters, Ruth, which triggers feelings of extreme jealousy in the other sister. Terry now reveals her darker side. She tries to drive Ruth into insanity, assume her sister's identity, and present the authorities with the wrong culprit. Dr. Elliott upsets Terry's plan and, in cooperation with the police, exposes Terry as the true murderer.

Siodmak's drama of twins echoes the prominent role of doubles in the expressionist films of the early Weimar period (fig. 1). But it would make little sense to impose dominant readings of the Weimar doppelgänger onto Siodmak's exile work in Hollywood.[20] A studio worker par excellence, Siodmak reinscribed the doppelgänger in *The Dark Mirror* in a way that was, to say the least, discontinuous: his film referenced the past as a symbol for present concerns. As she manipulates perceptions and mystifies minds, Terry Collins turns one of the principal elements of modernity—the experience of contingency—against itself. A grand enunciator of deceitful sights and sounds, Terry asserts totalitarian control over appearances, events, and people in order to obstruct knowledge, agency, and justice. She symbolizes a cinema of fatal attractions in which Machiavellian calculation subdues all residues of substantive reason. Siodmak, by contrast, instead of solely passing moral judgment on Terry, actively wrestles with the evil sister over the use of cinematic representation. In the last sequence Terry throws a lighter at a mirror in which she beholds Ruth's reflection. She shatters the glass and thereby produces a distorted image that recalls a shot we saw in the film's opening sequence: a shot of a broken mirror at the site of the murder. No longer able to maintain her role as the despotic enunciator, Terry effects a violent return of the repressed. In the end refraction takes the place of reflection; discriminating perceptions and judgments triumph over Terry's cinema of mythic fear and deception.

Siodmak's *The Dark Mirror* enabled American audiences to see how a liberal modern order looked from an illiberal point of view. It encouraged contemporary viewers to engage with the enemies of liberal dialogue in

Figure 1.   Reflections/refractions: Olivia de Havilland in a dual role in Robert Siodmak's *The Dark Mirror* (1946). Courtesy of Filmmuseum Berlin—Deutsche Kinemathek.

order to interrogate their own rationalist commitments. At the same time, however, the film also allegorized the unsettled position of German exiles in Hollywood, a position marked by deceptive reflections, multiplied identities, and the "politics of make-believe."[21] Dominant understandings of exile have emphasized the émigrés' traumatic experience of loss, dislocation, and fragmentation. Adorno's famous description of exile as a state of inescapable mutilation and expropriation has expressed this paradigm most forcefully.[22] Although it would be cynical to deny the hardship that separation from homeland brought for the majority of Jewish-German film workers in Hollywood, it is equally important to understand that Adorno's paradigm might not fully describe the status of German film practitioners in exile. Many of these expatriates perceived their forced emigration to Hollywood as a continuation of careers that already in Germany had been deeply involved in American mass culture and Hollywood conventions. Hollywood, rather than confronting the exile with illegible scenes of cultural alterity, was often encountered as something quite familiar, something much closer to home than displaced writers or philosophers were willing to admit. In spite of all loss and trauma, the émigré's experience of Hollywood was one of uncanny half-involvements and half-detachments,[23] of "liminality and incorporation, of ambivalences, resistances, and slippages."[24] Similar to Siodmak's *The Dark Mirror,* the exiles' lives in Hollywood were beset with perplexing mirror images and false appearances. And, as I will argue in this book, it is through their eyes and films that we can best recognize the discontinuous dynamic of German cinema after 1933 in general, its heterogeneous locations in-between the local and the global.

Siodmak's *The Dark Mirror,* then, offers an emblem for this study, not because this film encourages us to search for causal connections linking Weimar expressionism, Nazi entertainment films, and the Hollywood culture industry but, on the contrary, because it urges us to map this relationship as a dialogical and refracted one—as a relationship structured by the figure of the double. Whether produced in Berlin or Hollywood, German cinema was replete with sights and sounds of cultural mimicry and performative identity, of hybridity and cross-dressing. It must be understood as a cinema in which different political, institutional, technological, and aesthetic visions mimicked each other to propose competing interpretations of what it meant to be modern. Like Siodmak's *The Dark Mirror,* this study intends to discriminate among different visions of modern experience. In all chapters I ask how German film practitioners negotiated different traditions and cultural conventions and how they sought to create new meanings out of transitory and contingent presents.

The classical canon of film historiography and film theory provides few examples of how to recognize contingency as one key to the making of modern history. Early film historians had often been attracted to finalistic perspectives and teleological models. Whereas one scholar traced the history of film as a linear development toward greater realism, expressiveness, and subtlety, the other chronicled the story of cinema as the exfoliation of film's inherent technological possibilities.[25] Both might have taken recourse to biological metaphors to describe the evolution of film language and technology as an aging process from infancy to maturity. Both saw history as a linear chain of cause and effect that would subsume discrete developments for the realization of a unified goal. Although clearly breaking away from how earlier generations had thought about film and film viewership, the by now canonical texts of 1970s film theory largely eliminated difference and individual agency from the books of film history. Whether they conceptualized cinema as a Platonic cave, infantilizing the spectator, or whether they theorized classical editing as a mechanism to program the spectator-subject, the theoretical orthodoxies of the 1970s understood the viewer's subjectivity as a direct effect of the film and every film as an effect of the ideological apparatus of dominant cinema. Asserting that thought, perception, and reception were merely functions of larger discursive paradigms, 1970s film theory left no conceptual space to account for alternative practices, historical changes, normative transgressions, and the voice of the viewer's qualitative experience. Informed by Althusser's, Foucault's, or Lacan's vocabulary, 1970s film theory ontologized discourse as the monolithic ground of all experience and thus—like early film historians—took individual agency and contingency out of film culture.

In accord with the more recent opening of film studies toward culture studies, *The Dark Mirror* wants to put back the conceptual possibility of agency and nonidentical acts of reception. Because the contingencies of historical experience matter even to the operations of industrial mass culture, neither teleological historiography nor poststructuralist discourse theory proves adequate for the attempt to assess the locations of German cinema between Hitler and Hollywood. At the same time, however, the present study aspires to evade some of the potential traps of today's culturalist scholarship, which by celebrating individualized reception often loses sight of how mass cultural expressions may implant ideology, orchestrate collective fantasy, and execute political domination. If German exile cinema in Hollywood alerts us to the pitfalls of deterministic and universalist historiographies, the case of Nazi cinema warns us against any misdirected heroization of cultural particularism and intentionality. Nazi film culture pressures cultural studies to develop historiographical strategies that can critically reconstruct historical contexts in which certain choices resulted in the erasure of choice, articulations of difference cemented hegemonic norms of unity, and the invocation of concrete experience neutralized sense perception and obliterated the individual body as an autonomous site of desire.

The task of this book, then, is one not of recuperation or deconstruction but of reconstruction. In all eight chapters I situate texts and modes of film consumption in their historical contexts. All of my readings seek to reconstruct what kinds of choices were available and why some choices prevailed over others. *The Dark Mirror* thus conceives of both film practitioners and film recipients as potentially active agents who can use, reuse, synthesize, reject, and renew given symbols, styles, and meanings. Yet because neither the production nor the consumption of films takes place in a vacuum of power, interest, and ideology, choices do not necessarily signify autonomy or emancipation. Rather, every choice must be seen in relation to the larger and historically variable force field of film culture in which individual events are products of diverse aesthetic, cultural, technological, social, economic, and political determinants. The point is therefore neither simply to record the course of individual films and their stylistic solutions nor to describe the institutions of film production and consumption. Instead, the aim is to chart the shifting role of cinema as a fragile and stratified public sphere where texts and audiences interacted with each other, films helped articulate or contain experience, and individual practices of consumption reinforced or challenged institutional environments.

The point of any reconstruction lies in the present. It rests on the assumption that many historical developments become fully intelligible only in hindsight. Because the concept of film culture designates a space at once symbolic and material, historians do well to avoid notions of linear causality and determination. To regard, say, economic or ideological mandates as distinct causes of certain symbolic events obscures the potential multiplicity of film culture and explains away in what form films really entered their viewers' heads. Individual elements by themselves, as Hannah Arendt has written in a different context, "probably never cause anything. They become origins of events if and when they crystallize into fixed and definite forms. Then, and only then, can we trace their history backwards. The event illuminates its own past, but it can never be deduced from it."[26] Following Arendt's suggestion, *The Dark Mirror* recalls the course of German popular cinema between the 1930s and the 1950s in a series of crystallizations that aspire not to sacrifice the principal possibility of contradiction and discontinuity for the sake of historical totalization. Although I, like any historian, clearly hope to cohere past temporalities in the course of my analysis, I am also guided by the assumption that any history of modern culture must reckon with the possibility of messy incoherence and simultaneity. Because this past itself was structured by conflicting temporalities and competing narrativizations of history, critical reconstruction will read events both backward and forward. Its task is to establish meaningful constellations in which specific texts and practices illuminate the era in all its complexity. I do not claim to offer an exhaustive survey of German-American film relations. The case studies of this book aim at what one might call paradigmatic validity. They are meant to galvanize the course of German cinema between Hitler and Hollywood into typological situations. In the final analysis the selection of materials is justified not by their prominence or canonicity but by their capacity to produce persuasive views of how texts interacted with their contexts and how historical contexts defined frameworks of meaning, perception, and practice.

The primary aim of this book is to draw attention to the historical indexes of meaning, pleasure, spectatorship, and identity. Yet insofar as it questions the notion of a specifically fascist or antifascist film aesthetics, *The Dark Mirror* must face the question of how to deal with the legacy of Nazi cinema today. If the political effects of Nazi entertainment features in no small measure rested on contextual factors that are no longer in place, can contemporary television audiences simply relax and zap back and forth between showings of Luis Trenker's *Der Kaiser von Kalifornien* and Robert Siodmak's *Phantom Lady*, of Curtis Bernhardt's *Der Tunnel* and his *Interrupted Melody?* If we have moved beyond the historical conditions that enabled fascism, has history consumed the very need to watch the products of Goebbels's film studios with critical eyes and ears? Does the reconstructive perspective, in pointing out the historical relativity of meaning, thus not secretly feed into the project of historical normalization after all?

To put it simply: no. The reason for this negative answer is neatly illustrated in a short passage from Leslie Epstein's 1997 *Pandaemonium*. This novel is a story about a Hitleresque German exile director in Hollywood as seen through the eyes of Ladislav Loewenstein, a.k.a. Peter Lorre. The passage narrates a Hollywood gala held in October 1940 to aid the victims of Nazism. Everyone of standing and reputation in the Hollywood studio system seems to be present: powerful studio moguls, star directors, charismatic actors, exiled writers and composers. Lion Feuchtwanger explains how he escaped from Nazi Germany, Charles Laughton mimics Winston Churchill, Fritz Lang boasts about how he rejected Goebbels's recruitment efforts, Otto Klemperer conducts the L.A. Philharmonic through set pieces of European nineteenth-century music. Suddenly, the houselights dim and the orchestra offers soft, shimmering string and woodwind sounds. The audience is shocked. Arnold Schoenberg jumps up and insists that such music cannot be allowed; Albert Bassermann calls Klemperer crazy. Loewenstein / Lorre relates:

> I knew the notes the Philharmonic was playing. They were by Wagner. *Parsifal? Tristan?* No, *Lohengrin.* I could hardly believe my ears. How, on such an occasion, could they play the work of Hitler's favorite composer?
>
> Suddenly there was a gasp throughout the hall. Out onto the edge of the stage a tramp came tripping over his cane. Charlie! Chaplin!

There was a burst of laughter and applause. The tramp turned, just in time to catch a large rubber ball that someone tossed from the wings. Not a ball, but a giant globe, the same inflated world that all of us knew from the actor's new picture. Now, to the vibrating strings, he performed the Great Dictator ballet, embracing the earth, tossing it skyward, wooing it, then caressing it like some great breast he meant to suck dry. I stood in awe. Amazing how the vagabond's familiar moustache became that of the tyrant, how the stance of a man submissive to the world became the stride of one who was its conqueror.[27]

Frames guide perception. They enable aesthetic experience and delineate a range of possible judgments. In reframing Wagner's music for Hollywood, Chaplin not only elicits pleasurable responses but simultaneously opens up the possibility for critical insight and perceptual self-awareness. Loewenstein/Lorre's appreciation of Chaplin—the observer's movement from shock to awe—emerges from the active recognition of fundamental differences between how Wagner works under Hitler and what he can do for Hollywood. This differential experience of Wagner's music offers a glimpse of how we might want to approach the legacy of Nazi cinema today. The point, in my view, is neither to lock the products of Goebbels's culture industry into the poison cabinet of cultural fascism nor simply to applaud them as by now innocent vehicles of escapism. Whereas the first strategy wants to see only the frame, the second presents the framed as all there is. This book, by contrast, suggests that one of the tasks in viewing the films produced during the Third Reich is to recognize our own cultural distance to what made German feature films successful under the rule of Hitler. The work of exile film practitioners in Hollywood will help us to assess this distance not just along diachronic but also along synchronic axes. Rather than level crucial distinctions, the reconstructive case studies of *The Dark Mirror* intend to reframe and refract Nazi audiovisions from multiple points of view. They ask how entertainment films of the Third Reich may have acted on their historical audiences not in order to recuperate the legacy of Hollywood in Berlin for contemporary consumption but to probe what made classical Hollywood cinema and what makes our own frames of perception qualitatively different. Ultimately, this recognition of our own cultural distance might be the greatest pleasure we can still obtain from viewing Nazi feature films today.

Part 1

HOLLYWOOD IN BERLIN, 1933–1939

1 Sounds of Silence

Nazi Cinema and the Quest for
a National Culture Industry

The examination of Nazi film culture remains challenging not only because of the German film industry's remarkable familiarity with classical American cinema but also because Hollywood elements were often not seen as opposed to the creation of a self-consciously national mass culture. Nazi entertainment cinema aspired to be highly popular, a distraction factory that proliferated upbeat scores and impressive production values. In common with international trends of the 1930s, it cultivated stars and promoted new films with elaborate publicity campaigns, it capitalized on popular genre formulas, and it used individual films to showcase the latest commercial products. To be sure, in contrast to the Hollywood studio system, Nazi cinema was commanded by powerful politicians rather than almighty studio moguls. Minister of Enlightenment and Public Propaganda Joseph Goebbels supervised scripts, coordinated opening dates, defined star salaries, directed technological developments, chose film awards, and ordered the construction of new studio facilities. Unlike Hollywood tycoons, "film minister"[1] Goebbels believed that only state interventions, by separating the artistic from the commercial aspects of film production, could ensure the formal quality of German cinema. Yet in spite of such differences in ideology and institutional makeup, Nazi cinema perceived Hollywood as a measuring stick of creativity and spectatorial appeal. Like Hollywood during the classical era, Nazi cinema adopted industrial methods of production and distribution to reach the widest audience possible. It understood studio filmmaking as a means to reclaim domestic territory and conquer foreign markets. American-style distractions thus became primary tools to establish National Socialist hegemony. They served the Nazi state to win and secure legitimacy, not by means of political agitation or direct coercion but by molding a new public above class and conflict.

It has often been pointed out that the National Socialist regime employed modern industrial culture to give twentieth-century politics the appearance of resolute action. Nazi politics, following such readings, blurred the boundaries between reality and fiction, appearance and essence. It recycled decadent notions of artistic practice with the intention to convert the political into a self-referential space of authenticity and existential self-assertion. The 1,086 German feature films that premiered between 1933 and 1945 in many respects complemented this project. Nazi cinema was meant to convince people that they would all pursue the same goals and desires—living prosperously and amassing fashionable goods. Integrating dissimilar meanings and traditions, Nazi feature films broke older bonds of solidarity and displaced configurations of experience that originated from socially specific contexts of living. As the other side of aesthetic politics, they fostered the illusion of a new collective of consumers that would overcome economic competition, social struggle, regional difference, and gender conflict.

Following the understanding of Nazi society as one in which spectacular illusions replaced post-Enlightenment codes of legality and political emancipation, postwar scholarship has focused much of its attention on the peculiar organization of visual elements in Nazi cinema. Accordingly, Nazi cinema has been described as a laboratory of primal effects silencing spectators with the spellbinding power of images.[2] Similar to propaganda spectacles such as Leni Riefenstahl's *Triumph of the Will* (1935), Nazi feature films entertained the scopic drive with fantasies of wholeness and harmony.[3] They first overwhelmed the viewer with fascinating sights and then reintegrated the shattered body in fascist mass ornaments.[4] In doing so Nazi film upheld structures of domination that obscured their actual effects.[5] Joining visual pleasure and shrewd repression, Nazi cinema caused audiences to identify with what forced them into submission and, ultimately, brought about their destruction.

Nazi Germany, in the realms of both politics and cinematic entertainment, aspired to transform diverse publics into spectators. It homogenized conflicting viewing positions and redefined people with different social, cultural, religious, and gender backgrounds as members of one and the same national audience. Although it is difficult indeed to overlook the focal role of vision in this process, the use of sounds in Nazi cinema and their contribution to the coordination of distraction have remained largely unexamined. This lack of attention becomes particularly striking if we consider the historical juncture at which Hitler rose to power and Goebbels assumed control over German cinema. After all, the passage into the Third Reich coincided with both the economic and aesthetic consolidation of the sound film, which had been introduced to German audiences in 1929. In the early 1930s sound film was often seen as a remedy for what many loathed as the ever-increasing leveling of cultural differences. Not only did the breakthrough of the talkies activate feverish hopes to overturn the rule of Hollywood over the European film market. It was also embraced as a unique chance to re-articulate nineteenth-century constructions of German national identity, constructions that defined the substance of national belonging in terms of linguistic properties and domestic musical traditions. With this in mind we should not be surprised that the coming of sound film really mattered to Nazi film ideologues. In spite of technical transition problems and international patent battles, Nazi film officials and filmmakers endorsed talking pictures as a viable method to develop a popular, nationally specific, vernacular. As we will see in a moment, Richard Wagner's nineteenth-century visions of language and art inhabited a prominent place in this nationalization of cinematic pleasure. Revamping Wagner's longings with the help of industrial culture, Nazi sound film set out to fuse acting, dialogue, and music into a seamless total work of art, an audiovisual cocoon that stirred German emotions and forged contradictory experiences into fantasies of reconciliation.

Obviously, the establishment of sound film around 1930 did not constitute a necessary condition for Hitler's rise to power in 1933. Silent film, too, had proven instrumental to rouse emotions and move bodies for populist agendas, and there are of course many more significant reasons for the rise of National Socialism in Germany than the historical course of film technology.[6] But given the fact that the Third Reich turned out to be the first full-fledged media dictatorship in world history,[7] the concurrence of Hitler's march to power and the triumph of sound film remains intriguing. It in fact poses a series of both historical and theoretical questions that have been largely neglected. To what extent was the arrival of the talkies in Germany essential to the Nazi vision of a homegrown German Hollywood? Did Nazi cinema shape cinematic sound practices into a nationally specific style? How did German sound films of the 1930s in both ideological and formal terms negotiate Goebbels's call for national specificity and European success? And how did the actual use of film sound in Nazi cinema correspond with certain ideological dictates of the Nazi movement, a movement valorizing resolute action over feminine talk and bourgeois debate?

This chapter attempts to provide some preliminary answers to these questions. Sound in Nazi cinema served as a welcome technology of fantasy production. Nazi sound tracks recalled earlier popular traditions and at the same time heralded coming attractions. They transported viewers to other places and times but at the same time impeded any recognition of the other as a source of insight and self-reflection. Although Nazi entertainment films were often fraught with precarious self-contradictions, their sound played a critical role in managing the viewer's attention. Whether it overwhelmed, held in check, or was subordinate to the image track, sound helped appropriate desire, undercut rather than empowered communication, and recast diverse publics as textually anchored spectators. For the new masters of Babelsberg, the legendary home of the UFA film studios, the talkies did not lead to a Babel-like cacophony of different languages, voices, and musical idioms; rather, they offered welcome opportunities to nationalize entertainment and promised new lifestyles through consumption.

DISSONANT BEGINNINGS

Sound film entered the German scene in the form of a spectacle, a cinema of audiovisual attractions. German technicians had experimented with sound technologies ever since 1922, but it was an imported Hollywood film that broke the sound barrier in German cinemas.[8] Opening in the Berlin Gloria-Palast on the evening of June 3, 1929, the Warner production *The Singing Fool* (1928, Lloyd Bacon) was immediately hailed as a historical turning point in the history of film (fig. 2). Significantly, most reviews of the premiere night focused not on the film itself but on the viewers' response to Al Jolson's voice. Much of the audience's enthusiasm apparently had little to do with any sudden expansion of narrative realism or illusion. Instead, the true star of the evening was the new apparatus itself.[9] Recalling the reception of the very first moving pictures in the 1890s,[10] *The Singing Fool,* through the presence of Jolson's voice, once again accented the extraordinary nature of cinema to restructure human perception and the individual's spatiotemporal relations. As one critic put it, the arrival of sound transformed the space of the theater into "something uncanny. Voices have always been there since the beginning of the universe, but now we have an apparatus which makes a voice and a singer or an actor immortal."[11]

Only six months after the premiere of *The Singing Fool* the public's understanding of sound film had undergone significant transformations. The first 100-percent-German sound production, *Melodie des Herzens* (Melody of the heart, 1929, Hanns Schwarz), no longer struck reviewers and audiences as uncanny. Rather, the addition of sound in this film was seen as a highly effective amplification of illusion, thanks to the way sound reinforced the actors' corporeal presence onscreen. Although some reviewers complained about the film's multilingual voice track (German and Hungarian),[12] most agreed that the use of sound bestowed the image with heightened in-

Figure 2. Breaking the sound barrier: Ad for the German-language release of *The Singing Fool* (1928, Lloyd Bacon) (*Film-Kurier,* June 1929).

tensity and realism. In spite of dramatic flaws and uneven performances, the first German sound film thus already anticipated what was to become dominant international sound-film practice: the joining of sound to the dynamic of the image, the articulation of sound and image into seemingly natural unity. But *Melody of the Heart,* as many critics pointed out, not only revolutionized cinematic illusion but also offered a new approach to filmmaking according to which the popular imagination could be based in culturally specific strata of thought, feeling, and speech. "What a relief," wrote Ernst Jäger for the *Film-Kurier*, "sound film without a saxophone."[13] Whereas Al Jolson's success earlier that year had reinforced the Weimar fascination with foreign rhythms and different sounds, jazz music in particular, *Melody of the Heart* portended a future in which native voices and domestic musical idioms would recenter German spectatorship and halt the increasing internationalization of leisure activities.

The German film industry entered the sound age from a comparatively strong position. In the second half of the 1920s UFA—the largest German film studio of the time—had taken crucial steps toward rationalizing production schedules and restructuring market operations. Hollywood imports during this time lost much of the attention they had captured during the early 1920s.[14] Meanwhile, the German film industry bought out American interests and strengthened its export position on the markets of central Europe. By 1928 the industry "was sufficiently diversified and innovative to keep pace with American cinema."[15] German industry representatives therefore endorsed sound emphatically, hoping to strengthen local revenues and expand the marketability of German cinema abroad.[16] Whereas in 1925, paralyzed by the costly production of Fritz Lang's *Metropolis*, UFA had suspended its "useless experiments" with nascent sound technologies,[17] the industry now hailed the arrival of the talkie as an opportunity to reduce American market shares in Germany and German-speaking Europe. By late 1929 UFA and other German production companies pursued the production of sound films aggressively. In 1929 German studios still produced 175 silent and only 8 sound films; in 1930 the ratio diminished to roughly 2:1. In 1931 the total number of silent film productions decreased to 2, and in 1932 German studios shot no more silent pictures at all.[18]

Retrospectively, many have come to think of the silent era in terms of a lack, a juvenile stage in film's maturing toward comprehensive illusionism and spectatorial identification. The arrival of the talkie, according to this line of reasoning, fulfilled what audiences had desired all along, namely the mutual integration of sights and sounds into organic representations. Historical research reveals a different picture, however. Synchronized sound in actual fact had very little appeal to the popular imagination prior to 1929, and the installation of sound equipment in German theaters had less to do with mass demand for new avenues of consumption than with the pressures of industrial production and marketing. Producers, not exhibitors, urged rapid conversion, driven by the belief that sound allowed for a more efficient managing of resources and revenues. "Silent film presentations had been notoriously variable. Works could be projected at different speeds, with operators advised in some manuals of their trade to vary the rhythm of projection within a given film. A single work could exist in different versions: black and white, or colored by one of several methods; long, short, or medium length; accompanied by large orchestras using carefully planned cue sheets, or by a single drunken pianist."[19] Synchronized sound streamlined these variable relations of production, exhibition, and consumption. Whereas meanings, as well as profits, in early silent cinema had been highly contingent on local exhibition contexts, sound film—in the eyes of the industry—promised new possibilities to shape a unified mass-cultural audience. Talking films helped standardize production codes and exhibition practices. In doing away with what in early silent film had been "at the mercy of relatively *unpredictable,* aleatory processes,"[20] sound film shifted the public's attention away from the peculiar projection situation, for example the interior of a local cinema or the particular style of a musical accompaniment. Instead, it refocused both the act of reception and the amassing of box office returns on mostly the film itself, while at the same time enforcing spectatorial silence and passivity as middle-class standards of respectability.

Whatever the actual driving force behind the conversion from silent to sound film, German audiences embraced the talkie quickly and decisively. In spite of the fact that sound reduced stylistic diversity in the long run, the new rhythms, noises, and voices that filled German theaters struck an immediate and favorable chord in the popular imagination. The speed of this approval remains perplexing. It seems legitimate to argue, however, that given the complete absence of any previous signs of dissatisfaction, the irresistibility of sound film had less to do with aesthetic concerns than with larger transformations that disrupted the fabric of everyday life. We should remember, after all, that the breakthrough of sound film coincided with rampant social, economic, and political upheavals. Synchronized sound helped audiences fill the void that had suddenly opened up in the wake of the Great Depression. Whereas the economic crash of 1929 resulted in an unprecedented convulsion of global spaces and temporal coordinates, sound film seemed to offer an ordered and recognizable space where it became possible to articulate or even counteract feelings of displacement, to restructure memory and readjust fantasy. The rhythms and streamlined temporalities of the talkie actualized structures of experience that differed from the chaotic flexing of time during the late Weimar Republic. More than simply an expression of escapism, the new vernacular of the sound film echoed real needs and provided a means of working out—in however distorted forms—fundamental, group-specific anxieties.

Against this backdrop we may also better understand why the talkie sparked acerbic criticism among some of the leading film critics of the Weimar period. "The talking film," Herbert Ihering wrote as early as 1922, "is a danger not only because it mechanizes the word, that which is the soul and spirit of a human being; but also because it undermines the laws of film that have emerged in the development of cinema."[21] Locating the laws of film in the primacy of the image, in the work of the camera and the virtuosity of editing, prominent critics rejected sound as redundant. Although directors such as G. W. Pabst, Fritz Lang, and Robert Siodmak quickly developed imaginative strategies to integrate sound and image, many critics remained skeptical and described the shift from silent to sound film as a move that would undo the poetry of film art. According to Rudolf Arnheim, for instance, the addition of sound reduced the difference between screen and reality and thus leveled the artistic status of the visual medium of film. Béla Balázs, by way of contrast, considered the introduction of sound to film the death knell for the universal nature of cinema and its ability to reveal the deeper magic of the visible world.

Noël Carroll and Rick Altman suggest that we ought to understand this critical rejection of sound film as an expression of a fundamental crisis in film aesthetics around 1930.[22] Sound, for critics such as Arnheim, signified a precarious return to canned theater, to film's earlier association with the principles of the stage. The coming of sound, for the partisans of the art of silent filmmaking, represented a monstrous return of silent cinema's repressed. It obstructed camera mobility, subjected the image to extraneous imperatives, and thus invalidated the purity of film as artistic expression. That many, such as the celebrated actor Emil Jannings,[23] conceived of Germany's considerable acting traditions as a powerful means to give sound film a uniquely German cultural elevation only added to Arnheim's and others' misgivings. Film, for the talkie's critics, achieved artistic originality not by incorporating literary traditions or mimicking stage practices but by operating with an aesthetics of its own. Sound was seen as antithetical to this end. Composite and heterogeneous in nature, the talkie no longer allowed film to define its difference from other arts and thus unfold its full artistic possibilities.

To reconstruct the dissonant beginnings of sound film in Germany in terms of conflicting aesthetic standards and expectations is helpful, but what is missing in this kind of conceptualization is any reference to the public dimension of cinematic reception and spectatorship. After all, the struggle over sound film was not just a struggle over the poetic logic of the medium. It was also, and perhaps foremost, a confrontation between different notions of cinema as a public trading ground of meaning and experience. Many of the talkie's critics envisioned (silent) cinema as a twentieth-century manifestation of the bourgeois public sphere. It opened a space of public discourse based on the educated reception and edifying valorization of aesthetic artifacts. Sound, according to this view, poisoned the formal integrity of filmic texts and hence undermined the structural possibility of public discourse. Seen with historical hindsight, the popular success of the talkie might therefore be understood as testimony to the rudimentary existence of different types of publicity and spectatorial initiative around 1930. Although the consolidation of sound film standardized formerly diverse acts of reception in the long run, sound film offered a space in which viewers could embrace the products of commercial culture to negotiate needs and identities within an industrial-commercial context. Although it would no doubt go too far to celebrate this new site per se as one of popular resistance, it seems reasonable to conceptualize early sound film as an ambiguous juncture at which desire, fantasy, and experience could be expressed through commodity consumption itself, through cultural practices that differed from the work of bourgeois publicity and that become legible only if seen against the turmoils of the time.

Nazi film culture sought to do away with the understanding of cinema in terms of bourgeois publicity and critical discourse and with the conception of the movie theater as an alternative public sphere allowing for the articulation of vernacular experiences, including those of blockage, displacement, and speechlessness. Nazi feature films were designed to emancipate the spectator from the restrictions of time and place. They supplanted audiences into a dream world radically different from Nazi realities; they subdued critical thought and simulated the advent of new communities beyond class, conflict, and discontent. The use of sound was an integral part of this project. Sound helped erase what had been locally specific about spectatorship during the silent era and caused empirical viewers to surrender their experience to the affective spectacle onscreen. Borrowing from Goebbels's own rhetoric, one might describe this approach to film sound as one based on an orchestra principle. In the performance of an orchestra composition every group of instruments has its own part, but with the help of a good score and conductor all result in one symphonic whole. "We do not expect everyone to play the same instruments, we only expect that people play according to plan." [24] Nazi feature films tapped into the new possibilities of cinematic audiovision not to propagate agitational sound bites so much as to define the general plan—a unified horizon of meaning, knowledge, and sense perception—that would tune different voices into one larger symphony. The use of sound in Nazi cinema introduced German film culture to what Adorno, with his eyes on the American culture industry, called the principle of pseudoindividualization—the "halo of free choice" on the basis of standardization itself.[25] It is to this ideological function of sound in Nazi film, its coordination of choice and its leveling of conflicting configurations of publicity, to which we now turn.

SPEAKING BODIES, SILENCED MINDS

Semiotic and psychoanalytic film theory suggests that we may understand the coming of sound as a revolution in the representation of bodies and a reconfiguration of spectatorial pleasures. Sound carried with it the potential danger of uncovering the heterogeneity of the filmic medium, but it also offered ample means of conjuring fantasies of wholeness and corporeal self-presence: "The addition of sound to cinema [introduced] the possibility of re-presenting a fuller (and organically unified) body, and of conforming the status of speech as an individual property right."[26] Sound in dominant cinema reanchored the body in the space of the narrated world. It positioned the spectator as an "auditory subject"[27] and amplified illusions of oneness, of identity and meaning, sustained by a body situated in space.

According to this argument one might think that German film theoreticians and filmmakers of the 1930s would have considered the presence of speaking bodies onscreen as a timely blessing playing right into the hands of their ideological designs. After all, Nazi Germany set out to counteract the fragmentation of identity and meaning in modern life; it promised to empower German men to become men again, to reassert themselves as resolute, unified subjects. Strangely enough, however, German films of the Nazi period by and large lacked the economy and precision that typified Hollywood dialogues of the same time. As my discussion of *The Tunnel* in chapter 2 will illustrate, Nazi feature films were often populated with protagonists who relapsed into silence or assumed stylized positions of muted suffering—think, for instance, of the heroes in *Morgenrot* (1933), *Hitlerjunge Quex* (1933), *Der verlorene Sohn* (1934), *Patrioten* (1937), *Friedemann Bach* (1941), *Carl Peters* (1941), and *Der große König* (1942). Over and over again, we witness heroes struggling for verbal expression or withdrawing from speech entirely, heroes who never seem to be quite at home in their language. Other films presented speech itself as the primary site of heroic action and self-assertion. As we will see in chapter 4, films such as *Der Kaiser von Kalifornien* and *Wasser für Canitoga* fed on the voice and allowed men, by merely emitting a voice, to become masters.

All films discussed in the following three chapters are marked by often-contradictory efforts to identify new bodies and spaces from which proper German voices could emanate. In all films we will notice either an assertive overabundance or a puzzling deficiency of speech. At first, one might be tempted to blame the low status of screenwriting in Nazi cinema for this. It is a well-known fact that—with the exception of star dramatists such as Gerhard Menzel *(Morgenrot, Flüchtlinge, La Habanera, Robert Koch, Heimkehr)*[28]—screenwriters did not enjoy much recognition for their work under Goebbels. Yet to attribute the dearth or the surplus of film dialogue simply to clumsy screenplays, we would have to overlook how the linguistic properties of Nazi features resonated with larger political configurations. Three possible reasons come immediately to mind when trying to account for the unsettled role of recorded voices in Nazi cinema. First, one might see the vocal repose of many protagonists as a direct application of Nazi film theory and its definition of cinema as a "biocentric" rather than logocentric organ of national education.[29] Because speech onscreen appeals primarily to the viewer's rational cognition, it was seen by some as antithetical to film's explicit goal of shaping moods and feelings, of overcoming discord and resentment, of conquering the deepest recesses of the unconscious. Heroism, it was claimed, "does not always need big words at all, and it can be expressed in film much more compellingly with other means."[30] Recorded voices, it was argued, spoil images of immediacy, and they interrupt spectatorial identification. Spoken dialogue led fantasy back to the real world and thus thwarted collective dreaming and spectatorial bonding.

Second, what often seems compulsive about spoken dialogue in German films of the 1930s might also be seen against the backdrop of Goebbels's intention to make cinema into a visceral mass event that, in order to beat American competition, had to break with the legacy of German literary and stage traditions. An outspoken cineaste, Goebbels surely favored a cinema of formal excellence and artistic merit, but he did not intend to accomplish this goal simply by raiding the treasures of eighteenth- and nineteenth-century German literature or stagecraft. German cinema, he argued, should shun canned theater or wordy introspection. Narrative film is driven by conflict and action, and therefore it needs to learn how to translate cultural values into compelling visual surfaces. Americans in fact had it much better in this respect, Goebbels explained in 1941: "They entered film production as young peoples, without being somehow burdened by the ballast of the work of many hundreds of years. They therefore also found in a natural way what we were able to find only via detours, namely to emancipate film from literature, to sever its ties to the theater, and to make it into an autonomous and self-centered art form."[31] Learning from American culture, Goebbels insisted that philosophical eloquence and poetic locution had no place onscreen. Only a resolute privileging of gesture over word, of emotion over reason, could help build a national film culture that would deliver something for everyone.

Third, and finally, to better understand the unstable position of speaking bodies in Nazi film space, one might refer to what Karsten Witte has called the Nazis' fear of decadence and decay, of flowing into dissipation.[32] Nazi film aesthetics hallowed the freezing of individual bodies in ornamental configurations. It fragmented movements and bodies only to convert them into rigid and ritualized expressions. "Film narratives of the Nazi era generally privileged space over time, composition over editing, design over movement, sets over human shapes. Compared to Hollywood movies, most features of the Third Reich appeared slow and static. They were more prone to panoramas and tableaus than to close-ups, decidedly sparing in their physical displays (very little nudity, few stunts and action scenes)."[33] Driven by deep-seated fears about spontaneity and desire, Nazi film tried to desexualize the body and contain what could thwart the appearance of consecration and control. The design of spoken dialogue in Nazi film was deeply implicated in this project of halting dissipation and de-eroticizing the body. Many Nazi features, on the one hand, endorsed what one might call antilanguage. They involved a grave mistrust about linguistic expressions simply because oral communication signaled a loss of mastery, an emasculating opening toward the contingencies of the real. When the hero talked, his language was supposed to be minimalist and self-effacing. On the other hand, however, spoken words in Nazi movies were also meant to shift the viewer's attention away from the body. Excessive dialogue displaced desire, contained physical displays and movements with emotive sounds, and bonded the viewers' pleasure to larger compositions and designs. Spoken dialogue in Nazi film thus played an important role in channeling perception and regulating desire. What may strike today's viewers as awkward about recorded voices in Nazi film is the often self-contradictory use of dialogue: to frame and domesticate pleasure in cinema, that most pleasurable of all sites of modern entertainment.

SPECTACLES OF SYNCHRONIZATION

Heide Schlüpmann has argued that Nazi film configured image and sound in a strictly hierarchical relationship.[34] Sound in Nazi cinema deepened and dramatized diegetic space, but, similar to dominant Hollywood practices, it remained subordinate to the image track. My comments on dialogue in Nazi film so far urge us to modify Schlüpmann's findings: the hero's voice, whether it speaks too much or too little, was considered not as secondary but as an integral moment in a larger aesthetic gestalt. The point, therefore, is not to theorize whether Nazi cinema privileged one over the other but to understand how Nazi feature films readily and equally exploited the power of the visual and the sonic in order to organize attention and regulate desire. Speech in many feature films of the 1930s is meant to be sensuous and emotive. As I will argue in particular in my analysis of the Nazi cowboy in chapter 4, the perlocutionary aspects of language—the ability of words to make something happen in the world—overrule the power of discourse to enable rational insight and noncoercive forms of human interaction. Speech here assumes the status of a nonrepresentational sign.[35] It generates meaning in ways that differ from conventionalized processes of signification; it emphasizes that which knows no real referent in language, that is, the material rhythm, texture, and color of verbal expressions. In a sense film dialogue—as discussed in the following chapters—mimics the role leading Nazi film theoreticians ascribed to the power of film music: to emancipate the viewer from discursive thought, to silence the spectators' censor, and to cue them into shared narrational positions.[36]

Nazi sound films placed great emphasis on the timbre of regional dialects and variegated accents, on the tessitura of local German vernaculars. Regional actors and their regional modes of speaking enjoyed great popularity in Nazi cinema. Furthermore, many films cultivated strategies of what I call linguistic sampling: they gave voice to various German dialects even if the plot's setting did not warrant the presentation of this kind of diversity.[37] It seems reasonable to suppose that this regional grain of Nazi film dialogue, at the level of discursive construction, was meant to recall the emphasis nineteenth-century discourse had placed on the German language as a catalyst of ethnic identity. Richard Wagner's by no means original linguistic theories found a curious echo in Nazi film practice. For Wagner, language reflected national essences, and the coloratura of speech provided a sign of ethnic identity. Language, for Wagner, essentially belonged to the realm of natural history and biology; its nonreferential textures would always be imperfectly accommodated by those who were foreign or physiologically different, particularly the Jew and the French.[38] Nazi film practitioners applied these theories to the domain of industrial culture. They espoused film dialogue as a means to set specifically German moods and orchestrate ethnically specific affects. With its many regional voices, Nazi dialogue hoped to inundate audiences with typically German patterns of intonation. The sound of speech was designed to function as a sign of mythic Germanness; it was thought to amplify cultural difference and tie the viewer into the national community.

Yet Nazi cinema, of course, aspired not only to become "German through and through"[39] but also to conquer foreign markets. Commercial imperatives clearly set limits to the way feature films could broadcast the German language as a catalyst of national identity. The remarkable number of foreign-language versions produced by Nazi film studios even during the second half of the 1930s bears testimony to the often-contradictory coexistence of economic and ideological protocols in Nazi cinema. Nazi film officials may have considered sound as a tool to conjure a homogeneous community integrated via the regional textures of the German language, but they were no less willing to produce feature films in foreign languages, as well, in an attempt to end Hollywood's postwar dominance in Europe and refashion German cinema as the most successful European cinema of all time.

The practical design of film dialogue in Nazi cinema, therefore, clearly exceeded the discursive construction of language as a conduit for typically German affects. The actual function of speech in Nazi feature films, I suggest, was in fact less to accentuate national specificity or celebrate community than to restrain desire and restrict the power of language to enable symmetrical forms of human interaction. As we will see in chapters 2 through 4, Nazi feature films often identified male and female voices with the materiality of their vocal idiosyncrasies. Speech incorporated the subject into the diegesis. Although protagonists may speak lavishly, no one in Nazi cinema really becomes a subject of discourse. Instead, the grain of both men's and women's voices communicates their bodies as objects of control that elude any control over the mechanisms of signification. Although Nazi feature films aspired to push linguistic expressions beyond the coded and, by foregrounding the materiality of speech, gave language the appearance of an unmediated sensory experience, they at the same time presented speech as entirely in the image. Dominant editing rules privileged the speaking body, even in shot/countershot scenarios. Throughout the 1930s they restricted the role of disembodied voices, whether they speak offscreen or as a voice-over. Nazi feature films thus attempted to arrest the migratory potential of the human voice and inhibit its power to establish new bonds and solidarities. Arresting speech within established boundaries, Nazi film dialogue excelled in what Michel Chion has called de-acousmatization: "a sort of enclosing of the voice in the circumscribed limits of the body—which tames the voice and drains it of its power."[40] Speech in Nazi film dissociated people much more than it allowed them to open up for each other through the medium of language, whereas it became the task of film music, as we will see in a moment, to reunite the isolated as isolated and to fulfill, under conditions of domination, popular demands for play, plenty, and community.

WAGNER IN BABELSBERG

It has become a commonplace for film historians to point out the influence of Richard Wagner on Hollywood film scores of the classical studio era. European émigré composers such as Erich Wolfgang Korngold, Miklós Rósza, Max Steiner, and Franz Waxman played a critical role in the process of adapting Wagner's compositional techniques to the narrative demands of Hollywood feature films.[41] Hollywood film composers since the early 1930s had evoked Wagnerian harmony, chromatism, and unending melody to ameliorate dramatic action. They used Wagner's leitmotif technique to illustrate thoughts, feelings, or motivations and, thereby, to supplement the diegetic world with glimpses of anticipation, remembrance, or irony. Whereas Nazi Germany embraced Wagner as an icon of national and racial self-assertion, Hollywood's film composers utilized the master's compositional methods to extend impressions of narrative integrity and roundness, to unveil putative truths and essences that amplified the work of dialogue, narrative, and image track.

Theodor W. Adorno was little surprised about Wagner's popularity in Hollywood. Like Wagner's mature music dramas, which for Adorno already contained the seeds of twentieth-century industrial culture, studio film music was designed for audiences no longer capable of concentrated structural listening. But, according to Adorno, in its very effort to complete Wagner's individual techniques with the means of a Fordist culture industry, Hollywood eluded the utopian elements of Wagner's aesthetics. Let us briefly recall that Wagner's famous concept of the total artwork envisioned future artworks that would reintegrate the alienated siblings of music, dance, and poetry. For Wagner the total artwork intended to restore the possibility of sensual plentitude and communal solidarity, to recenter experience and overcome cultural fragmentation. The total artwork aspired to nothing less than reclaiming the role of tragedy in ancient Greek society. It was to reestablish aesthetic experience as the principal path of communal integration and identity. In the critical perspective of Adorno, Hollywood failed to recognize how Wagner sought to couple aesthetic innovation with political reform. Studio film composers, pressed by Hollywood commercialism, reified Wagner's leitmotifs into mere signposts that captured the viewer's attention like advertisements. Void of any substance and complexity, Hollywood leitmotifs merely typified heroes and announced situations. Their sole purpose was to facilitate the audience's perception. For Adorno Hollywood Wagnerianism in fact rendered music a mere lackey to image and narrative. It valorized musical expressions that remained below the threshold of conscious perception and critical awareness. Although film music—like Wagner's monumental style—was designed to be seductive, it was said to do its job best whenever we don't hear or, as Hanns Eisler argued, see it.[42] Although for Wagner "the unity of the music drama was achieved through the synthesis of its elements, with the total effect equaling more than the sum of its parts, classical film music critics and practitioners believed cinematic unity was attained through redundancy and overdetermination—not through a true synthesis of elements."[43]

Adorno is of course an unlikely candidate to defend Wagner's total work of art against Hollywood. In Adorno's view Wagner himself already delivered false goods because he neither lived up to his own project of restoring spontaneity nor ever contemplated the possibility of creating art through collective labor. Nonetheless, Adorno's criticism can help us better understand the popularity of Wagner's larger aesthetic program in the self-reflection not only of exile film composers but also of Nazi filmmaking. Wagner's concept of the total work of art deeply informed the way leading film practitioners of the Third Reich aspired to use narrative film to stimulate national awakening. Looking more at Wagner's general program than at his individual techniques, Nazi film theorists and filmmakers assigned music—understood as that most German of all arts—a much more audible and visible place than did their Hollywood counterparts (fig. 3). In often granting diegetic and nondiegetic music the possibility of energizing the image track, they also professed the final coming into being of Wagner's original vision of future art—the advent of a truly synthetic form of public art that would close the gulf between the aesthetic and other domains of modern experience.

Whether we consider the electrifying sound tracks by film composers such as Giuseppe Becce, Hans-Otto Borgmann, Theo Mackeben, Willy Richartz, Herbert Windt, and Wolfgang Zeller or the prominence of the revue and music-film genre,[44] Nazi cinema accentuated music as an equal participant in the composite art of filmmaking. It cultivated many stars

Figure 3.   Music matters: Ads for music films shown in Germany in 1933
(*Film-Kurier*).

combining proficient acting and singing skills, but it also opened many a door for current opera and operetta celebrities to appear on German screens (for example, Maria Cebotari, Beniamino Gigli, Louis Graveure, Maria Jeritza, Jan Kiepura, Tresi Rudolph, Erna Sack, and Joseph Schmidt).[45] Far from simply fulfilling an auxiliary role, music—diegetic and nondiegetic—took center stage in a great number of Nazi entertainment films and genres. Instead of subjecting film scores to what Eisler called Hollywood's "vanishing function,"[46] Nazi cinema put it on display in what one might call a cinema of sonic attractions: a cinema privileging spectacle, exhibitionism, and sensuous immediacy over narrative development, voyeurism, and dramatic closure. The comparatively large proportion of diegetic music performances— from classical symphonies to contemporary hit songs—gave voice to the effort of converting (German) sounds into appealing sights, into showcases of what nineteenth-century romanticism had constructed as the primal source of German identity. Unlike classical Hollywood practice, Nazi film music was often meant to be heard and seen. It wanted to seduce and lull the mind, but it also wanted to impress, astound, and overwhelm, with the aim of incorporating German viewers into the national community.

In July 1936 Joseph Goebbels declared that Wagner's work had "conquered the world because it was consciously German and did not wish to be anything else."[47] Goebbels suggested on numerous public occasions that Wagner's international success should inspire the film industry to develop a distinctly German and stylistically assured film language that could revive domestic popularity and increase revenues abroad. Significantly, however, in the eyes of Nazi filmmakers and film composers—with the exception of explicit Wagnerians such as Becce *(Hans Westmar, Der verlorene Sohn, Der Kaiser von Kalifornien, Condottieri, Der Berg ruft)* or Borgmann *(Hitlerjunge Quex, Gold, Verwehte Spuren, Die goldene Stadt, Opfergang)*— it was less Wagner's compositional technique itself than his metaphysics of sense perception that was seen as the most important medium of giving German cinema Goebbels's desired Wagnerian turn. Except for the diegetic staging of Wagner's music in Erich Waschneck's 1934 *Musik im Blut* (Music in the blood) and Karl Ritter's 1941 *Stukas,* Nazi feature films strangely shunned any direct references to Wagner's music dramas. Whereas Hollywood Wagnerians such as Korngold and Steiner consciously adopted Wagner's intricate methods of weaving voice and music into a dramatic syntax, their German counterparts considered Wagner primarily an ideological soul mate, a nineteenth-century soothsayer foretelling film's power to engineer utopian states in which neither the arts nor the human senses would suffer their modern condition of separation.

In an instructive essay of 1939, director Wolfgang Liebeneiner *(Du und Ich, Bismarck, Ich klage an),* who would serve as UFA production head from 1942 to 1945, explicated these Wagnerian undertones of Nazi cinema.[48] The basic law of silent *and* sound film, Liebeneiner argued, lies in film's musicality, in how cutting and editing impute images with rhythm. Film is music with other means; therefore, it is the primary function of sound to accentuate the basic musicality of the image track and ameliorate cinema's work of enchantment. "We know that the word, the dialogue, has a formulating and sobering function, and that it on the other hand deepens, spiritualizes, and interiorizes. But it can only fulfill the demands of film if it adheres to the musical rhythm of the image and becomes its equal."[49] It is not what actors say but how they say it—not discursive logic but intonation, stress, and accent—that makes film dialogue persuasive.[50] Film music, too, should emphasize the rhythmical structure of film instead of simply illustrating emotions or stitching narratives together. According to Liebeneiner, scores meet the laws of film whenever they crown a movie's principal rhythm with harmony, melody, color, and timbre, whenever they fulfill the "old Germanic longing to include the whole world into one artwork and to combine all art forms into one powerful experience."[51]

Silent film, Liebeneiner continued, was only the first step toward the full unfolding of cinema's musicality. It left the acoustical space open for the viewer's own imagination, and it is for this reason that undubbed or subtitled American features enjoyed great popularity in Nazi Germany, simply because spectators falsely rendered the sound of foreign voices as music and melody. But when seen from a more critical perspective, Liebeneiner insisted, Hollywood lacks the cultural resources to produce aesthetically relevant sound films. Driven by greed and the whim of industrial progress, modern America has endorsed pure, disenchanted rhythm and thereby obliterated the community-building power of harmony, melody, and timbre. Contemporary Germany, by way of contrast, sustains rich musical traditions in spite of all signs of modernization. As the most immediate expression of the German soul, music saturates daily life literally at every corner; it emanates from coffee shops and entertainment places, from domestic gramophones and the public marching grounds. It is Germany, therefore, the country that "created music and conquered the world with it,"[52] that provides what is essential to perfect the musical logic of film, to synthesize cinematic sounds and sights, and thus to fulfill Wagner's dream of future art as a public medium of plenitude and communal integration. Babelsberg, not Hollywood, is the privileged site at which authentic sound films can come into being.

Informed by Wagner's programmatic vision of future opera as a space of cultural synthesis, Nazi film theorists and filmmakers such as Liebeneiner recognized film as the most effective instrument of modern culture to unify experience and reshape sense perception. Film was seen as essentially melodrama, and by definition Germans did best in infusing the drama of images with *melos,* with emotional timbre and an imaginary sense of plenitude. What Liebeneiner and others envisioned as Wagnerian film art was meant not only to unify the heterogeneous elements of cinematic representation but in so doing to reform the nation's body politic. Similar to Wagner's quest for a musical idiom that would speak to the entirety of the German people, film music was meant to close the great divide of modern culture: the gap between legitimate art and mass culture that had existed since the late nineteenth century. As conceived by Nazi film theorists, film music proved essential to set collective moods and bond the people, to mobilize desire and regenerate lost experiences of community.

MUSICAL POACHING

In 1878 Richard Wagner declared that the essence of German national identity could be found in music, yet at the same time he acknowledged the difficulties of defining exactly what made German music German: Bach's work had relied on French and Italian models; Händel had achieved his fame in London as a composer of Italian operas; the Austrians Haydn and Mozart had been heavily influenced by Italian music of the time. Confronted with the dilemma of the international character of German musical traditions, Wagner ended up explaining the Germanness of German music by pointing to the remarkable ability of German composers to rework foreign sources and unlock the true meaning of other aesthetic traditions: "[H]is is no mere idle gaping at the Foreign, as such, as purely foreign; he wills to understand it 'Germanly.' . . . [H]e strips the Foreign of its accidental, its externals, of all that to him is unintelligible, and makes good the loss by adding just so much of his own externals and accidentals as it needs to set the foreign object plain and undefaced before him." [53]

Nazi musicologists, in their attempt to define the essence of German music, largely followed Wagner's reasoning. Vague assumptions about the German ability to adapt foreign models persisted throughout the Nazi period, in spite of various projects to find more rudimentary forms of musical Germanness in folk music, local traditions, and Gregorian chant. [54] Nazi film music, I suggest, at once reflected and exploited this dilemma. To be sure, Goebbels in 1933 had quickly ordered roughly 45 percent of all film composers to be removed from their positions, the majority of them Jewish, in order to make German film music "German."[55] But similar to both Wagner and Nazi musicology, Nazi cinema failed to clearly define essentially German musical traits. In fact, responding to the continued receptivity of German audiences and composers to international compositional practices, Nazi film sound tracks featured many musical idioms that official Nazi doctrine deemed inauthentic, including jazz and swing. Nazi film music, particularly during the prewar era, often overstepped the boundaries of what its ideologues prescribed, yet it did so not to give voice to some kind of aesthetic resistance but rather to meet popular demand halfway and bring it safely home. It poached on the foreign, transposed the exotic into the familiar, to address and simultaneously domesticate the entire spectrum of modern musical pleasure and thus to contain possible aesthetic resistance within the dominant order itself.

The interaction of sounds and images in *Glückskinder* (Lucky kids, 1936, Paul Martin), a German remake of Frank Capra's 1933 *It Happened One Night,* is a good case in point. *Lucky Kids,* as Eric Rentschler has argued, "replicated a Hollywood film on a Babelsberg studio set, imitating a generic pleasure made in a foreign dream factory, in effect creating the illusion of an already illusory world, raising artifice to a higher power by frankly admitting its own derivation and desire."[56] In contrast to Capra's original, which engaged a multitude of visual puns and erotic metaphors, *Lucky Kids* is at pains to bracket sexuality and desire or—at best—to relocate desire from the visual level to the much safer and more controllable sphere of dialogue. Cosmopolitan music styles, although mostly constructed by Nazi ideology as overly sexualized and degenerate, play a significant part in this project of displacement. Peter Kreuder's sound track for *Lucky Kids* appeals to the continuous popularity of jazz and swing in the Third Reich,[57] yet at the same time it helps discipline the actors' bodies as much as the viewers' perceptions. This effort to contain pleasure and perception culminates when Lilian Harvey, Willy Fritsch, and two friends engage in a brief song-and-dance interlude, performed in Fritsch's New York apartment to the sounds of Kreuder's hit song "Ich wollt' ich wär' ein Huhn" (I wish I were a chicken [lyrics by Hans Fritz Beckmann]).[58]

A remarkable exercise in cultural redress, Kreuder's song for *Lucky Kids* borrows from various musical traditions to set the stage for a series of ever-shifting dance formations. Allusions to French, Russian, and American folk songs intermingle swiftly with the citation of Viennese waltzing music, American fox-trot, and the habanera from Bizet's *Carmen*. Everything seems possible; indeed, nothing seems to halt the song's grasp for distant realities and exotic modalities. Nevertheless, camera work and editing throughout the performance number are motivated by a fundamental fear of corporeality, a fear that a sudden ecstasy may yield a dissolution of identity and, hence, anarchy. Instead of tracking dancing bodies with imaginative travel shots, pans, or shifting perspectives, Martin's camera remains extremely static. It renders motion from a stifling frontal point of view; it freezes speed and activity into images of rigidity. Several times the camera pulls back straight along a central axis as if to increase the frame's defining and confining power. Even when the number, featuring jazzy big band sounds, involves all four actors in eccentric activities such as step- and belly-dancing, the camera remains in a safe position of control and in fact recruits the help of an additional framing device, a door frame, to transform horizontal movement into vertical stasis. The interlude ends with a series of tilted, disconnected close-ups of all four singers. This final montage not only reveres what is to be understood as the superiority of embodied yet curiously desexualized voices, but it also shows us the quartet's amused reaction when the needle of the record player gets caught in a crack and endlessly repeats a single phrase. What camera movement and editing have already established is thus affirmed by the failure of mechanical reproduction. The film urges disavowal to emerge from the very space of ecstasy. It exorcises the objects of its own fascination.[59]

Like speech, music in Nazi feature films is routinely subjected to processes of narrative and visual containment. Although on the one hand music is considered an unmediated expression of passion and the German soul, on the other hand it should resound from the visual field itself, from a visible body framed and contained by the cinematic image. Rather than help the body to communicate or signify, singing and music in films such as *Lucky Kids* communicate the body as an object of control, a captive within the material textures of the diegesis. As a container of song and music, the body becomes contained itself, situated and excessively diegeticized through audiovisual spectacles of embodiment. In the final analysis, then, foreign sounds in *Lucky Kids* offer the National Socialist body yet another chance to chicken out. Thoroughly domesticated by what Liebeneiner understood as the Wagnerian edifice of German cinema, "un-German" music helps stage affective outbursts that end up cementing given identities and prohibiting any decentering experience of alterity. *Lucky Kids* incorporates word, dance, and music into a compelling aesthetic synthesis. It frames alternative pleasures, synchronizes different traditions and tastes, and implicates music in a repressive project of disciplining the senses.

ANAESTHETIC POPULISM

Nazi music politics was characterized by continuous conflicts over the relationship between serious and light-entertainment music. Goebbels's dismissal of composer Richard Strauss as head of the *Reichsmusikkammer* (Reich Music Chamber) in July 1935, for example, resulted largely from Strauss's reluctance to place greater weight on popular music as an instrument of cultural politics. Goebbels, by contrast, "who had some elitist tastes and certainly scorned the masses, nonetheless was a consummate politician and realized that if he was to co-opt the largest number of people to satisfy the aims of the regime, they would have to be wooed, and this could be achieved only with the help of popular culture, not Bach or Beethoven."[60] The idea of film as a Wagnerian total work of art offered a compromise to these controversies. It allowed for the possibility of satisfying popular demand for hit songs and cosmopolitan idioms and at the same time justified film as a comprehensive art form grounded in high cultural traditions. Such synthetic aspirations became best exemplified by the way Nazi cinema used opera stars in order to proliferate light musical entertainment. Although films such as Georg Zoch's *Ein Lied klagt an* (A song accuses, 1936) and Carl Froelich's *Frühlingsmärchen* (Spring fairytale, 1934) problematized musical crossovers, Nazi film music readily exploited vocal talent in order to bestow popular material with cultural aura and thus close the pernicious gap between high and low. Following the lead of Wagner's ambitious aesthetic program, music in Nazi film played an important role in fusing contradictory elements into a synthetic whole that could gratify diverse tastes, interlock different auditory media channels, and disseminate sounds that could be consumed at all times. Many leading film composers may have expressed their unease about using classical music in their scores,[61] but on the sets of Babelsberg the conception of film as a total work of art helped justify the parallel existence of Beethoven and popular hit songs, of eighteenth-century marches and easy-listening music, of symphonic extravaganzas and cliché-ridden sing-alongs.[62]

Nazi film music during the 1930s clearly fell short of actualizing the kind of German musical essences that many zealous ideologues assigned to Wagner's music.[63] Similar to the implementation of film dialogue, the use of film music in Nazi cinema was characterized by many disjunctions between discourse and practice, intention and reception, ideology and commercialism. Nevertheless, in its endeavor to integrate high and low, familiar and foreign, old and new, Nazi film music did assume some of the same gestures that had characterized Wagner's own compositional practice. Adorno's work on Wagner once again captures the full scope of Nazi populism: "As advocate of the effect," Adorno wrote about Wagner, "the conductor is the advocate of the public in the work. As the striker of blows, however, the composer-conductor gives the claims of the public a terrorist emphasis. Democratic considerateness towards the listener is transformed into connivance with the powers of discipline: in the name of the listener, anyone whose feelings accord with any yardstick other than the beat of the music is silenced."[64] Similar to Wagner, who assimilated nineteenth-century high art to public taste at the expense of structural coherence, the German sound cinema of the 1930s aspired to control all possible effects. Nazi film music beat audiences into delightful submission. It poached on various musical traditions, not to intermingle competing cultural codes but to exorcize the other and remake the viewers' desires in the film itself. Musical sound tracks in Nazi cinema were designed to seize and overwhelm the audience. They rendered domestication and discipline a pleasure. As they encouraged viewers to become universal German spectators, they put sound in the service of silencing minds and bodies.

National Socialism and fascism have often been characterized by their surplus of aesthetics, that is, the aestheticization of politics. Nazi sound film practice reveals that if we recall the original sense of the word *aesthetics*—the sensory experience of perception—the opposite seems much closer to the truth. Like Wagner's compositions (in Adorno's reading), Nazi sound film excelled in *anaesthetics*. Although appealing to the viewer's emotions, Nazi cinema hoped to neutralize sense perception and deny the corporeal nature of experience. Understood as a Wagnerian total work of art, Nazi sound film aspired not only to arouse powerful sentiments but at the same time to obliterate the private body as a site of spontaneity and experience. It assaulted the body and disregarded sentience with the intention of arresting the individual mind and body in isolation. As Simonetta Falasca-Zamponi has put it: "[T]he lack of aesthetics, rather than its excess, made fascism totalitarian."[65]

HEGEMONIZING SPECTATORSHIP

Although film historians generally agree that in the long run the coming of synchronized sound supported the dominance of Hollywood in Europe,[66] for Nazi cinema sound played an indispensable role in the attempt to build a viable alternative to Hollywood filmmaking during the 1930s.[67] Nazi cinema embraced sound not as a means of overt agitation so much as a tool to set collective moods and channel emotions, to move minds and mobilize bodies. Cinematic sound appealed to Nazi film practitioners and industrialists alike because it opened new possibilities to capture the entire range of modern diversion and thus, in Goebbels's words, "to produce ever more films that are accessible to the whole folk, to high and low, rich and poor, young and old."[68] Surely, as we have seen in the preceding pages, neither the use of film dialogue nor that of film music entirely followed the ideological mandate of elevating the viewer's soul to the ineffable substance of Germanness. But in historical hindsight, what must be seen as the most notable aspect of Nazi audiovision is the much more elementary project of remaking the viewer's sense perception and restraining reciprocal relations between self and other. Like Wagner in Adorno's reading, Nazi sound cinema aimed at merging expression and repression into one and the same mechanism. It set out to neutralize desire and coordinate memory, to reshape the viewer's temporal and spatial relations, to frame competing definitions of reality, and in so doing to reify rather than open up given boundaries of meaning, articulation, and identity. Put into the service of the Nazi culture industry, talking pictures became a primary tool to make existing frameworks of power, social integration, and cultural signification appear legitimate and natural.

In the eyes of Nazi film ideologues the relatively new possibility of synchronized sound allowed German cinema to develop a nationally specific film language powerful enough to achieve international success: "The national rejuvenation in Germany," boasted *Film-Kurier* in 1934, "has done away with this nonsense of imitating foreign styles and customs. Today the German film is what it should and must be: German."[69] But Nazi film culture, as we have seen already, was far less unified than its ideologues wanted. It contained elements that do not meet the textbook definition of totalitarian rule and mass coordination: a recurring split between theory and practice; a tendency toward administrative confusion and provisional decision making; an often-incoherent concurrence of opportunism, populism, and authoritarianism. Reckoning with the continuous popularity of American sights and sounds, Nazi filmmaking as a result often sought to co-opt rather than simply deny the persistent hunger for Hollywood-style genre products. It appealed to Americanist fantasies but at the same time articulated highly anti-American agendas (fig. 4). America was perceived as the harbinger of innovative technologies and fearless rationalization, but it was also seen as a laboratory of decentered and feminized identities, a site of emasculated, degenerate, and Jewish hybridity. At once incorporating and disciplining what endured as fascinating about America, Nazi cinema referenced

Figure 4.   American fantasies: Ad for Luis Trenker's *The Prodigal Son*
(*Film-Kurier*, 1934).

Hollywood with the ambition of reminding German viewers of older sights
and pleasures but also of building bridges to the new order. However paradoxical in nature, the emulation of Hollywood thus functioned as a crucial catalyst for the construction of Nazi hegemony, that is, the articulation
of national consent beyond previous frictions of class, status, and gender.

The notion of hegemony implies ongoing contestation and historical contingency at the very center of modern society; it rejects narratives of all-inclusive determination and acknowledges that "unfixity has become the condition of every social identity."[70] Hegemony is never a given; it is in constant need of sustenance and reproduction. The following three chapters discuss in greater detail how feature films of the Third Reich helped win and refix Nazi hegemony by anticipating desired viewing positions and thus gaining control over whatever remained contingent about the act of reception. In paradigmatic readings all three chapters argue that both the presence of synchronized sound and the ambivalent appeal of American popular culture were central to the rendering of history as nature and fate and thus to the hegemonization of spectatorship in the Third Reich. Although we cannot reconstitute the contours of empirical acts of viewing, we may infer, primarily by way of negation, what the interaction of image and sound in Nazi feature films really meant to individuals in their everyday lives by analyzing the various strategies intended to curb unwanted fantasies and control what Alexander Kluge has called cinema's moment of unpredictability: the film as it unfolds in the spectator's head.[71]

2 Incorporating the Underground

Curtis Bernhardt's The Tunnel

Rudolf Arnheim, one of the most belligerent German critics of the talkie, rejected sound well into the 1930s as something foreign to the art of filmmaking. In Arnheim's view synchronized sound polluted the film medium; it curtailed the camera's poetic power.[1] Arnheim's critique of sound might seem puzzling in retrospect, but the early years of sound film did indeed bring an alarming loss of refinement in the areas of camera work and editing. The new pragmatics of sound effectively transformed a sophisticated visual language that had been shaped by silent directors such as Friedrich Wilhelm Murnau and Fritz Lang. As Claudia Gorbman explains,

> synch sound visually rooted actors to the spot, and limited the possibilities of exploring space within a scene. . . . Actors were obliged to remain close to the microphone[s], which . . . were hidden behind props; early mikes not only had poor sensitivity to voices but paradoxically seemed to pick up every other stray sound around the set. The camera, imprisoned in its soundproofed booth, would not generally regain freedom of movement until the development of the blimp and rolling camera carriages in 1930–31.[2]

In the early 1930s cinematographer Fritz Arno Wagner (*Westfront*, 1930; *Kameradschaft*, 1931; *M*, 1931) was central to the reinvention of camera mobility. It was not until at least 1933, however, that editing practices, too, could fully recuperate their former flexibility. For only then did it become possible to record speech, music, and sound effects on separate tracks, to layer dialogue and film music, and, in doing so, to overcome the often stilted sequencing of early sound sources and scenes.

Throughout the 1930s almost all important innovations in cinema technology served the effort to produce the illusion of real people onscreen speaking real words.[3] Industrialists and filmmakers alike aimed at technological solutions that would place sound and image in natural harmony. German theater owners were often unable to keep pace with the industry's speed of transformation. By 1932 only 60 percent of all theaters in Germany had been wired for sound projection. German audiences, however, quickly embraced what contemporary commentators routinely discussed as a gendered drama—the marriage of sight and sound, including the one of imported images and dubbed voices. By 1933 lip synchronization and sound remixing had improved to such a degree that German audiences gave up their earlier rejection of dubbing.[4] For German spectators, dubbing no longer flattened diegetic space or drove bodies and voices apart. While technological advances had helped integrate sound and image into a myth of principal unity,[5] audiences had learned how to imagine natural links between body and voice even where those links did not exist.

Given the domestic approval of dubbing, it might surprise us that Nazi film studios continued to produce foreign-language versions of domestic films in order to deal with the language problem in early sound cinema. For export-oriented film industries prior to 1933, multiple language versions had provided the most feasible method of selling sound films abroad. Foreign-language productions had raised artifice to a higher degree to communicate the marriage of image and sound across given linguistic boundaries. That Nazi cinema extended the production of multiple language versions well beyond the point of technological necessity, on the one hand, must be seen as a result of purely commercial considerations. Because foreign-language versions could draw on the appeal of local stars and familiar faces, they promised a much more thorough penetration of foreign markets. On the other hand, the endurance of multiple-language productions throughout the 1930s must also be understood as a response to ideological mandates. Unlike subtitled or dubbed films, foreign-language versions allowed Nazi cinema to exploit foreign markets while upholding a sense of national difference and sonic segregation. Nazi filmmakers and ideologues cared much more than their audiences about who really owned the voices that came out of the loudspeakers. They embraced multiple-language productions in the hope of capturing foreign consumers without blurring linguistic boundaries and national affiliations.

Curtis Bernhardt's *Der Tunnel* (The tunnel, 1933) was one of these "freak"[6] multiple-language productions (fig. 5). Based on Bernhard Kellermann's popular 1913 science fiction novel of the same name,[7] *The Tunnel* premiered on November 3, 1933, at the Capitol Theater in Berlin. Bernhardt, one of the last directors of Jewish background working for Nazi film studios, was brought back to Germany from Paris to shoot this film, in no small part because the film's production company, Bavaria, intended to draw on Bernhardt's French experience to produce a second-language version for French audiences.[8] One of the few science fiction films produced during the Nazi period,[9] *The Tunnel* narrates the construction of a subway connection between Long Island and Europe. The film draws the viewer into a domain of special effects in which modern technology becomes an awesome spectacle and in which disciplined (German) work in the end prevails over the destructive force of Jewish capital and American greed. *The Tunnel* engages the viewer in a struggle over sound and its national ownership. Similar to the task of multiple-language production in the Nazi film industry at large, the film renders cinematic audiovision of critical importance to the marketable conversion of cultural difference into radical alterity. While presenting a narrative of geographical transgression and spatial conquest, *The Tunnel* enlists synchronized sound in the effort to rework spectatorship, separate different cultures, and revoke the rule of Hollywood over Europe.

Many initial reviewers applauded *The Tunnel* as a great success, not least of all because the film's futuristic narrative was able to reawaken childhood fantasies and early reading adventures. As one critic commented, "Bernhard Kellermann's novel *The Tunnel* was a remarkable sensation when it appeared for the first time. This reviewer still recalls very clearly how at that time, shortly before the war, as a sixth-grader he devoured the novel with a pounding heart and hot cheeks."[10] According to this and many other reviewers, *The Tunnel* invited the viewer to envision the future with a certain kind of nostalgia. A product rooted in fantasies from the past, the film projected memory as coming attraction; its appeal relied on how it brought present audiences back to the future. It is in this curious fusion of conflicting temporalities, desires, and memories that the following pages locate the political project of Bernhardt's *The Tunnel*. The film's fascination with America and modern technology, I argue, produced meanings intended to capture the past for the present and shape a new view of the world. Unlike the original novel, the film presented America as essentially memory, and it is as memory that America here became part of the effort to mobilize generic conventions for a political cause. Casting sound and image into seemingly natural unity, *The Tunnel* redefined German film as a showcase of renewal and mobilization, and it thereby realized Goebbels's simultaneous call for a self-consciously German and internationally viable cinema.

Figure 5. Networking the national community: Ad for Curtis Bernhardt's *The Tunnel* (*Film-Kurier*, 1933).

IN SEARCH OF SOUND

André Bazin once suggested a number of editing strategies that could bring greater realism to the imaginary world of science fiction features.[11] According to Bazin science fiction should progress from alternating long shots to climactic images that show the strange and the normal together in the same frame. Drawing from Bazin, Vivian Sobchack has concluded that spectatorial pleasure in conventional science fiction films results primarily from successful visual collisions, that is, the compelling coexistence of the real and the imaginary in one image. Science fiction films, she contends, arouse delight through unique strategies of authentication that allow the spectator to simultaneously avow and disavow the work of special effects: "The satisfaction comes from seeing the visual integration of actual and impossible in the same frame, from the filmmaker's ability to make us suspend our disbelief at the very moment we are also wondering, 'How did they do it?'"[12]

It is not difficult to see that the setting of *The Tunnel*—an enclosed underground tube—mostly prohibits the strategies of persuasion suggested by Bazin and Sobchack. A straight and dark underground passage hardly allows for the extreme long shots that establish spatial depth and set up the visual integration of the unknown (the gigantic tunnel) with the familiar (the masses of working bodies). It therefore is no surprise that the camera—once in the tunnel—remains extremely passive. Although praised by various reviewers as magical,[13] Karl Hoffmann's underground cinematography is dominated by stifling frontal shots and awkward angular viewpoints. It omits lateral tracking shots or daring crane vistas, and it thus recalls the kind of cinematography that typified sound cinema prior to the development of mobile recording devices around 1931. In accord with the majority of later Nazi features, the film valorizes display over movement, well-defined sets over shifting perspectives and alternating focal lengths. Although offering a narrative of spatial conquest and technological triumph, *The Tunnel* transforms action into stasis and in so doing frustrates the viewer's desire for a climactic union of the actual and the possible. So restrictive is this underground that the meeting of the strange and the familiar, in a sense, has always already happened. What we see is always the same dark hole, a hole that hardly suffices to make the spectator believe in the magic of future engineering.

That *The Tunnel* nevertheless succeeds in creating the illusion of coherent and expansive space results from strategies of persuasion that transcend Bazin's and Sobchack's image-centered suggestions. On the one hand, it is the differentiated use of diegetic sound that shapes the viewer's sense for the plasticity of the underground locale.[14] Off- and onscreen noises from sirens, trains, drills, and other construction gadgets deepen diegetic space, define auditory points of view, and emplace the spectator in the diegesis itself. Many of the film's sound effects lead the viewer's imagination beyond what is merely visible. They open up the frame's defining power, add different compositional planes, evoke the illusion of documentary footage, and thus add realism to the image. Walter Gronostay's galvanizing music track contributes actively to this construction of spatial depth and diegetic texture. Modeled on Ernst Lubitsch's 1929 *Love Parade,* Gronostay's workers' march infuses the film with rhythm and direction. It creates illusions of resolve and mobility that counteract the camera's lack of motion.

What compensates for the overall lack of visual credibility is, on the other hand, an interesting framing device, which transports the viewer from the New York prologue to advanced stages of the digging activities. After showing the bankers' decision to pursue the enterprise, the film immediately directs us into a cinema to witness a newsreel broadcasting the progress of the American crew. Filmed from a frontal perspective, with the movie screen's edges still visible, the film-within-the-film condenses a whole series of newscast sequences into one continuous event. It informs about the recruitment process, the first installation of train tracks on Long Island, the impressive movements of soil, and finally—after a smooth ride through space and time—it sets the stage for the film's first tunnel episode, in the third year of digging. In order to prove the spatial progress, this montage of newscasts repeatedly displays maps; graphic lines indicate the route and current position of the American crew, and intercuts and superimpositions picture the flat surface of the ocean in extreme long shots. Bernhardt arrests us in this cinema-of-attraction for the remainder of the film: without rupture the newsreel frame suddenly dissolves; the inner screen becomes the main screen; the newscast transforms into narrative action, and internal and external audience become one and the same.

Instead of making us wonder about the question "How did they do it?" the newsreel sequence appeals to the look of documentary footage in order to naturalize the space of the unfamiliar and to help us suspend our disbelief. By staging a newsreel report and drawing the viewer into a play with different forms of cinematic representation, the film creates its own myth. Additionally, as it dissolves the framing device and collapses documentary and narrative, *The Tunnel* models the cinematic apparatus itself as the ultimate enactment of futuristic special effects. The blurring of newscast and fiction designates film as the ideal vessel of science fiction themes, insofar as cinematic representation relies on a whole inventory of special effects it-self: the tricks of shooting, cutting, and splicing that belong to the practice of filming, not to what is being filmed.[15]

Introducing the fantastic underground as a realm of believable special effects, the newsreel sequence involves the spectator in a multiple process of persuasion. It seems to establish—as Steve Neale has argued in a differ-ent context—the film's very "regime of credence—the rules, the norms and the laws by which its events and agents can be understood and ad-judged."[16] Yet much more is at stake in this sequence than simply the need to generate realism. Although enormous loudspeakers can be seen on both sides of the screen, the cinema in this newsreel sequence predates the ar-rival of synchronized sound. The musical sounds and voices that bathe the auditorium in grandiose effects clearly emanate from a separate sound source, whereas the actual film-within-the-film remains technically silent. Past technologies thus guide the film's viewer into the future. Remarkably enough, at several points this four-minute sequence intercuts to shots that depict a proletarian, all-male audience, pictured from the point of view of the screen itself. When the engineer Mac Allan (Paul Hartmann), in the newsreel, waves directly at the camera, a reaction shot captures the amused response of his spectators. Far from being distressed about Mac Allan's muted voice, the audience in this moment assumes the role of ventrilo-quist. We see and hear how the viewers add their own interpretations to Mac Allan's lip movements and thus, in their imagination, transform the film they witness onscreen into a talkie.

In stylistic terms this brief scene recalls the use of speech in René Clair's first sound films of the early 1930s, *Sous les toits de Paris* (1930) and *Le Million* (1931) in particular. Clair, in these films, frequently relied on imaginative plot situations that involved an absence of speech, and this mo-tivated lack of dialogue allowed him to maintain many values of silent cin-ema while endorsing asynchronous sound as a viable method of expression in the age of the talkie.[17] Bernhardt's cinema sequence, likewise, integrates aspects of silent film aesthetics into the era of sound film. It recuperates the old with the help of the new to bridge historical ruptures and uphold mem-ory. What is equally important, however, is the fact that in picturing Mac Allan's direct address to the diegetic audience, the film imagines a viewing public very well aware of the act of looking, an audience emancipated from the codes of dominant narrative cinema, silent *and* sound. In the film's newsreel sequence cinematic sights and sounds seem to interrupt the voyeuristic pleasures of "invisible" spectatorship, pleasures that derive from forms of representation that bond the viewer to a fictional world and its dramatic drive. Although the newsreel sequence celebrates sound film as a teleological culmination of silent cinema and its viewer's innermost desire for speech, it also endorses forms of spectatorship that appear fundamentally decentered and distracted, not arrested by silent passivity or disembodied identification.

It is in this sense that *The Tunnel*, at first sight, seems to situate cinema as what Oskar Negt and Alexander Kluge understand as an alternative public sphere, a place that allows for the articulation of group-specific needs, anxieties, fantasies, and memories within industrial or commercial contexts. Opposed to the speech-centered and exclusive model of bourgeois publicity, the emergence of alternative and proletarian public spheres in modern culture entailed "principles of inclusion and multiplicity, an emphasis on concrete interests and self-organization and, most crucially, an insistence on the concreteness of human experience across dominant divisions of public and private, including the experience of fragmentation and specific blockages."[18] Similarly, the newsreel sequence of *The Tunnel* seems to valorize spectatorship as a medium of articulation and exchange that indeed fosters the identity of the proletarian collective. Preceding a kind of cinema that absorbs diverse empirical viewing acts into textually centered positions of subjectivity, Bernhardt's silent-cinema-within-sound-cinema seems to define cinema as a trading place of concrete experience and fantasy across existing private and public demarcations.

A closer look, however, reveals something quite different. First, it is noteworthy that the newsreel sequence purchases its praise of decentered and embodied forms of viewership with a curious denial of technological mediation. As the film entertains illusions of reciprocity between screen space and auditorium, it renders invisible—in accord with the formulas of classical Hollywood cinema—the materiality of representation and its codes of enunciation. When greeting Mac Allan, the film's diegetic audience disavows the work of cinematic technology and mediation; it views films as self-contained realities. Believing that there is a real body out there present on the screen, Bernhardt's spectators perceive images produced by modern machines as direct extensions of the body. Like ventriloquists, they render mediated effects as natural presences, and, in so doing, they fall prey to fantasies of reconciliation that deny class difference and unite engineer and worker, brain and hand, in consensual harmony.

Second, any reading of the newsreel sequence and its implied model of spectatorship will remain incomplete if it fails to address its counterpart at the end of the film, which depicts the climactic rendezvous between the American and European crews. In this sequence a long shot shows the

American workers gazing at the front wall of the tunnel, when—through a vaginal opening—a face suddenly appears, shouting "Hello, America! Here is Europe!" (fig. 6). The tunnel's wall here clearly resembles the screen in the earlier newsreel episode, and the image of male bodies confined to the dark tunnel refers back to the earlier depiction of cinema spectators. In addition, on a more formal level, the shot/reverse-shot pattern, the frontal long shot perspective, and, finally, the forms of address directly parallel the strategies used in the earlier sequence. Mise-en-scène and editing thus seem to substantiate what the viewer suspected all along: Bernhardt's workers are moviegoers in disguise; his underground walls are emblems of projection screens, and vice versa; his film posits direct links between spectatorship and heroic work, between the mobilization of fantasy and the mobilization of the body for a higher cause. Yet what makes both sequences different is of course that, contrary to the ventriloquism of the newsreel interlude, the final breakthrough scene depicts proper bodies speaking with proper voices. Whereas in the earlier sequence speaking bodies emerged as silent cinema's innermost fantasy, the climactic scene presents the attractions of sound film as the most viable tool to elicit awe amid industrial culture. Whereas Mac Allan's silence in the newsreel sequence allowed the diegetic viewers to lend their own voice to the spectacle onscreen, in the film's end the worker-spectators are struck with silence themselves. Cinema here assumes spectatorial silence as its new standard of respectability. It recenters pleasure and perception to incorporate earlier forms of spectatorship and publicity into a new hegemony.

Hegemony, Antonio Gramsci has argued, does not necessarily annihilate or fully replace undesirable ideological positions of the past or the present. Rather, it is characterized by the principle of articulation, that is, the effort to sift through competing ideological possibilities and experiences and integrate them into "the nucleus of a new ideological and theoretical complex."[19] Bernhardt's film follows this logic of hegemonization. Recapitulating the historical course from nonsynchronized to synchronized sound, from viewer involvement to spectatorial silence, from decentered to textually inscribed modes of spectatorship, *The Tunnel* absorbs different traditions and intends to transcend class affiliations and reach the widest audience possible. That this project of absorption reflects a political agenda can hardly be overlooked: the film articulates earlier forms of proletarian publicness to what it shows as the new hegemonic principle—masculine willpower and resolution, self-sacrificial labor, and submissive collectivity. It is therefore by no means tenable to argue that cinema here emerges as a public horizon of proletarian self-organization and self-expression in Negt

Figure 6. "Hello, America! Here is Europe!" *The Tunnel.* Courtesy of Film-museum Berlin—Deutsche Kinemathek.

and Kluge's sense. Rather than recognizing cinema as a group-specific site of difference and autonomy, *The Tunnel* endorses in the final analysis nothing other than the Nazi remake of earlier forms of publicness. The film, in its final moments, supplants experience and difference instead of promoting their independent organization. It consecrates the advent of a unified public sphere whose function is to engineer consent from above, not to express critique from below.

Given the Americanist predilection of both Kellermann's original novel and Bernhardt's film, it might seem odd that the final sequence pictures Mac Allan's American crew as passive onlookers of the European workers, a European sound cinema gone underground. Although the film's narrative focuses entirely on the American digging efforts, it is the European team that effects the final breakthrough and, in so doing, assumes control over the terms of representation. Fear of penetration, we must recall, characterizes the overall body of Nazi film. Nazi features are preoccupied with drawing borders, shutting out foreign voices, bracketing sexuality, and containing media of exchange such as money in order to uphold both the purity of

German space and the "armored man's self-preservation."[20] To propose a possible answer to this perplexing role reversal at the film's end, one needs to take into consideration not simply the Americanism debates of the 1920s and 1930s but more specifically the German film industry's attempt during the 1930s to challenge the foremost signifier of Americanism, Hollywood, on its own grounds. Like the majority of feature films produced during the National Socialist era, the film might aspire to become "readable in terms of classical narrative in much the same way as do Hollywood films of the 1930s."[21] On the other hand, however, the film prefigures the efforts of Nazi cinema to replace Hollywood with a domestic version of industrial mass culture. That Bernhardt, in the end of his Americanist fantasy, pictures America as the passive spectator of Europe prefigures the advent of a new media culture not in America but at the home front—a media culture in which moving images of bodies and voices serve the cause of political mobilization.[22]

Nazi film theorist Hans Traub proposed in 1933 that movement and rhythm are themselves tools of ideology and propaganda. What counts, according to Traub, is not sheer monumentalism but how a film offers shifting perspectives that draw the viewer into the depicted flow of crowds and overwhelm the audience with a sense of physical immediacy.[23] In the final sequence *The Tunnel* combines Traub's definition of ideology as movement with what Wolfgang Liebeneiner, as discussed in the previous chapter, understood as the principal task of German cinema, namely to convert film as sound film into a total work of art. If the newsreel sequence heroized the sights of modern America, the breakthrough scene in the end introduces German sound cinema as a viable, in fact, superior substitute for the attractions of Hollywood. In line with a long-standing trope of German anti-Americanism, the film in the end taxes America as an emasculated site of decadent consumption, a culture dominated by the "desires, tastes, and world views of women,"[24] whereas Germany alone embodies a nation of resolute and recentered, of uncompromising and self-asserted, men. In the final shots the film literally consumes Hollywood, hoping to instill the popular fascination with American mass culture and technology with the power of a resolute vision and political movement.

NETWORKING THE NATIONAL COMMUNITY

It has often been pointed out that radio played an important role during the Third Reich to deliver Nazi ideology and secure political control. Airwaves, particularly during the war, became a crucial medium to generate a sense of spatial continuity and bond the people's emotions to their leaders. As David Bathrick has written, "Father and mother and newborn babe are brought together again in ether space, enabled by an apparatus that will link their individual destinies spatially and communally to the now expanded familial Reich."[25] Melodramas such as *Schlußakkord* (Final accord, 1936, Detlef Sierck) or *Wunschkonzert* (Request concert, 1940, Eduard von Borsody) have cast this ideological use of radio during the Third Reich into powerful cinematic images. Radios in these films, and the kind of music they transmit, signify the advent of a national community produced by the power of modern communication technology. Understood as a conduit to the deepest recesses of the German soul, radio here ties together individuals dispersed in geographical space; it is meant—in the words of a contemporary trade journal—"to leave the marketplace and return to the church, to a church, which will encompass all its listeners with the same atmospheric powers and which is capable of bridging distances just like the all uniting House of the Lord."[26]

Radio was surely instrumental in elevating the Nazi movement to power. In the electorate of 1932 Goebbels's voice entered more than four million households through radio loudspeakers.[27] Unlike the speeches of the democratic leaders, Goebbels and Hitler mesmerized their listeners with vocative resolve, visionary appeal, and fierce emotionalism. Yet, considering the fact that film practitioners at the same time were at pains to articulate voice and body into persuasive harmony, radio must have had something uncanny, particularly for a movement rallying against the functional differentiation of modern life and promising a resurrection of unified identities. Radio, in the views of early commentators, destabilized space and unhinged temporal coordinates. It severed voice from body, split sounds and sights, fragmented the audience's perception, and thus—potentially—ran counter to the Nazis' call to recenter self and community.

The Tunnel echoes some of this early unease about the decentering force of radio. Contrary to Weimar science fiction films such as *F.P.-1 antwortet nicht* (F.P.-1 does not answer, 1932, Karl Hartl), in which wireless communication successfully bridged space and prepared narrative solutions, *The Tunnel* remains quite ambivalent about radio as a tool of mediating human voices. In the film's hierarchy of media the wireless, in fact, comes in third. It is shown as inferior to both the charisma of unadulterated speech and the technical reproduction of the voice through sound film. Radio, in Bernhardt's film, fails to unite the masses in a new House of the Lord. Nor does it succeed in leaving the marketplace. According to *The Tunnel* it is only when attached to images, when elevated to the higher plane of sound cinema, that the mechanical recording of voices can serve the cause of mass mobilization.

In contradistinction to the opening of Kellermann's novel, Bernhardt's *The Tunnel* immediately marks its futuristic world as one deeply familiar with various mechanical means of sound transmission. After a complex series of high- and low-angle montage shots of Manhattan the film's first sequence confronts us right away with the issue of voice recording and audio transference. In order to spy on the illustrious society invited by Mac Allan to the roof garden of a New York hotel, the journalist Harris installs a microphone in one of the garden's plants. Harris's efforts recall the strategies of early sound film technicians, who prior to the invention of postproduction sound recording had to hide their mikes all over the set. Ironically, however, Harris's transmission channels get cut off when Mac Allan begins to disclose his tunnel project. The banker, Woolf (Gustaf Gründgens), discovers the bug and places a fan in front of the microphone. Much to the dismay of Harris, Woolf thus produces undifferentiated noise instead of marketable sensations. Subsequently, microphones and radios reappear in scenes similarly marked by sensationalism and a ruthless commodification of spoken language. Witness Mary (Olly von Flint), Mac Allan's wife, pulled in front of a mike to comment on the approval of the project; and witness Hobby (Attila Hörbiger), who is snatched by a radio reporter in the tunnel and forced to deliver a statement immediately before the final rendezvous of the American with the European crews.

Radio microphones in *The Tunnel* connect the main characters to the commodified world of mass information and sensation. Telephones transmit functional messages in repeated states of emergency. Over and over telephones sound an alarm, relate surprising news, immediately stir panic, or launch uncontrolled emotions: when Mac Allan, Hobby, and Mary are informed about the approval of the project; when Mac Allan learns about a flood in the tunnel while attending a party; when Mac Allan uses a phone to broadcast the sabotage activities instigated by Woolf yet fails to warn the workers on the front line because the telephone wires have been cut; and during the prologue in Manhattan, when we see reporters knock violently on three telephone booths occupied by their fellow journalists.

Rudolf Arnheim's 1936 essay *Radio* is instructive in accounting for the use of communication technologies in *The Tunnel* and their role as media expressing urgency and threatened reality control. In this essay Arnheim emphatically embraces the electric media of aural communication because they allow for an exploration of the "effects of pure sound."[28] Radio's focus on acoustic expressions reverses what Arnheim considers the unfortunate separation of music and speech in modern civilization. Radio reinstates the poetic materiality of spoken language. To be sure, inextricably bound to a certain here and now, aural media, according to Arnheim, fail to give adequate representations of movements in space. Yet such limitations are actually the media's unique strength. They provide a sense of closeness virtually unknown in all other forms of art and mass communication: "The wireless addresses those millions not as a mass but as individuals. It talks to everyone individually, not to everyone together . . . , as if 'à deux.'" [29] According to Arnheim radios deterritorialize human communication and at the same time set up new zones of intimacy. In effect, aural media—properly used—can shape new democratic communities that are based on the principle of polyphony. Shrinking space, radio enables new networks of cultural exchange. As a result, Arnheim argues, the wireless might even redraw the borders of traditional nation-states as it undermines nationalist strategies of polarization, strategies that primarily rest on "a certain distorted caricature" [30] of the other as enemy.

Arnheim's theory of radio culminates in a humanitarian redemption of liberal individualism. Bernhardt's *The Tunnel,* in contrast, presents media of aural communication in the context of what Herbert Marcuse in 1934 called the battle against liberalism in the totalitarian conception of the state. [31] *The Tunnel* depicts telephones and radios as flawed and unsettling means of exchange. They effect emotional destabilization, signify critical losses of control through spatial, and hence visual, deterritorialization; they promote the transformation of human communication into a meaningless spectacle, a commodity. Denigrating the efficacy of wireless oral exchange, *The Tunnel* rejects Arnheim's utopian vision of radio on at least two planes.

First, in contrast to Arnheim's portrait of aural media as instruments for an exploration of the poetic side of language, *The Tunnel's* project of picturing a community of working bodies relies on a primarily instrumental view of language. Where Arnheim wants the radio to play with the materiality of language, *The Tunnel* pictures a process of social homogenization that requires both the commanding voice *and* the visual presence of Mac Allan. Instead of polyphony and poetry, monologue and strategic modes of address mark *The Tunnel's* practices of speaking and listening. Language here is mostly antilanguage. Unless spoken in the imperative, words are feeble and misleading. What counts are resolute actions and gestures of submission alone. Instead of exploring the noninstrumental and mimetic sides of language, *The Tunnel* champions the direct force of the speaking image and visualized voice rather than the humanist openness and intimacy of aural media.

Second, whereas Arnheim insists on privacy, *The Tunnel* invokes new forms of collectivity in which the individual male body merges into an all-encompassing labor machine. Bernhardt's telephones and radios, although populating a futuristic world, are clearly figured as outmoded technologies of the age of individualism; they are carriers of single voices. What they bring to the fore are forms of bourgeois identity that are on the verge of losing or have already lost their authority and authenticity: telephones and radios connect emotionally unstable, corrupt individuals. According to Arnheim the radio addresses its listeners as individuals, not as a mass. *The Tunnel,* by contrast, stigmatizes media of aural exchange only to hail cinematic audiovision as a mode of address that overcomes bourgeois concepts of individuality, interiority, and emotional authenticity. As I will detail in a moment, *The Tunnel* accomplishes this stigmatization of aural media by displaying bourgeois privacy as a messy and—underneath its surface—highly dangerous sphere, governed by unfulfilled female desire that threatens paternal authority. Mouthpieces of the bourgeois subject, radios and telephones carry the hazards of domestic life and emotional interiority into the open. Film and newsreel shows, on the other hand, help contain the threat of sexual difference and repressed emotionality, of sensationalism and commodification, and they most efficiently cast the individual in the mold of a new male community, in the cast of industrial sameness and fascist mass politics.

Arnheim understood the shrinkage of space through aural media as a means of exploring new forms of communication and bridging cultural gulfs. In Arnheim's view the radio promised a progressive mediation of collective and individual identities; it undid reified polarities and enabled the mutual interpenetration of the global and the local. Radios stretch spatial relations and diversify cultural experiences. Bernhardt's denigration of radios and telephones, by way of contrast, is part of a discourse that rejects Arnheim's utopia of cross-cultural contact and replaces it with an imperialist vision of spatial appropriation and cultural segregation. In *The Tunnel* radios and telephones decenter the body and impose the fear of flowing into dissipation. They blur the protective boundaries of the armor-plated subject as much as of the nation-state. Only the natural integration of voice and image helps maintain a clear sense of physical identity, of who is a friend and who a foe. Only the putative immediacy of cinematic audiovision can suture the individual body into the fascist collective.

In 1933 Hans Traub ranked sound cinema as the second most important means of transporting language and propaganda to the masses, anteceded only by the führer's unmediated voice itself. Film "is full of surprises in the rhythm of emotional intensification and displacement";[32] therefore, it can disseminate the spoken word much more effectively than radio or print media, which arrest rhythm in static expressions. The use of radios and telephones in *The Tunnel* conforms to Traub's formula. Pictured as a technology far superior to the wireless, the audiovisual wonders of film constitute a perfect instrument of engineering emotions and commandeering space. Although in the final breakthrough sequence sound brings the Weimar fascination with America home to Nazi Germany, the film's phobic representation of radios and telephones, by way of negation, celebrates the self-assertion of body and body politic as a prime value. Fascism needs the other, yet it is always afraid to recognize itself in the other's features. In *The Tunnel* German fascism successfully snatches cinema away from Hollywood, leaves America with its emasculating radios and silent films, but nevertheless—as I will detail in the remainder of this chapter—remains constantly threatened by what might amount to a monstrous return of the repressed.

MEN, WOMEN, AND THE JARGON OF AUTHENTICITY

As it presents the underground as a world of technological wonders, *The Tunnel* sustains a form of technophilia that opposes the paradoxical technophobia—the technological discourse on the dangers of new technologies—expressed in most science fiction productions. Conventional science fiction films tend to stress the danger of machines and invoke traditional values as antidotes to the fear of mechanization.[33] They pit the realm of the human against technology, nature against culture, feeling against reason only to obscure the fact that the figure of nature itself might be nothing other than a cultural construct, an ideological device that authorizes existing inequality. Even highly modernist and self-reflexive texts have often failed to resist technophobic inclinations and their denial of historical agency. In Fritz Lang's *Metropolis* (1927) social harmony becomes possible only after the threats of dehumanization and the alleged regime of the machines have been defeated. Lang's final tableau of social reconciliation restores proper demarcations between culture and nature, feeling and reason, human body and machine yet leaves everything the way it has always been.

Welcoming the triumph of instrumental reason over nature, *The Tunnel* clearly departs from the ambivalent technophobia depicted in *Metropolis*. Bernhardt's film does not seem troubled by a dehumanization of the body or a humanization of the machine. It renders the worker's arm a corporeal extension of the hammer drill, the screen of the cinema an extension of the spectator's retina. Yet this peculiar blurring of nature and culture is far from releasing emancipatory potentials and unlocking spaces of autonomous human agency. Bernhardt's film construes the underground as the site of a concerted functioning of the human body, one that integrates the individual into an all-encompassing labor machine. Using the human body as an architectural element,[34] The Tunnel foreshadows the dehumanization of the individual body in Leni Riefenstahl's notorious images of Nazi parades. Down in Mac Allan's tunnel metallization takes command. Cinematic and industrial machines of (re)production project the image of the human body as a prosthetic device. They fuse human being with machine rather than to enable any exchange of parts or functions. "Within this economy of identification," as Jeffrey Schnapp explains in a somewhat different context, "machines stand for an ideal: not that of a body without fatigue or of a society without alienation, but instead the distinctively fascist ideal of constant exertion and fatigue coldly resisted . . . in other words, metallization."[35]

The visual style of The Tunnel mirrors this quest for anaesthetic dehumanization. Hoffmann's camera remains detached throughout the film— in stoic distance, never touched by anything, never attempting to assume the perspective of the protagonists or to reveal inner thoughts and visions. The camera thus underlines what is at the core of The Tunnel's ideological project: the transformation of bourgeois subjectivity into what Ernst Jünger called the "type," a metallized body machine whose "gaze is calm and fixed, trained to observe objects which are grasped in conditions of high speed."[36] Like Jünger's type, Bernhardt's workers have learned how to assimilate to the technological orders of the day. Domination and reality control, self-discipline and the repression of passion have become second nature for them. Whatever might trouble the male above ground loses its grasp in the tunnel. Dehumanization, for these workers, offers salvation from the contingencies of life. It subjects spontaneity and sentience to the imperatives of total mobilization, and it replaces the challenges of the real with a curious utopia of technological self-birth and self-armoring.

But why, then, Mac Allan's final forlornness, his downcast eyes after the climactic breakthrough? Why his psychic absence and speechlessness in the last scene? Do these signifiers simply express the melancholia of a rapidly aged engineer?[37] Or do they evidence Mac Allan's powers of repression and the bad conscience of a pioneer who has employed expansive human resources to carry out stubborn fantasies?[38]

One way to explain Mac Allan's rather unheroic presence in the final frames is to refer to what Ernst Bloch in 1929 called the "engineer's anxiety": the engineer's fear of unleashing through technology—like the magician's apprentice in Goethe—uncalled-for powers.[39] This fear results in a desire to see technological projects undone rather than crowned as spectacular triumphs. Reminiscent of Bloch's inventor, Mac Allan is an engineer paralyzed by self-doubt. Struck by anxiety, he escapes into melancholy. He views technology as magic and thus disavows the monstrousness of his initial visions. In the last sequence Bernhardt's science fiction thus turns into a melodrama in order to assure the spectators' identification with the film's unheroic hero.

But Mac Allan's final melancholy exceeds Bloch's notion of anxiety, for what Mac Allan's last appearance simultaneously conceals and reveals is nothing other than the costs of metallization, the price of his attempt to protect patriarchal authority against the fascist engineer's own anxiety about (female) sexuality. Mac Allan becomes melodramatic because he must concede that his bias for male self-affirmation and instrumental reason culminates in a Pyrrhic victory: the construction of the tunnel required the symbolic and physical demise of Mary, Mac Allan's wife, who died in an accident when she tried to enter the tunnel. If male authority succeeds in the end of *The Tunnel*, it does so only because it had to go to the extreme, namely, to erase the very difference that patriarchy needs to sustain its operation. In contradistinction to the self-congratulatory gesture of all the others—the workers, the foremen, the radio reporters—Mac Allan's melancholy encodes the unsettling, albeit repressed, insight that such a victory is no victory at all (fig. 7).

Nazi feature films often base their images of ecstatic community on highly misogynist narratives: "Crucially and consistently, the projected weak images of women form the basis of signification for many Nazi films, reflecting a vulnerable and ultimately paranoid order . . . Nazi cinema goes far beyond the institutionalized sexism of Hollywood movies and the way in which the classical narrative recuperates even the strongest women in the male discourse. Nazi cinema does not leave it at simple recuperation, though; women are to be overcome, indeed sacrificed." [40] *The Tunnel* provides a curious variation of this denial of femininity, offering a narrative of male camaraderie reminiscent of Klaus Theweleit's study on male bonding after World War I. [41] In contrast to Theweleit's potentially homophobic argument, [42] however, I suggest that *The Tunnel* requires the viewer to conceive of homoeroticism not as a necessary corollary of collective technobodies and their (proto)fascist politics but rather as a disposition shaped into a highly regressive fantasy by both Mac Allan's diegetic and the film's metadiegetic technologies of power. In accord with a long tradition of linking homosexuality and fascism, the film stages homoeroticism as a desire for repression: the homosexual's desire in the final analysis desires the end of desire, an annihilation of the desiring body. [43] The liminal space of the

Figure 7.   The engineer's melancholy: Paul Hartmann as Mac Allan in *The Tunnel*.
Courtesy of Filmmuseum Berlin—Deutsche Kinemathek.

underground allows for the articulation of what cultural conventions censor above ground, and the film ends up casting a carnivalistic release from
censorship and inhibition into an even more effective structure of control.
Exploiting homoerotic desire, Mac Allan's tunnel project stages a supreme
male fantasy. It pictures women as self-marginalizing and self-repressing.
They willingly sacrifice their own lives to protect men from the threat of
femininity and otherness. Like many other Bernhardt films—German,
French, or American—*The Tunnel* presents an image of woman scarred
with the wounds of self-denial.[44] Remarkably enough, Mary knows even
better than Mac Allan that she poses a risk to the engineer's projects; therefore, in a gesture of utter subordination she silences her own voice and arrests her own desire. Neither her body nor time is on her side.

    Already known for his depiction of claustrophobic spaces and enclosed
interiors—of orphanages (*Die Waise von Lowood* [The orphan from Lo-
wood], 1926), army posts (*Das letzte Fort* [The last fort], 1928), mills (*Die
letzte Kompagnie* [The last company], 1929), or railway cars (*Die Frau,
nach der man sich sehnt* [The woman one desires], 1929)—Bernhardt de-

picts Mac Allan's subway as a niche of male comradeship. His tunnel is a site at which the spectacle of modern technology appeals to and instrumentalizes homoerotic desires only in order to overwhelm the individual with a regressive utopia. Machines, muscles, and marching tunes meet here to overcome phobias concerning female agency. Whereas sexuality above ground remains transmuted into cathartic rituals, Mac Allan's underground opens a space in which men may enact their desire to break free from compulsory heterosexuality as much as from any possible dependence on the female as other and as mother. Mac Allan and his working armies dig ever farther through the dirt, not to connect the two continents but to pursue their dream of male self-procreation through technology, a dream that establishes male identity as a completely autonomous system of desire and signification but that ultimately only reproduces already given structures of power. Mac Allan's enterprise, in other words, enables homoerotic desires only in order to promote a phobic erasure of difference and alterity.

It hardly needs mentioning that in Mac Allan's underground, the imagery of displaced intercourse (the phallic drilling devices) intersects with the desire for a regressive reunion with a self-constructed mother (the womb of the tunnel). Both moments culminate, ironically but not surprisingly, in the ultimate materialization of male self-procreation, accomplished in the final sequence when the European worker appears in the vaginal opening to welcome the American crew—a striking image of male technological self-birth, of clean and safe sex indeed. Although it may seem claustrophobic, then, the underground actually delimits a space of shelter and escape, a site at which emancipation from everyday repression coincides with acts of regression. Woman has to die so that the tunnel, so that fascist solidarity and male redemption, so that technological progress may live.

But then again, who does really live down in Bernhardt's tunnel? "Your grief is not so important," Hobby comforts Mac Allan after Mary's death. "Your life no longer belongs to you." *The Tunnel* cloaks the various practices of work, spatial appropriation, domination over nature, and erasure of difference with a rhetoric of heroic self-sacrifice and duty: what counts is not the individual but the project, not particular interests or pleasures but the larger vision of the tunnel, the digging male collective. "Every work," Mac Allan once declares in front of his working armies, "is a battle, and there are casualties in every battle, in the mines, on the oceans, in the machine halls in the cities. There is no life without danger." Resolute words here try to recontain what the film's images fail to deliver. Fierce speech is meant to reanchor the body in space so as to mask the film's many layers of displacement and projection. Danger and death, Mac Allan wants his workers to believe, constitute the most valuable force of any human existence; he who rules over the moment of danger, he who overcomes his own body and desire, deserves all authority and sovereignty.

DISTRACTION AND CROWD CONTROL

On the opening day of the New York subway on October 27, 1904, the city's police commissioner revealed to the public an unforeseen use of the new transportation system. What had been anticipated in decades of public discussion as a triumph of urban sanitization, safety, and speed suddenly emerged as an effective vehicle of crowd control.[45] For the police commissioner the subway's main achievement was not simply to alleviate dreadful traffic conditions and to obliterate the proverbial foul air that prevailed in the overcrowded cars of surface transportation. Instead, the police commissioner hailed this new technological device as an instrument to contain future social uproar, one in fact that "is going to absolutely preclude the possibility of riots in New York. . . . [For if] a riot should break out at any time now we could clear the road and send out a trainload of a thousand men, dropping as many of them off at every station as necessary, and have an armed force in Harlem in fifteen minutes."[46] Just as Haussmann's Paris boulevards had prevented the building of barricades, the New York subway—in the eyes of the police commissioner—provided a new technology of power, inaugurated to increase control over the urban masses.

Produced at the threshold of the Third Reich, Curtis Bernhardt's *The Tunnel* similarly rendered the underground as a perfect technology of power—one, however, that by far surpassed the New York commissioner's vision of unrestricted police mobility. The film and its rhetoric of sacrifice and mobilization extended the imperatives of crowd control to the realms of fantasy and distraction. It integrated cinema's sights and sounds into a seemingly natural harmony so as to align perception and coordinate sentience from above. Reckoning with what in 1933 was left of Weimar's fascination with America, with the appeal of American speed, technology, and mass culture, *The Tunnel* thereby inaugurated Nazi cinema as a site of domestication, incorporation, and transformation. Transporting the past into the present, the film coaxed the viewer from silent to sound film, from Weimar Americanism to Nazi sovereignty, from Hollywood to Germany. It provided generic pleasures with the intention of precluding the organization of experience in self-regulated and socially specific public spheres.

One of the many multiple-language versions that German film studios produced during the 1930s, *The Tunnel* fulfilled urgent ideological functions at home, but at the same time it intended to endow Nazi politics and entertainment with respectability abroad. As Heinrich Fischer wrote in the exile journal *Die neue Weltbühne, The Tunnel* "is the shortest intellectual connection between Hitler Germany and other countries; it has the task to submerge audiences abroad, who are not yet totally infected, with the ideological bacteria of the Third Reich; its method is so dangerous because it does not propagate the political reality of the new Germany but, by the allegorical means of a seemingly private individual fate, the naked heroic view of inhumanity." [47] With a film elevating the marriage of cinematic voice and body to a formula of political transformation, no risks were to be taken. The perfection of dubbing techniques by 1933 notwithstanding, Bavaria hired Bernhardt to direct a second version with the same sets for the French market, using French actors and their voices. Under the sign of a new order *The Tunnel* thus catered to demands as different as domestic mobilization and international revenue amassing, national self-assertion and Americanization, politicization and distraction, recentered identity and national difference. As a sort of bricolage integrating different temporal and spatial coordinates, the film enlisted cinematic sound as a tool of moving the masses *as* masses; it sought to redefine German cinema as a laboratory of a new national community. However, although produced at the very outset of the Third Reich, *The Tunnel* at the same time already foreshadowed the final self-destruction of Nazi fantasy production. Just as the film presents labor and technology as agents of metallization, so it constructs the cinema as a mechanism in which the unity of sights and sounds prepares humanity to "experience its own destruction as an aesthetic pleasure of the first order." [48] Mac Allan's final melancholy bears testimony to what Bernhardt's Americanist fiction—against its own ideological intention—cannot fully repress: that the film's figuration of both the subterranean world and the cinematic apparatus, far from providing collective rejuvenation and sensual renewal, far from bringing American wonders safely home to Nazi Germany, in fact only recycles the mythic image of Hades, the Greek underground realm of the dead.

3 Engendering Mass Culture
Zarah Leander and
the Economy of Desire

Curtis Bernhardt's *The Tunnel* illustrated how Nazi cinema tried to establish a fully controlled production and reception process, an autonomous culture industry dedicated to capturing dormant utopias and shaping these into politically effective responses. The film navigated the Weimar fascination with American urbanity, speed, and mass culture into the arms of Nazi mobilization. Significantly, however, *The Tunnel*'s peculiar way of showcasing muscular bodies and armor-plated subjects remained an exception rather than the norm among the overall output of German film studios during the Nazi era. Contrary to long-held assumptions about Nazi cinema, only a minority of the more than one thousand feature films produced during the Third Reich evidenced the kind of iconography that Hollywood itself and many scholars since 1945 have reified into fascism's fatal and fascinating aesthetics. Seen with historical hindsight, *The Tunnel*'s project of exorcizing America remained incomplete. Often seemingly at odds with the call for a unified weltanschauung, the signifier "America" endured popularity throughout the 1930s as a repository of diverse attractions and diversions, a utopia of modern consumption and private leisure activity.

Challenging the stereotype of Hitler Germany as a perfectly organized machine of domination and mobilization, historians during the last decades have increasingly turned their attention to the hiatus between the imperatives of Nazi propaganda and the existence of a relatively apolitical sphere of private distraction and commodity display. In many of these revisionist accounts the relationship between National Socialism and American-style modernization is understood as incongruous. The fact that the Third Reich's consumer culture "could be described with the jargon of authenticity, that is, slogans celebrating immediacy, experience, the self, soul, feeling, permanence, will, instinct and finally the race," is seen as an effect of ideological displacement.[1] Historian Hans Dieter Schäfer, for instance, reads the contradictions between ideology and everyday practice as a sign of the pathological nature of Nazi society, a schizophrenia characteristic of the psychopathic disposition of Nazi politics.[2]

Contrary to Schäfer's attempt to pathologize Nazi Americanism, I suggest that we need to understand the heterogeneity of Nazi culture not as a symptom but as an integral part of the Nazi project. Nazi cultural politics provided seemingly apolitical spaces of American-like diversion in order to set moods, define norms, and align conflicting interpretations of reality. Although often at variance with the strict demands of ideological correctness, American-style consumerism, in particular during the prewar years, provided a stage for what Adorno in his analysis of American hit songs considered pseudoindividualization: spurious expressions of spontaneity and choice that already anticipated resignation. "By pseudo-individualization we mean endowing cultural mass production with the halo of free choice or open market on the basis of standardization itself. Standardization of hit songs keeps the customers in line by doing their listening for them, as it were. Pseudo-individualization, for its part, keeps them in line by making them forget that what they listen to is already listened to for them, or 'predigested.'"[3] Nazi film culture followed this formula to the letter. Entertaining the viewer with the illusion that within this highly politicized society certain spaces remained free of control and coordination, Nazi entertainment features sought to organize the viewer's spontaneity. They offered predigested choices that defined points of view and—with the help of film music's beats and rhythms—organized emotions. Nazi Americanism disabled earlier forms of solidarity to produce lonely crowds. It co-opted the popular's "ineradicable drive towards collectivity"[4] and blocked alternative definitions of modern German identity that were coupled to notions of individual autonomy and political emancipation.

During the years 1935 to 1938 the Nazi regime tried frantically to build up a German Hollywood and endow pseudoindividualization with a political task. Severely hit by slumping profits around the middle of the decade,[5] the film industry was first put under direct state authority. Production schedules were streamlined, and stronger budgetary controls were implemented at all levels of operation. Second, the regime sought to rekindle domestic consumption, not—as Victoria de Grazia has shown—"by promoting the fan club, the movie magazine, or the giveaways typical of U.S. marketing campaigns during the Depression and widely imitated in Europe, but by mobilizing the Nazi political apparatus (Kraft durch Freude and traveling cinemas), discounting tickets, and sponsoring the UFA 'revivals.'"[6] Third,

and finally, the regime tried to broaden the film industry's export operations, in part through coproduction arrangements with its European neigh-
bors and improved marketing strategies in areas as remote as the Balkans
or Latin America. Coordinating the various aspects of film production, distribution, and consumption, the Nazi film industry became a multinational
venue. It manufactured genre films whose plots and styles were often meant
to speak to audiences abroad as much as to domestic viewers.[7] It produced
light-entertainment fare that omitted all overt references to Nazi agendas,
to the aesthetics of metallized bodies in motion, or to specific party icons,
yet it aspired to stir national sentiments and exploit Germanness as a conduit to international success. In many cases this simultaneous inscription
of political and economic directives resulted in far less homogeneous texts
than its proponents and many later historiographers would have liked. The
products of Nazi cinema during the prewar era, in fact, were often based on
surprisingly contradictory concessions, on gestures of cultural appropriation pregnant with fragile syntheses and glossed-over fault lines, gestures
that "left the government caught in ludicrous forms of self-redress and
strategic withdrawal before the commodity fetish."[8]

Nowhere is this ideologically ambivalent attempt at producing mass culture from above more obvious than in the ways the German film industry of
the mid-1930s constructed female star images. All of the most important female stars of the Third Reich—Zarah Leander (fig. 8), Marika Rökk, Lilian
Harvey, and Kristina Söderbaum—entered the German culture industry
from abroad. In the cases of Leander and Harvey these stars also deviated
from the image of woman as the domestic soldier of racial reproduction.[9]
Imported stars projected cosmopolitan sensibilities onto the German screen.
Frequently cast in roles that thematized their foreignness, these stars embodied forms of sexual agency that—although a far cry from the aggressive
female sexuality in contemporary Hollywood screwball comedies—challenged the general inhibition of pleasure so characteristic of Nazi cinema.[10]
Song and dance played an essential part in the popularity of these film divas.
Inaugurating new commercial relations between film and record industry,
singing stars such as Leander, Rökk, and Harvey elevated sound film to a
domineering position in the marketing of light-entertainment music.[11]
Their voices traveled across different media and could be consumed through
various channels at once; they offered a sense of cultural mobility by means
of their sheer ubiquity.

Nazi film stars proved highly instrumental in the transformation of German film into a mass cultural product package. Their stardom linked particular films to the extrafilmic arenas of musical consumption, fashion,

Figure 8. Mirror, Mirror on the wall: Zarah Leander in *The Heart of a Queen* (1940, Carl Froelich). Courtesy of Filmmuseum Berlin—Deutsche Kinemathek.

makeup, and tourism, arenas central to the Nazis' modernization of German leisure culture. Whereas Nazi film theorists—somewhat anxious about the bourgeois vocabulary of commodification—tended to rephrase the cult of stars in cherished nineteenth-century notions of aesthetic genius,[12] musical film stars such as Leander essentially helped redefine film spectatorship in middle-class terms of respectability and privatized consumption. Playing to popular desires for American-style leisure and melodramatic identification, these star personae became the trade winds of Nazi cinema: their performances gently reminded viewers of powerful attractions beyond the domain of ideological mobilization yet at the same time assisted the National Socialist political agenda by blowing the vessel of everyday culture into the harbor of a unified German distraction industry.

Georg Seeßlen locates the political moment of apolitical Nazi feature films in the fact that they were intended to offer not outright propaganda but individual strategies of survival and models of conformity under the condition of fascism.[13] Rather than leveling crucial differences between Nazi modernism and Hollywood film culture of the 1930s and early 1940s, Seeßlen reminds us of the political task of the Third Reich's "apolitical" entertainment films. Nazi features provided people with shared dreams and emotions; they standardized desires for attractive lifestyles and modern distractions and in doing so produced the impression of one body politic engaged in a common project. What was political about the apolitical products of the Nazis' dream factory therefore must be seen not simply in internal textual characteristics but in the context of the distinctive projection situation and a set of external systems of signification that attributed meaning to a visit to the movie theater: the newsreel shows and cultural education films that framed individual screenings, the iconography of stardom as proliferated through the mass media and in advertising campaigns, the party galas meticulously staged for individual film premieres, and the intertextual dynamic of generic conventions and formulas. Against this broader notion of the cultural politics of Nazi film the following pages will examine the making of the UFA star Zarah Leander around 1937 and her first appearance on German screens in *Zu neuen Ufern* (To new shores, 1937) and *La Habanera* (1937), both directed by Detlef Sierck. Leander's star persona, I suggest, constituted a site at which Nazi society negotiated ideologically unstable relations informing gender identity, modes of spectatorship, the location of mass culture in fascism, and the meaning of German identity. Understood as an intersection of different textual and contextual registers of meaning, the image and voice of Leander, I argue, bear witness to the perplexing syntheses of the Nazi culture industry, the shrewd ways in which Nazi mass culture allowed ideologically ambivalent representations of cultural alterity and sexual difference to enter the heart of a cinema whose implicit function was to bond the individual to the community of the people and redefine industrial mass culture as an art of and for the folk.[14]

EMPOWERING SUBMISSION

In one of the episodes of Edgar Reitz's TV series *Heimat* (Homeland, 1984) Maria and her sister-in-law, Pauline, fashion their hair in front of a mirror according to the exotic coiffure of the film star they have just seen at the movies: Zarah Leander in Detlef Sierck's *La Habanera*. Highly prominent in Sierck's stylized mise-en-scène itself, the mirror enables both women to project Leander's cosmopolitan appearance onto their own bodies. It provides temporary release from the constraints of rural life and allows Maria and Pauline to articulate a surprisingly autonomous notion of female identity. Relying on the magnetism of stars, melodramatic excess, and exotic diversion, prewar mass culture here is shown as a site of individual empowerment. As if inhabiting a niche unfettered from Nazi politics, both women appropriate the popular in order to perform nonconformist gestures of self-expression and redress their position within everyday life.

Reitz's ethnography of female spectatorship challenges the notion of Nazi mass culture as a functional engine of ideological manipulation, as one continual "communal celebration that eliminated the brain and led to ecstasy."[15] Although this is not the place to discuss the problematic nature of Reitz's historiographical method, it is interesting to note that his portrait of Nazi popular culture can muster ample support in the postwar reception of Leander, on the one hand, and in critical discussions of Sierck's melodramatic authorship, as practiced during both his tenure at UFA and his later career in Hollywood, on the other. Leander's often-exotic screen presence has inspired many later critics to heroize her as an icon of transgressive sexuality and ideological subversion. Through excess and stylization, so the argument goes, Leander unmasked the constructedness of gendered identity under Nazi rule. Leander's masquerade debunked what society considered natural in the constitution of identities and thus undermined the Nazis' politics of gender.[16] In particular Leander's voice, similar to the deep tones of Dietrich and Garbo, has served for postwar critics as evidence of her subversive effects.[17] More attractive to women and to gay men than to straight men, these critics contend,[18] Leander's exotic baritone voice mocked the repressive conception of sexuality and gender identity under Nazi rule.

Seemingly similar narratives of nonconformity and social commentary have informed the academic assessment of Sierck's melodramas. Ever since the 1970s critics have emphasized that Sierck's films used mise-en-scène, chiaroscuro lighting, and textual manipulation to subvert what the viewer sees at the film's surface. Rendering style and rhythm instead of dialogue and narrative progression as the primary catalysts of meaning, Sierck's films exposed the constraints society imposes on the individual; surplus sentimentalism unraveled the hypocrisy of twentieth-century civilization.[19] Although Sierck's German films of the 1930s have found much less attention than his 1950s Hollywood productions, they too have been read primarily as ironic works of subversion. Sierck's German films, critics have argued, played out sophisticated formal characteristics against overt narratives and ideologies. They somehow succeeded in smuggling modernist or even countercultural sensibilities into the domains of Nazi mass culture. For Jon Halliday Sierck's German melodramas constituted "a sign of what the German cinema could have been after 1933." For Marc Silberman films such as *To New Shores* probed the limits of Nazi politics and ideology.[20]

Although resulting in similar claims about the possibility of resistance and nonconformity in Nazi Germany, both lines of argument rely on very different and in fact incompatible premises that reflect different understandings of cinema as a site of ideological signification. Those who attribute subversive meanings to Leander's exoticism and feminine masquerade conventionally refer first and foremost to the spectacular surplus of Leander's performances. Leander deconstructs the Nazis' politics of race and gender because through excess she cancels out her own appearance. As she stages her body as spectacle, she undoes any attempt to fix individual bodies in mythic conceptions of national specificity and gendered identity. By way of contrast, Sierck's melodramas are seen as sites of defiance because they group different layers of meaning in volatile force fields: Sierck pushes the limits of Nazi culture by fusing image, dialogue, narrative, and music into disruptive constellations. Whereas Leander's noncompliance allegedly originates in the operatic tableau of her look and voice, Sierck's nonconformity lies in his art of cinematic counterpoint; Leander draws on the power of spectacle, whereas Sierck is at pains to sabotage it.

In spite of such crucial differences, both positions share the assumption that a film's ideological status rests primarily on particular strategies of textual expression and cinematic self-reflexivity. Therefore, both positions, I would argue, overlook the complex ways in which the political status of cinema is constituted and contested at historically contingent crossroads of texts, institutions, modes of reception, and ideological, as well as economic, mandates. Furthermore, reducing the individual text to the exclusive site of a film's political meaning, both positions also forfeit a more thorough understanding of the function of mass culture in prewar Nazi Germany. As they focus on the economy of formal structures, neither position considers discrete structures of perception by means of which viewers received the outputs of the Nazi distraction factory, nor does either address the often-astonishing ways in which the Nazis themselves allowed aesthetic resistance to overwrite political ideology. What in the eyes of the astute critic emerges as a subversive effect of textual features, in other words, might have very well offered in the context of the films' original reception a stage for consumer practices long accustomed to the logic Schäfer calls the split consciousness of Nazi culture. What for the textual critic looks like a violation of the ideology of closure might have constituted for the mass cultural bricoleur a crucial compromise with Nazi politics, a state powerful enough to permit apolitical distraction amidst an otherwise highly politicized society.

There is surely no reason to question the self-reflexive intentions of Detlef Sierck, a director ostensibly familiar with Brechtian distanciation and self-commentary. What is striking, however, is that several generations of Sierck scholars have accessed his films' cultural status solely through formal analysis, unearthing instances of rupture or ambiguity underneath the texts' glossy veneer. In the most extreme cases they have not hesitated to claim that Sierck's historical audiences, incapable of recognizing irony, camp, or trash in Sierck, simply got it wrong when indulging in the hyperbolic emotions of the films' respective narratives and characters.[21] Although Sierck's contrapuntal manipulation of textual arrangements might indeed have pushed the limits of Nazi ideology, one cannot neglect the fact—as I will detail in a moment—that his two Leander films were also clearly marketed as showcases featuring the sights and sounds of a new star. For the greater public, Sierck's mise-en-scène—whether or not it was meant to be ironic—provided ample opportunities to consume the star doing her peculiar thing. Leander's star image buttressed the relationship between cinema and modern consumerism. It encouraged the spectator to desire not only the body of the star but also the kinds of spaces and objects that in their fetishized form as commodities helped display the star's body: houses, rooms, furniture, appliances, and fashion items. Sierck's Leander served a double mission. Whereas her voice and look pointed the viewer to newly emerging arenas of commodity consumption beyond the theater, her star persona at the same time anchored different viewing positions in the filmic text itself. Leander's peculiar presentation admonished the female spectator-consumer of the time to, as Mary Ann Doane has written in a different context, "concern herself with her own appearance and position—an appearance that can only be fortified and assured through the purchase of a multiplicity of products."[22] As a trigger of feelings of immediacy and affective intimacy, Leander's voice allowed the mass-cultural consumer to reconcile the curious split between the experience of cinema as a collective space on the one hand and a newly emerging notion of spectatorship as private, albeit mass-produced, experience on the other.

Commodities are mysterious things. They appear in a dreamlike framework that eclipses their actual source of value; they reduce an object to a means of its own consumption.[23] Leander's star persona documents the extent to which the Nazi culture industry captured emotions not in recourse to the use value of ideology but the mysticism of cultural commodities and consumption. Leander's appeal, as Eric Rentschler writes, derived "from an ability to unite opposites: a tender physiognomy and a thick body, silent suffering and animated expressivity, domestic charm and foreign allure, solemn spirituality and playful sensuality, maternal warmth and vampish sadism."[24] Leander's sights and sounds produced spectators who were eager to convert cultural expression into personal property, who knew how to reify the object of desire into a thing the spectator thought "he can put in his pocket and take home."[25]

Leander's work with directors other than Sierck magnifies what is precarious about any redemptive approach to her star image or the power of melodramatic excess. In 1942 spectators such as Reitz's Maria and Pauline would be invited to transfer their delight to the image of Leander playing the role of Hanna Holberg in the UFA melodrama *Die große Liebe* (The great love), one of the biggest box office hits between 1933 and 1945. Directed by Rolf Hansen, this film was to boost the morale of those waiting and working at the home front. It has become famous for Leander's infamous "Durchhaltelieder," her melodramatic songs of perseverance. The film's final shot links what Reitz presents as female defiance directly to the German war effort; it inscribes—as the reviewer for *Der Film* saw correctly—"the order of the day" as a rhetoric of "greatness and relentlessness" in the realm of what is left of private life.[26] In this last shot we see Holberg, temporarily united with the aviator Paul Wendlandt (Victor Staal), attentively watching the skies, not in order to discover shooting stars but to behold a bomber formation en route to the front. Far from experiencing war as an antagonistic element, Holberg detects in war a figure that fascinates: war emerges as the very condition that makes great love possible in the first place. Leander's star persona, in this final shot, glorifies warfare as the telos of melodramatic attentiveness and female spectatorship. Watching Leander watching, listening to Leander listening, the 1942 spectator was asked to understand war as a melodramatic spectacle of the first order. "Ich weiß, es wird einmal ein Wunder geschehen" (I know a miracle will happen at some point), Leander intones in this film in what is perhaps her most illustrious song ever—both a consolation to those fighting at the home front and a tribute to Hitler's myth of the "Wunderwaffe," the vision of a missile magically undoing the enemy.[27]

"HABANERA VS. CHRISTMAS CAROL"

Zarah Leander was born on March 15, 1907, as Zarah Stina Hedberg in Karlstad, Sweden.[28] Although never promoted by Hitler to the position of a state actress, Leander captivated the emotions of German audiences between 1937 and 1943 with her curious mix of renunciation and determination, exoticism and "German" faith, fatalism and autonomy, sensuality and spontaneity. As UFA's highest-paid star during this period, Leander in fact provided the film industry with a charismatic flagship giving direction to the entire star system. Even before she was seen in a German production for the first time, Leander's image was shaped into that of a metastar whose primary function was to set up a framework in which Hollywood-like elements—including the media stardom of political leaders—could assume their respective operations.

What originally incited UFA to attract Leander to Germany was her success in Ralph Benatzky's *Axel an der Himmelstür* (Axel at heaven's gate, 1936) in Vienna, an operetta in which Leander played a glamorous film star. In contrast to the domestic actresses who populated German screens circa 1936, Leander promised to supply German audiences once again with the image of a powerful femme fatale, an ideal stopgap to fill the void left after both Garbo and Dietrich had turned their backs on the German film industry. From the moment of its inception, Leander's star persona was therefore characterized, and jeopardized, by ostensible signatures of simulation. Whereas film stars commonly derive their charisma from peculiar signatures of individual authenticity, from presumed continuities between on- and offscreen persona, Leander entered the German film industry as a substitute, a mere copy measured against what she was supposed to replace. Hence an extravagant press campaign accompanied her move to Nazi Germany: an attempt to naturalize her stardom, don her in an aura of exceptionality, and make audiences forget about the fact that her stardom designated the presence of an absence. Masterminded by Carl Opitz, the public relations manager of UFA, Leander's promotion built up mass expectations long before the new star had even appeared in front of the UFA cameras. "I was supposed to be found so high above the audience," Leander herself recalled the fabrication of her aura, "that it became possible to see me distinctly as the 'star' who I was, yet not so distinctly that the common man would be unable to fancy and add details according to his own desires."[29]

Finally projected on the screens of Nazi cinema, Leander's composite star image did not embody collective mentalities so much as it offered a projection screen itself, an imaginary space open for multiple and often contradictory desires and uses. For Detlef Sierck, her first UFA director, Leander's face resembled Garbo's owing to what he called its flatness. Accordingly, it required the modeling work of the camera and the director to endow Leander's physiognomy—a silent mask and virtual "cow face"[30]—with allure in the first place. For a columnist in a 1938 issue of *Filmwelt*, by way of contrast, Leander's face introduced to German cinema not a malleable surface but a perfect embodiment of the essence of Germanic femininity: "This incredibly impeccable and sculptured face mirrors everything that moves a woman: wistfulness and pain, love and bliss, melancholy and resignation. In her attitude as an actress, Zarah Leander is the epitome of 'spiritualized sensuality.' As dark as her low, indefinable alto—which is able to represent so excitingly the expression of hidden female desires—is also her essence."[31] Alternatively seen as an empty signifier or an archetype of eternal womanhood, Leander's face carried either less (Sierck) or more (the *Filmwelt* reviewer) than necessary to propagate the idea of self-determination and self-authorship so central to the Hollywood star cult of the time.[32] From the moment UFA inaugurated Leander's aura, her face simultaneously meant nothing and everything. Instead of simply giving form to the viewer's daydreams, it defined a liminal space in which it was possible to play out one's desire seemingly without being disturbed by the reality principle.

But more than her face and looks, Leander's voice was perceived as the hallmark of her stardom. Musical numbers and revue elements within Leander's films suspended narrative progress and invited the film's audiences to consume the aural presence of the star. Significantly, however, the popularity of Leander's voice and singing relied on an array of ambivalences similar to the one that concerned the discursive construction of her face.[33] Whereas her baritone indeed probed given constructions of femininity, her Swedish accent infused the rigorous idiom of the German fatherland with a melos culturally coded as feminine. Like her face, Leander's voice had something in stock for everyone. As one reviewer wrote in 1937, this voice "is intoxicating as heavy dark wine. It can sound as powerful as the sound of an organ. It can appear as transparent as glass, as low as metal. Everything is in this voice: jubilation, happiness, the drunken melody and the wild pain of life."[34]

Leander's film songs were typically broadcast on radio several weeks prior to a film's premiere, a marketing strategy that built up audience expectation and allowed distributors to advertise particular films as showcases of Leander songs. Reminiscent of Fred Astaire's concurrent media popularity in the United States,[35] Leander became simultaneously a film star and a radio personality; she entered German hearts and minds through her performance onscreen as much as over the *Volksempfänger*. Significant shifts in the diegetic position of Leander's musical numbers quickly reflected the commercial value of her voice. In her first UFA feature, *To New Shores,* Leander's singing still remained relatively subordinated to the narrative; most of her numbers are interrupted halfway through. It is only with *La Habanera* that Leander's films developed narrative arrangements that allowed the star to perform entire songs and thus deliver what audiences (and industrialists) expected from their new idol. Some critics responded to the latter strategy with understandable suspicion. They were concerned that future features might completely disregard the star's skills as a dramatic actress[36] or breach the laws of narrative film by "unconditionally and with violence heading for 'the Song.'"[37]

It is interesting to note that whatever in Leander's inner-diegetic performances provoked sexual mores and gender definitions was typically corrected by the overall lines of narrative development. Here, too, spectators could have their cake and eat it too. Gloria Vane in *To New Shores,* for example, appears onstage as a lascivious and aggressive femme fatale, rousing her audiences through direct forms of address and pulsating refrains, whereas beyond her performance she emerges as a faithful and reclusive lover. What most deserves our interest, however, is the extent to which Leander proliferated musical forms clearly at odds with Nazi cultural politics. Only a few of Leander's hit songs during her UFA period really adhered to the musical vocabulary defined by Nazi ideologues as German music. Clearly dominating Leander's performances, "Foxtrot, tango, habanera, and czardas, strictly speaking also polka, were musical forms that had to be considered as 'racially degenerate' within the National Socialist ideology because of their Afro-American or Slavic origin."[38] In most of her films Leander's sounds transported the listener beyond the boundaries of the National Socialist worldview and its essentializing definitions of what it meant to be German. Typically, however, such moments of transgression summoned a variety of narrative devices that realigned exotic pleasure with the ideological orders of the day. Leander's songs provided a prime example for the exorcising tasks of Nazi film music. They exploited desire for the unknown with the intention of segregating self and other and making the individual body disappear in larger constellations of power.[39]

Intoned in the role of the Swede Astrée Sternhjelm, who becomes entrenched in a love triangle in Puerto Rico, Leander's musical numbers in *La*

Habanera are a good case in point. Composed by Lothar Brühne, her most memorable song, "Der Wind hat mir ein Lied erzählt" (The wind has told me a song), borrows from the Caribbean habanera tradition. It uses balalaikas, castanets, and stuffed trumpets, instruments that were on the official blacklist of the Nazi music board. Set in duple meter and a slow tempo, the habanera idiom originated from Creole and African American sources at the beginning of the nineteenth century, although some of its compositional features can also be found in Iberian music. Sometimes called "contradanza criolla," it provided the rhythmical basis for many varieties of Latin American dance music, including the tango.[40] Like jazz, the habanera emerged as a popular response to the experience of cultural displacement; it defined itself as an intrinsically hybrid mode of expression, the intersection of different cross-cultural trajectories. In Sierck's film habanera rhythms yield a recurring sonic background to the dramatic action. They intensify Sternhjelm's despair and melancholy, her desire to break away from the despotic Don Pedro and to return home to northern Europe. While the narrative stages the triumph of European rationality over southern lust and greed,[41] the musical sound track intermingles the familiar with the foreign and invites the viewer to travel across cultural boundaries. Whereas the film first imagines Puerto Rico as a structured opposite to the Aryan state and then destroys the island's idyllic façade,[42] Leander's song espouses an exoticized other as a playground for the imagination to underscore that there is no place like home (fig. 9).

Most contemporary reviewers, in order to channel exotic distractions back into the Procrustean bed of ideological correctness, deemphasized Leander's habanera and instead praised the film's Teutonic "Kinderlied," a Christmas carol Sternhjelm intones for her son at that most bourgeois and "feminine" of all musical instruments, the piano.[43] Whereas the habanera was seen as a generic number, signifying the kind of seduction, blindness, and racial miscegenation that prevail in Puerto Rico, the rather pedestrian "Kinderlied" was hailed as Leander's most compelling musical performance in *La Habanera*.[44] At once a language primer and a vehicle to express the protagonist's yearning for her Northern origins ("A, B, C, D, E, F, G, the whole garden is full of snow"), the carol, for most reviewers, articulated the immutable melos of Sternhjelm's ethnic identity. She, wrote the *Film-Kurier*, "sings the 'Kinderlied' to her boy who originates from a marriage with a Southerner. It is in this simple and hearty melody that her heart beats, her memory of and longing for the homeland."[45] Understood as a counterpoint to "Der Wind hat mir ein Lied erzählt," "Kinderlied"—in the eyes of the majority of reviewers—provided a glimpse of a better, unified

Figure 9. Exotic pleasures: A festive scene from Detlef Sierck's *La Habanera* (1937). Courtesy of Filmmuseum Berlin—Deutsche Kinemathek.

world amid southern hybridity. The song expressed desire for ethnic par-ticularity, for forms of identity anchored in nationally specific sounds and materialities of language. Whereas the habanera, then, was downplayed as inauthentic and mere pretense, it was in the straightforward tonality and rhythmic uniformity of the "Kinderlied" that most critics heard the film's redeeming voice of authenticity, a voice that recuperated lost utopias and fused them with the order of the day.

In many respects the reviewers' selective praise for Leander's songs echoed UFA's overall advertising strategies for *La Habanera*. The film was released shortly before Christmas, and in tandem with Luis Trenker's mountain spectacle *Der Berg ruft!* (The mountain calls), it was meant to become the year's most captivating holiday attraction—a must-see, adding exotic adventure to days of familial and national recluse.[46] UFA's advertising campaign for *La Habanera* in fact mapped the film's ambivalent themes of cultural dislocation onto the all-too-familiar topographical myth of North and South. Leander's delicate immersion into a "degenerate" musical idiom was turned into an Italian journey, a journey that takes one beyond oneself but does not revise existing formulations of cultural boundaries and collective identities. During a promotion of the film two members of *La Scala*, accompanied by a former accompanist of Enrico Caruso, presented Italian arias, songs, and duets. In a curious exercise of cross-cultural redress, UFA here mobilized the aura of high culture and spiritual refinement in order to bring Leander's exoticism—her engagement with Caribbean popular culture—safely home to Germany. Italian opera staked out a space in which the audience could consume its star in various positions and against all signs of ideological inconsistency (fig. 10).

Most stars of Nazi cinema were designed to fetter the dreams of the spectator, to immobilize desires and identifications that threatened to escape political control.[47] Shaped into a multivalent signifier, Leander at first seems to deviate from this norm in her performances. Her star persona invited the viewer's imagination to wander off in various directions at once and, particularly in her early films, to transgress the realms of conformity. On closer inspection, however, we see that Leander inhabited a discursive site at which ideological imperatives and cultural commodification struck a curious compromise. Fashioning her image into a repository of contradictory emotional investments, UFA inflated Leander's meaning to such an extent that the star came to embody a wholesale market of spectatorial delight and consumption. Leander's fans got whatever they wanted, which at first sight seemed a lot, yet in truth Leander only extended an invitation to cathartic assimilation. The pleasure of consuming the star Leander—to modify Adorno and Horkheimer's famous dictum—promoted the resignation that it ought to help forget.[48] For the German audience of 1937 Leander's voice and image meant everything and nothing. As a screen site of highly contradictory investments, the star Leander became indeed "the falsest woman of the century."[49]

Contemporary cultural studies is quick to assign subversive meanings to the popular appropriation of mass cultural symbols, to the ambivalent pleasures of consuming a star such as Leander. John Fiske does not hesitate to understand the mass cultural consumer as a "poacher, encroaching on the terrain of the cultural landowner (or textowner) and 'stealing' what he or she wants without being caught and subjected to the laws of the land (rule of the text)."[50] Yet the Americanist inclinations of Nazi mass culture reveal some crucial blind spots built into such theories of cultural poaching. I would argue that German Hollywood clearly anticipated what contemporary audiences might have seen and today's revisionists celebrate as enactments of resistance. A counterpart to a highly politicized public sphere, Nazi consumer culture reckoned with cultural poachers. Particularly in the case of Zarah Leander, it invited people to steal according to desire, to consume the

Figure 10.　Southern exposure: Zarah Leander in *La Habanera*. Courtesy of Filmmuseum Berlin—Deutsche Kinemathek.

illusion that within Nazi Germany certain spaces could remain free of politics. What the institutions and—as we will see in the remainder of this chapter—the texts of Nazi mass culture granted were predigested expressions but no rights: they enticed poachers to poach; they provided spaces of individualization and empowerment, only to strengthen—to extend Fiske's metaphor—the laws that regulated the distribution of land outside of the distraction factory. The cultural poachers of the Nazi era transformed cultural poaching into a pleasurable experience of consumption itself, a commodity. Instead of consuming illegitimate meanings, they ended up being consumed by the very objects of their pleasure.

POACHING A STAR

Stars stimulate modes of spectatorship that tend to undermine what formalist film scholarship considers the primary engine of a film's meaning, namely the mandates of narrative unity, closure, and motivation. To the extent to which publicity campaigns and tabloid journalism define a star's persona as a public affair and social event, the star's presence within a peculiar text blurs the boundaries between an "address relying on the identification with fictional characters and an activation of the viewer's familiarity with the star on the basis of production and publicity intertexts."[51] The star's performance interrupts narrative progress in favor of spectacular interludes solely there to exhibit the star's features to the viewers' consuming glance. Recycling constitutive elements of the early cinema of attractions, stars promote viewing pleasures that encourage the viewer to become not a hermeneutic reader but a textual poacher who isolates moments of spectacle when the image of the star can be consumed most intensely. The desire to possess displaces the urge to follow a narrative as the primary mode of reading a film.

In accord with international trends of the time German cinema of the 1930s redefined in no small way how stars appeared onscreen and appealed to their viewers' emotions. One of the many stylistic effects of the coming of synchronized sound circa 1930 was a clear reduction in close-ups. As Hugo Zehder observed as early as 1929, "The close-up is being used ever more rarely, it is losing its expressive value because the sounds of voices and songs draw the audience's attention to the hero and characterize the event exhaustingly."[52] Synchronized sound altered the methods by which narrative cinema aspired to the status of spectacle. It placed the star's physical appearance at some greater distance, but at the same time it offered new technological opportunities to position her or him at very close range. What one might call the sonic close-up—shots that allowed the star's voice as speech or singing to speak intimately to the viewer—became an important vehicle not simply to compensate for lost technologies of spectacularization but even to enhance the textual fabrication of star charisma. The making of stars in particular during the 1930s must be understood as a decisively audiovisual event.

Detlef Sierck, in his two Leander films of the 1930s, turned out to be an imaginative authority in this new art of audiovisual spectacularization. *To New Shores* was clearly meant from its very inception to endow the imported icon Leander with the visual and sonic spell of personality. It is one of the many ironies of Sierck's career that he met this task by making a film that examined modern stardom itself. Intended as a piece of social criticism according to Sierck himself,[53] *To New Shores* takes issue with the role of the star in postautonomous aesthetic culture. The film, in fact, tells a story about a peculiarly modern battle over the location of culture, about the division of modern culture into the commodified realms of popular entertainment, on the one hand, and the exclusive domains of aesthetic refinement and social representation, on the other. Torn between these two spheres, the Leander character experiences her popular consumption as a form of violence and self-alienation, and she learns to view the elite's rhetoric of cultural refinement as hypocritical, as a strategy that links certain cultural practices to class positions in order to cement given structures of power. At the same time, however, the elaborately choreographed mise-en-scène of Sierck's film caters to the new logic of the star system and the popular's practices of audiovisual poaching. Set first in England during the heyday of colonial capitalism and then in Australia, the film uses shifting locations to deliver effectively the image *and* sound of UFA's new star to the audience. Whether we see Leander in the role of Gloria Vane in London or as a prisoner in the Parramatta jail, Franz Weihmayr's cinematography conjures a panoply of attractive perspectives that suspend the viewer from the film's overall narrative and supplies him or her with close-ups of Leander's "beguiling music" and looks.[54]

Both in England and in its colony Australia, the practices of cultural refinement occupy a space in which the social elite represents class position and negotiates the terms of social mobility. Although the film leaves no doubt about the corruption that prevails behind the façades of cultural distinction, it presents the cultural activities of the colonial upper class as part of a symbolic order that derives its strength from continual mechanisms of marking difference, of indicating inclusion or exclusion. At a party at the governor's palace in honor of Queen Victoria, the elite come together to engage in a minutely staged ritual of social exchange while an anonymous crowd gathers outside passively watching the elaborate gala. Significantly, what provides diversion for the crowd offers the elite a platform to affirm and reconfigure the channels of power. The governor's party and its sequence of formation dances serve as a spectacular backdrop to announce the marriage between the governor's daughter and Gloria's former lover, Albert Finsbury, and thus to reinscribe the lineage of colonial rulership. The traditional institutions of cultural refinement and high art operate here as stages on which power represents itself. Reserved for the colonial elite alone, the rituals of aesthetic cultivation transform the members of the crowd into cultural window-shoppers who consume their own exclusion from power as a spectacle of the first order.

Popular culture, on the other hand, is far from offering a space of democratic participation and empowerment either. In fact, it exhibits deformations and duplicities similar to the ones that mark high culture. Popular diversion emerges as a realm of excess and exhibitionism, of aggressive sexuality and voyeuristic pleasure—a spectacular foreplay enticing desires but endlessly delaying their gratification. Although Gloria's performance in the opening sequence challenges the moralism of the Victorian bourgeoisie, the viewer is soon to learn that her provocative stage persona is only a pretense, a second skin catering to her male consumers. Gloria's successful "Yes, Sir!" that mocks the Victorian watchdogs brings into relief—as the film's narrative is quick to reveal—anything but Gloria's true backstage personality. Already during Gloria's performance Sierck provides the viewer with a clear sense of the artificiality of the singer's frivolous stage persona. The camera follows and reframes her movements onstage from ever-changing points of view and focal lengths. Frequent cuts and abrupt shifts draw the film viewer's attention to the fact that what we see is not the recording of an artistic expression but a violent process of dismemberment—male desire mapped onto Gloria Vane's body. Allowing us to see Gloria through the eyes of her delirious onlookers and listeners, Sierck's editing denounces popular diversion as meaningless: Gloria's spell of personality is fake, a reflex of projective activities, a male fantasy (fig. 11).

Sierck's double critique of Victorian moralism and popular diversion as inauthentic becomes obvious in a later sequence when the former star of the Adelphi Theater, released from the Parramatta jail, performs in front of an Australian audience characterized by desires similar to those of the London public. In contrast to the London spectacle, however, Gloria now refuses to transform her body into a pleasurable commodity. Not surprisingly, her effort to use the stage as a screen of her true feelings meets with

Figure 11. Spectacle as male fantasy: Zarah Leander in Detlef Sierck's *To New Shores* (1937). Courtesy of Filmmuseum Berlin—Deutsche Kinemathek.

the rude rejection of the audience, which is unwilling to endure Gloria's melancholy slow fox-trot "Ich stehe im Regen . . ." (I stand in the rain . . .). As if to endorse Gloria's exercise in expressive authenticity, the cinematography and editing during this second performance avoids oscillating between various points of view from the audience. Instead, the camera immediately zooms in on Leander's face and presents her throughout the performance in uninterrupted and motionless medium close-ups. These shots isolate her from the unruly diegetic audience and redeem the melodramatic power of her artistic virtuosity for modes of spectatorship that valorize contemplative identification over distracted appropriation. If the film's camera work and editing in the earlier London sequence defined the popular dimension as one in which male audiences exploit women, during the second performance they try to reinstate for the film's audience a legitimate notion of popular culture that incorporates principles, such as originality, authenticity, and attentiveness, typically associated with bourgeois high art. Melodrama and its emotional intensity, in this way, rearticulate auratic experiences in the heart of the most pertinent site of modern mass distraction itself, the cinema. Mechanical reproduction reproduces the magic it— following Walter Benjamin's famous postulate—originally set out to destroy. Fusing high and low, the popular form of melodrama aspires to become an "intensified, primary, and exemplary version of what the most ambitious art, since the beginnings of Romanticism, has been about."[55]

In a sense the film's passage from London to Sydney, from cultural consumption to aesthetic elevation, closely follows the logic described by Gertrud Koch as the sadistic impulse behind Sierck's melodramatic imagination.[56] The film first construes what amounts to a repulsive image of female sexuality only to then resort to ritual acts of cleansing. Sierck privileges a gaze that moves from aversion to purification, and in so doing he arrests the female body as a deformed, disciplined fetish.[57] *To New Shores* links this authoritarian logic to a conservative project of cultural criticism. True to Sierck's lifelong preoccupation with religious themes and images, the end of *To New Shores* resorts to the sights and sounds of organized religion in order to foreground Sierck's vision of a homogeneous culture consolidating aesthetic refinement and popular traditions. Sierck literally exorcizes Leander's voice and body in a final purgatorium so as to hammer home his vision of a new community integrated via affects and intuitions rather than formal principles, legal procedures, or economic relations. When Gloria marries the faithful farmer Henry in the last sequence, the church's altar, the choir's "Gloria in Excelsis Deo," and the final close-ups of the choirboys all allegorize what lies beyond the end of the gap between high and low. However baroque they may seem, the film's final images encrypt Sierck's dream of a culture in which melodramatic pathos and contemplative attentiveness heal the rifts between legitimate art and popular culture and thus revitalize social integration and identity formation. Religious sights and sounds here channel conflicting voices, tastes, and perspectives into a symphonic whole. Popular culture becomes art, art popular culture, so that the formerly divided community may live again.

Narrative development and mise-en-scène in Sierck's *To New Shores*, then, delineate what appears to be a strangely ambivalent force field. On the one hand the film clearly supplied Nazi consumer culture with a spectacular commodity; it opened a series of seemingly private windows on the new star, her good looks as much as her perplexing voice. Focusing on Leander, the film's image track and sound track appealed to modes of spectatorship associated with a Hollywood-like star system so as to fuel the audience's desire for cultural consumption. On the other hand Sierck's film exposes the very mechanisms that make and mark stars. The narrative seeks to undo the split between high and low and, thereby, to overcome what makes stars into cultural commodities in the first place. *To New Shores* denounces the triumph of commodified consumption over artistic expressivity as a step into a realm of inauthenticity. In addition, it renders melodramatic sensibilities as catalysts for acts of spiritual purification and elevation. Melodrama is meant to redeem the individual from the respective excesses of both popular distraction and the elite's hypocritical discourse of aesthetic refinement.

To New Shores, then, with its final images of religious redemption, seems to articulate a utopian vision that leads beyond the instrumentalization of the aesthetic in modern industrial society in general and National Socialism in particular. Sierck's melodramatic reunification of high and low, of aura and distraction, seems to point at what transcends the organization of pleasure and desire in twentieth-century modernity. Does it really, though? For Horkheimer and Adorno, we should recall, this melodramatic vision of cultural homogenization constituted the signature of industrial culture itself. Sierck's dream of unification was Horkheimer and Adorno's nightmare. When analyzing the fate of cultural modernization under the sign of organized capitalism, Horkheimer and Adorno came to the conclusion that the culture industry collapsed former divisions between high and low into a "ruthless unity."[58] Symptomatic of a postliberal market society in which all aspects of production and consumption were controlled through bureaucratic organizations, industrial mass culture provided everyone with everything; it forged into a false unity what no longer could add up to a whole. "Light art has been the shadow of autonomous art. It is the social bad conscience of serious art. The truth which the latter necessarily lacked because of its social premises gives the other the semblance of legitimacy. The division itself is the truth: it does at least express the negativity of the culture which the different spheres constitute. Least of all can the antithesis be reconciled by absorbing light into serious art, or vice versa."[59]

Unlike Sierck, Horkheimer and Adorno tried to break away from binaries such as high and low, authentic and inauthentic, true and false. Their criticism of modern culture differentiated between older forms of popular culture and the peculiarly modern formation of Fordist mass culture and at the same time separated traditional dogmas of high culture from the notion of aesthetic modernism as a mouthpiece of determined negation.[60] Neither Sierck's understanding of the modern gulf between high and low nor his desire for cultural synthesis is therefore compatible with the argument of the *Dialectic of Enlightenment*. On the contrary, the melodramatic utopianism of *To New Shores* directly echoes the synthetic tasks of industrial mass culture itself. Sierck's utopia of reconciliation encodes what was also at the top of Goebbels's cinematic agenda, namely the mutual absorption of high and low, of artistic merit and popular appeal. Reminiscent of Wagner's nineteenth-century aesthetic visions, which intended to overcome the fragmentation of art in modern society, Sierck's film merges word, image, and music into a new form of public art. The final sequence of *To New Shores* unifies nonidentical particulars under the hallmark of some new kind of aesthetic totality and thus converts visions of wholeness into consumer items.

Eric Rentschler has argued that Sierck's melodramas "fit well into Nazi constellations, both as ideological affirmations and as the sites of what appeared to be transgressive designs. Aesthetic resistance was part of the system; it provided a crucial function in a larger gestalt."[61] My reading of *To New Shores* confirms and in fact expands this proposition. A composite of Sierck's melodramatic craftsmanship and Leander's star presence, the film highlights the often contradictory, albeit no doubt effective, ways in which the National Socialists in their pursuit of a homogeneous community of the folk relied on the power of cosmopolitan distractions and the demand for commodity consumption, social mobility, and the accoutrements of a bourgeois lifestyle. On the one hand *To New Shores* illustrates the Nazis' hope to exploit Fordist mass culture as a *political tool,* a crucible of fantasy production powerful enough to break older bonds of solidarity and fragment the body politic into a multitude of pleasure-seeking monads. Part of a project that sought to establish an economically viable alternative to Hollywood, the film draws our attention to the way Nazi leisure culture entertained the poachers of industrial culture with the illusion that within this highly politicized society certain spaces remained beyond politics and coordination. On the other hand *To New Shores* informs about the curious telos of fascist cultural politics in general, the fact that sweeping narratives and the outright imitation of American patterns often went hand in hand with the intention to organize national consent within an autonomous yet marketable German mass culture. The film exemplifies how Nazi mass culture, far from subverting the dictates of ideology, hoped to fabricate a new national community through American-style consumption. It is difficult to see, therefore, how Sierck's simultaneous avowal and disavowal of the popular dimension in *To New Shores,* of distraction and consumption, could have really pushed the limits of Nazi politics, as one branch of Sierck scholarship would like us to believe. Instead of heroizing Sierck's ambivalences as signs of aesthetic resistance,[62] it seems much more appropriate to read the negotiation of mass culture, gender, and community in films such as *To New Shores* as an integral element of prewar Nazi cultural politics. The film exemplifies how Nazi cinema enlisted cultural consumption—including the identification with ideologically inconsistent representations of gender and cultural otherness—for the project of displacing politics with aesthetics, society with community.

CODA: HEALTHY WOMEN AND BUSY BEES

According to Benjamin's famous thesis fascism implemented technologically advanced communication technologies such as film in order to simulate a utopian community of equals.[63] Mass spectacles and their mechanical reproduction onscreen addressed the modern hunger for distraction and scopic pleasure, yet they did so solely to give the masses emotional expressions but no rights. Within the context of fascist mass culture, distraction and modern spectatorship constituted forms that reproduced as a sensational event what mechanical reproduction allegedly rendered obsolete: the charisma of auratic experiences.

Implicitly challenging Benjamin's account of modern mass culture, Patrice Petro has argued that the category of distraction as a peculiar mode of experiencing modern life was far less universal and gender-neutral than Benjamin assumed.[64] Benjamin's category of distraction, she argues, might encode the experience of those permitted to participate in the processes of modernization since the middle of the nineteenth century, but it omits the experiences of those who, owing to given landscapes of power, remained at the margins of these processes, in particular women. Highly popular in Weimar cinema as a "female" genre, the melodrama—according to Petro—bears testimony to the existence of modes of spectatorship different from those described by Benjamin under the rubric of distraction. In the melodrama mechanical reproduction addresses those for whom distraction has not become the norm, those whose "concentrated gaze involves a perceptual activity that is neither passive nor entirely distracted"[65] and who therefore desire contemplative identification and emotional intensity.

Petro's insistence on the diversity and gender specificity of modern spectatorship, on the parallel existence of industrialized and emotionally attentive modes of film viewing, should make us wonder about the accuracy of Benjamin's theory of fascist mass culture. If, following Benjamin, fascism musters distraction in order to engineer political homogeneity, then do we have to assume that those committed to melodramatic spectatorship and consumption escaped the suturing effects of the Nazi spectacles? One might be tempted at first to answer this question in the affirmative and thus attribute a rather ironic moment of resistance to those who found themselves

positioned at the fringes of technological modernization in a patriarchal society. But such an answer, after more careful consideration, would blindly
fall prey to false alternatives suggested in the question itself, that is, the
definition of Nazi cultural politics solely in terms of the stage managing
that Benjamin called the aestheticization of politics. What it would overlook is the fact that—in contrast to Benjamin's model—Nazi politics relied
on both at once, on "proletarian" mobilization as much as on bourgeois
leisure and modern commodity consumption. Melodrama helped essentially build bridges between the ideological and temporal disjunctures of
Nazi politics. As a genre of excess and operatic intensity it ameliorated the
"fuzzy totalitarianism" that characterized fascist modernism.[66] Melodramatic narratives recalled earlier viewing pleasures, but in doing so they also
bonded diverging experiences to the new order.

The making of the star Zarah Leander circa 1937 reminds us that we
must not mistake the very existence of competing cultural practices during
the National Socialist period for signs of ideological opposition, let alone
political resistance. In its effort to achieve a Wagnerian alliance of word,
image, and music, Nazi feature films advocated the pleasures of pseudo-
individualization. They watched and listened for their viewers in order to
bond different modes of reception to one calculated product package. Clearly
aware of cinema's historical possibilities as a heterogeneous and often unpredictable horizon of public experience, Nazi cinema in fact did not spare
any effort to monitor the entire act of going to the movies. Advertising campaigns and press coverage played an essential role in protecting the studios'
products from undesirable interpretations; they contained surplus meaning and directed the reception process. The kinds of short films that accompanied the actual screening of Leander features illustrate this in an instructive manner. *To New Shores,* during its opening week in Berlin, was
preceded by the short "Healthy Women—Healthy Folk,"[67] which propagated the desirability of women's sports, of shaping women's bodies for the
sake of the nation. *La Habanera,* by contrast, was initially featured in tandem with a film celebrating the community and hierarchy of a beehive.
This film left little doubt about the fact that biological wonders should
serve as blueprints for human societies as well.[68] Shorts such as these offered predigested meanings and set the stage for the pleasures of melodramatic excess. The "apolitical" consumption of stars such as Leander might
have been the primary attraction of a night at the movies, but it took place
in a public sphere organized and orchestrated from above, a public sphere
exploiting the viewer's desire rather than encouraging the articulation of
concrete needs and interests.

Figure 12.   Home, sweet home: Zarah Leander as Magda von Schwartze on a film poster for Carl Froelich's 1938 film *Heimat* (*Illustrierter Film-Kurier*, 1938).

The TV series *Heimat*, to return for a last time to Reitz's collection of ethnographic snapshots, seems to know about this reconstruction of cinema as a melodramatic space of pseudoindividualization, yet it struggles to suppress further insight under a highly subdued visual veneer. In a second film-within-the-film sequence Reitz confronts his spectators once again with a movie theater and a Leander spectacle. The film's color switches back to black and white, and a curtain opens and brings into view the screening's title: Carl Froelich's 1938 *Heimat*. A director definitely not known for non-conformist intentions ever since his 1913 bioepic *Richard Wagner*, Froelich in his *Heimat* situated Leander in a father-daughter melodrama, a tale of renunciation and reconciliation (fig. 12). Once more Reitz's spectator will find Maria and Pauline in the audience, mesmerized by their idol, although now watching the film side-by-side with their respective husbands and ersatz husbands. Similar to the earlier sequence, Reitz renders the audience a gathering of weeping listeners and cultural poachers. Leander's extravagant apparel onscreen stimulates Pauline to muse about her own fur coat and the lack of possibilities for showing it off. Two other spectators parody what they see onscreen as they exchange and eat apples. In contrast to the earlier sequence, Reitz's camera pictures the women's acts of melodramatic viewing in one and the same frame with the matter-of-fact responses of their male partners. In a series of highly controlled images the film's cinematography thus reinstates patriarchal order and compulsory heterosexuality. "I'm so happy to be back here," we hear Leander sobbing onscreen at the chest of her father. In the end of this sequence Leander intones passages from the *St. Matthew's Passion*, "Repentance and remorse cleaves the sinner's heart asunder," while her father and daughter watch attentively. Intimately resonating with Froelich's patriarchal conception of female identity, Reitz's *Heimat* in this second Leander sequence belies any redemptive approach to the Leander/Sierck productions, as much as to instances of cultural poaching in Nazi mass culture. Women's place on and in front of the screen might have changed in comparison to the earlier sequence, yet their modes of melodramatic looking at and listening to the star have not. For the women there seems to be no perceived difference between consuming Leander in a film by Sierck and enjoying the icon in a film by the Nazi activist Froelich, between the putatively subversive image of an exotic woman gone astray and the close-up of a prodigal daughter returning to her patriarchal masters. Froelich's 1938 *Heimat*—as it reappears in Reitz's 1984 *Heimat*—does not negate or recontain Maria and Pauline's earlier pleasures of watching *La Habanera*. It simply complements them, adds to the opulent buffet of emotions that Nazi mass culture had to offer. Americanist articulations of multiplicity and difference in Nazi culture thus by no means signify subversive intentions or emancipatory practices. The curious genre of the Nazi Western and its cross-cultural constructions of assertive masculinity, to which I will turn my attention in the following chapter, provide further evidence to support this thesis.

4 Siegfried Rides Again
Nazi Westerns and Modernity

In spite of its appeal to an explicitly modern demand for technological spectacle *(The Tunnel)* and commodity consumption (Leander), Nazi cinema built heavily on the fact that not everyone inhabits the same present and that many continue to adhere to seemingly outmoded thoughts, memories, and utopias. Nazi feature films were designed to assist audiences in negotiating major transformations in their contemporary lifeworlds. They helped carry viewers of diverse backgrounds across the threshold of the Third Reich in such a way that much older meanings could find a place amid the new order. The reconstruction of German cinema as a genre cinema was essential to this effort. Nazi genre films provided a sense of continuity in the face of radical transitions; they soothed emotions and displaced conflicting experiences. As Klaus Kreimeier has argued, "For twelve years genre cinema functioned as an advocate of the ordinary people, their everyday worries and desires, their demand for security, their visions of happiness, their brief escapes and, most of all, their longing for normality. In a world that seemed to topple all measures genre films not least of all warranted that normality existed and life continued to go on."[1] German cinema during the National Socialist period bridged temporal disjunctions and became German not because it subscribed to an intrinsically fascist aesthetic but because it consolidated the many elements of Weimar film practice into an economically viable genre cinema. Synchronized sound proved indispensable for this project. Neither what was understood as the *German* comedy, costume drama, or problem film nor as the *German* melodrama or revue film of the time would have succeeded without the magnetism of speaking and singing bodies onscreen.

Often seen as a kind of contract between the industry and the viewer, film genres occupy the space in-between specific films and the cinematic apparatus.[2] Genres involve changeable structures of expectations and conventions that link the film industry, the individual text, and historically contingent modes of spectatorship. Like other expressions of the popular, genres therefore do not necessarily represent forms of standardized consumption. Instead, they may constitute an "active process of generating and articulating meanings and pleasures within a social system,"[3] a process clearly marked by the imperatives of the industry but nevertheless also actuated by shifting audience expectations and structures of perception. Genre texts are shot through with markers that indicate not only how political and economic agendas shape the contours of culture at a specific historical moment but also how people make use of the products of industrial culture, how they embrace textual meanings in order to articulate them into their everyday life. Understood as transmission belts between industry and audience expectations, film genres encrypt historically specific anxieties and wish fantasies; they evoke meanings that maintain identities and secure action beyond individual irritation, desperation, and speechlessness.

It has often been pointed out that the category of genre has been essential to the way that classical Hollywood cinema has come to dominate global markets since World War I. Genres helped streamline production processes, cut the costs of making films, and rationalized distribution. They supported an aesthetics of instantaneous recognizability that could easily traverse cultural boundaries. As a result genre cinema has often been seen as an essentially American mode of telling stories and organizing pleasure, as a ruthless application of assembly-line production to the arenas of cultural expression. Americanism in a nutshell, the art of genre in this view has often been condemned as an instrument of homogenization leveling the semantic wealth of group-specific experiences and national particularities.

Against the background of this suspicion that film genres promote a quasi-automatic Hollywoodization of local cultures, this chapter examines the way Nazi cinema appropriated that most American of all film genres, the western. Goebbels designed Nazi cinema as a genre cinema that would be at once entertaining, ideologically effective, politically useful, and financially profitable, a cinema dedicated to Hollywood illusionism yet at the same time devoted to a German mission. I will argue that during the 1930s, Nazi western productions such as Luis Trenker's *Der Kaiser von Kalifornien* (The emperor of California, 1936), Herbert Selpin's *Sergeant Berry* (1938) and *Wasser für Canitoga* (Water for Canitoga, 1939), and Paul Verhoeven's *Gold in New Frisco* (1939) were part and parcel of this project. By exploring issues of charismatic leadership, masculine identity, organic communality, and technological progress, Nazi westerns aspired at once to absorb

Figure 13. Frontier fantasies: Native Americans in Luis Trenker's *The Emperor of California* (1936). Courtesy of Filmmuseum Berlin—Deutsche Kinemathek.

older aesthetic utopias and to fulfill urgent ideological functions. Part of a cinema that largely eschewed overt agitation in order to achieve popular appeal, the Nazi western genre helped redesign film "as a mechanized means to animate primal emotions, a modern technology to stir the soul's inner speech. It was to move the hearts and minds of masses while seeming to have little in common with politics or party agendas."[4] Far from simply erasing national particularity, the Nazi western genre inundated the viewer with a fake sense of normality, yet at the same time it solicited politically effective meanings and subjectivities. Nazi western features stirred fantasies about forms of geographical expansion that did not involve cultural intermingling. They evacuated foreign spaces, or remade the other in the image of the self, to warrant the particularity and hierarchical segregation of different cultures. German westerns of the 1930s may have distracted their viewers with exotic adventures, yet simultaneously they elevated the representation of bodies, language, and music to the status of a total work of art, a laboratory of affective enthrallment that promoted vitalist power and imperial domination (fig. 13).

COWBOYS AND MODERNIZATION

An anecdote of World War II history relates that Hitler, in 1943, ordered his general staff to read Karl May's western novels about the Apache Winnetou and his friend Old Shatterhand. Vis-à-vis the dwindling fortunes of the German war machinery, Hitler wanted May's imaginary West to become a source of moral inspiration.[5] Seen through the lenses of May's American frontier, technological warfare for Hitler emerged as a western adventure, a shoot-out between greedy Jewish Yankees on the one side and noble savages and superhuman German cowboys on the other. Spellbound by May's romantic western fantasies, Hitler in the very last days of the war did not even hesitate to apotheosize himself as a double of the last of the Mohicans, a representative of a race of heroically dying, yet morally infallible, warriors.[6]

Writing in American exile, Klaus Mann exposed the role of popular western imagery in Nazi ideology as early as 1940. As Mann argued, May's hero, Old Shatterhand, incarnated a "fascinating blend of young Siegfried and Tom Mix."[7] Shatterhand personified an amalgam of romantic longing and existential resolution that was destined to culminate in Nazi Germany:

> One of the most ardent Karl May fans was a certain good-for-nothing from Brunau [*sic*], Austria, who was to rise to impressive heights. Young Adolf was seriously smitten by Karl May, whose works were his favorite, if not his only reading, even in later years. His own imagination, his whole notion of life was impregnated by these Western thrillers. The cheap and counterfeit conception of "heroism" presented by Karl May fascinated the future Führer; he loved this primitive but effective shrewdness: the use of "secret weapons" and terrible tricks, such as carrying prisoners as shields, the brutal cunning of wild animals in the jungle; he was delighted by the glorification of savages. . . . He could see no reason why Old Shatterhand's convictions and tactics should not work if applied to national and international politics. One might conquer civilization by going back to the principles of the jungle.[8]

It is not difficult to see that Mann's rage against May and his disciple Hitler, although highly perceptive, relied on rather fragile assumptions. According to Mann, May's and Hitler's westernism resulted largely from a falsified picture of American frontier life. Only because Germans, in Mann's view, had misconstrued the western frontier in the first place could they transform the Far West into a source of political legitimation. What Mann overlooked was of course the mythic status of the frontier itself, the fact that ever since Frederick Jackson Turner's 1893 speech in Chicago American frontier fantasies had helped define American identity one-sidedly, in terms of agrarian democracy and heroic individualism rather than of ethnic difference, European immigration, and urban conflict in East Coast metropoles. Instead of falsifying history, as Mann believed, Hitler, when taking recourse to western themes, simply elevated myth to a higher level.

More important, however, what makes Mann's argument insufficient is the fact that he completely elided the diversity of German western fantasies prior to the Nazi takeover. By suggesting direct continuities from May to Hitler, Mann obscured the host of western images that had swept over Germany during the 1920s, mass reproduced through a variety of different media and institutions, in particular the urban movie theaters.[9] Weimar images of the Far West were thoroughly marked by contemporary debates about the costs and blessings of technological, cultural, and political modernization. The Nazi cowboy must therefore be viewed as a discontinuous reinscription of nineteenth-century fantasies rather than as their direct continuation. Only after containing the discursive heterogeneity of German western images could Hitler impose himself as a descendant of Old Shatterhand and his blood brother Winnetou. As we will see in this chapter, Nazi western films played an essential role in this process. They unified competing interpretations of the American West to arouse desire for ideology.

It is useful when trying to examine the curious existence of the Nazi cowboy first to retrace briefly the trail of German western fantasies from the nineteenth into the twentieth century. The popularity of western themes in Germany originally evolved from the same historical context that gave birth to the notion of "Heimat" (homeland).[10] The idea of both "Heimat" and the "Far West" expressed anxieties about the unsettling effects of industrial technology, rapid urbanization, monetary exchange, and functional abstraction. Portraits of bucolic homeland settings and idealized images of the American West became catalysts of fantasy production. Western fantasies offered imaginary places of action, heroism, individualism, and liberated wilderness.[11] They symbolically reduced complex political or economic issues to questions of morality. In a truly Wagnerian move, the early literary western genre portrayed economic instabilities as products of egotistical materialism and corrupt ethical dispositions, not of restraints placed on the individual by inadequate social structures. Often counterposing American greed with true German spirituality, German western stories reconstructed the homeland somewhere else and in doing so became a screen on which to project what nineteenth-century German discourse considered the essential elements of home: individual authenticity, temporal continuity, spatial closure, and harmonic interaction between a homogeneous social body and its natural environment.

In the nineteenth-century texts of Otto Rupius, Balduin Möllhausen, Friedrich Armand Strubberg, and Friedrich Gerstäcker countless and often barely literate readers found vehicles for imaginary travel to the New World. Yet these early western fictions offered much more than simply fantastic escape. They participated in the construction of an alternative public sphere, one inimical to bourgeois reading practices and the increasing dissemination and commodification of printed news. Western novels, however unrealistic, served as maps and manuals. They prepared for what, around 1850, seemed like a mass exodus over the Atlantic—pulp fiction instructed the disempowered on how to succeed in their quest for a new homeland abroad. As Ray Allen Billington writes, western novels might not have been "the most accurate purveyors of information, but they were better than nothing."[12]

Karl May's success around the turn of the century, that is, after the actual heyday of German emigration, indicated a fundamental transformation of the German western genre from a swatch of migration aspirations to a catalyst of exotic fantasies and transfigurations.[13] May rendered the West as a tabula rasa that awaited the inscriptions of imaginary new social orders, symbolic structures, and the kinds of "customs" that abound in his novels.[14] Although overflowing with nostalgia for the romantic, May's novels exported contemporary architectures of authority and submission from Germany to the Far West. As he projected onto Indians the seasoned picture of the noble savage,[15] as he embraced the western setting to rail against American materialism and greed, May recast the American West as a realm of spiritual salvation. In the heroic figures of Old Shatterhand and Winnetou, Wagner's heroes Siegfried and Parsifal continued their respective voyages to the final frontier of mercy and redemption. In his writing May fed directly into the imperialist projects of Wilhelminian Germany around the turn of the century. As his texts traversed fictional geographies, envisioned new social orders from scratch, and relocated traditional meanings, especially the rhetoric of Christianity, to exotic settings, May played a pivotal role in the proliferation of the cultural vocabulary necessary for imperial rule: the hierarchizing of different cultures, the aligning of narrative and spatial practices, and the jargon of unquestioned authority and domination.[16]

May's late-nineteenth-century search for paradise, as Eric Santner has pointed out, took place "at precisely that historical moment when psychoanalysis was becoming a science, when a mass popular culture was beginning to emerge in a form that could become a new market and industry proper, and finally, when film was being introduced as a new medium for the exploration of fantasy."[17] Small wonder, then, that for twentieth-century audiences western themes kept much of their appeal and actuality even though the western genre's proper subject domain had more or less been reduced to anachronism by the historical process. During the first decades of the new century, images of the Far West invited newly emerging mass audiences to embark on passages through space and time—voyages not simply to an imaginary past of unhampered individualism and archaic nature but also to one's own childhood fantasies, shaped by the reading of adventure literature and the experience of ethnographic exhibits so popular around 1900. The many second-rate American western films that were dumped on the German market after 1921[18] were thus all grist to the mills of Germany's desire for the West. In the field of Weimar visual art, representations of the West as a result often engaged directly with the way modern technology itself shaped fantasy and produced memory. In many instances these representations revealed that the popular historiography of the West had become concomitant with the history of cinematic representation, that the western film, as a genre, was a product of the very conditions that made its heroes disappear.

Consider, for example, Karl Hubbuch's drawing *Lederstrumpf* (Leatherstocking, c. 1921), which depicts an urban sidewalk tableau with electrical appliances and a truncated film advertisement (fig. 14). At first one is tempted to read the movie poster within this sketch as an incentive to imaginary escape, but Hubbuch draws his ad for a western film in a conspicuously dismembered fashion, severing the very dramatic event, the struggle that—we are led to believe—occupies the center of the poster. Further, he invades the romantic representation within the representation with markers of economical instrumentality, the sticker "Kartenverkauf hier" (Tickets sold here) glued right over the face of one of the internal onlookers. Surprisingly, what is excluded from our vision of the movie poster, action and heroic combat, reemerges synecdochically in the form of the arrow inscribed in the hardware of modernity. As a result of a curious symbolic exchange between the Wild West and the modern city, the arrow on the electric box signifies the very drama that escapes our view in the movie ad. Electric modernity and American frontier thus constitute an intricate play of presence and absence, one that calls attention to the modern moment that triggers the invocation of the West and transforms it into a commodity. Hubbuch's drawing reveals the technological apparatus that prompts Weimar fantasies of western heroism. It betrays the fact that cinematic modernity shapes the very content of such fantasies.

Figure 14.   *Lederstrumpf,* by Karl Hubbuch (c. 1921). Courtesy of Miriam Hubbuch, Freiburg (Germany).

Compare Hubbuch's drawing with Paul Gangolf's 1922 lithograph *Kino* (Cinema), which radically blurs the borders between the representation of western themes, the cinematic apparatus, and the forms of modern urban life (fig. 15). Gangolf's *Kino* depicts a chaotic crowd of people in a nocturnal German city. Over the heads of the mob looms a film poster announcing the western movie *Land without Sun.* Here urban life appears as a dark amalgam of hardly discernible, anonymous individuals, and the street becomes an extension of the cinematic auditorium. The picture show, in a

Figure 15. *Kino,* by Paul Gangolf (1922). Courtesy of Bildarchiv Preußischer Kulturbesitz, Berlin (Germany).

movement of ironic inversion, has become the witness and interpreter of the city's Kafkaesque hustle and bustle; it exposes modern urbanity as a savage spectacle of cowboys and Indians. In contrast to Hubbuch, Gangolf shows a city that is still ensnared in the mythic patterns of the western. Cinematic projection and urban traffic here endlessly reproduce the mythic past. Whereas for Hubbuch the western owed its very existence to modern technologies, Gangolf contends that westerns tell the inner truth about metropolitan life. Westerns, he suggests, reveal to urban audiences the mythic captivation of their putative modernity.

Hubbuch's and Gangolf's drawings indicate the extent to which Weimar imagery of the Far West constituted a site of competing political and aesthetic agendas, a psychic extension of what was perceived as the uncanny nature of modern Germany. Seen as a genuinely cinematic enterprise,[19] the West on the one hand revealed the hidden truth about the present. It allegorized the many ways that modernity replayed the immediate past as movie, myth, and commodity. On the other hand, however, western images also transcended the given moment in order to elicit charismatic hopes and formulate utopian desires. Westerns propagated forms of nonregulated agency clearly at variance with the contemporary rationalization of social space and the acceleration of traditional lifeworlds. For many German western aficionados of the 1920s Weimar modernity thus emerged both as a precarious perpetuation and a liberating reinvention of a more primitive past, a traditionalist as much as an anarchic rodeo of asphalt cowboys and city Indians.

At the end of the Weimar period the painter Rudolf Schlichter described this ambiguous rediscovery of the western during the 1920s: "For me, Wagner's world fused with American jungle poetry into a peculiar myth of legendary adventures."[20] Westerns of the Weimar era, according to Schlichter, transported half-forgotten dreams to the present, not simply to offer imaginary escape but to launch utopian residues against the order of the day. Similar to the genre of the mountain film, popular around 1930,[21] westerns mediated natural shapes and melodramatic story lines, sublime wonders and human conquests. They explored primal nature with modern technologies and thereby allowed the audience either to create powerful myths of modernity or contest the mythic attractions of modern culture. As I will show in a moment, Nazi westerns aspired to contain these ambivalences of Weimar's desire for the West. They blocked out any dialectical understanding of myth and modernity and thereby obliterated the conditions for critical references to and subversive uses of mythic or utopian elements. Unlike Weimar artists such as Hubbuch, Gangolf, or Schlichter, Nazi westerns chose to deify modern technologies of representation via the image of the cowboy rather than to examine the Far West as an uncanny effect of cinematic technologies. Nazi westerns were deeply implicated in the reactionary modernism of fascism. The image of the cowboy posited Nazi modernity as a realm of legendary adventures and Wagnerian authenticity. It suspended political modernity—the ideals of emancipation, equality, and justice—with the help of peculiarly modern technologies of domination and distraction.

. . .

BULLETS AND WORDS

André Bazin described the western as "the American film par excellence." [22] Classical Hollywood westerns dramatized the breakthrough of modern civilization. They depicted the western frontier as the mythic origin of modern American identity. Located at the interface between burgeoning civilization and anarchic nature, classical westerns staged violent encounters among different attitudes toward morality and legality, individualism and community. If the good hero killed, if he turned savage, he did so only to redeem the power of the law and ensure the final victory of civilization.

Meditations on violence and justice, classical westerns relied on relatively coherent conventions and iconographic trademarks. Their centerpiece was the six-gun and the climactic shoot-out on Main Street. Guns feature prominently in the classical duel situation, which unfolds in a highly conventionalized public aesthetic defined by face-to-face combat, undistorted ocular exchange, and the absence of speech. Bullets take over where words fail to uphold the standards of good living, justice, or communal integrity. The public duel enacts discourse with other means. It offers an ideal speech situation in which the rigor of guns replaces the feeble force of language. Colts may be succeeded by the power of words, yet words often need dueling colts to gain their power in the first place. Westerns, by celebrating the manly shoot-out, annul women's invasion of the public domain in late-nineteenth-century America. They envision the public sphere as a "woman-less milieu, a set of rituals featuring physical combat and physical endurance, and a social setting that branded most features of civilized existence as feminine and corrupt, banishing them in favor of the three main targets of women's reform: whiskey, gambling, and prostitution." [23] In the hand of the duelist, the six-gun redeems the community from the threats of feminization or institutional disintegration—a community that hides behind shutters to watch its redeemer on the public square, just like the cinematic audience hides in the auditorium to watch its stars onscreen.

Following the opening of Luis Trenker's *The Emperor of California* in New York in 1937, the reviewer for the *New York Times* applauded the film's impressive production values, but he did not fail to suggest that Trenker's attempt at copying the American genre par excellence involved a "few historical slips and anachronisms." [24] For the American reviewer one of Trenker's generic faux pas must have been that *The Emperor of California* completely eluded the aesthetics of gunfights. Guns in Nazi westerns do not attain the importance they have in the classical Hollywood model. Their presence is random, their use explicitly censored or accompanied by

Figure 16.   Men with guns: Carica-
ture of Hans Albers in Herbert
Selpin's *Sergeant Berry* (*Film-
Kurier,* October 1938).

awkward gestures of panic or embarrassment—a narrative context alto-
gether devoid of the classical duel's resolve, control, and firm masculinity.
In the hands of German western heroes like Trenker or Hans Albers guns
appear like uncanny objects; they induce klutzy gestures instead of subdued performances. Albers, in Selpin's *Sergeant Berry,* may utilize his two
guns, his "mighty Ottos," for a never-ending series of shootings, but as the
initial German reviewers were eager to point out, the film's primary aim
was to satirize the "nonsense of all-too heroic Wild West films" and thus to
mock the stern metaphysics of the Hollywood six-gun (fig. 16).[25]

Guns in German westerns of the 1930s fail to distill dramatic action
down to a climactic scene of confrontation. If shown at all, the gunfights of
Nazi westerns take place in enclosed and distinctly private locations; they
forgo the ritualized execution of violence in the classical duel situation. Be-

fore the Albers character in the prologue sequence of *Water for Canitoga* kills the villain Westbrook, he bars the door of his hut with his own body. Thus, a private interior becomes the only witness of Monstuart's (Albers) rather clumsy shot at Westbrook, who is fumbling for a gun stuck in his pocket. Similarly, when Sutter (Trenker), in *The Emperor of California*, tries to keep a friend from broadcasting the discovery of gold, he is at pains to confine the conflict to his home, drawing the gun while blocking the antagonist's way to the door. Although celebrated even by some American critics for its action sequences,[26] Trenker's film frustrates our hope for a heroic face-to-face shoot-out. Sutter is in fact so unacquainted with the logic of guns that he allows his opponent to seize control over the weapon and escape Sutter's villa.

This privatization of gunfights in interior settings correlates with the tendency of German westerns to translate the classical model's quest for law and order into a romantic struggle between materialism and spirituality. Because Nazi westerns tend to shift our attention away from the classical showdown between different conceptions of legality and morality, and because Trenker and others omit the classical authorization of legality through violence in order to pit capitalist modernization against individual virtue, shoot-outs—*the* generic mechanisms of solving conflicts—are moved from the main street, the public domain of the law, to the interior, the private realm of economic activity and moral propriety. Guns in German westerns reveal the moral justification of conflicting economic projects instead of inaugurating legal orders and bestowing them with moral sanctity. Whereas the final showdown in the classical western encodes a retrospective discourse on the emergence of the American public sphere, the removal of gunfights from public spaces in German westerns aspires to collapse private and public realms, an aspiration whose ideological function will become clear by examining the Nazi western's use not of bullets but of words and modes of linguistic address.

German westerns of the 1930s abound with language. They drown the linguistic austerity of the classical American model in a flood of words, verbal sidelines, puns and jokes, arguments, descriptions, and public speeches. Where the American hero shoots, the German one starts to explain, to argue, to joke, or simply to babble. Trenker, in *The Emperor of California*, inundates other characters and the viewer with both dictatorial orders and lavish small talk. His thick Tyrolean accent, as the reviewer for the *Film-Kurier* remarked, endows his role with the jargon of Germanic hominess, with a sense of "rooted-in-the-soil-ness" (Bodenständigkeit).[27] Albers, on the other hand, in both *Water for Canitoga* and *Sergeant Berry* professes the grandiloquence of a self-styled tramp and daredevil. His linguistic self-assertion entertained German audiences of the time with a German equivalent of Hemingway's masculinist prose.[28] Albers's parlance expressed fundamental fears about any unrestrained articulation of physical desire, yet at the same time it opened pockets of subversive laughter and unpredictability.[29]

In the classical American western, written and oral language are primarily relegated to the domestic spheres of Victorian women. Cowboys, trappers, and bounty hunters, in turn, practice forms of linguistic minimalism. They clip their sentences, mutilate grammar, and often communicate through one-liners only. When the western hero speaks, he in fact seeks to efface the very language he deploys, for words open his quiet masculinity to a multiplicity of relations that threaten what he esteems most: control, action, and pure physical experience. The western is driven by antirepresentational impulses; it is "at heart antilanguage. Doing, not talking, is what it values."[30]

Given the antibourgeois thrust of Nazi ideology, its promise to recenter identity by engineering a sense of unmediated physicality, it may seem surprising at first that Nazi westerns completely ignore the antirepresentational urges of the classical model. After all, the Hollywood western's antilanguage should have matched very well the image of a decisive Nazi cowboy in search of new communities and primary modes of belonging. Why, then, this hesitation to use the gun and the attempt to replace bullets with words? Why this lack of resolution, which according to the classical model borders on a state of emasculation? Why representation and rhetoric rather than action and the physical dialectics of the shoot-out?

In a speech of March 1937 Goebbels used the edifying setting of the Berlin Krolloper to promote a consciously German cinema, a homemade Hollywood integrating artistic merit and popular appeal. The sensitive execution of film dialogue, according to Goebbels, was to play an essential role in this nationalization of mass culture. "Luther once said: In order to affect people, we must listen to what people really say. He learned his language among the people, and in his German bible translation—so important for the history of the German language—he sought only to use expressions which could be understood by everyone. He dealt with problems that were very close to the people. It would be good if our film dialogues would do something similar."[31] In Goebbels's view film dialogue ought to be folksy, tuned to the ear of the layperson, in order to reach and affect the widest audience possible. It should eschew highbrow deliberation and reproduce instead the thick materiality of local accents and regionally specific lexicons. Rather than asking actors to speak like marionettes, German cinema should discover the grain of film dialogue as the royal road to mass popularity, economic success, and ethnic identity.

The use of abundant dialogue in Nazi westerns follows Goebbels's formula to the letter. The two most prominent Nazi cowboys, Trenker and Albers, may break with the antilinguistic codes of the Hollywood western, but by speaking in their folksy, accent-ridden tongues they at once fulfill ideological tasks and help establish a distinctly German alternative to Hollywood. Dialogue in Nazi westerns is, to use Roman Jakobson's terms, largely emotive and phatic in function. On the one hand, it is meant to transport information not by cognitive but mostly by expressive means, by the nonreferential sound patterns that flavor utterances on different levels of articulation. Emotive speech in Nazi westerns aims at "a direct expression of the speaker's attitude toward what he is speaking about,"[32] and in so doing it seeks to solicit affective reactions in the listener. On the other hand, the Nazi cowboy's wordiness is largely ritualistic. It seeks "to establish, to prolong, or to discontinue communication, to check whether the channel works . . . , to attract the attention of the interlocutor or to confirm his continued attention."[33] Putting into effect what Jakobson calls the phatic function of language, the wordy Nazi cowboy assumes manly authority not by means of his six-gun but by talking himself into unquestioned mastery over the terms of discourse and representation. Authority and power in Nazi westerns feed on the hero's voice, on a vocal imperative. Speech in Nazi westerns is highly sensual. It appeals to the viewers' emotions and guides their attentions in the text itself.

The use of richly textured speech and the absence of stylized shoot-outs in Nazi westerns reveals in an exemplary fashion how Nazi cinema reshaped seemingly apolitical conventions in order to bond the viewer's emotions to ideology. In the classical American western, guns and dueling partake of a charismatic foundation of legality, a spectacular redemption of law and order through violence. By way of contrast, the absence of shoot-outs in German westerns and the abundance of speech bestow legitimate authority, not to universal legal orders but to the individual hero, a leader whose charismatic presence provides the cement that may hold his ethnic communities together. Whereas bullets in American westerns negotiate the threshold between anarchy and legality, the German western resorts to emotive and phatic speech to reinforce the social fabric and justify forceful leadership. In contrast to the classical paradigm, then, which pictures discourse as a threatening feminization of the cowboy's public sphere, German westerns render orality the pathway to success and heroic mastery. Linguistic austerity in the Nazi western is not a distinction of the hero but of those who submit to the hero's talkative enactment of charismatic authority.

In the remainder of this chapter I will detail this fusion of charismatic leadership, modernity, and "cowboydom" with regard to the two single most important German western productions of the 1930s, *The Emperor of California* and *Water for Canitoga*. These films not only linked the rhetoric of home to practices of colonial appropriation, but they also enlisted the full spectrum of cinematic possibilities in order to engineer highly affective and politically effective responses. Providing dramatic, elaborately controlled choreographies of action, speech, and music, *The Emperor of California* and *Water for Canitoga* demonstrate how Nazi cinema stimulated desire so as to make people desire repression, how it appealed to the whole array of modern sense perception so as to negate the senses, how it cannibalized Hollywood elements so as to mold the national community.

CALIFORNIA DREAMIN'

William Everson once described Trenker as "Germany's John Wayne and John Ford rolled into one, . . . an auteur long before that term came into common usage."[34] Grossly exaggerated though this comparison may seem, Everson's claim concerning Trenker's peculiar auteurism—the fusion of director, offscreen personality, and onscreen character—is useful in approaching the hardy world of Trenker's films. Trenker's popularity during the Nazi period documented larger transformations in the construction of star images during the 1930s. His tanned physiognomy, windblown hair, and kinetic body replaced the pale and dismal faces of expressionist cinema; it opened up new kinds of commercial tie-ins with the burgeoning tourism, alpinism, and skiing industries.[35] Ford and Wayne in one, Trenker in fact never hesitated to connect his outdoor masculinity to the art of filmmaking. The act of filming itself was supposed to reflect the rugged nature of a film's principal characters. Not just the product but the making of a film was meant to be heroic, muscular, commanding—a "tough performance," as a *Film-Kurier* critic reported in February 1936 about the shooting of majestic mass scenes for *The Emperor of California*.[36]

Grand panoramic vistas, in colonial discourse, often yield commanding views in which aesthetic sentiments, the production of knowledge, and the assumption of authority become one and the same. Mapping unknown territories as spaces of future appropriation, majestic views are often presented as the first gesture of colonization itself.[37] In Trenker's *The Emperor of California* ocular practices of this sort—intensified by Giuseppe Becce's film score—recurrently signify Sutter's efforts to establish an agrarian community in Northern California and ensure his authority over the new homeland. What occurs in *The Emperor of California,* in other words, is a fusion of power and audiovision that climaxes whenever the hero places himself in a "monarch of all I survey" position.[38] In the film's opening sequence Sutter, persecuted by the Napoleonic police, takes refuge on top of the church of his Swiss hometown. As he climbs the stairs, striking superimpositions conflate his image with a slow upward tilt following the tower's rise into the sky, a motion that fuses camerawork and heroic ascent into a sublime vista point that, in turn, will become the setting for a scene of spiritual introspection and redemption. Once on the tower's peak, Sutter meets his alter ego, the apparition of Ernst Moritz Arndt (Bernhard Minetti), the icon for a national resistance against French foreign rule in Germany both in the early nineteenth century and after the Treaty of Versailles.[39] Arndt, in the posture of a magician, conjures a sequence of panoramic audiovisions that capture Sutter's attention: mountain ridges and lakesides, wide open prairies, the Grand Canyon, empty deserts, and, finally, the ocean, the utopian signifier of emigration and escape. Becce's operatic sound track in this scene endows the images with overwhelming magnetism. Ascending and accelerating chord progressions signify coming attractions, and triumphant brass fanfares and dreamlike harp glissandos provide a sonic impression of sublime wonder and compelling monumentality. "Isn't the world still beautiful?" asks Arndt as the master of the imaginary. Dressed like a cowboy, the poet Arndt sketches out a program of colonization that translates the power of audiovision directly into a spectacle of power. "You can serve your people everywhere," he encourages Sutter. "You can fight everywhere."

In selecting Arndt as a spokesman of westward expansion, *The Emperor of California* employs an ideological trope characteristic of right-wing anti-Americanism ever since the Weimar period: the image of the German as the good American immigrant resisting Jewish American greed, functional abstraction, cultural hybridization, and racial miscegenation. Unlike other immigrants, the German in America, according to this trope, preserves a typically German sense of belonging, a sense—as Adolf Halfeld wrote in 1928—of "his morals, his homeland, and his blood."[40] German immigrants remind multicultural America that ethnic differences matter. As they sustain organic relations to geography and ethnicity, German Americans—according to this view—infuse the accidental nation America with existential vigor and meaning. Trenker's Arndt projects this anti-American trope on the most American of all film genres, the western. Arndt's cinema of attraction inspires Sutter to become the model Germanic settler who defends

Figure 17.   Colonial optics: Luis Trenker as cowboy Johann Sutter in *The Emperor of California* (1936). Courtesy of Filmmuseum Berlin—Deutsche Kinemathek.

agrarian virtues and ethnic identity against the evil forces of capitalist abstraction, racial mixing, and—by implication—Jewish migrancy.[41]

Like Arndt, Sutter himself on several occasions operates as a cinematic audiovision machine in whose perception aesthetic pleasure, spatial appropriation, and the execution of power over fellow immigrants become one and the same. Consider the California sequence showing Sutter at the height of his success as he rides through his estates. A low-angle close-up frames the hero's face, proudly gazing left and right, and the deliberate overexposure of the image endows his features with an almost divine aura (fig. 17). This close-up intercuts several times with what the spectator must assume is Sutter's point of view, although Trenker's montage editing disappoints our desire for spatial continuity among the scenes that we will see through Sutter's imperial eyes. The first intercut maps a grand orchard with trees neatly arranged in geometrical lines and shapes: rough nature turned into an ordered garden. The second displays a gigantic wheat field exposed to the gentle rhythms of the winds, a scene that literally displays the writing of nature on the surface of the visible. The third consists of four different shots of farmworkers who swing their scythes in harmonious rhythms. Presented to Sutter's and our own gaze as a unified configuration of bodies and synchronized movements, these harvesters appear forged into a mass ornament. In a manner strikingly consonant with Nazi ideologies of labor, individual work is rendered not as exertion but as a form of music, a ritual of communal communication that allegedly transcends the confinements of modern subjectivity and routine. The fourth intercut pictures a large group of sheep transformed into *one* body by a black sheep dog that approaches from the left and stimulates the herd to a single movement to the right. This last shot, drawing from the formal tradition of Eisenstein's intellectual montage, presents a visual metaphor for what we have seen before: the charismatic creation of integrated communities in which the unified shape counts more than the individual body.

Becce's sound track throughout this sequence underscores this project. During the first close-up Becce once again bathes the audience in what has been clearly established as the score's leitmotif for Sutter's colonial aspirations: ascending brass fanfares that extend sublime impressions of power. Subsequently, Becce's richly textured score emulates a highly melodic peasants' song and in so doing traverses, in a sense, the boundaries between diegetic and nondiegetic spaces. The bucolic humming we hear weaves working bodies and natural settings into one powerful experience. Social integration, we are meant to understand, results from the melodic alignment of individuals and natural environment. It requires the presence of a commanding subject, a compelling choreography of sights and sounds powerful enough to establish a nexus between aesthetic experience and social discipline.

Christopher Frayling has emphasized the antimodern impetus of scenes such as this in Trenker's film.[42] Trenker, for Frayling, embraces the western genre in order to escape modern urban life. His western conveys mystic desires for redemption; it wanders into the past with the intention of displacing the technological outlook of the present with images of reciprocal harmony between humanity and the elemental. Although Frayling's analysis is insightful, it seems necessary to elaborate on the distinctively modern moment that drives Trenker's search for agrarian salvation. In the abovementioned sequence Trenker not only marks the hero's gaze as a distinctively cinematic one, but he also indicates that his idyllic images of harvesting are technological constructions, conjured by modern recording devices and the skill of editing. In a manner that recapitulates the Weimar mountain film genre,[43] and in surprising agreement with the antimimetic elements of modernist painting, landscapes in Trenker's films of the 1930s often achieve almost abstract qualities. Assuming the gaze of the film's hero, the camera in the harvest sequence venerates natural topographies as screens featuring abstract bodies, outlines, shapes, and movements. Modern machines here create the natural sublime; they are to become nature again. Like Arnold Fanck, Trenker seems to claim that "nature remains mute and unexpressive unless captured by the camera." [44] Like Fanck, Trenker elevates mediated effects to natural presences. As the film's director and cinematographer in disguise, Sutter advocates an authoritarian concept of nature that calls for individual and collective subjection to alleged laws of natural circularity. Although the film's choreography of sights and sounds replaces the timetables of history with the "rhythmic principle" of nature,[45] it also actively converts natural forms and human formations into ornamental configurations. Yet in containing the imagined elemental as ornament, Trenker masks the instrumental reason that fuels Sutter's very project of California colonization. As it maps agrarian space through Sutter's commanding gaze, Trenker's cinema renders political authority solely a function of aesthetic beauty. Like fascism in Benjamin's famous reading, Trenker's antimodern modernism replaces politics with aesthetics. Trenker's uncompromising desire for form, his pathos of creation and control, becomes in the final analysis an attack on the viewer's senses, an assault on the human body as an unpredictable site of pleasure and corporeal experience. In likeness to the fascist spectacle Trenker's agrarian total work of art wants to rouse powerful emotions, yet at the same time it strives "to neutralize the senses, to knock them out." [46]

Trenker's *The Emperor of California* is shot through with longing for premodern wonders, as Frayling rightly observes, but it also endorses a modernist project in a twofold manner. On the one hand, Trenker wants to restore contemplative experiences through a deliberate use of modern machines. Twentieth-century technologies of representation here endow colonial countrysides with a renewed sense of metaphysical depth and a mystical unity between humanity and nature. On the other hand, and in a manner similar to that of Rudolf Borchardt's modernist sketch of the Italian landscape in "Villa" (1908),[47] Trenker relocates aesthetic experiences from the secluded sphere of bourgeois art to the ranges of farm life as seen through the ordering perception of patriarchal autocrats. Sutter's audiovision explodes the limits of bourgeois art, but it simultaneously recontains what has been unleashed by the hero's imperial perception in the first place. In achieving this Trenker proposes nothing less than a modernist attack on autonomous art, redefining art—like Borchardt—as "a practical expression of power, stripped of any commitments to emancipation." [48] Trenker's cinema summons the elemental in such a way that his film pictures the

West as a site that renders power and art, form and domination, mutually exchangeable. Trenker embraces advanced tools of representation as vehicles that overthrow liberal rationalism: to the extent that the cinematic apparatus—in likeness to the settler or cowboy—transforms nature into an ordered garden, it installs a public space in which personal charisma undoes the legacies of bourgeois culture.

Like Hitler in his 1943 order to read May novels, then, Trenker's western invites the viewer to understand modern constellations as effects of mythic structures. Trenker's *The Emperor of California* turns an idealized image of the cowboy as colonial explorer into an authoritative metaphor for modern life and the cinematic process. Emulating the Hollywood western genre, Trenker suggests that the cinematic apparatus itself, in spite or even because of its modernity, operates according to the same logic that once appeared in the perceptual regime of the Far West, in the westerner's imperial perception of pristine landscapes and virtuous farmworkers. Trenker's film does not therefore simply seize the western as a source of escapist fantasies. Quite the contrary, the rugged world of the West here defines the generic structures and possibilities of film itself. What triumphs at the end of the film is not so much Sutter's political intervention as the logic of the camera, the film's evocation of elemental forces and their recontainment in a highly controlled mise-en-scène. So triumphant is the victory of Trenker's sights and sounds that they can even outlive the destruction of Sutter's New Helvetia. The final shot of Sutter as a trekking cowboy, literally projected on a screen of clouds,[49] articulates this powerful persistence of cinematic recording. Trenker's last shot encodes cinema as an instrument preserving the imperial spirit of western heroes. Cinema recuperates the power of colonial appropriation and stimulates contemporary spectators to channel their energies into new geopolitical projects, whether at the western frontier or the eastern front. Mobilizing images from the West, Trenker's ethereal cinema of clouds thus becomes a cinema of emotional mobilization.

It should therefore come as no surprise that one of the most emblematic New Helvetia scenes is directly modeled on a sequence of *Triumph of the Will*, Leni Riefenstahl's Nuremberg film released only a few months before *The Emperor of California* went into production. In this sequence Sutter walks along a line of workers eagerly shoveling an irrigation canal. While he offers each worker a cigar, he asks the men to identify their geographic origins, prompting them to name a host of locations spread all over central Europe. Although executed with less cinematic artistry than its textual predecessor, this scene relocates the labor force sequence of *Triumph of the Will* from the Nuremberg rally grounds to the shores of the Sacramento River. Similar to Riefenstahl's elaborately choreographed parade, in which the spade workers' linguistic accents attest to the powerful bonds of nature, tradition, and ethnic identity, Trenker's sequence takes recourse to the regional textures of the German language to orchestrate the impression of a new folk rooted in agrarian myths of community. Riefenstahl's spade workers reemerge as colonial heroes, and the power of Hitler's ordering perception is transferred to the patriarch Johann August Sutter. In an astounding exercise of cinematic intertextuality, the jargon of blood and soil becomes the core of California politics. Although worlds seem to separate *Triumph of the Will* and *The Emperor of California,* both films thus represent a curious double that documents the affinity of aestheticized politics and American-style consumption in Nazi Germany. What both films celebrate is the homogenizing effects of charismatic leadership strong enough to mold social and natural topographies into direct expressions of power. What triumphs in both films is also and foremost the power of cinematic audiovision to make viewers desire repression, to elicit desire for representation as repression.

INTERLUDE: WAGNER, COWBOY STYLE

Officially rated as "politically and artistically especially worthwhile," *The Emperor of California* premiered in July 1936 at a gala in the Reichsministry in Berlin and subsequently earned considerable box office returns in Germany. In late August 1936 the film won the Mussolini Trophy at the Biennale in Venice, demonstrating that, according to a *Film-Kurier* commentator, German "film art is a living organism that actively strives towards its self-proclaimed goals and withstands international competition with astonishing successes."[50] Although after the end of the Nazi period Trenker denied any political affiliations of the past—in his notoriously unreliable autobiography he emphasizes Hitler's discontent with the conclusion of his western[51]—there can be little doubt that *The Emperor of California* hit a gold mine in artistic, economic, and political terms all at once.

Yet it was Trenker's treatment of gold in *The Emperor of California* that struck a nerve with some of the initial reviewers. Because of his scathing anticapitalism and anti-American Americanism, Trenker, in the eyes of the critic for the *Licht-Bild-Bühne,* mystifies gold; he fails to understand that gold "turns destructive only when it becomes an end in itself," that is to say, enters profit-oriented, and by implication Jewish, circulation.[52] Trenker, the reviewer implied, mistakes historical contingencies for ontological facts, and in doing so he remains ensnared in the kind of delusions Jewish capitalism imposes on the individual. In fact, one might extend this reviewer's reservations to argue that Trenker did not read his Wagner carefully enough.

After all, in Wagner's *Ring of the Nibelung* gold becomes calamitous only after greedy dealers such as Alberich insert it into the circuits of power and exchange, whereas it constitutes an object of aesthetic delight as long as it remains confined to the bottom of the Rhine, the bosom of nature.

The reviewer's dissatisfaction with Trenker's treatment of gold must surprise. It points to the general confusion that marked Nazi economic thought in the aftermath of the Roehm crackdown of June 1934 and the elimination of anticapitalist voices within the Nazi party. For it is not difficult to see that Trenker, contrary to the reviewer's assumption, clearly follows the critique of modern life spelled out by Wagner and that Trenker's figuration of gold closely adheres to the political agendas prefigured in the master's magnum opus. Once turned into an object of possessive desire and exchange, gold, in both Trenker and Wagner, enables infinite circulation, traverses traditional boundaries, and thus fosters a dangerous loss of *Heimat*. Gold in Trenker—like in Wagner—must be expelled from circulation so that homogeneous communities may live again. In unison with Nazi westerns such as *Water for Canitoga* and *Gold in New Frisco*, as well as nonwesterns such as Karl Hartl's *Gold* (1934), Trenker ascribes to gold "a social-psychological power, a sublime essence independent of its real presence."[53] Gold hunters in Trenker, as much as in Wagner, deify gold's exchange value and eclipse its actual use value. Trenker and Wagner, in turn, fetishize gold because they believe that the use value of commodities can be separated from their exchange value, that value can be measured outside social contract and economic exchange. Doubly fetishized, gold in both Trenker and Wagner haunts communities with a monstrous return of the repressed. It rouses powerful fears of penetration and signifies a dangerous opening of the social organism to the contingencies of history and the real.

Let me focus my attention now on other echoes of Wagner's work in Trenker's western project. I want to explore how *The Emperor of California* takes recourse to Wagner's aesthetic practices in order to manufacture a nationally specific and politically effective German mass culture. For Wagner not only informs Trenker's conception of gold; his nineteenth-century aesthetics inspired the way in which Giuseppe Becce's score synthesizes sounds and sights into one overwhelming experience and gives, as the reviewer for *Der Film* wrote, "action and image their final effects."[54]

Becce debuted in film with a drumroll that in many respects set the tone for his later scoring work for directors such as Arnold Fanck, Gerhard Lamprecht, Leni Riefenstahl, and Luis Trenker.[55] Becce commenced his film career in 1913 by arranging the score and playing the title role for Carl Froelich and William Wauer's bioepic *Richard Wagner*. Because of copyright struggles with the Wagner family, Becce, when arranging the score for *Richard Wagner,* was forced to draw mostly on musical sources other than Wagner, Viennese classicism in particular. Aside from legal reasons, however, Becce's choice of Haydn, Mozart, and Beethoven "evidently had to do with the film's overall aim of glorifying Wagner unconditionally. Entirely in line with Richard Wagner's own teleological perspective, Becce suggests to the audience a history of German music where the Viennese classics lead directly to Bayreuth. Even Giacomo Rossini, whom Wagner, in his writings, considered one of his main adversaries, is used by Becce to underscore this perspective."[56] Wagnerian effects, in what can be safely named the first German film score,[57] were thus achieved by means of a musical language that far surpassed Wagner's own. Already in his very first film score, Becce envisioned a Wagnerian cinema that would integrate various traditions and idioms, including extant repertory pieces, into an effective whole, one that would formally adapt to and thematically consummate a film's narrative.

The combination of disparate elements and conflicting classical legacies became Becce's trademark as a film composer throughout the 1920s and 1930s. Characterized by Wagnerian leitmotifs and open forms, film music was meant to extend impressions of heroic courage and operatic grandeur, to establish irresistible continuities between past and present. The task of film music, according to Becce, was to articulate heterogeneous styles into one new expressive syntax. His orientation toward premodernist idioms notwithstanding, Becce advocated a quasi-Taylorist division and Fordist organization of scoring practices. Developed between 1919 and 1929, Becce's *Kinothek* compiled hundreds of scoring segments that could be easily moved among different contexts and applied to highly diverse film subjects.[58] Likewise, the *Allgemeines Handbuch der Film-Musik,* coauthored in 1927 with Hans Erdmann, aspired to systematize the aesthetic possibilities of film scoring as it provided a multitude of atmospheric set pieces that intermingled allusions to nineteenth-century idioms from Weber via Wagner to Liszt's symphonic poems. The best film music, Erdmann and Becce explained in the *Handbuch,* "is the one which dissolves with a particular film scene into one inseparable unity."[59] A bricoleur of the first order, Becce aimed even prior to the arrival of synchronized sound to put industrial principles of rationalization and interchangeability at the service of conjuring eighteenth- and nineteenth-century illusions of wholeness, of remaking industrial culture in the image of Wagner's preindustrial visions of sensual synthesis and organic totality.

In the close cooperation with Luis Trenker throughout the 1930s Becce's cinematic Wagnerianism became bonded to a political mission. Similar to

Herbert Windt's sound tracks for Riefenstahl's spectacles,[60] Becce's lyric-heroic scores aimed at joining cinematic sights and sounds into a dramatic synthesis of overwhelming effects. Drawing heavily on eighteenth- and nineteenth-century styles, Becce's musical language of the 1930s clearly avoided Hollywood's contemporary experiments with modernist or even atonal idioms. Instead, it was in the German masters of the past, as well as in popular folk traditions, that German cinema was to find the sonic resources to extend impressions of perfection and integrity, to celebrate manly action and resolution, and thus to recuperate heroism for a postheroic age of machines and bureaucratic administrations.[61] Although Becce's scores incessantly aroused expectation and catered to the demand for novelty and mobility, strictly speaking—to recall Adorno's critique of Wagner—nothing new took place in them. Advocating the viewer's desire in the film itself, Becce's scores exalted in industrial sameness. They communicated identical materials "as if they were something new and thereby substitute[d] the abstract succession of bars for the dialectical progression of substance, its inner historicity."[62] Everything in these scores seemed to undergo dynamic change and development, yet in the end we get that which has putatively always been the same, the mythic as a calculated effect of the modern.

In Trenker's film a three-minute intermezzo, which directly precedes Sutter's discovery of California, demonstrates how Becce's score translates disparate idioms into an overpowering language of authority and self-assertion. We see Trenker's body mastering the cliffs of the Grand Canyon with Alpine virtuosity—an ecstatic display of physicality that advances the lonesome cowboy to the legitimate leader of New Helvetia. In the previous sequence we witnessed the hero's voyage through the Arizona desert. Trenker's mismatched, handheld desert shots here conveyed a quasi-neorealist impression of suffering and depravation. The succeeding climbing sequence, however, reverses this pathos of resignation. Instead of exploring the uncanniness of the desert, the camera now identifies with the muscular performance of the hero. In a rhythmic series of shots from ever-changing angles we observe Sutter carefully scouting the terrain, traversing rocks and crevasses, resting his head against the wall, and finally reaching the rim of the canyon, where a joyful explosion of physical power emancipates both the hero and the spectator from the emasculating gloom of the desert.

Becce's score effectively illustrates the climber's shifting positions and moods throughout this spectacular ascent. Melodically stagnating violins signify moments of hesitation; towering brass fanfares proclaim the resurgence of resolve and vitality. Driven by ever-more accelerating rhythms and assertive beats, Becce's score in the first half of this sequence emulates the pulse of American two-step marches and the kind of chromatic arrangements well known from American western films. Toward the end, however, it turns to a more hymnic idiom that floods the listener with passionate melodies in the manner of Wagner, Strauss, or Puccini. Once atop the rim of the Grand Canyon, in a geographically somewhat astounding move, Sutter poses as a conqueror, triumphantly shouting "California!" A low-angle close-up pictures his proud act of looking, immediately followed by a subjective shot that scouts the wide-open spaces of California, the territories of Sutter's colonial mission. It is in this moment of imperial triumph that Becce's sound track performs one of its most stunning bricolages as it reaches out for a grandiose fanfare, a dazzling variation on the *Star-Spangled Banner,* modulated into a rather parodic flat key. Becce's composition in this moment of triumph bonds the viewer's affects directly to a breathtaking language of charismatic leadership. Not simply Sutter's imperial resolution but also Becce's irresistible sound track here takes command over America. It arouses desire for a unified, mobile, and extraordinary body, for a synthesis of words, music, and dance, but at the same time this score, by means of its monumental gestures, also hits the viewer over the head. The triumph of Sutter's will includes a triumph over the viewer's will.

Adorno and Hanns Eisler, in their critique of Hollywood film music, argued that dominant scores aid in conjuring illusions of reality and physical immediacy. Film music presents the mediated effects of mechanical reproduction as natural and unmediated. Hollywood scoring practice, they wrote, "brings the picture close to the public, just as the picture brings itself close to it by means of the close-up. It attempts to interpose a human coating between the reeled-off pictures and the spectators."[63] Part of a project to bring Hollywood home to Nazi Germany, Becce's sound track for *The Emperor of California* far exceeds this function. Becce's fusion of popular and classical idioms—like Hollywood scoring practice of the time—wants to offer glimpses of a better life; it caters to a nostalgia for lost periods of imagined integrity and unity, of mythic wholeness and mimetic immediacy. At the same time, however, in its peculiar interaction with the film's image track, film music here becomes a medium to suppress the very desire it arouses in the first place. Becce's Wagnerian attempt at integrating the different channels of sensual expression and perception offers a highly organized imitation of magic practices, the mimesis of mimesis.[64] The score mimics mimetic behavior with the help of mechanical reproduction; it enlists "primitivist residues"—a utopian rebellion against domination—as a useful tool of domination itself. Grafting Nazi folklore and führer ideology onto the scenes of popular exoticism, Becce's score opens up a mythic space in which suppressed nature—sentience, spontaneity, and the desire to become an other—may articulate itself only in order to succumb even more effectively to the powers of repression.

ENGINEERING THE NAZI COWBOY

Nazi westerns explore the American West to rouse a paradoxical protest against capitalist modernity. Although the Nazi western, as I have argued with regard to *The Emperor of California,* sanctifies technological achievements as fascinating spectacles, it simultaneously mourns the disappearance of preindustrial lifeworlds, traditional identities, and unproblematic ethnic communities. Herbert Selpin's 1939 *Water for Canitoga,* to which I now turn, further illuminates this ambivalent modernism. The film, as one reviewer wrote, "is of such closure and power, of such colorfulness and atmosphere, it is so polished in its details and made with such virtuosity, that it does not take second place to the most shining examples of the grandiose and fascinating American adventure film. We are thus in a position to equal Hollywood, indeed to surpass it with regard to a film's ethical tendency." [65] Shot exclusively at the Bavaria studios in Munich-Geiselgasteig, *Water for Canitoga* pictures the Far West as a space where rugged individuals and greedy racketeers struggle over the meaning of technological progress and masculine identity, modernity and morality, labor and money. In contrast to the American western formula, it is not the sheer presence of modern machines here that disrupts the primeval integrity of the western landscapes but rather the confrontation between those who consider technology a triumph of the human spirit over nature and those who use modern machines solely to satisfy their egotistical demands for wealth and leisure. Although the advent of technological modernity in the West at first seems to undo the image of cowboy masculinity, the existential battle over the use of modern machines yields a modernized notion of masculine heroism. "Some will always have to perish so that a great work may succeed and last," the Albers character proclaims in the end, positing the figure of the engineer as a twentieth-century reincarnation of the cowboy.

Set in 1905, *Water for Canitoga* introduces Oliver Monstuart (Hans Albers) as the principal engineer of a pipeline project that is to bring water to the Canadian frontier community of Canitoga (fig. 18). The project prompts frequent sabotage activities, sponsored by American gold trusts that fear the emergence of new mining areas. After he kills one of the saboteurs, yet fails to produce justifying evidence, Monstuart has to flee the construction site. Later in the year, and transformed into a serious alcoholic, Monstuart returns to Canitoga and, in disguise, seeks reemployment with the construction company. Despite his being rejected by Captain Trefford, an old

Figure 18. Engineering masculinity: Ad for *Water for Canitoga* (1939, Herbert Selpin) (*Film-Kurier,* March 1939).

soldier friend from British colonial enterprises and now the head of the project, Monstuart appears on the site and assumes a leading role in the project again. Quickly, Monstuart detects faulty structures and unveils some of the saboteurs, led by Lily Westbrook, the flamboyant owner of the local saloon. To rescue the project, Monstuart suggests the assembly of a high-pressure caisson in whose protection the workers can fix the dam. Another sabotage act, however, threatens the underwater tank, whereas a number of the workers, after learning Monstuart's true identity, want to lynch the engineer. Monstuart convinces the mob of his integrity and, despite his physical condition, descends into the tank. Meanwhile, Trefford remembers the power of male friendship and persuades the Canitoga dignitaries of Monstuart's goodwill. When Monstuart, after his heroic intervention, arrives at the town meeting, the gathering absolves him from his murder charges and celebrates him as a hero. The engineer asks for a glass of water and staggers out of the room—literally dropping out of the frame—to die.

Resolute commitments to technology in *Water for Canitoga* overcome the emasculating effects of alcohol and unearth the civilizing powers of male camaraderie. In the traditional western the male heroes drink, on the one hand, coffee, the bourgeois goad to intellectual attention and self-control,[66] and, on the other hand, hard liquors, normally consumed in the West's saloons and ingredients of a ritual in which the lone ranger temporarily drowns his self-inflected animosity to communal bonds.[67] In *Water for Canitoga*, in contrast, Monstuart's alcoholism brings to the fore the social stigmata rebuked by temperance movements in Europe around 1900.[68] Liquor, far from enabling a public male ritual, here promotes a weakening of masculinity. It subverts what holds society together: the dynamic will to collectivity and solidarity. Yet if Monstuart rediscovers in the course of the film his willpower, he does not do so in order to exchange whiskey with coffee, narcotic intoxication with a drink that sharpens the senses. Instead, Monstuart's fusion of engineer- and cowboydom culminates in a final request for a glass of water, the very resource his technical work mediates to Canitoga. Not the rationalism and restraint of the classical western but rather the technological recuperation of the natural is the motto of Monstuart's last toast.

Monstuart's change of drinks illuminates what drives the film's overall representation of technology. Engineers and their technological projects in *Water for Canitoga* appear endowed with a cultural mission, a calling for spiritual purification that bolsters both the individual and the collective against the egotistical aspirations of mere profiteers. According to the film's notion of modernization, social crises do not result from the sudden colonization of the Far West with modern machines and technological projects per se but rather from the implementation of modern technology in the symbolic system of capitalist exchange: the will to material wealth ruins technology, which ruins nature, which ruins society. Whereas Monstuart sacrifices himself for the pipeline project to ensure the aura of a technological work, the saboteurs destroy the manifestations of modern engineer-dom and in so doing also expunge the very spirit that provides the cement for social harmony.

Monstuart's technological spiritualism—his fusion of idealist, anticapi-talist, and antirationalist sentiments into a jargon of physical immediacy—clearly reflected the signs of the time. Leading theoreticians of technology during the Third Reich, such as Heinrich Hardenstett, Rudolf Heiss, Eugen Diesel, or Werner Sombart, rendered modern machines and technologies as an emanation of the spiritual realm of *Kultur* rather than the material one of *Zivilisation*.[69] The sublime presence of technological works, for these engineers and ideologues, gave form to the chaos of life and thereby elevated the individual to the timeless realm of the national spirit. In influential journals such as *Technik und Kultur* Nazi engineers, in fact, de-veloped a philosophy of technology that sought to unearth mythical di-mensions of modern machines and turn their thrust against the achieve-ments of social and political modernity, against procedural politics and the normative substance of liberal democracy.

Similar to Monstuart, ideologues of engineering during the Third Reich understood technology not as a product of abstract reasoning but as a mys-tic mediator between the realms of the spirit and the material demands of the day. Whereas scientists, they argued, would create dead knowledge through abstract theories, the Faustian engineer generated beautiful forms that could last for eternity. In Heiss's writings this hostility against sci-entific abstraction gave cause to the portrayal of the engineer as an artistic genius. For Heiss "the natural sciences existed in a world of laws, regular-ities, and impractical abstractions, rather than in the creative and heroic immediacy of the inventor and engineer."[70] To secure this cultural mission of technology, Nazi ideologues argued for a separation of technology from the demands of the market: it was only through the intervention of an au-thoritarian state, they contended, that technological creativity could be de-fended against profit seekers and the anarchic domain of exchange values. To the extent that they insisted on a political, not economic, hegemony over technology on the one hand, while emphasizing the superiority of pragmatic creativity over scientific abstraction on the other, Nazi engineers hoped technology could provide a renewed sense of existential authenticity and cultural homogeneity. Steeped in a cleverly generated aura of precapi-talist craftsmanship, technology was meant to resuscitate a world of natu-ral rhythms and uncontested values. Fascism's engineers sought to recu-perate "modern man's lost rituals with the help of the very factor that has threatened them in the first place: technology."[71]

Water for Canitoga grafts Heiss's reactionary modernism onto the figure of Oliver Monstuart. What is at stake in constructing Monstuart's pipeline is not the project's actual use value so much as the realization of existential pathos and the reassertion of masculine identity. Similar to the way in which the *l'art pour l'art* movement around 1900, in its protest against the commodification of nineteenth-century art, cut all links between art and social life, Monstuart aims to redefine technology as an autonomous realm of existential self-referentiality. He marshals instrumental reason to sanctify technology as an overwhelming presence. Albers, who according to Nazi film ideologue Oskar Kalbus embodied nothing less than "the German idea of masculinity,"[72] proved an ideal choice for this task. In the film's musical interlude, "Goodbye Jonny,"[73] Albers establishes himself as a roughneck whose aim is to evacuate women and uncontrolled passion from the Far West. Modeled on the New Year's Eve sequence of W. S. Van Dyke's 1936 *San Francisco*, Albers's song articulates a crude attack on difference and female sexuality that aspires to reinvent the West as a sphere free of whatever could distract the cowboy-engineer from his existential mission. Albers's song intends to make language rough and dangerous again, to transform orality into a conduit for manly action.[74] In opposition to a scientist's putative intellectualism and abstraction, Monstuart's song recasts language into a direct expression of male resolution and physical immediacy.

Long before the film's release, press reports applauded the work invested in the making of *Water for Canitoga* as a sign of authenticity. What became a particular object of fascination was the caisson, which was built according to real models exhibited in the *Deutsches Museum*, Munich. As *Der Film* informed its readers in minute detail, the technical staff "manufactured a wood caisson which holds a pressure of 2.5 atm and which is 2.2 meters high, 6 meters wide, and 6 meters long. Its walls are 60 centimeters in depth."[75] In the film itself Monstuart resorts to rather different methods of marketing the caisson. To illustrate its operation, he cuts a whiskey bottle in half and submerges it in a small aquarium (fig. 19). Casually commenting on his procedure, Monstuart captures a fish underneath his model and pressurizes the bottle with air. As the fish desperately seizes because of the lack of water, it proves that men could work in the suggested underwater container and fix the dam's faulty constructions. Like his tough talk, Monstuart's fishbowl presentation typifies modern engineering as an existential quest for Faustian creativity and physical immediacy in which technology figures as an expression of the engineer's will to power. Relying on the power of visual display rather than on discursive modes of reasoning, the engineer overcomes the alleged captivation of scientific reason in regularities, laws,

Figure 19.   Recuperating resolve: Monstuart's (Hans Albers) fishbowl experiment in *Water for Canitoga*. Courtesy of Filmmuseum Berlin—Deutsche Kinemathek.

routines, and orthodoxies. Implemented by a cowboy-technician, techno-logical breakthroughs become stages of charismatic revelation, sites that recenter identity and help describe modern technology in terms of essen-tial meanings—of the soul, the will to form, and unhampered virility.

In *The Emperor of California* Trenker explored the western genre as a metaphor for the cinematic apparatus. For Trenker it was not such a leap of faith from the cowboy's colonial to the camera's techno-ideological work. Selpin's *Water for Canitoga,* by way of contrast, deploys the phallic rheto-ric of the traditional western in order to suggest surprising continuities be-tween the nineteenth-century world of cowboys and the twentieth-century cosmos of engineers. Monstuart's engineerdom valorizes forms of labor that challenge the impact of both scientific reason and finance capital. The western's toughness, in Selpin's film, elevates technology from the realm of *Zivilisation* to the realm of *Kultur,* from the spheres of abstraction and con-ceptual reflection to the ones of immediacy and the soul, from images of polyphonous confusion and formlessness to strong enactments of the will to form and order. Technological progress, cloaked in the imagery of the western frontier, thus helps recuperate what it threatened in the first place: masculine identity and authentic expressiveness.

Monstuart's existential engineerdom clearly resonated with what Goebbels, in a famous speech of 1939, was calling the contemporary age of "steel-made romanticism,"[76] the Nazi attempt to give a soul to technology and to put it in the service of the German folk. Small wonder, then, that Goebbels's distraction factory spared neither trouble nor expense to market *Water for Canitoga* with the most advanced technological means of the time: television.[77] On the evening before the film's Berlin premiere, Selpin and some of his actors chatted about their western on Berlin's still experimental TV program.[78] At the end of the show all guests suddenly decided to intone one of the film's most marketable attractions, "Goodbye Jonny." Albers himself, on the other hand, when asked in a different context, left little doubt about the political index of *Water for Canitoga.* In an interview with *Film-Kurier* the star drew direct lines between Monstuart's spectacular caisson and Hitler's *Autobahns.* The film, Albers pointed out, "plays around the turn of the century, but it is rather attractive to compare the technical problems of the past with our monumental constructions of bridges and roads today."[79] Albers's remarks point to the fact that, similar to *The Emperor of California, Water for Canitoga* engages different cultural codes in an attempt to engineer a unified sense of identity. Rugged cowboys such as Monstuart reveal through technological mediation the organic essences of the German soul and folk. They prevent modern Germany from falling into the same trap of degenerate feminization that Nazi discourse attributed to the federal system and plutocratic order of the United States.[80] At once cowboy and engineer, Monstuart embodies the Nazi call for a strong, masculine state resolutely defining the course of technological modernization. Challenging what Nazi ideology perceived as the polycentric gestalt of modern America, the film envisions a self-sufficient state that defies both the liberal-democratic separation of power and capital's manipulation of politics. Whereas the cowboy-politician Sutter perished not because of a want of will but because American settlers failed to live up to Trenker's image of the faithful cowboy, the cowboy-engineer Monstuart redeems the West from the detrimental force of exchange, greed, and competitiveness. If America itself cannot uphold what German filmmakers consider the legendary world of the western, then German cinema must film the legend and activate it against its actual adversaries.

WESTERN ADVENTURES AND WARFARE

One of the economically most viable American genres of the silent film era, the Hollywood western went mostly underground in the early years of the talkies because of fundamental transformations of American film culture during the Great Depression and New Deal period, the technical problems of on-location sound recording, and the highly competitive attraction of new genres such as the musical and the gangster film.[81] It was only by the end of the 1930s, with John Ford's celebrated *Stagecoach* (1939) and George Marshall's *Destry Rides Again* (1939), that American westerns experienced an impressive renaissance lasting far into the 1950s. In spite of the great popularity of the western in prewar Germany, German audiences had to wait until the postwar era to witness this rebirth of the American western genre around 1940: Ford's masterpiece was never screened in Nazi Germany.[82]

In contrast to the American development, the outbreak of World War II ended the German cowboy's trek through Nazi cinema. Westerns such as *The Emperor of California, Sergeant Berry, Gold in New Frisco,* and *Water for Canitoga* had used the absence of American competition during the 1930s to bond the German viewer's desire to a different and nationally specific interpretation of the genre. A site of multiple temporal and spatial dislocations, the German western of the 1930s was designed to carry viewers across fundamental social and political transformations of the time. Men in search of charismatic power and the technological sublime, German cowboys such as Sutter and Monstuart played a critical role in unifying the controversial evaluation of the western frontier and American modernity so typical for the Weimar period. Nazi westerns absorbed competing views into one hegemonic interpretation, yet rather than empowering communication across the boundaries of different cultures, Nazi Westerns reified cultural particularities and coupled desire with ideology. That the trail of the Nazi cowboy through German cinemas in 1939 ended abruptly does not reflect a sudden change in Nazi film politics. Instead, it must be seen as resulting from the fact that the German western's primary audience had now been effectively relocated from the urban movie theaters to the eastern and western fronts. By 1939 the Nazi cowboy had more or less served his preparatory mission. His former fans, converted into soldiers, were now called on to prove what they had learned.

A conduit to a seemingly lost world of masculine virility and unhampered physical immediacy, Nazi westerns captured the age's constitutive nonsynchronicity. As they aligned new technologies with popular utopias, these westerns aspired to cater to both at once: to those who lost and to those who gained from Nazi modernization. Far from simply escaping into the past, Nazi westerns embraced modern machines and the "American" art of genre to engineer the power of elemental forces. Cinematic and other machines here yielded access to a world where modern distraction seekers could hope to reconstitute an imaginary sense of corporeal plenitude and wholeness. Fusing exotic images and operatic sound tracks into total works of art, modern apparatuses thus helped align antimodern impulses with the tasks of the time. As they rendered the old as a product of the new or presented the new as the latest manifestation of the always same, Nazi westerns rolled myth and modernity into one overpowering experience. They ventured into the Far West in order to rewrite history as fate and replace historical contingency with the self-sufficient timetables of nature and charismatic leadership.

The Nazi cowboy's quest for virility and charismatic authority fit well into the larger political constellations of Nazi Germany at the threshold of World War II. Nazi ideology strongly opposed the refraction of the modern state into competing apparatuses of domination. In the view of Nazi ideologues the liberal-democratic state—in particular in the United States—effaced the existential dimension of the political. Politics was supposed to become Great Politics again, and to achieve this goal it was necessary to re-center the state and emancipate it from economic, administrative, or social imperatives. But Nazi politics by no means lived up to these ideals. Although penetrating most aspects of public and private life, the Nazi state entailed a great number of subcenters of bureaucratic domination. The Nazi elite therefore redefined politics as the art of maintaining distance among competing agencies of domination. They hoped to recenter the state by personalizing politics and making the head of state, Adolf Hitler, into a charismatic judge who ruled out possible struggles among diffuse centers of power. The closer the Third Reich approached war, the more Hitler emerged as occupying "the nodal points between the partial fields of power."[83] The drive toward war in fact provided the only means by which the Nazi state was able to keep its organizational jungle in check. War was essential in giving politics the appearance of unified and resolute action. Combat, military leadership, and imperial exploitation alone could finally satisfy the call for autonomous politics.

Like the calculated presentation of Hitler as a mythic führer,[84] Nazi westerns aroused desire for forms of political action that defined the political as a site where authenticity could come into being. Nazi cowboys offered what helped gloss over the gap between ideological demands and political realities, past utopias and present realities. They rode in the service of an order that tried to sell war as the telos of all desire, a desire to undo the unpredictability of desire. The outbreak of World War II may have discontinued this ride, but if we are to believe Goebbels's megalomaniac visions, this war also promoted the final triumph of the Nazi film cowboy and film culture. For imperial warfare, in Goebbels's eyes, provided an important strategy to increase the export shares of the German film industry.[85] War was meant to open up new markets for German film exports. It was designed to drive Hollywood out of Europe. If German film's mission was to spread German culture and the German language abroad,[86] then Nazi warfare was supposed to secure a radically expanded field in which Nazi cinema could serve as a new lingua franca. In the self-perception of Goebbels, World War II was therefore not just a war against the verdicts of the Treaty of Versailles but also against Hollywood and its dominant position in the world market.

On August 17, 1940, even prior to the American entry into World War II, Goebbels ordered Metro-Goldwyn-Mayer to close its German offices and prohibited any future screening of American films in Germany or in German-occupied territories.[87] Eager all along to protect the art form of film from commercial imperatives, Goebbels's intervention concluded the way prewar entertainment features had sought to recast cultural difference as radical alterity and overpower any recognition of other cultures as possible sources of critique or emancipation. Although Nazi mass culture throughout the war clearly continued to supplant concrete experience with powerful illusions, Goebbels's ban against American films effectively emancipated German cinema from direct Hollywood competition. It ended the narrative of Hollywood in Berlin as a narrative of cross-cultural transaction and rivalry. How Hollywood itself responded to the ambitions and formulae of Nazi cinema, and how German exile film practitioners employed American mass culture during the 1940s and 1950s to articulate their experience of cultural dislocation, is the focus of part 2 of this study.

Part 2

BERLIN IN HOLLYWOOD, 1939–1955

5 Wagner at Warner's

German Sounds and Hollywood Studio Visions

The breakthrough of sound not only radically changed Hollywood industry structures and production operations. It also gave rise to a number of new genres that occupied what we have come to understand as the cinema of the classical studio era. The coming of synchronized sound enabled Busby Berkeley's backstage musicals, the wisecracking vernacular of Warner's gangster dramas, the sonic effects of Disney animation features, and the witty dialogue of the screwball comedy. Sound enhanced cinematic illusionism, yet it also made possible a new kind of realism, which gave film a new footing on the material contexts of Depression-ridden America. But even though sound gave the movies unprecedented possibilities to articulate social messages, explicit political references or interventions were seen throughout the 1930s as antithetical to the task of cinema. As Will Hays, the first president of the Motion Picture Producers and Distributors of America (MPPDA), put it in 1938, "Entertainment is the commodity for which the public pays at the box-office. Propaganda disguised as entertainment would be neither honest salesmanship nor honest showmanship."[1] Hollywood films of the 1930s by and large concealed economic distress and social discord from their audiences, implying that even if they existed at all they had no impact on people's real lives. It is therefore no exaggeration to say, as David Cook has pointed out, that "with regard to the social, sexual, and political dimension of human experience, the American sound film throughout the thirties remained quite effectively 'silent.'"[2]

Solicited by the studios themselves, the PCA (Production Code Administration) regulations of 1934 defined entertainment as a moral undertaking, "rebuilding the bodies and souls of human beings."[3] Sound film was understood as an inherently universal art form that transcended given social divisions. Unlike music, literature, or drama, sound cinema—the authors of the PCA code argued—can and must speak to both the cultivated and the uneducated, and consequent to this popular task sound films carry a higher moral responsibility than other art forms. But this universalist mission of popular entertainment, according to the PCA code, not only called for respect for religious feelings, for the sanctity of marriage and the home, and for the integrity of law and social order. It also demanded the "fair" representation of the "history, institutions, prominent people and citizenry of other nations."[4] In spite of the universal nature of sound film, it was not seen as the task of Hollywood cinema to pass judgment on nationally particular ideologies or political practices. One predictable result of this was Hollywood's stunning silence on current events in Europe during the 1930s, a silence that fitted well with the industry's desire to keep international markets open and secure global hegemony. It took not only the beginning erosion of studio control and the influx of innovative talent around 1939 but also the outbreak of World War II in Europe and the final closing down of the important German export market in 1940 to convince Hollywood studio bosses to reinterpret the code and make European fascism an explicit theme in American narrative film.

No longer driven by commercial imperatives to please German censors with "fair" representations of contemporary Germany, Hollywood commenced its first series of anti-Nazi movies with Anatole Litvak's *Confessions of a Nazi Spy* (1939). As Jan-Christopher Horak has shown in ample detail, the primary impulse of Hollywood's engagement with German realities around 1940 was less to draw a realistic picture of Nazi domination than to delineate the enemy and—particularly after Pearl Harbor—win American audiences for the war effort.[5] Hollywood cinema depicted Nazi Germany as a totalitarian society in which military dictates coordinated all aspects of private life. Anti-Nazi films valued American democracy as a bulwark of bourgeois freedom (freedom of speech, trade, religion, passion, and fear). Nazi Germany, by contrast, was seen as a revolutionary state destroying traditional social structures, dissolving family bonds, annihilating the possibility of romantic love, eliminating universal moral principles, and thereby doing away with the very notions of individual agency and psychological accountability that defined the cornerstones of classical Hollywood cinema.[6] According to Hollywood circa 1940, Nazism aimed at mind-numbing discipline at home and imperial warfare abroad, but it also leveled the ideological foundations on which the studio era based its character-centered narratives. American cinema, one might therefore argue, declared war on Germany in 1939, not only because fascism could simply no longer be ignored but also because Hollywood finally came to see in Hitler its own antithesis. Anti-Nazi features of the early 1940s aspired to the impossible. They represented the unrepresentable in the hope of overcoming the nemesis of Hollywood entertainment with the means of American mass culture itself.

Hollywood anti-Nazi features of the early 1940s clearly served their function to assist the American war effort on the home front. In their predominant reading of Nazism as a totalitarian militarism, however, films such as *Confessions of a Nazi Spy, The Mortal Storm* (1940, Frank Borzage), *The Cross of Lorraine* (1943, Tay Garnett), *Hitler's Madman* (1943, Douglas Sirk), *Hitler's Children* (1943, Edward Dmytryk), or *The Hitler Gang* (1944, John Farrow) missed some of the most provocative aspects of the Nazi state. By explaining Nazi domination simply as an extreme offspring of Prussian authoritarianism, these films ignored the curious modernity of Nazi society: its devotion to technological progress, commodity consumption, and mass entertainment. Hollywood Nazis yelled and howled, but they hardly ever forged sounds and sights into compelling objects of mass cultural consumption. Neither the Nazis' prewar passion for things American—for speed, fashion, and cosmopolitanism—nor Goebbels's attempt to outdo Hollywood with a self-consciously German culture industry were part of the picture anti-Nazi movies extended to American audiences. The anti-Nazi film genre instead followed an uncompromising *Sonderweg* thesis of German history.[7] Anti-Nazi features read the Hitler state as a peculiarly German product of preindustrial traditions that had blocked the development of democratic institutions and modern consumer culture. Accordingly, Hitler became possible because eighteenth- and nineteenth-century Germany had not witnessed the emergence of an active bourgeoisie powerful enough to sustain parliamentary institutions and a liberal civic culture. Hollywood anti-Nazi features, in other words, understood the rise of Nazism not in terms of a disastrous dialectic of modernization but rather as a full-fledged revolt against modern life. With their naive belief in the linearity of progress, early anti-Nazi features thus ironically granted Nazi propaganda a second triumph. Rather than examining how modern tools in Nazi Germany reproduced older meanings and captured disparate longings, Hollywood reiterated the Nazis' many attempts to deny the heterogeneous nature of Nazi ideology and society, its structured confusion.[8] As it ignored the role of industrial culture in Nazi society, the Hollywood anti-Nazi film silenced the very echoes American mass culture had found in contemporary Germany.

The most striking exception to the rule is Charlie Chaplin's *The Great Dictator* (1940). Chaplin's Tomania is a state of archaic ideologies and premodern social structures, but it is also one of eminently modern technologies that penetrate all aspects of public life and private expression. In the role of dictator Adenoid Hynkel, Chaplin speaks German double-talk, yet the Chaplin gibberish aspires to do more than simply poke fun at Hitler's Austrian accent and warped intonation. Instead, what Chaplin's idiosyncratic idiom brings to the fore is a language of power that replaces rational communication with performative effects, a language that acts directly on the listeners' hearts and minds. Theatrical through and through, Hynkel's voice is prosthetic. It reflects conditions in which speeches in front of large crowds have become the norm and in which microphones have turned into extensions of the vocal chords. Chaplin's gibberish in this way draws our attention to the many ways that Nazi Germany appropriated the cinematic apparatus to silence the articulation of concrete experience. What sounds like primal murmur is exposed as mediated by modern machines.

Although shot more than a decade after the introduction of synchronized sound, *The Great Dictator* was Chaplin's first real talkie. It seems as if the outbreak of World War II in Europe finally prompted the master of silent comedy to acquire a voice and speak out against Nazi Germany. Unlike the majority of anti-Nazi features, *The Great Dictator* challenges Nazi media culture on its own grounds. To do so, however, the film defies some of Hollywood's most sacred conventions. In the film's final five minutes Chaplin inhabits Hynkel's stage in order to step out of his role and speak directly to the film's audience. Poised in front of two microphones, Chaplin proposes a humanist critique of instrumental reason that hails modern technology as an organ to bring people together: "We have developed speed but we have shut ourselves in. Machinery that gives abundance has left us in want. Our knowledge has made us cynical, our cleverness hard and unkind. We think too much and feel too little. . . . The airplane and radio have brought us closer together. The very nature of these inventions cries out for the good in men, cries out for universal brotherhood, for the unity of us all." Chaplin in his final address celebrates the space-contracting force of modern media as their very message. Fascism turns technology against itself. It enslaves the communicative substance of mechanical reproduction in order to rule over people's inner and outer nature. Chaplin, on the other hand, wants to overturn this enslavement of humanity and technology from within. He literally learns the art of sound onscreen so as to take the talkie away from the fascists and actualize film's potential to foster solidarity and re(de)fine, not assault, human sensuality.

The final sequence of *The Great Dictator* suggests a powerful alternative to the Wagnerian aspirations and anaesthetic fantasies of Nazi cinema.

Strangely enough, however, at the apex of the speech, the film takes recourse to Wagnerian sounds themselves in order to intensify Chaplin's
message: the overture to the first act of *Lohengrin*. Wagner in this instance
is meant to extend utopian impressions of unity and sensual integrity. The
delicate lyricism of *Lohengrin* is used to underscore glimpses of a right life
amid a wrong one. Chaplin's musical choice might seem surprising at first,
in particular if we recall that the same music is also used to capture
Hynkel's desire for imperial domination during the famous globe ballet.
How can Wagner at once help emphasize a progressivist vision of human
individualism and a fascist preview of absolute domination? How can the
master's music simultaneously signify a desire for lost emotional integrity
and for authoritative grandeur?

Chaplin's dual use of *Lohengrin* points toward unsettling junctions of
Nazi culture and Hollywood entertainment. Similar to Adorno, Chaplin in
The Great Dictator understands Wagner as a signifier of both: the birth of
fascism out of the spirit of the total work of art, and the origin of modern
mass culture out of the spirit of the most arduous aesthetic program of the
nineteenth century.[9] Unlike Adorno, however, for whom American mass
culture and fascism were virtually identical, Chaplin wants his audience to
make crucial distinctions between the competing Wagnerianisms of his
time. Both the fascist spectacle and Hollywood rely on the driving force of
utopian desires, on mass culture's Wagnerian promise of self-transcendence
and authentic collectivity, but they channel these mythic longings in fundamentally different directions. Although *The Great Dictator* exposes the
puzzling modernity of Nazi politics, Chaplin is unwilling to write off either
Wagner or industrial culture. In fact, Hollywood sound film, Chaplin suggests, needs Wagner as never before in order to at once condemn the abuse
of fantasy in fascism *and* warrant the utopian possibilities of industrial
culture.

Walter Benjamin wrote as early as 1934 that "Chaplin shows the comi-
cal aspects of Hitler's serenity; whenever he plays the refined man we know
the whole story about the *Führer*."[10] Premiering only a few days before
Benjamin committed suicide in the Pyrenees, Chaplin's *The Great Dictator*
tried to tell the whole story about how Nazi culture summoned industrial
means to consecrate modern power as an auratic presence. But in denounc-
ing Hitler's media dictatorship the film at the same time drew attention to
the role of German sounds and cultural traditions in contemporary Hollywood mass culture. A tale about a doppelgänger and mistaken identities, *The
Great Dictator* pointed toward the uncanny relationship between Hollywood filmmaking and the aestheticization of politics in National Socialism,

between the Americanist elements of Nazi Wagnerianism and the Wagnerian syntax of American popular culture. It is the task of this chapter to follow Chaplin's lead and set the stage for a more detailed discussion of Wagner's ambivalent function and the uncanny role of "Germany" in Hollywood filmmaking from the 1930s to the disintegration of the studio system in the late 1940s and early 1950s. The point, however, is neither to write a comprehensive history of German exile work in Hollywood nor to trace the various representations of German culture and history during this time. Rather, what is at stake is to think through how Hollywood studio filmmaking absorbed selected German sounds and cultural traditions into its universal ambitions, how studio films drew on German exile talent and an imaginary sense of Germanness to warrant product differentiation, and how in turn both exile film composers and directors—although often asked to playact what they had left behind—used studio filmmaking as a means to bridge different cultural codes and renegotiate Wagner's legacy to twentieth-century mass culture.

STANDARD AMERICAN AND ITS DISCONTENTS

The story of how the breakthrough of sound ended the career of many Hollywood film stars has often been told. Synchronized sound upset a number of dominant conventions concerning acting styles and gesticulation patterns. It put actors out of work who did not live up to the new and more naturalist performance codes, but it also opened new roads to stardom for performers trained in theater, vaudeville, and burlesque. Norma Desmond's declaration in *Sunset Boulevard* (1950, Billy Wilder) that it was the films rather than the stars that became small with the transition to sound ignores, therefore, at least half the truth. Desmond, however, clearly has a point, even though the "shrinkage" of Hollywood movies after 1930 may have had less to do with the dwindling aura of silent film stars than with the way sound induced the studios to level former representations of ethnic specificity and social diversity. Synchronized sound triggered a process of industrial standardization that reflected the kind of cultural homogenization that characterized the post-Depression era and New Deal at large.

The cinema of the 1930s marked an era of largely accelerated sounds and sights.[11] The verbal and visual dynamism of Berkeley's musicals, of Cagney's gangsters, or of Hawks's screwball comedies extended an idea of tempo that was at odds with the experience of stagnating economic realities throughout the Depression era. The verbal hyperactivity of Hollywood films was indicative of the fact that directors had relinquished some of their former control to screenwriters and dialogue coaches. It was also a part of concerted efforts to capture viewers across differences of class and race and to dramatically expedite the universal reach of cinematic pleasure. At the end of the 1920s many East Coast dramatists and writers had moved West to help Hollywood studios refine dialogues and tighten narratives. Joining professional screenwriters, these "word workers," as Giuliana Muscio has called them, "produced a linguistic naturalism that standardized geographic and social gradations to make them comprehensible. This fundamental work on language undertaken by Hollywood cinema, alongside that of the radio, constructed the American way of speaking in the 1930s." [12] Screenwriters and voice trainers elaborated a new vernacular that eluded both the perceived arrogance of upper-class rhetoric and the putative vulgarity of working-class or regional idioms. The Hollywood studios of the early 1930s did not by any means do away with class-specific or local accents, but in their hope to streamline the spoken word they increasingly abandoned what had populated the screens of late silent cinema: the representation of ethnic immigrant cultures. Hearing the accents of immigrants onscreen seemed to abrade "the senses of the broad center of the audience and therefore obliged studios to soften otherness into mere difference, ethnicity into sentiment, and hardship into nostalgia. In any case, ethnicity became too much for classical Hollywood to handle and was easily rendered into a 'structured absence.'" [13]

There is clearly something profoundly deplorable about the way American sound films during the early 1930s eliminated the flavors of ethnic, regional, or class-specific accents. In their efforts to deliver standardized consumer products Hollywood studios engineered a marketable lingua franca that muted the other by remaking it in the image of the self. They constructed an allegedly neutral language that denied traditional links between linguistic properties and particularistic identities. Yet if we recall how Nazi film theorists and practitioners, at the level of discursive construction, tried during this same period to remake film dialogue in terms of racist ideologies, Hollywood's linguistic modernization of the 1930s might be viewed in a somewhat more favorable light. Nazi ideologues understood the coloratura of the German language and its dialects as transmission belts of national essence. Hollywood's word engineers, on the other hand, remained distant to this ideology of sound. Instead, the new vernacular of the 1930s— at least in the self-understanding of the studios—aimed at what one might call a post-traditional form of civic culture. Language standardization carried the seeds of a postnationalist definition of citizenship. It divorced notions of national belonging from nineteenth-century discourses on racial homogeneity or cultural superiority, and it advanced the formal recognition of shared institutions to the primary meaning of national identity. Paradoxical though it may seem, capitalist mass culture thus ended up propagating a pragmatic view of language as a tool of mutual recognition and rational exchange.

Given Hollywood's anxiety about the ethnic patinas of American English, it should come as no surprise that of all German exiles in Hollywood during the 1930s, film and theater actors experienced the greatest loss of status and artistic self-expression. In stark contrast to the late silent period, when Hollywood exploited transatlantic studio relations to attract foreign talent and stardom, classical Hollywood sound films allowed for linguistic particularism and foreign inflection mostly in character roles—and primarily for comic effects. Thus, even the most distinguished German actors such as Fritz Kortner, Ernst Deutsch, or Albert Bassermann found themselves relegated to the extreme margins of the studio system. Playing side roles as butlers, doctors, composers, or waiters in the popular costume films of the 1930s, their principal function was to provide vague aural impressions of Europeanness or cultural refinement.[14] With the exception of a very few (for example, Marlene Dietrich, Peter Lorre, Hedy Lamarr, and Paul Henreid) who succeeded in aligning their foreignness with the studio's need for exotic femme fatales, odd-ball villains, or charming cosmopolitans, most émigré actors had to experience their German accent as a signature of multiple displacement. It triggered a kind of heightened self-consciousness and latent self-hatred documented in the paranoid questions émigrés would ask after hearing other exiles speak: "No, my accent isn't as bad as that?"[15]

The popularity of the anti-Nazi genre between 1939 and circa 1944 temporarily increased the presence of German exile actors on Hollywood screens although not exactly in the way these émigrés must have desired. In a cynical twist of fate exile actors were suddenly contracted by Hollywood studios to typify the very personae responsible for their original dislocation: SS and Gestapo officials, Wehrmacht soldiers, Nazi spies. Dressed up as their enemy, German exile actors were now allowed to speak their native tongue and grant the German language a curious inroad into American entertainment. What most film scripts asked these actors to say, however, had little to do with what they had vocalized prior to their exile, for Hollywood reinvented German around 1940 as a bellowing idiom solely designed for sadists and tyrants. "What a strange stroke of fortune," commented Alfred Polgar, "to gain prestige and maybe stardom as the performer of a kind of bestiality that has made oneself into a victim."[16] According to Horak's analyses, 54 percent of all anti-Nazi features placed at least one German emigrant in a major or supporting role, whereas a total of 130 German-speaking exile actors were involved in the overall production of anti-Nazi films throughout World War II. Their precarious stardom, however, vanished again as early as 1943, when studio executives began to register the public's growing unease with Hollywood's new multilingualism and drastically reduced the number of foreign actors in domestic productions. As Hans Kafka wrote in September 1943 in the leading Jewish exile journal *Der Aufbau:* "Most of the studios now object to casting accent parts with accent people. In some of the most important forthcoming films, Nazis, Russians and Chinese are being played by Americans."[17]

It is interesting to note in this context that German exile directors did often very little to reverse the marginalization of German émigré actors in Hollywood. Fritz Lang's casting policy for *Hangmen Also Die*, the 1943 United Artist production about the assassination of Reinhard Heydrich in May 1942 in Prague, is a good case in point. Against the will of both his co-producer, Arnold Pressburger, and the film's coscriptwriter, Bertolt Brecht, Lang insisted on casting only actors without middle-European accents in the roles of Czech resistance fighters. In order not to threaten the audience's emotional identification with the courageous Czech, Lang deliberately wanted to Americanize the film's heroes. His ideal cast consisted of what he called middle Americans (midwesterners) or Britons with flawless—that is, "inaudible" and hence putatively universal—diction.[18] Brecht was greatly disappointed by Lang's quest for linguistic homogenization.[19] Not only did Lang's policy crudely contradict Brecht's aesthetic program of affective distanciation, but it also frustrated Brecht's hope to place both his wife, Helene Weigel, and his friend Fritz Kortner in prominent Hollywood roles.[20] In the end *Hangmen Also Die* had only three exiles among its credited cast: Alexander Granach, Hans von Twardowski, and Reinhold Schünzel, all of whom played Nazis or Nazi collaborators.[21]

Edward Said has described the life of the exile as an always precarious existence in-between. In the modern world the exile's fate is not simply to live away from home in a state of surgical separation but to live with many reminders that his or her home is in fact not that far away, that old and new may intermesh yet never produce any real sense of fulfillment. The exile, Said argues, "exists in a median state, neither completely at one with the new setting nor fully disencumbered of the old, beset with half-involvements and half detachments, nostalgic and sentimental on one level, an adept mimic or a secret outcast on another. Being skilled at survival becomes the main imperative, with the danger of getting too comfortable and secure constituting a threat that is constantly to be guarded against."[22] Hollywood studios of the 1930s and early 1940s were far from creating conditions under which German-speaking exile actors could indulge themselves in too much comfort or security. Studio filmmaking left little room for the exile actors' mimetic faculty, their professional ability to liquefy the boundaries between self and other. Rather than lending American mass culture their various talents, these exiles became in many cases unwilling executioners of how Hollywood around 1940 pictured the whole of German culture, including its language, as intrinsically eliminationist.

In 1941 *Der Aufbau* published an almanac of American everyday phrases to facilitate the émigrés' process of cultural survival.[23] For German exile actors, however, a mere lexicon of ordinary speech was simply not enough to find them a place in Hollywood. Burdened with their German accent, these actors experienced "home" as something faraway, and they therefore hardly ever entered that state of cultural hybridity Said describes as the condition of the exile in a modern world. Unlike their much more successful and—to use Said's term—comfortable émigré colleagues in the studios' scoring departments, the majority of exile actors after the end of the war quickly returned to whatever was left of their former home. It is this curious triumph of those other engineers of "German" sounds in exile, the middle-European film composers of the classical studio era, that concerns us now.

ROMANTIC UNIVERSALISM

Between the early 1930s and the early 1950s, film music fulfilled a more or less uniform set of tasks and expectations.[24] It was designed to intensify dramatic moments, create narrative continuity between scenes, stitch together the various spaces of the cinematic experience, and transform the viewer into "an untroublesome (less critical, less wary) viewing subject."[25] Film music cued the viewer into desired viewing positions. It appealed to the irrational, the dreamlike, to make audiences more receptive to the power of fantasy. To fulfill these functions, studio film music relied on a fairly stable inventory of stylistic elements deeply influenced by the compositional practice of late-romantic composers such as Richard Wagner and Richard Strauss. Classical Hollywood film music capitalized on romanticism's quest for expressive excess and emotional plenitude, on its melodic intensity and harmonic abundance, and on its interweaving of musical motives into an all-encompassing texture of sensual stimulation.

Although classical film music was characterized by a quasi-Fordist division and acceleration of labor, the romantic cult of genius continues to inform the widespread understanding of classical film music even today. If we were to follow most popular accounts, classical film music was almost single-handedly invented during the 1930s by a few European émigré composers, in particular the Viennese-born Max Steiner and Erich Wolfgang Korngold; the German Franz Waxman; and, the son of Eastern European immigrants, Alfred Newman. Jewish exile and emigration, according to Hollywood folklore, was the primary engine behind the romantic extravaganzas of the studio era. Hollywood, we are led to believe, owes the triumphs of classical film music to nothing other than the rise of Hitler and the effects of the Great Depression in Europe. Did it, though? And did Hollywood Wagnerianism and romanticism differ in any significant respect from the way in which Nazi film practitioners aspired to forge cinematic sights and sounds into Wagnerian configurations?

Hollywood scoring practice throughout the classical studio era largely followed the romantic conception of music as a pure language of emotions, a language of excess that transcended specific social or discursive contexts. Like the masterpieces of nineteenth-century romanticism, classical film music understood itself as the other of conventionalized representation: a direct conduit to universal meanings and passions. Music, according to this construction, conjured forth forgotten pasts and unheard-of futures. Similar to the nineteenth-century masters of the concert halls, Hollywood composers based their practice on the idea that music is inherently "seditious, sensual, pre-literate, pre-Oedipal, precultural—terms which all relegate music to something close to a Lacanian imaginary."[26] Music, following this understanding, referred the listener to places where human subjectivity could indulge in unhampered presence. For Hollywood's new romantics, then, music may have had no real referent, but it had the ability to take us out of ourselves and make us experience something ethereal and timeless. Music transcended culture. It extended universal truths that were free of ideological distortions and therefore carried the viewer beyond the contingencies of the real.

This romantic ideology of music clearly appealed to the Hollywood film industry long before the arrival of synchronized sound or the exodus of Jewish composers to Southern California. During the silent era, piano accompanists had already based their background play on catalogues of putatively "natural" emotive significations. They explicated narrative turns and intensified moods with the help of Wagnerian leitmotifs and romantic orchestrations. In 1911 W. Stephen Bush suggested in the *Moving Picture World*, "Every man or woman in charge of the motion picture theatre . . . is a disciple or follower of Richard Wagner."[27] Although it thus would be silly, as Caryl Flinn contends, to insist that middle-European immigrants basically invented the classical conception of film music and its Wagnerian principles around 1935,[28] it might not be so silly to argue that the development of sound recording techniques between 1931 and 1934 modernized the position of Wagner in Hollywood to such an extent that they offered new creative possibilities for composers such as Steiner or Korngold, who were trained in negotiating the conflicting elements of late romanticism and twentieth-century modernism. With the new technologies of sonic postproduction and multiple-track recording, Hollywood scoring methods entered a phase of rationalization that seemed to contradict not only romanticism's quest for organic totality but also Wagner's own refusal to share the labor invested in the creation of total artworks. If we were to follow common wisdom, then, Steiner, Waxman, and Korngold succeeded under these conditions because their upbringing at the intersection of nineteenth-century idioms and twentieth-century modernism allowed them to revitalize the pathos of romanticism with the means of modern culture. Trained under the sign of Wagner and Strauss, immigrant composers intuitively knew how to give a human coating to what had been engineered with advanced technologies. They infused twentieth-century images with the primal power of nineteenth-century sounds and thus contributed to an entertainment industry whose primary purpose was to make capital out of the individual's utopian longings and nostalgic attachments.

It is not difficult to see that this argument, in a rather perverse fashion, parrots Adorno's apocalyptic equation of Nazi coordination and American mass culture. Similar to Nazi film practitioners, Jewish exile composers in Hollywood—the above argument suggests—relied on mechanical reproduction in order to produce nature; similar to Nazi film practice, Hollywood scoring departments under the guidance of Hitler refugees hoped to produce the old as an effect of the newest technology. But things are of course much more complicated than this line of reasoning implies. What, for example, do *old* and *new* really mean in this context? And why should we assume that nineteenth-century sounds had the same effects on audiences in Berlin and in New York during the 1930s? What makes the argument unsound, in other words, is that, like the romantic ideologues of music themselves, it naturalizes music as a prediscursive language of pure emotions. Instead of quickly proclaiming the compatibility of, say, Giuseppe Becce's monumentalism and Max Steiner's Wagnerian excess, we therefore need to ask what kinds of links Hollywood scores sought to establish with the past and what sorts of (imaginary) pasts and utopian futures Jewish exile composers communicated to the present.

FILM SCORES AS POPULAR MODERNISM

The introduction of synchronized film sound had a profound impact on contemporary American music production. It put several thousands of film accompanists out of work at the same time that it transformed Hollywood virtually overnight into a center of musical production in the United States second only to New York.[29] Hollywood's exile Wagnerians played a significant, although often ambivalent, role in the transformation of American music during the 1930s. Their eclecticism upheld endangered continuities, but it also undercut the antimodernist credos of many post-Depression American composers. In the first decades of the century European modernism had placed a taboo on harmonic, melodic, or coloristic beauty. Serious concert works no longer afforded romantic expressiveness or flowing tonalities and relied instead on a quasi-scientific or explicitly constructivist conception of music. American concert hall compositions of the 1930s and 1940s, on the other hand, were in the majority dedicated to overcoming the abstractions and formal experimentations of modernism. American composers of the post-Depression era were turning to "native" resources and rural folklore in the hope of finding an indigenous American musical style.[30] The work of Charles Ives, Henry Cowell, Aaron Copland, and Virgil Thomson defined musical Americanism as the order of the day. Although there was clearly some dispute about what could or should be counted as authentic American traditions, composers of serious music nevertheless sought to promote musical forms that expressed a distinct sense of national identity.

The Wagnerianism of the Hollywood studios occupied an ambivalent position between the legacy of European modernism and this domestic vogue of musical nationalism. Like the Americanist composers of the 1930s and 1940s, émigrés such as Steiner and Korngold relied on compositional techniques that had lost currency among modernist composers since the turn of the century. Unlike some of the ideologues of musical Americanism, however, Hollywood's new romantics did not really deny the fact that their musical recourse to the past relied on a number of modernist principles—on constructivism, performative self-reflexivity, and antiorganicism. Classical film scores drew from highly heterogeneous sources and often resulted in eminently hybrid configurations. Studio composers saw no potential contradiction in intensifying medieval narratives with nineteenth-century idioms. Nor did their work—in spite of the standardization of musical motifs, phrases, and themes—imply that musical expressions were particular to one specific culture.

Seen from the vantage point of modernist aesthetic theory, studio film music may indeed be considered the mere shadow of autonomous art. Studio composers, one might contend, raided the past so as to provide their audiences with a marketable sense of universality that was otherwise denied to them. But given the peculiar function of film music within the studio system, it seems far from appropriate to lump Steiner's or Korngold's Wagnerianism together with the dominant currents of contemporary American music and, as a result, argue that their work typified a concerted backlash against aesthetic modernism. Seen in their historical context, the scores of émigré composers were in fact far more modernist than is often recognized. At its best, exile Wagnerianism, in following its principal task to rouse emotions and define viewing positions, opened curious avenues toward what one might understand as a form of popular modernism: an alternative modernism that within the bounds of a modern leisure culture of consumption gathered selected artistic innovations in a popular *and* modern vernacular of its own. Instead of aiming at organic fusions of dissimilar sources, the exiles' Wagnerian scores absorbed conflicting materials into an open framework in which cinematic sounds were meant to communicate universal human passions.

Hollywood and Nazi sound practitioners, then, may have both subscribed to essentializing conceptions of music, but they operated within discursive frameworks that attributed fundamentally different meanings to the legacy of nineteenth-century romanticism in general and Wagner in particular. Film music in Nazi cinema, as I argued in chapter 1, served the purpose of containing desire and orchestrating Germanness. In classical Hollywood cinema, by way of contrast, Wagnerian sounds were mostly seen as part of a musical language that transcended national boundaries and ethnic particularity. Defined as the other of conventional representation, neoromantic film music had the power to rouse the individual's emotions, stimulate the viewer's desire for desire, and thus intensify the marks of human subjectivity. Far from hitting audiences over their heads, Hollywood's Wagner echoed the ideological projection of unencumbered individualism, that is, the utopian view that under ideal conditions an individual's determination would be rewarded with plenty, freedom, and wedlock.

WAGNER AT WARNER'S:
THE CASE OF ERICH WOLFGANG KORNGOLD

It has become commonplace to say that Hollywood studio obligations crippled the artistic talents of exile composers by forcing them to score ever more films in ever shorter periods of time. The working conditions in the studios' scoring departments, in particular at Warner Bros. and Twentieth Century–Fox, were surely different from those that composers had experienced prior to their emigration. Hollywood studios expected even "stars" such as Steiner or Waxman to streamline their compositional practice according to the model of industrial assembly-line production. In many cases, however, rather than simply containing creativity, the studios' expectations released new energies and triggered unexpected stylistic breakthroughs. Studio conditions could open spaces in which émigré composers would transcend their initial background in lighter idioms and turn more serious or even dissonant than they might ever have intended. Exile studio composers, in particular after 1940, in fact encountered many occasions that forced them to masquerade themselves as aesthetic modernists and thus to mimic musical styles that clearly did not meet their original aesthetic preferences.

Erich Wolfgang Korngold's career in Hollywood between 1938 and 1946 is a good case in point. Korngold was born in 1897 in Vienna. Raised under the ambitious tutelage of his father, music critic Julius Korngold, Korngold was celebrated in the first two decades of the century as a new wunderkind— a second Mozart, excelling in both performance and composition, a musical genius no less prodigious than Gustav Mahler.[31] Korngold's first compositions were published when he was only thirteen, and from the ballet-pantomime *Der Schneemann* (The snowman, 1910) to the three-act operas *Die tote Stadt* (The dead city, 1920) and *Das Wunder der Heliane* (The miracle of Heliane, 1927), from his Trio in D major (1910) to the Piano Sonata no. 3 in C major (1930), Korngold's music prior to his exile was already marked by strong melodic writing and emotive intensities, by dance-like rhythms and delicate chromatic harmonies, by spectacular fanfares and atmospheric mood paintings. Although Korngold clearly developed his own personal signature, his work remained deeply affected by the works of Brahms, Wagner, Puccini, Richard Strauss, and Johann Strauss. Possible echoes of the Second Viennese School, on the other hand, remained muted. Dedicated to tonality and melodic beauty, the prodigy child Korngold was far from carrying out any Oedipal revolt against the world of his fathers, including his own. The basic parameters of his music barely changed at all while the world around him went topsy-turvy.

Korngold's work for Hollywood commenced in 1934, when he arranged the score for *A Midsummer Night's Dream* (William Dieterle/Max Reinhardt). But public recognition did not come until 1938, when after the *Anschluß* Korngold settled permanently in Hollywood and started to score prestigious A pictures such as *The Adventures of Robin Hood* (1938, Michael Curtiz), *Juarez* (1939, William Dieterle), and *The Sea Hawk* (1940, Michael Curtiz). In contrast to Steiner or Waxman, whose contracts required them to work on one film after another, Korngold's arrangement with Warner allowed him to score as few as two films per year and to have much more control over the scoring process. Although Korngold never used a "click track," his sense of timing, of coordinating images and sounds, proved exceptional. As Jessica Duchen writes, "[Korngold's] use of large blocks of music, complex interweaving of Leitmotivs, and sensitivity to music's interaction with speech left an indelible impression on the future of the field. . . . Korngold showed how music could be woven integrally into the structure of a film; he not only raised the quality of the music but also its relevance to the movie as a whole."[32] Throughout his years in Hollywood, Korngold sought to refine existing techniques of pitching music just beneath an actor's voice so as to intensify speech but not to interfere with the audience's understanding of the words. The aesthetic program behind this scoring practice was positively Wagnerian. It aspired to weave speech and music into a dramatic syntax powerful enough, as Wagner had demanded in *Opera and Drama,* to emotionalize the intellect. Unlike Wagner, however, whose mature musical language was intended to unfold the primal substance of the German language, Korngold's Wagnerianism aimed primarily at the amplification of dramatic action and speech, not at a mythic interpenetration of word and music in Wagner's sense. That Korngold's compositions for film clearly prioritized the intelligibility of spoken dialogue over the rhetoric of musical effects, yet at times could sound like opera without words, evidences the distance between Korngold's Wagnerianism and Wagner's own project of organic synthesis.

Korngold's success in Hollywood, one might speculate, resulted largely from the fact that he had already composed film music long before he had ever entered a film studio. Trained in the late-romantic language of emotional intensity and chromatic beauty, Korngold understood intuitively how to bridge the gaps between German classical music, the lightness of turn-of-the-century operetta, and the demands of contemporary mass culture. What is more important for our purposes here, however, is that Korngold argued during his Hollywood career against any view of film music as merely incidental. Instead, he publicly promoted Hollywood Wagnerianism as an equal brother of serious concert hall expressions. In an interview with *Overture* toward the end of his Hollywood career Korngold did not even hesitate to present film music as a means of cultural edification and self-transcendence:

It is not true that the cinema places a restraint on musical expression. Music is music whether it is for the stage, rostrum or cinema. Form may change, the manner of writing may vary, but the composer needs to make no concessions whatever to what he conceives to be his own musical ideology. . . . Fine symphonic scores for motion pictures cannot help but influence mass acceptance for finer music. The cinema is a direct avenue to the ears and hearts of the great public and all musicians should see the screen as a musical opportunity.[33]

One may surely read Korngold's credo as a naive misinterpretation of dominant Hollywood production practices, yet Korngold's emphatic defense of film music has the virtue of clarifying what we need to conceptualize as the utopian and universalist function of Hollywood Wagnerianism: its task of providing audiences with glimpses of integrity and reconciliation and its role as a whole to promise cultural transformation and mobility. Unlike the Wagnerian ideologues of Nazi cinema, who embraced film music as a conduit to some kind of mythic past and essentialized identity, Hollywood Wagnerianism à la Korngold conceived of itself as a project, as building the road toward a better and principally open future.

Studio filmmaking was less a process of collaboration among different creative talents than of ongoing negotiation and struggle.[34] Films were not simply the product of individual human expressions but rather the outcome of an always contested melding of various institutional forces. Film music occupied its own territory within this force field, and notwithstanding all attempts to understand the effects of music scores in terms borrowed from the vocabulary of nineteenth-century genius aesthetics, we do well not to evaluate Hollywood Wagnerianism simply according to one-dimensional categories such as subversive authorship or subservient assimilation. To speak of studio filmmaking as a structured process of negotiation means to draw attention to how particular forces within this process may have altered intended meanings by taking recourse to peculiar sets of signs, practices, and traditions. It enables us to see the contingency of studio operations and products, that is to say, the fact that in spite of all stylistic uniformity nothing about the making of films during the studio era was simply natural or inevitable.

It is against the background of this understanding of studio filmmaking as a delicate equilibrium of conflicting forces that we need to conceptualize what Korngold presented in his 1946 interview as the "musical opportunities" of film scoring. For in spite of dominant conceptions of music as a preconventional language of pure emotions, it was this negotiated character of classical film music that in certain cases enabled Hollywood's exile

Wagnerians to transcend dominant neoromantic codes and mimic aesthetic modernism. Korngold's last Hollywood score, for Irving Rapper's 1946 *Deception,* is a good example. This Warner film starred Bette Davis, Paul Henreid, and Claude Rains in a tragic love triangle comprising unfaithful pianist, virtuoso cellist, and star composer. The Rains character, the fictional Alexander Hollenius, was designated as a moderately modern composer. Henreid, in the role of the emigrant musician Karel Novak, identifies Hollenius as a master "who unites the rhythms of today with the melodies of yesterday" while citing Stravinsky as the unsurpassed hero of the present and Richard Strauss as his favorite composer of the past. Korngold's one-movement Cello Concerto in C major, op. 37, was written specifically as the technically challenging work Hollenius composes in order to embarrass Novak. Parts of Korngold's composition serve as nondiegetic film music, as well as for the climactic diegetic concert hall performance (played by Eleanor Aller). Compared to Korngold's other compositions of the time, the Cello Concerto op. 37 is relatively discordant. Including numerous passages that violate chromatic harmonies and straightforward tonality, the cello concerto not only encodes the conflicts between the film's main players but also signifies Novak's experience of destruction and dislocation during World War II. In spite of its modernist stances, however, the eleven-minute concerto contains deeply melodic and emotionally intense moments as well, and it is this calibration of old and new that sheds light on Korngold's own peculiar position in Hollywood. A stylistic conservative, the late-romantic Korngold in his last Hollywood picture masqueraded as a modernist who piped a number of postromantic sounds through the ducts of Fordist mass culture. Cello Concerto op. 37 illustrates the extent to which studio filmmaking could empower forms of popular modernism that overstepped the composer's own aesthetic preferences.

Adorno and Eisler, in their 1947 *Composing for the Films,* insisted that we cannot understand Korngold's or Steiner's music without general references to the dynamic of commodification and rationalization in organized capitalism. Film music, for Adorno and Eisler, reproduced the grammar of contemporary advertising. "The basic structure of all advertising: the division into conspicuous pictures or words and the inarticulate background, also characterizes motion-picture music."[35] Studio film music tried to bathe listeners in affects so as to bond their desire to a unified product. This manipulation of sense perception, in Adorno's and Eisler's view, paralleled the overall fusion of meanings and values under the rule of organized capitalism. Commodification operates as a universal equalizer, and its logic of homogenization includes the integration of picture, word, sound, script, acting, and photography into the seemingly unified configuration of the talkie. Although this flight from differentiation clearly already operated in Wagner's music dramas or in the symphonic poems of Franz Liszt and Richard Strauss, it was consummated only in Hollywood "as the amalgamation of drama, psychological novel, dime novel, operetta, symphony concert, and revue."[36] Dominant film music, in its primary function of rounding off the rough edges of mechanical reproduction, embodied a primary form of ideology. It amplified the way Fordist capitalism hid its own logic of fragmentation and bestowed the isolated individual with a false sense of universality and totality.

Adorno and Eisler's reading of dominant film music is surely helpful. It enables us to go beyond the essentializing concepts normally attributed to the work of Hollywood film scores and to understand the historical indices of film music's utopian function. Similar to Adorno and Horkheimer's larger culture industry thesis in *Dialectic of Enlightenment,* however, the neo-Marxist critique of classical film music as false consciousness tends to level different formations of industrial culture. Possible differences between the Wagnerian aspirations of Nazi film practitioners and of Hollywood dream workers are therefore categorically denied. Unless we wish to subscribe to a homogenizing view of twentieth-century industrial culture ourselves, we therefore need to explore not only the fact that film music is ideological but *what kinds* of ideologies it proliferated and to what end. German sounds and Wagnerian ambitions, as I have argued, echoed differently in Nazi and classical Hollywood film practice, and these differences had largely to do with the different tasks performed by mass cultural expressions in Hitler's Germany and Roosevelt's America respectively. The final sections of this chapter therefore turn to the basic operations of the Hollywood studio system during the New Deal, to its beginning disintegration after 1939, and to the ways in which exile directors such as Robert Siodmak, Douglas Sirk, Fritz Lang, and Curtis Bernhardt wove in their own audiovisual agendas.

STUDIO FILMMAKING AND THE DIALECTIC OF EXILE

In 1939 Lewis Jacobs described the Hollywood studio system as a bureaucratic and intrinsically conservative apparatus hostile to any artistic innovation. Relying on contract stars and genre formulas, Hollywood filmmaking, according to Jacobs, destroyed all forms of individual creativity, taste, and imagination. "Production methods," Jacobs wrote, "under this rigid system became mechanized: the 'assembly line' appeared in Hollywood. The resulting standardization of pictures caused the downfall of the most important directors during the late twenties. The various branches of production were divided and specialized so specifically and minutely that directors had a lessening opportunity to contribute to the whole. Most directors became 'glorified foremen' under the producer-supervisor."[37] According to Jacob's Weberian reading of classical Hollywood, studio operations transformed Hollywood into an iron cage of specialists without spirits and sensualists without hearts.[38] Rationalization either negated individual talent from the very outset, or it caused a few charismatic geniuses to rebel against and be crushed by the studios' front offices.[39]

Jacobs's desolate account has informed several generations of film scholars in their attempts to assess the basic procedures of studio filmmaking. Similar to Max Weber, who ended up favoring a return of personal charisma in order to halt the bureaucratization of modern life, scholarship in Jacobs's wake has privileged the image of the creative auteur who challenges the system and leaves personal signatures against all signs of standardization. It is only during the last two decades that scholars have moved away from the Weberian model of Hollywood filmmaking and, by and large, embraced what one might understand as a Gramscian paradigm of negotiation and hegemonization. According to this newer model classical Hollywood was engaged in a war of positions in which diverse wills were fused together with the studios' specific production and management structures, their technical resources, their narrative repertoires, and their marketing strategies. Classical Hollywood, as Thomas Schatz explains, was a period when various social, industrial, technological, economic, and aesthetic forces negotiated a delicate compromise: "That balance was conflicted and ever shifting but stable enough through four decades to provide a consistent system of production and consumption, a set of formalized creative practices and constraints, and thus a body of work with a uniform style—a standard way of telling stories, from camera work and cutting to plot structure and thematics."[40] Unlike Goebbels's German Hollywood, in which each individual aspect of filmmaking remained subject to extrinsic supervision and political control, Hollywood studios endorsed internal struggles between industrial and aesthetic imperatives as viable sources of formal quality and financial gain. Studio films became classical to the extent to which they articulated different institutional and stylistic forces into coherent conceptions.

The year 1939 has often been seen as a year of the studio system's greatest successes, yet it also marked the beginning of a new period in which the integrated major studios started to lose some of their former control over the production, distribution, and exhibition of feature films. New tax laws caused an unforeseen surge of freelance talents and independent production companies, and internal and external pressures resulted in the sudden rise of new producer-directors, a greater demand for product differentiation, and significant modifications to the studios' hierarchy of A and B productions. The extraordinary boom of the Hollywood film industry during World War II surely delayed a full-blown manifestation of what started to upset the classical studio system around 1940. But seen in retrospect, it is evident that a general sense of pending realignments struck Hollywood as early as 1939 and, hence, that ominous signs of decline and reorientation, of confusion and dislocation, loomed over studio filmmaking long before the Supreme Court separated production from exhibition sectors in 1948 and thereby triggered the protracted death of the studio system in the course of the 1950s.

Industry conditions in the immediate prewar era opened an exceptional window of opportunity for film directors eager to infuse studio filmmaking with new creative impulses. "Significantly enough, many of these filmmakers came from outside the studio system, bringing a strong sense of personal style and individual creative authority to their work in Hollywood. Indeed, the early 1940s saw the sudden explosive emergence of a new generation of Hollywood directors who would have tremendous impact on American film history."[41] It was the time of Hitchcock and Welles, of Ford and Hawks, and of Sturges and Huston, who all understood how to translate their creative ambitions into commercially viable products. But it was also the time of German-speaking exile directors such as Bernhardt, Lang, Preminger, Siodmak, Sirk, Wilder, and Zinnemann, who either were finally contracted by the studios for their technical expertise and versatility or whose American work suddenly experienced both critical and commercial successes. As we will see in further detail in the following chapters, the positions of these émigré directors differed greatly. What they all shared, however, was an often passionate dedication to things American, a desire for cultural adaptation and transformation that had clearly preceded their exile from Hitler Germany.

The irony of the remarkable rise of German exile directors during the 1940s, then, was that it took place against the backdrop of fundamental industry changes challenging the classical Hollywood studio system. Unlike pre-Nazi émigrés such as Ernst Lubitsch or William Dieterle, late-arrival exile directors confronted a film industry eager to modernize its formal syntax and cultural reach. What is even more ironic, however, is that in spite of their outspoken desire for cultural transformation and self-redress, exile directors were often expected to do precisely what they had left behind. Like exile actors and émigré composers, German directors, too, were hired by Hollywood studios to replay the past and thus to perform "Teutonic clichés as a mimicry of survival."[42] But if the Hollywood employment of most émigré actors rested, as we have seen, on their ability to act out a limited number of decisively unmodern German stereotypes, the Hollywood fortunes of exile directors were tied to their former association with the eminently modern and economically adept German film industry. Notwithstanding what the Nazis were doing to German cinema at the time, in the eyes of Hollywood executives UFA continued to represent a laboratory of highly professional filmmaking, fusing cineastic proficiency with commercial viability. With UFA's trademark on their sails German émigré directors promised to help navigate studio filmmaking through whatever storm was approaching.

Contrary to common wisdom, German exile directors became influential forces in 1940s Hollywood not because their personal ambitions subverted dominant studio styles but because industry conditions rendered the 1940s a unique period of opportunity for outside talents anxious to merge their professional competence with the variable demands of the day. Whether they had surfaced as successful filmmakers already during the Weimar era (Bernhardt, Lang, Ophuls, Siodmak) or under Goebbels (Sirk), émigrés seemed to offer viable resources to warrant the future marketability of motion pictures. Professional success for exile directors resulted, therefore, from delicate negotiations between past and present, old and new. It crystallized within a force field defined by the studios' expectations for continuity and the exiles' personal quests for innovation, by the shifting ideological parameters of post-Depression America and the exiles' own imported and often hopelessly romantic Americanism. Performative repetition rather than radical metamorphosis often became the exile directors' password to initial recognition, even if it meant to masquerade as what one had never been before and, in the process, to manufacture copies without originals.

PROSTHETIC IDENTITIES

It is in this respect that the work of German exile directors during the last one and a half decades of the classical studio system provides a highly instructive test case for critical debates about the category of authorship and narrative control in Hollywood, about the interplay between innovation and standardization, art cinema and mass culture. George Wilson has advised us to be cautious when entertaining the view of cinema as authored, for there is "no grounds for recognizing in narrative film, a being, person-like or not, who fictionally offers our view of narrative events to us, although we are often tempted to do so."[43] David Bordwell, on the other hand, has acknowledged the critical role of directors in the 1940s as catalysts of product differentiation and stylistic change,[44] but similar to Wilson, Bordwell sees little evidence for an understanding of studio directors as sole creators of individual films weaving various narrative perspectives or aesthetic expressions into one unified fabric. European art cinema of the 1950s and 1960s may have seen the rise of a form of authorship that can be defined— retrospectively—as a set of formal, narrative, and thematic strategies that gradually emerged as a virtual trademark in the course of an entire filmmaking career.[45] But throughout the entire studio era, filmmakers rarely enjoyed the kind of autonomy and control that would allow later critics to reconstruct their works as strictly authored, as articulating a single author's style, agenda, or experience.

It is the premise of the following chapters that some of the most intriguing films by German exile directors after 1939 embrace this lack of authorship and expressive authenticity as a custodian of authorial control itself. Exile cinema at its best revels in masterful tales of impaired authenticity and mistaken identity, of mimicry, make-believe and masquerade, Lubitsch's *To Be or Not to Be* (1942) and Robert Siodmak's *Cobra Woman* (1943) representing perhaps the two most politically charged examples (fig. 20). In many instances exile directors aspired to forms of authorship in Hollywood by holding up a mirror to the workings of the studio system, by grafting their personal experience of forced displacement—the exile's lack of authorship over his own narrative of life—onto the work of representation. What Said calls the exile's median state of half-involvements and half-detachments, his or her performative and multiply imbricated identity, thus advanced to an often ironic allegory for the operations of studio filmmaking—and vice versa. Recurrently contracted by the studios to mimic their past and provide some kind of European flair, émigré directors exploited their peculiar state of in-betweenness, not only to complicate the relation of individual films to their genre but also to reflect, refract, and reconstruct the image of German cultural identity—of German music, literature, and cinema history—within the American imaginary of the time. Exile filmmaking as discussed in the following brought into view that any cinematic negotiation of past and present, home and homelessness, is deeply affected by cinema's "prosthetic memory,"[46] that is, the power of mass cultural technologies to enable individuals to experience different temporalities and memories as if they were their own.

Figure 20.   Allegory of fascism: Robert Siodmak's *Cobra Woman* (1943).
Courtesy of Filmmuseum Berlin—Deutsche Kinemathek.

The Wagnerian elements of Nazi Americanism, as we saw in the first
part of this study, served as instruments of fantasy production fusing disparate experiences with the cause of the Nazi movement. They functioned
as a vehicle of affective *Anchluß,* bonding mass cultural utopias to essentializing views of history as nature and of cultural identity as uncontested.
Although clearly involved in projects of ideological and temporal alignment themselves, the films discussed in the following chapters, by contrast,
examine the constructedness of cultural identities and explore the extent to
which—after Hitler—representations of inauthenticity subterraneously

salvage any reasonable sense of expressive authenticity and collective identity. Because they often worked in genres that involved multiple layers of representation (costume films, literary adaptations, musical films), exile film directors had ample opportunity to probe the processes of cinematic representation. As we will see, in many instances they not only reconfigured dominant relations between image and sound, as well as complicated the audience's modes of sense perception, but in doing so they also challenged—intentionally or not—the coordination of human sensuality in Nazi cinema. Exile filmmakers at their best made visible and audible the very process by means of which cultural identities may be put on or removed. They investigated why we always tend to assign transcendental meanings to music; they examined the impact of modern technologies on the human body and voice; they mingled "German" expressionist iconographies with domestic American literary traditions and visual styles, and in this way they helped draw attention to the prosthetic process of representation, projection, and remembrance that is at the center of all cinematic experience.

Given both Wilson's and Bordwell's legitimate reservations about seeing classical Hollywood cinema as authored, we need to be careful not to heroize the studio work of émigrés such as Bernhardt, Siodmak, or Sirk as expressions of genuine auteurism, even if their work rendered the representation of the inauthentic a placeholder for authentic expressiveness. As I will emphasize in the following interpretations, some of the most fascinating aspects of exile directorship in fact did not emerge out of a quasi-romantic defiance of mass cultural technologies but through their deliberate endorsement and gradual modification, not in spite of studio control but as a result of complex negotiations with the various forces that defined studio filmmaking. Likewise, rather than celebrating the textual meanings provided by exile filmmakers as subversive per se, we should inquire into how formal experiments interacted with industry demands for product diversification and how the sights and sounds of émigré films resonated with general transformations of the American imaginary. Only by positioning the work of exile filmmakers in their ideological and industrial context can we fully appreciate how some of their work aspired to de- and reconstruct larger structures of perception and identity and how for the exile director studio filmmaking could allegorize the traumatic experience of cultural displacement. Only if we, in other words, map the work of émigré directors against the interplay of sociocultural, industrial, technological, and ideological forces that define the history of film can we fully understand how their films opened up imaginary spaces in which different cultures and histories penetrated each other through the medium of mutual citation, interpretation, or imitation. Read forward, backward, and sideways at once, exile filmmaking after 1939 is thus reconstructed in the following case studies as an alternative to the way the mass cultural fusion of sights and sounds in Nazi cinema was meant to define the nation as a "repository of a unitary, immutable, and essentialized identity."[47] Seizing new possibilities that opened up in Hollywood after 1939, the best products of émigré studio filmmaking during the 1940s and early 1950s not only questioned naturalizing concepts of cultural singularity and absolute alterity, but they also proposed a kind of civic nationalism, a pluralistic framework in which oppositional identities and splintered narratives could cohabit the imagined community of the nation.

REFLECTIONS FROM A DAMAGED LIFE

In one of his most gloomy reflections on modern life Adorno wrote in 1944 that the combined realities of German fascism, Soviet-style socialism, and American consumerism have obliterated any possibility for properly dwelling in the twentieth century. The exile's life expresses metonymically what the dialectic of enlightenment has done to all of us. In a world in which disaster radiates triumphant, contemporary houses and apartments offer only a false sense of home. "The best mode of conduct, in face of all this, still seems an uncommitted, suspended one. . . . It is part of morality not to be at home in one's home." Yet even those who try to live according to this morality must guard themselves against the temptation to feel at home in their state of spiritual and/or physical displacement. For a loveless disregard for things cannot but lead to destruction, and "the antithesis, no sooner uttered, is an ideology for those wishing a bad conscience to keep what they have. Wrong life cannot be lived rightly."[48]

The following three chapters examine the extent to which selected products of émigré studio filmmaking during the 1940s and early 1950s reflected Adorno's paradox of exile. How did Hitler refugees in Hollywood use mass cultural technologies to offer reflections from damaged lives? How did they align their initial views of America with the significant transformations of American society during and after World War II? What strategies did they employ to elude the coupling of sights and sounds in Nazi cinema and thereby to redefine the possibilities of film as a public horizon of experience? At first sight, much of what will be said in the following might bear no direct relation to questions of German identity or film history. Data drawn from German history or culture appear as mere specters in the films discussed, as broken mirror images, as fleeting flashes of the imaginary. Yet it is precisely the gesture by which these films turn away from Nazi cinema and its essentializing definitions of individual and national identity and it is the methods by which these films experiment with *different* ways of merging images, sounds, and cultural codes into mass cultural products that mandate we see these Hollywood productions as an important chapter of German film history after all. If a wrong life cannot be lived rightly, if a proper sense of home after Hitler is no longer available, then cultural histories, too, transcend the physical boundaries of single nations and enter a state of fluid multiplicity and simultaneity. That émigré studio filmmaking turned "Germany" into a specter bears testimony to the fact that after Hitler nothing concerning the relation between modern mass culture and national identity goes without saying anymore. Their spectral audiovisions questioned conventional notions of the home and homeland and in so doing elaborated an emancipatory sense of Germanness that drastically broke with the essentializing concepts of the past yet has remained mostly unrecognized to the present.

6 Berlin Noir

Robert Siodmak's Hollywood

The American cinema of the 1940s "was an industry at war, fighting monumental battles at home and overseas, both on-screen and off."[1] From 1942 to 1945 Hollywood filmmaking found itself in a state of war production. Prodded by political elites and studio executives alike, wartime features explored unprecedented relationships between cinema and social conditions, mass diversion and propaganda. But the studios' most challenging wars during this decade were waged on the domestic front: over antitrust violations with the Justice Department in Washington, over communist infiltration with Congress and the House Un-American Activities Committee (HUAC), over employment issues with labor unions, over matters of artistic control with new independent producers and freelance talents, and over film distribution with unruly theater owners. Haunted by this ongoing state of emergency, the American cinema of the 1940s witnessed both a tremendous boom and, after 1946, a disastrous slump of revenues and studio confidence. The decade of the 1940s thus became an era of crises in the word's most literal sense: a time of instability and reorientation, a time in which political, economic, and cultural antagonisms upset what formerly had been taken for granted.

Crises are the signature of the modern. Rather than simply replacing something old with something new, the moment of crisis redefines the very parameters according to which we remember the past and envision the future. To speak of the American cinema of the 1940s as one of ongoing crises, therefore, means to draw attention to the ways in which studio filmmaking during this decade underwent a dramatic process of renewal and self-redress. It means to emphasize how economic, political, and aesthetic pressures urged classical cinema to probe its own limits, reinterpret former practices, and face an arbitrary tomorrow. Periods of crisis break up dominant perceptions of time, and in the American cinema of the 1940s this splitting of temporal experience produced competing models of how to organize time within the limits of a consistent tale. The war film genre and the anti-Nazi film genre, as Dana Polan has argued, still triumphed in the attempt to align the power of narrative with the need to shape community and produce political commitments. War features exploited cinema's "enveloping ability to take any element, even one that would seem oppositional or resistant, and represent it in forms of an overall masterplot, to transcribe it in a discourse of affirmation."[2] But in many other spheres of 1940s American filmmaking, we observe a questioning of coherent narrative patterns, a sudden emphasis on the arbitrariness of temporality and experience. We encounter repetition, stasis, and ambiguity. Men's and women's time in so many films of the 1940s entered into an unparalleled state of nonsynchronicity. In contradistinction to the escapist fare of the 1930s, there seemed "to be no single space in which all desires can come together in permanent and euphoric triumph."[3] In face of the continuing battles on- and offscreen many Hollywood films of the 1940s abandoned the teleological masterplot. They gave voice to a plurality of narratives and perspectives that no longer allowed one to think of history as a linear dynamic of development.

Film noir is widely—and rightly—recognized as one of the most fascinating responses to the many wars Hollywood waged in the 1940s. The film noir cycle was born out of the spirit of industrial crisis as much as out of social and political anxiety. It marked an important step in the maturation and diversification of American mass culture during and after World War II. With its stylized images of violence, paranoia, male hysteria, and legal corruption, with its narratives of social contingency and existential ambiguity, film noir simultaneously encoded and counteracted the experience of a world out of joint, including the world of classical studio filmmaking. Film noir can be understood in this respect as a heterotopia in Michel Foucault's sense: a site that differs from most other spaces but that allows us better to understand how society organizes human relations across space and time.[4] Heterotopias "are something like counter-sites, a kind of effectively enacted utopia in which the real sites, all the other real sites that can be found within the culture, are simultaneously represented, contested, and inverted. Places of this kind are outside of all places, even though it may be possible to indicate their location in reality."[5] Film noir often juxtaposed temporal and spatial experiences that were in themselves incompatible. In its most striking manifestations, film noir provided *other* spaces that complicated the ways in which American cinema and society emplaced the body in everyday space and time.

Common wisdom explains the prominent role of German exile directors in film noir by seeing film noir as a direct expression of exile and despair. Film noir, according to this argument, owed its existence in large part to the ways in which émigré directors such as Fritz Lang, Anatole Litvak, Otto Preminger, Robert Siodmak, Edgar Ulmer, and Billy Wilder stamped their personal past onto American entertainment. In the eyes of some critics film noir served Teutonic directors in exile as a platform to express nothing other than the torments of the German soul.[6] Other critics, arguing in more historical terms, suggest that German film noir directors all "shared a world view that was shaped by their bitter personal experience of living and then escaping from a nation that had lost its mind."[7] Separated from their home, these directors—we are told—revitalized the formal language of German expressionist cinema in order to challenge German fascism. They espoused the heritage of Weimar film—chiaroscuro lighting, canted angles, narratives of male anxiety—to convey personal gloom but also to explore forms of authorship in a film industry dedicated to standardized genre products. Film noir, in this understanding, was European art cinema in disguise, a calculated assault on classical cinema that grafted the exiles' experience of displacement and artistic blockage directly onto the syntax of Hollywood filmmaking.

The present chapter nudges debates about the German impact on film noir in a different direction by discussing how film noir itself undoes genealogical accounts that map the history of film in terms of linear determination and direct cultural transfer. Film noir, I argue, was not a product of German authorship in exile or a belated offspring of Weimar cinema. Rather, it marked an eminently modern moment in American film history at which conventional notions of authorship and generic unity, of cultural distinctness and cross-cultural influence, seemed to loosen their grasp. As I will detail with regard to the work of Robert Siodmak, whose directorship in Germany, France, and Hollywood prior to 1943 shows no expressionist predilections whatsoever,[8] film noir articulated diverse styles, cultural codes, and experiences into a performative and pluralistic hybrid. Understood as a heterotopia in Foucault's sense, Siodmak's work in Hollywood referenced the past as a symptom of present anxieties and concerns. Showcases of cultural absorption and redress, Siodmak's film noirs invite us to think through the metaphoric exchanges between Weimar cinema and Hollywood as part of a history of productive misrecognitions and highly mediated identifications.[9] They press us to think of film history as a space of multiple and nonlinear (over)determination, a space where present events may illuminate their own past but can never be directly deduced from it.

Siodmak's most productive phase in Hollywood dates from 1943 to 1949. For most of this time under contract at Universal, Siodmak directed a series of features that hold privileged positions in virtually all textbooks on film noir (for example, *Phantom Lady, Christmas Holiday, The Spiral Staircase, The Dark Mirror, The Killers, Criss Cross*). During the process of becoming a celebrated director of film noir, Siodmak in some sense departed radically from his own beginnings during the Weimar period. Confronted with studio pressures, Siodmak may have recalled some aspects of German expressionist cinema—Weimar film's vocabulary of anxiety and paranoia, of visual stylization and theatrical excess. But this reinscription was discontinuous to say the least. It resurrected a past that had never existed as such, and it reflected an imaginary other in the mirror of domestic traditions such as the hard-boiled detective novel or American cinema's own experiments with chiaroscuro lighting since the 1910s.[10] Yet it is precisely this calculated recreation of the past, the imaginary and nontransparent links Siodmak's films entertain with German materials, that helps us better grasp the position of film noir and exile filmmaking in the 1940s. In focusing in particular on *Phantom Lady* (1943) and *The Spiral Staircase* (1945) this chapter argues that Siodmak's exile films evidence his professional adaptability as much as they undo essentializing concepts of historical causality and cultural singularity. Siodmak's success in film noir did not result from some kind of innate Germanness or authorial vision. Instead, it ensued from his competent immersion into studio filmmaking, his intuitive understanding of Hollywood production processes as manifestations of what Fredric Jameson calls structural causality.[11] Films such as *Phantom Lady* and *The Spiral Staircase* urge us to conceptualize exile filmmaking in the contentious 1940s as a multilayered structure of semiautonomous elements whose relationships with one another were increasingly nontransparent and mediated. Siodmak's Hollywood is one in which uncertain causes and ambiguous effects become engines of narrative development, of textualization. Siodmak's work in Hollywood thus reveals that any historical reality is representable only as an absence, as a result of retrospective interpretation and reconstruction—that "history is *not* a text, not a narrative, master or otherwise, but that, as an absent cause, it is inaccessible to us except in textual form, and that our approach to it and to the Real itself necessarily passes through its prior textualization, its narrativization in the political unconscious."[12]

If it is the task of the historian to make the past somehow present again, then part of this project is to play through different patterns of nonlinear determination in the narrative space of the historian's reconstruction. If historical realities, in the final analysis, cannot be represented indeed, then one aspect of gaining access to the absence of the real is to reflect on the past's own modes of symbolization and narrative emplotment. This chapter argues that part of the political unconscious of Siodmak's film noirs is the confrontation with Nazi cinema and its Wagnerian ideologies of embodiment. Siodmak's films, I suggest, probe the composite character of modern identity not in order to yearn for some kind of prelapsarian state of immediacy but, on the contrary, to undercut any conversion of loss and fragmentation into fantasies of power and resolve. Whereas Nazi cinema tried to contain the migratory potential of voice and music, Siodmak's films of the 1940s complicate our understanding of cinematic audiovision by probing both the technological and ideological dimensions of sounds and images onscreen. An adept expert in the use of sound effects since the early 1930s, Siodmak explores in his American work how cinematic audiovision may either—as in Nazi cinema—amplify anaesthetic fantasies of wholeness and self-presence or promote more decentered forms of subjectivity that recognize lack, fragmentation, and nonidentity as peculiarly modern sources of meaning. Although we cannot deduce Siodmak's work from his German past, it is his German experiences that—like the psychoanalyst's voice—may illuminate what drives the conscious and unconscious of his protagonists in Hollywood.

EXPLORATIONS IN NONSYNCHRONICITY

Robert Siodmak's career is often told as a narrative of ruptures and fly-by-night departures. In his autobiography Siodmak summarizes the most critical caesuras of his life as such: he left Germany the day after Hitler had come to power; he departed from Europe one day before the outbreak of World War II; and he turned his back on Hollywood a year before the introduction of Cinemascope.[13] But to think of Siodmak's career simply in terms of unwanted dislocations underestimates what steered him to success in the first place. He may have left Germany when Hitler came to power, but—unlike many other German film practitioners in exile—he did not have much difficulty inserting himself into the French and later into the American film industry. He may have left Hollywood when the studios embraced widescreen cinema to reclaim their former hegemony, but in previous decades it had been, for instance, the arrival of sound and of more sensitive film stock that had propelled him into new creative directions. Driven by an enormous hunger for personal success and aesthetic recognition, Siodmak lived out four careers (Weimar, France, Hollywood, postwar Germany) that all shared the same eagerness to face new challenges and transform the unknown into a source of inspiration. Rupture and displacement were the very stuff Siodmak's successes were made of. Siodmak's career as a film-maker was a zigzag tale of masterful mimicry and visionary adaptation. The exile's state of displacement was his home, and the migrant's desolation became the price for his relentless grasp for fame.

In a report to MGM in the early 1940s, Hollywood agent Paul Kohner introduced Siodmak as a director of great versatility and competence: "Mr. Siodmak's films, although mostly treating difficult subjects, are vividly realistic and possess the spell of imagination which is the principal element of entertainment. The best argument for Mr. Siodmak's ability as a director is his pictures and I feel that he would be a definite asset to any production company." [14] Siodmak's work prior to his arrival in Hollywood indeed evidenced a remarkable ability to fuse entertainment values with technical experimentation. In particular Siodmak's response to the coming of sound contributed to his reputation as a pragmatic universalist, a zealous innovator eager to convert technological changes into new stylistic formulas. Although he had entered the scene of Weimar filmmaking with a silent feature, it was in the sound medium that some of his most striking accomplishments took place prior to the Nazi takeover. "A plain and mute shot," Siodmak explained in 1930, "can be contrasted with different sounds so effectively that the effect of this scene is much stronger than for example the effect of the pure rhythm of images in a silent film." [15] Already in Siodmak's first full-length sound film, *Abschied* (Farewell, 1930), speech, music, and atmospheric noises were brought into contrapuntal relations with the image track, achieving what Karl Prümm calls the film's "perplexing multitextuality." [16] Contradicting all those who considered film sound redundant, Siodmak's *Abschied* employed sound to multiply the film's levels of signification and allow the viewer's perception to migrate across the frame of the visible. Similar to Fritz Lang's *M* or G. W. Pabst's *Kameradschaft*, Siodmak's early sound films such as *Abschied, Der Mann, der seinen Mörder sucht* (A man in search of his murderer, 1930), and *Voruntersuchung* (Preliminary investigation, 1931) rendered the new medium itself as the message. These films featured sound not simply as a means to support but to comment or expand on the image, to fragment or explode the visual field, and thus to enhance both the imaginative and the realistic possibilities of cinematic representation.

Siodmak carried his fascination with the sound medium through his six years in France to the Hollywood studio system. In particular his film noirs of the mid-1940s are replete with instances of multitextuality. They offer highly acoustical mise-en-scènes that frequently, to say the least, ripple the primacy of the image in classical filmmaking. Unlike Max Ophuls, that other exile virtuoso of film sound, Siodmak, throughout his Hollywood period, showed little interest in using the sound track as an "acoustical panorama," an atmospheric texture offering thick descriptions of everyday experience.[17] Instead, Siodmak's use of sound relied mostly on principles of isolation, formalization, and stylization. He created hyperbolic collisions of sounds and sights that signify dramatic experiences of loss and fragmentation, outbursts of repressed desire and violence, but that at the same time explore narrative possibilities beyond the classical regime of closure and causality. The famous jamming session in *Phantom Lady*—an explosive interlude of frenzied jazz sounds and hyperkinetic images—may be the most stunning example of how Siodmak's Hollywood films employ the acoustical to puncture the frames of image and narrative and in so doing broaden the spectrum of sense perception.

In this sequence drummer Cliff Milburn (Elisha Cook Jr.) leads his putative date, Kansas (Ella Raines), into an obscure basement, an extraterrestrial space excessively cut into ribbons of light and shadow (fig. 21). What follows is an extended theater of musical passion that clearly exceeds the narrative task to detail Cliff's persona or highlight Kansas's brave deception. For a moment of unmitigated auditory and visual spectacle the film's narrative in fact comes to a standstill as Cliff joins the practice of a jazz quintet and, kindled by Kansas's erotic gestures, bursts into a delirious drum solo. Editing and camerawork in this sequence give formal impressions of Cliff's tension-ridden performance. The camera's canted perspectives emphasize Cliff's violent unfastening of desire, and the ever-accelerating montage of images translates explosive rhythms into a compelling iconic language. The visual field itself thus seems drawn into a musical vortex of passion and desire. The camera affords no stable position outside of the spectacle. It cuts bodies into pieces and shows facial expressions from grotesque proximity, intensifying the basement's claustrophobic design to the point of a virtual implosion.[18]

At first this sequence seems to employ jazz in an all-too-familiar manner: as a signifier of sex, ecstasy, and desire. African-American music here, we might argue, represents what dominant culture considers animalistic, unmediated, and uncontained. A closer look at the jazz interlude of *Phantom Lady*, however, should dispel this suspicion. The jazz sequence, in fact,

Figure 21. Jazz, desire, and representation: Robert Siodmak's *Phantom Lady* (1944). Courtesy of Filmmuseum Berlin—Deutsche Kinemathek.

foregrounds the very mechanisms of projection and exoticism according to which mainstream culture discursively constructs jazz as entirely nondiscursive. A film within the film, the jamming session features white musicians donning the dress of black culture to express what dominant stereotypes render the bliss of being carried beyond oneself. Aroused by Kansas's counterfeit, the rather feebleminded Cliff enters the basement, joins the band midway, bursts into an ecstatic solo, and then departs again without farewell or closure. In the role of the cunning enunciator of Cliff's desire, Kansas thus allows the viewer to see to what extent jazz may function as a language of representation after all. Although she herself fakes desire and heat, she reveals the status of jazz as a signifying system that can be used for different constructions of agency. Jazz may isolate Cliff from discourse and transform his body into an object of audiovisual spectacle, but for Kansas it becomes a means not only to take command over Cliff but also to lay bare the role of the cinematic apparatus as a tool of signification and fantasy production.[19]

Classical studio films, it has been argued, treated sound in analogy to the image and, therefore, underwent little stylistic change after the advent of synchronized sound. In classical Hollywood filmmaking "the recording of speech is modeled upon the way cinematography records visible material and the treatment of music and sound effects is modeled upon the editing and laboratory work applied to the visual track."[20] The jazz sequence in *Phantom Lady* undercuts this image-sound analogy. Sound, here, as in many of Siodmak's features, Hollywood or otherwise, does not simply add substance to the image track. Instead, the auditory is granted a certain kind of autonomy that enables sound and image to engage in a mutual process of denaturalization. Rather than incorporate music entirely into the visual field, the jazz sequence demonstrates the extent to which the effects of music and film sound rely on the power of discourse and representation. In this sense Siodmak's sound direction challenges what Michel Chion calls the scotomization of the microphone in classical cinema.[21] Inverting the image-sound analogy, the film contests the naturalist perspective according to which any reference to the process of sound recording must be purged not only from the visual and auditory field but also from the viewer's mental act of perception and representation. We may not see the mike that records Cliff's frenzied solo, but when the film invites us to hear what the musicians and Kansas hear, we start to understand how classical film sound usually wants to hear for us and thus render the rendered natural and organic.

Many of Siodmak's most successful films deliver speech, noise, and music from their subordination to the image track. Siodmak's sounds are custodians of nonidentity. They warrant the heterogeneity of cinematic representation, the brokenness of modern sense perception. In frequently splitting bodies from voices, sounds from sights, Siodmak's films allow the viewer's perception to slip beyond the visual field. They urge the spectator to keep the different modalities of human sense perception in a state of open-ended dissociation and crisis. Siodmak's film noirs explore the utopian potentials of nonsynchronicity. In doing so they not only convert the proverbial crisis mentality of 1940s America into a formal language, but they also revoke the Wagnerian undertones of Nazi cinema and its euphonies of standardized sameness and existential resolve.

PHANTOM BODIES, PHANTOM VOICES

Political existentialism, as conceived by Nazi theoreticians such as Carl Schmitt and Alfred Baeumler, considered the political a space of resolve, a privileged space where authenticity could come into being. Weary about the ever-increasing decentering of power and identity in modernity, political existentialists hoped to recast the modern state as a showcase of self-assertion and willpower. Politics, as some Nazi ideologues argued, is self-sustaining; political leaders justify their action not in recourse to normative debates or legal principles but their mastery of extreme situations and creative ordering of social space. Although claiming the radical autonomy of the political, Nazi existentialists, however, did not hesitate to interpret political action according to the principles of late-eighteenth- and nineteenth-century genius aesthetics. Goebbels summarized this affinity of art and politics in a speech to film practitioners in 1937: "Just as art shapes human beings, so does politics shape peoples and nations." [22] Both art and politics express humanity's will to form. For both the artist and the politician, form is a direct expression of power. In Goebbels's view industrial mass culture by no means eliminated this basic identity of artistic genius and political leadership. On the contrary, it offered unprecedented means of transmitting the aura of creative power to ordinary people. The task of German film was to transport the expressive authenticity of artistic genius and political leadership to the age of mechanical reproduction.

Siodmak's *Phantom Lady* moved Goebbels's nexus of art and politics to the center of a taut Hollywood thriller. Like Goebbels, Siodmak draws parallels between different arenas of human creativity, the ways in which people channel their talents into social projects and, thus, in a truly existentialist sense, hope to create themselves, as well as communal bonds. Unlike Goebbels, however, *Phantom Lady* reveals what is terrorist about the celebration of creative genius and authenticity in the era of machines. Staging a climactic conflict between genius aesthetics and liberal-democratic technocracy, *Phantom Lady* in the end exposes fascist modernism as an ideological practice that buries the arbitrary and sensual under a screen of anaesthetic reality control. Whereas Nazi existentialists envision art as an expression of power and a tool to intensify modern life, *Phantom Lady* suggests that this existential crusade for total form and identity culminates, at its most consequential, in the desire to administer death. Geniuses may aspire to interrupt the weary routines of modern existence, but they can do so only by silencing the voices of the other.

Produced by Joan Harrison for Universal, Siodmak's *Phantom Lady* premiered at Loew's State Theater in New York City on February 17, 1944. The film's plot was based on a 1942 novel by Cornell Woolrich, but it changed both the novel's original story line and character motivation in significant ways. With the figure of the psychotic artist Jack Marlow (Franchot Tone), a fascist modernist in thin disguise, Siodmak's *Phantom Lady*

added a dimension to Woolrich's original conception that not only permitted new narrative possibilities but also struck the political nerve of the
time. Siodmak's Marlow is an elitist sculptor who murders the wife of his
best friend, Scott Henderson (Alan Curtis), a young, energetic, and socially
committed engineer. The police arrest Henderson for the murder because
he is unable to provide a solid alibi for the night of the homicide. Having
gone out with a young lady without knowing her name or identity, Henderson fails to find any witness who would want to confirm his mysterious
night out on the town. Kansas (Ella Raines), Henderson's attractive secre-
tary, believes in the engineer's innocence even after the court sentences
him to death. Turning into a prototypical femme fatale, she traces the
anonymous lady by means of only one clue: a hat, the copy of a flamboyant designer model as it turns out, specially manufactured for an eccentric
Latin American singer. When Kansas, with the "help" of Marlow, finally
finds the phantom lady of the film's title—Ann Terry (Fay Helm)—it is time
for Jack to intervene in Kansas's unraveling of the case. Back at his apartment he reveals to Kansas the motive for his murder, recalling his love affair with Henderson's wife and how she refused to run away with him. Now
preparing to strangle Kansas too, Marlow discloses his true feelings about
his friend Henderson, this "mediocre engineer working in sewers, drain
pipes, faucets." In Marlow's eyes Henderson represents the aesthetic banality of Fordist modernity and liberal-democratic mass society. "I never,"
Marlow proclaims, "liked cities, noises, confusion, dirt, and the people in
them. They hate me because I am different from them. . . . What is any life
compared to mine?" When Inspector Burgess, suspicious that Henderson
might not be the murderer after all, knocks at the door of Marlow's apartment, Marlow jumps out the window and commits a spectacular suicide,
represented onscreen as sound and metonymical trace, the noise of breaking glass and the following image of a jagged hole in the apartment window. In the film's final sequence Kansas's originally neglected amorous investments are finally rewarded when Henderson returns to his office after
his release. Yet instead of revealing his own affection face-to-face, Scott
leaves a message on Kansas's voice recorder. He invites her for dinner
"tonight" and "every night"—a marriage proposal repeated to Kansas's
delight forever because of a malfunction of the apparatus.

Alain Silver and Elizabeth Ward praise *Phantom Lady* for Siodmak's ex-
quisite manipulation of mise-en-scène. The film's atmospheric images of
New York streets and jazz clubs, of jails and apartment interiors, of desire
and excess, they argue, recall the iconography of Weimar cinema. Assisted
by his cinematographer, Woody Bredell, Siodmak, in particular in the jazz

club sequence, "brilliantly interweaves expressionistic decor with American idiom. If watched without sound, the scene could be from one of the classic German films of the 1920s."[23] Silver and Ward make a convincing case for the visual qualities of *Phantom Lady*. Whether one considers the film's use of canted angles, disjointed continuity, expressive close-ups, visual allegory or synecdoche, spotlights, or chiaroscuro effects; whether one brings into focus the film's iconography of schizophrenia, hysteria, paranoia, or sexual stimulation—all might be understood as part of a performative recollection of Weimar expressionism authored by a nonexpressionist exile stranded in Hollywood. To suggest watching the film without sound in order to appreciate its artistic quality most distinctly, however, grossly misses the point, for it is precisely in the film's use of sound, in the layering and often deliberately mismatched juxtaposition of sound and image track, that Siodmak's *Phantom Lady* achieves its most notable qualities. *Phantom Lady* advances sound to the primary force that may breach the aesthetic excesses and perversions of Marlow. "Sound effects and silent track without dialogue," as the reviewer for *Variety* noted, "are used to maximum effect to heighten the suspense of the picture."[24] It is also in the use of sound, one might add, that the film's political unconscious affects the surface of the text most forcefully and urges the viewer to recognize the film's historical index.

In direct continuation of his first sound films for UFA, Siodmak's sonic experimentations in *Phantom Lady* primarily aim at severing sounds from their corporeal sources, at disconnecting acoustical events from visual representations. *Phantom Lady* in fact presents this peculiar disjunction of image and sound as the benchmark of modernity and its machines, institutions, and technologies of representation. Twentieth-century modernity, as film and experiential reality, in *Phantom Lady* decenters the unity of body and voice. It dissolves the traditional chains of signification people used in order to position themselves in time and social space. Yet whereas Marlow understands the modern unfixing of organic ties between the acoustical and the visual as a step into an apocalyptic state of inauthenticity, *Phantom Lady* endorses audiovisual disruptions as potential sources of agency and emancipation. The film splits voices from their bodies not only to foreground the constructedness of meaning but also to revoke Marlow's totalitarian coordination of sense perception, his rhetoric of aesthetic heroism and existential authenticity.

Consider, for example, the highly idiosyncratic and, arguably, farcical representation of Henderson's court trial, which grants the film's sound track a curious, albeit temporary, autonomy from the image track. Repeatedly throughout the sequence, rather than picturing those whose voice we hear—jurors, judges, or lawyers, even the accused himself—the camera pans over individual faces in the audience. Even more confusing are the various instances the camera zooms in on only the hand of a court stenographer recording the indictment speeches in shorthand. While the voices of jurisdiction achieve through their very invisibility a kind of heightened intensity, the court's audience is shown as transfixed in mute positions of voyeuristic spectatorship. The juridical system appears as a voice without body, whereas the public in whose name justice is spoken owns a body but no voice. *Phantom Lady* thus presents secular jurisdiction as both at once: as impartial argumentation and as spectacle. When the (invisible) judge proclaims the sentence, a visitor in the auditorium coughs so loudly that most diegetic and all extradiegetic spectators are kept from comprehending the final verdict. It is only by means of a reaction shot showing Kansas's consternation that the film finally discloses the outcome of the trial. Reconfigured into the conventional patterns of hierarchical dependency and mutual reinforcement, images and sounds thus come together again, but the spectator's trust in the unity of representation—the identity of sounds and images—has been irrevocably shattered. Temporarily sundering what conventional practices forge into an imaginary totality, the disjunctive courtroom sequence not only allegorizes the erroneous nature of the verdict—the fact that Henderson's sentence results from blind emotion rather than reasonable insight—but, more important, it questions epistemologies of jurisdiction that overlook the discursive character of truth. Inasmuch as the sequence plays various levels of representation against each other, it attests to the fact that any image of the past, as well as any evaluation of human action, is necessarily steeped in historically specific struggles over the forms, technologies, and contents of representation.

Many other instances in *Phantom Lady* could be cited in which temporary breaches between sounds and images drive a wedge between conventional assumptions about the identity of voice and body. In one of the two show numbers the voice of the Hispanic singer, Estela Monteiro (Aurora Miranda), dominates the sonic plane while the camera focuses on how Kansas exchanges erotic glances with the drummer, Cliff. Chased by Kansas, a hysterical bartender (Andrew Toombes Jr.) dies in a noisy car accident in the space offscreen while the camera shows us the response of Kansas and some pedestrians on the sidewalk. On Kansas's return to her apartment, Inspector Burgess (Thomas Gomez) seems to speak from a void, poised first in the darkness of her room and then with his head hidden behind a lamp shade. And last, but not least, Henderson's warped message on the voice recorder figures as a decisive vehicle for the film's happy ending. Romance here does not result in spite of modern technology but rather through its calculated employment—as if Walter Benjamin had it right after all, and mechanical reproduction indeed possesses the power to bring things closer to each other, spatially as much as humanly.[25]

For Marlow, to be sure, modern technology signifies the root of all evil. Insisting on the authority of the original, the here and now of the genius work, Marlow considers modern machines of reproduction to be catalysts of aesthetic banality; they enable an ominous dominance of *Zivilisation* over *Kultur*. Minus his psychopathology, the figure of Marlow closely follows the formula Nazi entertainment features had developed for the role of male artists. Nazi cinema privileged the representation of male artists involved in physically challenging, heroic genres: sculptors, battle painters, architects, or conductors of explicitly "masculine" music such as Bach and Beethoven.[26] Excessive masculinity, driven to the point of murderous paranoia, is also at the core of Marlow's aesthetic project. Marlow's New York studio, brightly lit and hygienically cleansed of all traces of modern civilization, is populated by a variety of sculptures that clearly recall the monumental work of Nazi artists such as Arno Breker and Joseph Thorak. Like Breker and Thorak, Marlow's art aims at what Nazi-philosopher Ernst Krieck theorized as a "realism of the *Volk*" (völkischer Realism).[27] Similar to the artifacts that dominated the aestheticized public sphere of Nazi Germany, Marlow's massive works hope to ground art in the vitalistic roots of collective life and, in order to do so, not only challenge abstract modernism and bourgeois utilitarianism but also promote the artist to the charismatic "prophet, educator, and *Führer* of his *Volk.*"[28]

Like Goebbels in his 1937 speech, Marlow insists on a fundamental nexus between the aesthetic and the political. Art, according to his view, has an essentially political function in that it shapes human emotions like clay into homogeneous public forms. For Marlow authentic art, just like politics, expresses the will to power and form. It structures corporeal expressions and recuperates what decisionistic theories of the state considered the existential determination of political life. Liberalism's valorization of justice, equality, and freedom thwart the political calling of authentic art. It causes Marlow to launch a double attack on modern life, one against the postaesthetic rule of mass art and diversion and one against liberal democracy and the equalizing rationality of social engineering. Henderson represents what aggravates Marlow most. By attending an entertainment show with an anonymous lady wearing a duplicate of an extravagant designer hat, Henderson, on the one hand, upsets Marlow's call for the aura of genius art.

Figure 22.   Marlow's hands: Franchot Tone (right), with Elisha Cook Jr., in *Phantom Lady*. Courtesy of Filmmuseum Berlin—Deutsche Kinemathek.

On the other hand, renowned—in Kansas's words—as an engineer for his "plans to build model cities, sunlight in every room, children's play yards everywhere for everyone," Henderson embodies in the eyes of Marlow an egalitarian liberal whose utopian commitments deplete the existential ground of the political: the moment of danger and enmity.

Reminiscent of the Austrian silent film classic *Orlacs Hände* (1924, Robert Wiene) and its 1935 MGM remake *Mad Love* (Karl Freund), Marlow's antimodernism is expressed most graphically in the artist's obsession with his own hands. Hands signify for Marlow the putative authenticity that preceded the industrial age of machines and masses. Preoccupied with his own hands, Marlow does not spare his victims lectures on the power of his hands (fig. 22). His speeches attest to the extent to which Marlow's attack on the institutions of social modernity is intimately tied to the desire to kill. Hands organize the chaos and anarchy of existence into stable shapes and meaningful structures for Marlow no matter whether they seek to preserve or to annul life: the aesthete's call for total form and reality control links directly to the killer's mode of reducing complexity through murder. It is fascinating to see, Marlow reflects before strangling Cliff, how hands can "mold beauty out of clay," "trick melody out of a piano keyboard," or bring "life back to a dying child." But it is even more mesmerizing, he continues, to imagine that "the same pair of hands can do inconceivable evil," how they can torture, whip, "even kill." As he promotes the act of murder to the most sophisticated artistic practice, Marlow in a perverse fashion joins the efforts of aesthetic modernism and the twentieth-century avant-garde to burst the boundaries of the aesthetic. Similar to the avant-garde, Marlow hopes to restore a more comprehensive notion of culture by means of a one-sided explosion of the aesthetic. Yet in simply replacing one form of putative excess (technology, democracy) with another (monumental art), Marlow drives both art and politics beyond any fact, code, or value. Prioritizing form radically over norm, he elevates death to the ultimate telos of all human action, for it is solely in death that life may adhere to the desired order and simplicity that fuel Marlow's discontent with modern civilization in the first place.

How modern, then, we must ask, is Marlow's antimodernism? To what extent does his aesthetic reduction of modern contingency and his search for moments of intensive life outside of the banality of bourgeois everydayness recall certain strains within aesthetic modernism itself that culminated in fascism? It is important to note in this context that Marlow himself appropriates toward the end of the film the split between voice and body that in previous passages of *Phantom Lady* signified the impact of modernity on everyday experience. As if temporarily slipping into the role of the film's director, Marlow seems to manipulate for his own purposes what the film at other moments employed in order to unmask Marlow's jargon of authenticity. After Marlow and Kansas finally discover the phantom lady, Marlow—panicked by the unraveling of the case—pretends to call Inspector Burgess and inform him about Henderson's innocence. To do so, he positions himself behind the windowpane of a gas station, tinkering with a public telephone without properly dialing. The camera alternates between Kansas's point of view, who is situated in the car outside and observes Marlow's gestures as if projected onto a big screen, and shots taken from the inside, allowing the spectator to know what Kansas doesn't know, namely, that Marlow's thumb has interrupted the connection. Faking a conversation, then, Marlow not only redresses himself as a director-actor who himself manipulates the terms of representation, but he also makes deliberate use of the peculiarly modern assimilation of the body to technology and the concomitant sundering of images and sounds. At the brink of a ruinous breakdown, Marlow selectively embraces technological modernity in order to warrant the future success of his antimodernist stance, his fight against the values of political liberalism and modern mass society.

Siodmak's *Phantom Lady* recognizes lack and fragmentation—corporeal absence and mechanical duplication, the separation of voice and body—as the modern hallmark of subjectivity and human reciprocity. Instead of signifying an ominous intrusion of the uncanny, the splitting of sounds and sights can offer antidotes to Marlow's deadly aesthetics of closure, uniqueness, and total presence. The gas station sequence, in this sense, testifies to the contradictory ways in which Marlow—like his fascist predecessors in 1930s and 1940s Europe—seeks to incorporate modern tools and experiences into a vitalistic rejection of civil society and modern liberalism. Switching back and forth between Kansas's space of viewership and Marlow's cinema of simulated speech, camera and editing expose Marlow as a skillful operator of the modern decentering of corporeal identity and sense perception but also as a dexterous forger of authenticity and existential resolution. Marlow's mise-en-scène, as seen by Kansas, is a counterfeit in multiple ways. What in Kansas's perspective appears to be a silent cinema generating powerful sounds of redemption is revealed by the film's alternating shots as a sound cinema producing vicious silence. What Kansas perceives as a homogeneous scene of incorporation and interiority is exposed as an actual site of heterogeneity and exteriority. Marlow may aspire to restore the aura of artistic genius and political authority, but what Marlow considers authentic expressions of the unified self are nothing other than the products of special effects and technologies of mediation. Marlow—like fascist modernism—makes use of modern machines to protect himself from recognition and self-recognition. He embraces technology and mechanical reproduction not in order to expand experience and connect nonidentical particulars but to project his own lack as trauma, scar, silence, and death onto the other.

SPEAK OR DIE!

Victorious in its very failure, Henderson's Dictaphone in *Phantom Lady* is no stranger to film noir. Whether they transmit, record, or amplify linguistic expressions, voice machines abound in Hollywood's dark cinema. They stitch narratives together, perforate the visible space, collapse different temporal registers, and often draw protagonists as much as viewers into a compelling dialectic of presence and absence. Film noir's voice machines—

telephones, Dictaphones, answering machines—feature speech as a narrative agent. They may communicate expressions of both individual self-assertion and human frailty, the desire to control narrative and diegesis as much as the failure to attain a space of one's own. In Billy Wilder's *Double Indemnity* (1944), Walter Neff's (Fred MacMurray) voice recorder emerges as a conduit of cinematic storytelling, an imaginary father figure authoritatively capturing a dying man's confession. Anatole Litvak's *Sorry, Wrong Number* (1948), by contrast, presents telephones as media administering death and thus ending all stories. "In the tangled network of a great city," titles at the film's opening explain, "the telephone is the unseen link between a million lives. . . . It is the servant of our common needs, the confidant of our inmost secrets . . . life and happiness wait upon its ring . . . and horror . . . and loneliness . . . and death." Voice machines in film noir make human speech transcend given boundaries between public and private, past and present, here and there. In so many cases the recorded voice in film noir wants to realign the borders of subjectivity. It employs speech as a tool to encroach on the other but also to articulate an existential need for recognition and self-preservation. In the paranoid universe of film noir, prosthetic speech is often marked and marred by strategic reason. You either speak or die, even if speaking may often result in death itself.

The telephones, Dictaphones, and prosthetic voices of film noir are part of the genre's exploration of what Chion calls "on-the-air" sound, of sonic possibilities that are not subjected to the "natural" principles of sound production: "Sometimes we hear them in sound close-up—clear and sharp, as if the film's loudspeaker were directly plugged into the radio, telephone, or phonograph depicted on the screen. At the other extreme they can be identified in the setting by acoustical traits to produce an effect of distancing, reverb, and the particular tone color of the speakers or whatever their onscreen source is. Between these two cases lie infinite degrees of variation." [29] On-the-air sounds such as the ones generated by Henderson's voice recorder fold different spatial and temporal layers into one textual representation. Although normally situated in a scene's real time, on-the-air sounds cross the boundaries of cinematic space and blur the zones of the onscreen, offscreen, and nondiegetic. Many noir thrillers surely exploit this mechanical unfastening of speech and corporeal source primarily to extend impressions of terror and anxiety; the splitting of body and voice encodes an uncanny return of something that should have remained hidden. [30] More generally speaking, however, film noir's on-the-air sounds can be seen as metonymies for the ways in which Hollywood cinema of the 1940s explored the narrative power of embodied voice-offs or even disembodied voice-overs. In stark contrast to Nazi cinema's phobic containment of sound and source within the visible, film noir is driven by an often-unresolved dialectic between sonic incorporation and disembodiment. As it depicts a world of murderous conflicts and never-ending trials, film noir presents the sounds and sights of cinematic representation in a situation of ceaseless struggle as well. Material experiences thus reappear as formal challenges, as antagonisms that potentially reveal the heterogeneous nature of the film medium.

Lacanian psychoanalysis has emphasized in many ways the pathological origins of human language. According to Lacan the symbolic is a realm of lack and loss. To speak means to depart from the undivided pleasures of the imaginary and forsake the original totality of the maternal. Whether they are prosthetic or not, film noir's voices evidence a curious variation—and inversion—of this apocalyptic figuration of language. For dominant voices in film noir speak over or against the image track to armor the human (and mostly male) body against possible pathologies. Film noir is driven by an existential necessity to speak, a relentless desire for the symbolic. Be they diegetically anchored or not, the various voices of film noir not only reveal what is inaccessible to the image track, but they also speak up against the visible in order to convert drastic circumstances into symbolic orders. The voices of film noir speak, as Kaja Silverman puts it, "in extremis."[31] As disembodied voice-overs they embrace narration as a last straw in the hope of casting the factual disarray of material experience into more manageable spatial and temporal structures. Film noir's protagonists speak in the performative. Their voices embrace speech as a medium that defines and reorganizes social relationships.

The stylized vocophilia and narrative obsession of film noir, it has often been pointed out, attests to the literary origins of the genre, its indebtedness to the hard-boiled stories of Cain, Chandler, and Woolrich. Diegetic and nondiegetic speech in film noir, one might add, espouses secondary orality—speech based on the paragon of the written[32]—as a source of meaning and orientation. More important to our present purposes, however, is the antagonistic and unreconciled character of film noir's embodied and disembodied voices. Film noir pictures speech as a realm of conflict and struggle, a realm in which neither meaning nor understanding is ever a given. Unlike the Nazi ideologues of biocentric dialogue, film noir presents the symbolic as an arena of discord and radical contingency. Speech is not natural; it is a product of articulation and hence deeply implicated in the individual's struggle to survive, to overcome fate and hostility. Voice machines in film noir in many respects amplify this view of human language as being articulated and contested. Telephones, for instance, in allowing communication from a distance, can work both as instruments of individual empowerment as much as of cruel subjection. As Amy Lawrence has argued with regard to women's use of phones in 1940s cinema, "To some extent the telephone empowers women, enabling them to combine their piecemeal knowledge and find out what is going on in the separate world of men."[33] Phone communications can puncture woman's confinement in the bourgeois home and thus disrupt the excessive diegeticization of women in dominant Hollywood cinema. At the same time, however, the telephone in film noir—as in Litvak's *Sorry, Wrong Number*—can also indicate a fatal lack of physical and intellectual control. Whether situated in the onscreen, the offscreen, or the extradiegetic, film noir's telephones accentuate the negotiated character of speech and signification. Part of film noir's inventory of on-the-air sounds, phones help broadcast the unfixity of meaning as the central feature of modern experience.

Feminist critics, with solid arguments and abundant examples, have theorized the use of sound in film noir as merely a split and deeply gendered project of unfixing the dominant codes of classical cinema. Far from rendering male authority problematic, the commanding voices in film noir, according to critics such as Kaja Silverman and Amy Lawrence, fortify the male subject against his own losses—at the cost of the female's body and articulation. Woman is spoken from the position of the sexual other. In particular the embodied male voice-over in films such as *Double Indemnity*, *Lady from Shanghai* (1947, Orson Welles), *Out of the Past* (1947, Jacques Tourneur), *D.O.A.* (1950, Rudolf Maté), and *Sunset Boulevard* (1950, Billy Wilder) functions like "a precarious hook on which to hang the phallus."[34] Film noir's women either speak too much and therefore need to be silenced by the intervention of the male voice, or they speak too little and must be brought to speech; yet once they open their mouths they are not really allowed to say anything. When women accede to the privilege of language at all, they do so only to become situated as dependent wives in the domestic sphere. Film noir thus projects male lack and paranoia—that which he cannot tolerate in himself—onto the female other as deformation, fragmentation, and impediment. As Silverman summarizes: "[T]he female voice, like the female body, is more frequently obliged to display than to conceal lack—to protect the male subject from knowledge of his own castration."[35] In the dark thrillers of the 1940s, illusions of male integrity and control are in fact reconstituted by going to the extreme—by extracting a scream from the female body. In accord with dominant practices women's voices are contained and excessively synchronized within the diegesis, whereas the male voice is allowed to wander offscreen into exterior positions of narrative authority and self-assertion.

Amy Lawrence, in *Echo and Narcissus,* has extended this analysis to Robert Siodmak's Gothic thriller *The Spiral Staircase.* The muteness of the film's character Helen (Dorothy McGuire) is for Lawrence "a lack she can overcome, but she can only do so within the narrative by assuming her approved social role as 'woman'—helpless, grateful, and dependent. The engine driving the narrative and providing the suspense is whether or not Helen will recover her ability to speak in time to save herself from the unseen killer who stalks her."[36] Although Lawrence's analysis is important and insightful, it underestimates the extent to which *The Spiral Staircase* itself addresses the role of cinema as a compensatory mechanism of male projection, an audiovisual machine that pits male empowerment against female subjugation. Moreover, Lawrence strangely elides the other ideological and highly contemporaneous subtext that drives *The Spiral Staircase.* In contrast to Ethel Lina White's original novel of 1941, entitled *Some Must Watch,* Siodmak's film presents the killer as an obsessed zoologist, Professor Albert Warren (George Brent), whose Darwinist quest for authenticity and social hygiene is fueled by Nazi rhetoric. Engineering words that speak over the killer's resolute appropriation of the imaginary, *The Spiral Staircase* allows Helen to speak so as to drive a wedge through Warren's existential quest for a vigorous and unified body politic. Helen's final ascent to language may qualify her indeed, as Lawrence suggests, for new domestic tasks, but at closer inspection it also emphasizes the performative aspects of speech and modern identity, as well as the noncoercive power of language to connect people. Helen's words in the last sequence matter because they posit language and meaning as contested. Speaking into a phone, her recuperated voice opposes Warren's fascist imaginary. The figuration of speech and muteness in Siodmak's thriller *The Spiral Staircase,* which according to one reviewer had the power to elicit from audiences "frequent spasms of nervous giggling and . . . audible, breathless sighs,"[37] therefore deserves closer scrutiny.

DIALING THE RIGHT NUMBER

Produced by Dore Schary for RKO and Selznick Productions, and shot in the summer of 1945, Siodmak's *The Spiral Staircase* explores the curious conjunction of existentialism, vitalism, and the aesthetics of horror. Similar to *Phantom Lady,* the film contains numerous references to the cinematic apparatus, to spectatorship, and to the work of special effects. Drawing on the remarkable success of earlier Hollywood gothics such as *Wuthering Heights* (1939, William Wyler) and *Rebecca* (1940, Alfred Hitchcock), *The Spiral Staircase* uses a late-Victorian setting to stage nothing less than a diegetic competition over cinema's production of sights and sounds—its capacity either to make bodies talk or to condemn them to silence. Set in a small town in New England in 1906, a time ostensibly characterized by many social and technological transformations, *The Spiral Staircase* tells the story of a zoologist who kills a series of young women because they do not match his standards of physical perfection and natural beauty. Son of a deceased big-game hunter, the socially respected Professor Warren lives together with his bed-ridden stepmother (Ethel Barrymore) and his dandy half brother, Steve (Gordon Oliver), in a mansion at the edge of town. Professor Warren's project of social hygiene leads him to hunt down Helen, his gullible servant who has become mute after having witnessed the death of her parents in a fire. All characters who populate the house—including Dr. Parry (Kent Smith), who seeks to heal Helen from what he considers her feminine hysteria—emerge at various times as the possible killer. Reminiscent of Hitchcock and Lang, Siodmak withholds essential information from the spectator's perception by means of strong narrative interventions. It is only in the film's final minutes that the camera reveals the true identity of the strangler. In the last sequence Mrs. Warren leaves her bed for the first and only time in the film in order to rescue Helen from her own stepson as she shoots the psychopathic professor on the mansion's spiral staircase.

Contrary to Victorian ideology, *The Spiral Staircase* depicts the domestic as a space not of security and refuge but of terror and anxiety. The mansion's interior resembles "a panopticum, a space of total control over all movements." [38] No one here can ever be by himself or herself. Any bourgeois notion of intimacy is inaccessible. Abundant mirrors seem to expand the spatial configurations, yet they do not yield any sense of physical liberation. Stuffed with remnants of the past, the mansion leaves no real room for residing in the present. Although the many animal trophies attest to the activism of the dead family patriarch, their crammed display casts paralyzing shadows on the present generation. Connecting the three different floors on which the narrative unfolds, the staircase intensifies the manor's fatalistic materiality. It dictates physical movements, punctures spatial borders, and thus overwhelms protagonists and viewers alike with impressions of inevitability. We see characters moving up and down but failing to escape their fate. No one in the film seems able to take flight from this flight of stairs. Initially, space here does not emerge, in Michel de Certeau's words, as "practiced place."[39] Only in the final sequence do the film's protagonists really appropriate the house as a space of the living and repossess the staircase as a location of agency and articulation. Poised at the very top of the staircase, the dying Mrs. Warren triggers the emancipation of the present from the grasp of the past. Her intervention ends Professor Warren's efforts to define history as nature and emplace human bodies in a fixed geography of power. Her gunshot discontinues the mansion's mythical order and reclaims the possibility of practiced place and historical experience.

True to what Mary Ann Doane has analyzed in her study of the woman's film of the 1940s, *The Spiral Staircase* introduces Helen as enthralled by specular pleasure, an excessive desire for desire for which the film's subsequent narrative will provide ample punishment.[40] The narrative opens in the town's improvised movie theater—lodged in the lobby of a hotel—with the showing of the silent film *The Kiss,* a gripping melodrama accompanied by a pianist playing dramatic Beethoven pieces. Unlike White's novel, which presented Helen as a by-no-means-mute simpleton who "could rarely afford a seat at the Pictures,"[41] *The Spiral Staircase* introduces its female protagonist as a cinephile intensely engrossed in scopic pleasure. Siodmak's editing, however, leaves little doubt that Helen's innocent act of viewing is more ambivalent than it may seem, as the film parallels the action on the screen with the film's first murder scene, which takes place right above the lobby on the hotel's second floor. The camera awkwardly tilts from the audience up to the ceiling, fades out and then in again in order to carry the viewer into the interior of a hotel room. At this point it is only the continuous, although now muffled, accompanist's music that warrants a sense of spatial continuity between the two locales, the site of melodramatic entertainment and the scene of psychopathic murder. Interestingly enough, the image of Helen's scopic bliss vis-à-vis *The Kiss* is replicated by a macro shot focusing on the eye of the murderer, who hides in a closet waiting to strangle the room's disabled tenant. Increasingly blurring the boundaries between diegetic fiction and diegetic reality, the subsequent shots suture both lines of action, the one on the screen in the hotel lobby and the murder in the hotel room, into one totality, authorized as it were by Helen's desire for distraction. What we see through her eyes on the screen of the makeshift theater in fact substitutes for what Siodmak at this point still wants to withhold from the spectator: the heroine's dramatic suicide in *The Kiss* coincides with the death of the strangler's victim upstairs, an act of murder relegated to offscreen space in order to prolong the tension.

The setting of this opening sequence brings to mind historical descriptions of female spectatorship in early cinema:

The high percentage of women in early film audiences was in fact perceived as an alarming social phenomenon, one which confirmed the
breakdown of traditional values elsewhere evidenced by the declining
birthrate, the rising marriage age, and the influx of women into the industrial labor force. The presence of a female audience, in other words,
not only represented a threat to traditional divisions between public
and private, cultural and domestic spheres; it represented a threat to the
maintenance of social legitimacy, to the distinctions preserving tradi-
tionally defined male and female gender roles and responsibilities.[42]

Emotionally captivated by the death onscreen, Helen, in the opening sequence, seems to pose a threat to traditional definitions of social spheres.
Her presence in a newly emerging public sphere qualifies her as a perfect
future victim. Helen's excessive spectatorship, on the one hand, magnifies
her muteness, which in the eye of the murderer justifies her elimination.
On the other hand, perverse though it may seem, Helen's fascination with
the cinematic apparatus strangely aligns her with the killer himself, whose
sadistic act of looking seems to constitute nothing other than the flipside of
Helen's own impassioned voyeurism. Invading the traditional lifeworld of
the town, the cinema of the opening sequence thus not only signifies the
controversial and hardly controllable proliferation of urban modernity and
mass entertainment, but it is also shown as implicated in a dramatic struggle
over the terms of perception, over scopic pleasure, control and mastery. Far
from implying that cinematic spectatorship per se exhibits a natural tendency toward a delight in the art of murder, the opening shots instead expose the way Warren's politics of social hygiene rely on a manipulation of
the cinematic apparatus and its peculiar pleasures. These shots draw attention to the way Warren—temporarily in control over the imaginary and
its effects on the spectator—blends filmic and nonfilmic reality and, hence,
appropriates the special effect that is cinema in order to pursue his antimodernist vitalism. Helen, it becomes clear in this opening sequence, will
need to overcome her speechlessness, and, by implication, her voyeuristic
desire for silent images, to survive Warren's aesthetics of horror.

Immoderate voyeurism and narcissistic pleasure, according to the narrative logic of *The Spiral Staircase,* feed into Professor Warren's sadistic mode
of perception, the imaging of terror in the iris of the killer's eye. In the view
of the vitalist who claims that "[t]here is no room in the world for imper-
fection," pleasurable looks signify a state of degeneracy: those who simply
look and even derive pleasure from it, those, moreover, who hope to fulfill
their desire amid the feminized institutions of twentieth-century mass distraction, demonstrate a form of weakness that fails to meet the demands of

Warren's Nietzschean anthropology. Interestingly enough, the film at crucial moments builds Warren's aesthetics of horror right into the film's system of representation itself only, as I will argue in a moment, to displace it in the end with a second and alternative perspective. The extent to which the film draws the viewer into Warren's sadistic point of view is best exemplified in the film's cinematographically most exciting sequence. In this scene we see Helen climbing the stairs to the mansion's second floor, in a shot that is later revealed as a reflection in a big mirror located in the middle of the staircase. When Helen stops in front of this mirror, looks intensely at herself, and finally imitates a person able to speak, the camera dollies back along the railing on the second floor until it brings into view the leg of a silent observer hiding behind a statue. The next shot shows us the wide eye of this secret onlooker, an eye in which we behold Helen's own image in the mirror. Literally defaced in the course of this double process of reflection, however, Helen now appears without a mouth. Warren's cinema of horror incorporates Helen's lack of speech as a bodily feature. It projects the female as a mutilated body, as wounded by anatomical deficiency.

Aside from the surrealist iconography, what is remarkable about this shot sequence is the way in which seemingly innocent pleasures of looking are forged into sadistic scenarios while overtly objective points of view are uncovered as the deranged perspective of a killer. Truly provocative, this sequence allows the killer's Darwinism to gain control over the movements of the cinematographic apparatus. What at first seems like a surprisingly arbitrary backward track of the camera, at closer inspection betrays the extent to which the killer aspires to dominate the film's means of representation itself. Momentarily elevating the psychopathic killer to a tyrant of the imaginary who infuses realistic images with violent fantasies, the film thus seduces its viewers into rather counterintuitive spectator positions as if to threaten them with the same kind of violence that strikes out against the mute onlooker Helen herself.

"What a pity," Professor Warren later lectures Helen while putting on his gloves in order to kill her, "my father didn't see me become strong. . . . He would have admired me for what I am going to do." To live up to his father's notion of what it means to be a man, Warren fortifies his masculine identity through the murderous silencing of women: not hunting but the obliteration of what he considers degenerate vitality constitutes the professor's mode of proving his manliness. Warren's male integrity, as Silverman has written in a different context, "is established through the projection onto woman of the lack he cannot tolerate in himself."[43] By associating Warren's project of male empowerment at various points with special ef-

fects, the film—similar to *Phantom Lady*—unmasks the professor's naturalism as ideology and self-deception. Warren's quest for wholeness,
toughness, and immediacy realizes itself solely through the mediation of
modern machines of projection, just like his crusade for intensity and presence is always mediated through the image of the past, a belated Oedipal
contest with his deceased father.

Furthermore, in rendering the old matriarch, Mrs. Warren, not only as
her son's antipode but also as the ultimately victorious competitor over the
terms of representation, *The Spiral Staircase* counteracts Warren's aesthetics of horror. Similar to Professor Warren, Mrs. Warren seems to have
privileged access to the mechanisms that inform the very making of the
film *The Spiral Staircase*. Although bound to her bed, she sees in her
dreams what we have seen earlier as part of the dramatic action and is
therefore able to warn Helen about the murderer's imminent attack. Like
the cinema in the opening sequence, Mrs. Warren's psychic anticipations
interpret the film's actual story line. In a curious sequence reminiscent of
E. T. A. Hoffmann's story *The Sand-Man*, Mrs. Warren hides a gun from
Helen under a piece of cloth on her bedside table. A second shot, however,
presents the image of a long tube, introduced by the old lady as her "spectacle case," even though in the final sequence this object will transmogrify
back into a revolver and permit the rescue of Helen from the murderous
hands of Professor Warren. This curious proximity between instruments
of intensified perception and instruments of shooting, as well as Mrs. Warren's magician-like authority over their representation and mutual substitution, is highly instructive. It demonstrates the extent to which *The Spiral Staircase* is not only about the perverse fantasy of a psychopathic killer
and his sadistic co-optation of the cinematic apparatus but also, and more
important, about the need to make use of cinema to redeem the individual
from Warren's vitalist aesthetics of horror. Instead of killing what a fascist
notion of natural perfection deems worthy of extermination, Mrs. Warren's spectacle-gun looks and shoots to protect the integrity of human life
against all dictates of "nature" and family lineage.

It is worth recalling at this point the rather mysterious opening shot of
The Spiral Staircase, which provides a seemingly nondiegetic background
for the credit scroll. The shot pictures the spiral staircase from a vertical
overhead perspective. A woman, struck by panic, is moving along the wall
in search of a way to escape something horrific (fig. 23). This title sequence
presents a disturbing enigma that of course foreshadows the final showdown involving Helen, Professor Warren, and Mrs. Warren on the old
mansion's staircase, the showdown that results in Helen's rescue from the

killer, Professor Warren's death, and Mrs. Warren's successive collapse from exhaustion. Significantly, it is only in the context of this later sequence that we learn more about the actual origin of the enigmatic opening shot as it becomes clear that the woman's horror was rendered through the eyes of Mrs. Warren, who in order to shoot her stepson in the final sequence takes position precisely at the top of the staircase. Interestingly enough, however, the actual shot of the opening does not appear as such in the later sequence. What we see in the credit sequence might therefore be best understood not simply as a window on coming events but rather as one of Mrs. Warren's visionary dreams. In retrospectively authorizing the opening perspective as Mrs. Warren's, the film establishes the old matriarch as the actual anchor of the entire narrative. Read from the perspective of the ending, the credit shot of the beginning introduces the Ethel Barrymore character as the legitimate authority over the diegetic process. In so doing the film endorses Mrs. Warren's redemptive intervention for the sake of both Helen and the cinematic apparatus as its own project. It valorizes Mrs. Warren's magic humanism over the professor's fascist cinema of incorporation and projective horror.

According to the activist-vitalist worldview, which Professor Warren shares with Nazi ideologues, modern civilization and bourgeois society confine the stream of elemental life. The rule of liberal democracy and bourgeois culture, following this position, hampers access to the existentially relevant layers of being. For any authentic being can manifest itself solely in the exceptional clearing of the will to power, in the aesthetico-political intensity of unregulated moments of danger. In its often-precarious amalgamation with the nineteenth-century tradition of biological naturalism, German vitalists embraced the category of the folk, of ethnic and racial identity, in order to warrant the desired community that any Nietzschean emphasis on heroic individuality may potentially thwart. Conservative revolutionaries of the interwar period established folkhood as a quasi-natural foundation of individual strength and existential meaning. It is only through identification with the racially homogeneous body politic that the individual can attain individuality in the first place and draw from the wellspring of community. Biology, in this view, not only becomes destiny, but it suggests strategies of social hygiene that annihilate all those who threaten communal identity through difference and otherness.

A film that delivers the present from the rule of the past, Siodmak's *The Spiral Staircase* testifies to the fact that the merging of biology and history, instead of shaping a new community, ultimately results in self-destruction. Professor Warren's ideology of physical perfection defines community neg-

Figure 23.   Defeating the dark: Dorothy McGuire in Robert Siodmak's *The Spiral Staircase* (1946). Courtesy of Filmmuseum Berlin—Deutsche Kinemathek.

atively: through the isolation and annihilation of "enemies." Driven by projective anxieties, he scapegoats whoever bears any sign of difference. He silences the other in order to constitute his own voice and suppress whatever could be other in himself. Warren's position thus becomes that of a radical solipsist, encapsulated in megalomaniac fantasies of power and reality control. True communal experiences, on the other hand, according to the narrative of *The Spiral Staircase,* reside with those who know how to inhabit modern life in ways that eschew Warren's many phobias and projections. In particular, Helen's rediscovery of speech during the climactic moments, first articulated in the form of a scream and then practiced on the telephone, manifests the films' simultaneous endorsement of technological *and* social modernity most graphically. Whereas telephones in Curtis Bernhardt's *The Tunnel* signify the male's fear of flowing into dissipation, in *The Spiral Staircase* they feature the imbricatedness of modern subjectivity as a source of meaning and agency. Helen's entry into language is not simply, as Lawrence seems to suggest, a new trauma, one that holds the female to the unity of sight and sound so as to discipline her body. Instead, in embracing the prosthetic device of the telephone, Helen's very first words aspire to transgress the boundaries of visible space and thus speak over and against Warren's cinema of incorporation. Awakening to language as an immediate expert in technological sound transmission, Helen embraces the migratory potential of the human voice—communicative reason—as a catalyst of redemption.

The film's final image is that of Helen in the mansion's telephone room as she calls Dr. Parry and whispers the number "189" into the apparatus (fig. 24). The camera then tracks out of the room, leaving the viewer with a shot of the phone's mouthpiece and of its elongated shadow on the wall. The shot hails speech technologies and on-the-air sounds as antidotes to the rendering of history as nature and biology. In the final analysis it is not simply the capacity to speak that breaks the spell of Warren's vitalism but rather the use of modern machines that can liquefy traditional boundaries, unfix the essentialist identification of body and voice, and bring people closer to each other—both spatially and humanly. While Warren aspires to contain the body in the image so as to control social space and eliminate the other, prosthetic speech secures an experience of community and solidarity that transforms modern space into practiced place.

HORROR'S HORROR

The newsmagazine *Time,* in its mainly positive review of *The Spiral Staircase,* wrote in February 1946 that "Siodmak is no lover of heavy horror, but the West Coast has him typed. He is now regarded with considerable awe by the Hollywood oracles as 'the new master of suspense.'"[44] On its first release in postwar Germany in January 1948, *The Spiral Staircase* received much less favorable reviews. Most German critics considered the film not an example of masterful suspense but of cheap entertainment and moral

Figure 24. Speak or die: Dorothy McGuire in *The Spiral Staircase*. Courtesy of Filmmuseum Berlin—Deutsche Kinemathek.

perversion. *Die Welt* discouraged sensible individuals from watching the film unless they hungered for the "torture of real thrill."[45] *Der Abend* and *Der Tagesspiegel* censured the film as an absurd amalgamation of colportage and bogus psychotherapy, a typically American invitation to moral corruption.[46] Whether Protestant or Catholic, the influential Christian organs of film criticism tried to persuade their constituencies not to attend any viewing at all. Although the Catholic bulletin *Filmdienst der Jugend* at least praised Nicholas Musuraca's cinematography,[47] *Evangelischer Film-Beobachter* considered *The Spiral Staircase* detrimental to the task of reconstructing German culture after Hitler: "Perhaps Americans need someone who shreds their nerves every once in a while. We, however, need our nerves; we have enough behind us and probably also enough ahead of us. Please spare us this kind of torture of our nerves. Let us as Christians avoid such import goods."[48]

The moralizing anti-Americanism of the Christian press found remarkable echoes on the left. In a lengthy essay written for *Tägliche Rundschau Berlin,* Hans Ulrich Eylau charged *The Spiral Staircase* with tastelessness and kitsch. The film, for Eylau, represented a typical expression of Hollywood imperialism and aesthetic banality. Germans, Eylau argued, have experienced enough terror and eliminationism during the Nazi period. They do not need Hollywood in order to confront their own murderous past as film and fiction. "Whoever as a victor of a war waged in the name of ethical principles, assumes the responsibility of reeducating and spiritually reshaping the Germans, should be able to recognize that murder films are not exactly an appropriate instrument to eradicate fascistic convictions."[49] In Eylau's view commercial Hollywood exports such as *The Spiral Staircase* rekindle fascism in postfascist Germany. They take German history away from the Germans and in so doing obstruct any authentic reformulation of German identity after the Nazis (fig. 25).

The hostile response to Siodmak's *The Spiral Staircase* in postwar Germany exemplifies a double process of displacement characteristic of German film culture in the 1940s and 1950s. It brings to view both the postwar failure to address the texts and meanings produced by Hitler refugees in Hollywood exile and the unwillingness to see in contemporary American film noir more than simply a harbinger of deviance and corruption. Throughout the late 1940s and 1950s German reviewers spoke of Siodmak vaguely as a director who had once left his homeland to become a Hollywood star, as an uprooted wanderer between the worlds, as an artist German audiences might still recall from Weimar days. But as if driven by some secret agreement, these reviewers categorically refused to mention the fact of Siodmak's exile and forced displacement in their respective accounts. Although German entertainment features of the 1940s and 1950s drew in large measure on the stars, directors, technicians, and generic formulas of the Nazi period, dominant discourses dehistoricized the paths of exile filmmakers by comparing their fortunes to those of prodigal sons and

Figure 25.   Pleasure or perversion? Poster for the German-language release of
The Spiral Staircase. Courtesy of Filmmuseum Berlin—Deutsche Kinemathek.

restless Ahasvers. Even more so than in the arena of literary expressions, German postwar cinema rendered the experience of exile taboo—it reminded one too vividly of what one was eager to forget. If reviewers mentioned the names of Siodmak, Bernhardt, Lang, Sirk, or Wilder at all, they did so either in seemingly neutralizing terms or, alternatively, to decry the extent to which Hollywood imports eroded the reconstructive mission of postwar German cinema.

Although film noir quickly entered the scenes of postwar German film culture, it failed to muster responses similar to the ones of contemporary French critics. Unlike their counterparts in France, German reviewers of the time rarely addressed the formal departures of Hollywood's dark cinema. Nor did they perceive these films as symptoms of crucial transformations in Hollywood studio filmmaking and American society. Film noir, in the eyes of German critics, attested to the inauthenticity of American mass culture, a claim that customarily included the work of German exile directors such as Lang, Siodmak, and Wilder. Siodmak's American productions, as Prümm reports, "were seen as sensationalist blockbusters, as part of a cinema that sought to overwhelm the viewer emotionally and lacked any moral foundation or clear-cut message."[50] Whereas Siodmak's best films of the mid-1940s questioned representations of history as nature and of identity as essentially unified, postwar German critics and audiences alike experienced any view of history as contingent—and hence constructible—as the greatest of all terrors. As a specialist in cultural transformation and redress, Siodmak and his dark films of the 1940s in fact threatened to spoil Germany's postwar quest for unquestioned traditions and transcendental securities. Deploring the growing influence of American mass culture on postwar Germany, middle-class audiences in particular rejected films such as *The Spiral Staircase* as debased because the majority of moviegoers were disinclined to recognize a cinema that interrupted narratives of continuity and explored horror's horror.

In spite of such anti-American resentments, however, German film culture in the immediate postwar era in many respects shied away from the outright fantasies of Hollywood competition and confrontation that had driven German filmmaking throughout the Weimar and Nazi era. After the end of World War II the Motion Picture Export Association of America (MPEAA), with the help of the U.S. State Department, inaugurated a number of regulations that granted Hollywood's major studios virtually unrestricted access to the ravaged German film market. Americans started to screen their films to German audiences as early as the summer of 1945. Unlike their Soviet counterparts they did not even hesitate to release American motion pictures without adding German subtitles or dubbing. Yet although original U.S. policies—implemented with the help of film émigrés such as Erich Pommer[51] and Billy Wilder[52]—conceived of American film as a powerful tool of moral and political reeducation, the Western zones of occupied Germany quickly emerged as a welcome dumping ground for all kinds of second-rate Hollywood fare.[53] German audiences before long rejected this ideological fusion of U.S. politics and export business. Once it was perceived as being directly associated with the directives of military occupation, the interwar fascination of Germans with Hollywood began to fade and to make way for a reprise of prewar German favorites—homemade musicals, glamour films, and comedies. But even when German spectators in 1946 started to rail against the then exclusive presence of American films in the U.S. zone, they articulated their appetite for domestic films less in terms of a clamor for national self-assertion than—turning "American" arguments against their American conquerors—by demanding freedom of consumer choice.[54] In face of a situation in which U.S. occupational policies had more or less eliminated the possibility of any German head-on confrontation, West German audiences in the late 1940s endorsed the vision of a peaceful coexistence of American and German products as the order of the day.

Beginning in 1948 (the year Siodmak's *The Spiral Staircase* opened in German theaters), West Germany started to develop a relatively viable film industry that relied heavily on former UFA directors, stars, and technicians and excelled in traditional genre films. "This domestic industry," as Thomas Elsaesser notes, "concentrated on the home market, and calculated its topics as well as its budgets accordingly." [55] In spite of Hollywood's postwar thrust into German territory, homemade genre films swiftly reclaimed the domestic market as they accomplished stunning box office returns. But in contrast to Nazi film policies, West German producers and film officials around 1950 had little ambition to build an industry that could really compete with Hollywood on a large scale; too many feared the social and cultural effects associated with any kind of cinematic cosmopolitanism. Dominant genres such as the *Heimatfilm* instead emphasized the timeless integrity of rural countrysides and local vernaculars. They glorified the aura of traditional lifeworlds so as to correct the putative emasculation of German men that had been caused by both the loss of the war and the presence of enemy soldiers on German territory. [56] In a climate of apolitical withdrawal and public amnesia these films promised spiritual regeneration through a rigorous reconstruction of the patriarchal family. As they engaged the viewer on a double front against what was seen as a self-destructive past and an increasingly boundless present, German films of the immediate postwar era articulated acute anxieties about the modern so as to fortify traditional boundaries and moral codes. In the *Heimatfilm*, in particular, "untouched nature replace[d] ruined cities, church bells resound[ed] instead of ubiquitous jackhammers, quaint panel houses offer[ed] a hominess the city's ugly and quickly erected concrete edifices could not." [57] Even though a good number of West German films of the 1950s incorporated noir elements, one can hardly imagine a cinema farther away from the lonely streets and fragmented spaces, from the broken dreams and shredded identities of American film noir than the German homeland cinema of the postwar era.

In spite of the escapist designs of postwar German cinema and the antagonistic response to his film noirs in the early 1950s, however, Siodmak left Hollywood in 1951 to return to Europe and, in 1955, to reinsert himself into the West German film industry. Siodmak could have given German postwar cinema a new voice, a formal language that would have spoken up against the postcard panoramas of 1950s feature films. But with the exception of

Die Ratten (The rats, 1955), *Nachts, wenn der Teufel kam* (The Devil strikes at midnight, 1957), and—arguably—*Dorothea Angermann* (1958), Siodmak's second German career remained one of unfulfilled promises and aborted ventures, a period of mere industriousness that ended in Siodmak's final retirement in Ascona, Switzerland, during the 1960s. To be sure, *The Devil Strikes at Midnight* did win more or less every award German cinema had to offer in the late 1950s; the *Süddeutsche Zeitung* hailed this tale about sexual murder in murderous Nazi Germany as an "oasis in the vast desert of formal boredom." [58] And both *The Rats* and *Dorothea Angermann*, similar to *The Devil Strikes at Midnight*, alluded to American film noir in order to picture West German society as a dystopian space of repression and displacement haunted by a past that would not go away. But when compared to the most productive phases of his earlier career (Berlin, 1929–1933; Paris, 1936–1939; Hollywood, 1943–1949), Siodmak's German films of the 1950s clearly lacked formal rigor and creative direction. "The long list of failed projects in the 1950s evidences the delicate circumstances [Siodmak] tried to master. In contrast to Hollywood, he encountered poor cinematographers; he had to fight arduously to finance his endeavors. Siodmak, who had always benefited from established configurations, who had been able to adapt and integrate himself, was now forced to create these connections himself, had to find stories, production facilities, and sponsors." [59] Leaving the Hollywood studio system at the brink of its disintegration, Siodmak failed to find in West Germany what throughout his earlier career had propelled him to excellence: a self-assured film industry driven by highly professional standards and a clear division of labor.

On his first return to Germany in 1952 Siodmak was struck by how the war had changed the light of his native city, Berlin.[60] As if Nazi warfare had realized what modernist architects had aspired to all along, Siodmak perceived the gaps in the urban landscape as a chance to start from scratch and build a culture of light and enlightenment rather than of darkness and terror. Three years later Siodmak was eager to attribute this sense of a new beginning to the position of postwar German cinema as well: "Certainly, technically a great deal is still to be desired here. But in Berlin what you do not have is the unbearable pressure of the big studio as in Hollywood, the industrial business to which every director must subject himself, whether he wants it or not. It is inevitable that creativity suffers under such pressure; one has to summon up one's whole power and energy in order to get one's way." [61] Oddly miscalculating the grounds of his own earlier successes, Siodmak's 1955 assessment proved to be right and wrong at the same time. Once he returned to West German filmmaking, Siodmak was soon to encounter high-handed producers, such as Arthur Brauner, who dictated contracts from above and—assured of domestic box office returns—radically pared down any investments in location work, production values, screenplays, and cinematographic quality. What Siodmak initially perceived as the blank slate of German filmmaking turned out to be an institutional vacuum that frustrated his remarkable ability to negotiate conflicting talents, agendas, and traditions. Whereas the contested force field of classical studio filmmaking indeed impelled Siodmak to unfold his full power and energy, the administered provinciality of German postwar cinema in the 1950s quickly resulted in a personal history of formal stagnation and ideological self-denial. Once a highly proficient engineer of universal stories and gripping audiovisions, Siodmak began his most onerous exile when he returned to what used to be home.

For a brief moment in 1959 it seemed as if Siodmak's second German career could take a dramatic turn for the better. In a review article for the influential *Filmkritik* Enno Patalas praised the visual style of *The Spiral Staircase,* placing Siodmak right next to the heroes of Weimar expressionist theater and cinema: "Here, the world of German silent film is still alive, the world of mirrors and shadows, of demons and of the demonically haunted. Already the title announces a well-known motif: the staircase—handed down by Jeßner's stage (Jeßner himself shot *Hintertreppe*)—provided a symbol for an 'inward turn,' an architectural means to integrate space vertically, to encompass human beings, to tie them to a specific path, to restrict their escape into the open." [62] Siodmak represented for Patalas a "better Germany," a German cinema that had subterraneously survived Nazi barbarism in exile. Moreover, Patalas endorsed Siodmak as a missionary for a new national art cinema powerful enough to displace the growing influence of American mass culture in Germany as much as the cloddish amnesia of the homespun *Heimatfilme.* Siodmak, Patalas implied, was to bring to West Germany what Bergman, Chabrol, Fellini, Godard, and Truffaut at the same time developed in other European film contexts: a modernist language of experimentation and transgression, a cinema of strong authorial signatures that escaped generic formulas and the star system.

But Patalas's praises of 1959, of course, only evidenced yet another facet of Siodmak's misrecognition in West German postwar culture. As I argued above, Siodmak had never been an expressionist in the canonical sense. Whatever was reminiscent of Weimar cinema in his Hollywood work was highly performative; it recalled the past as pastiche and masquerade to challenge reified notions of continuity and historical determination. Nor had Siodmak ever been an auteur in the emphatic perspective of the postwar generation. His place was clearly not among the young European cineastes who set out toward the end of the 1950s to rebel against Hollywood illusionism. In spite of Patalas's accolades Siodmak remained distant to the group of German filmmakers who at the Oberhausen festival in 1962 declared their intention to redo German film history and free German cinema "from the conventions of the established industry." [63]

Contrary to the program of young filmmakers around 1960, Siodmak's most remarkable films had evolved from within the bounds of a viable studio system. Whereas West German popular taste continued to reject Siodmak's American work of the 1940s, the young German filmmakers of the 1960s quickly came to scorn Siodmak as a representative of both Hollywood commercialism and *Papas Kino*. In part because of his own critical misjudgments, the former exile Siodmak was never able to fit any of the categories postwar German film culture was developing in order either to flee or to confront the Nazi past. He was seen either as too much or as too little of an avant-gardist, and he soon disappeared into oblivion. It was not until the Berlin Film Festival of 1998 that a broader public finally reassessed the troubled relationship of German cinema to Siodmak's many careers. In the festival's retrospective Siodmak reemerged as a director whose best features embraced studio filmmaking in order to explore the dialectics of modern contingency. The festival reestablished Siodmak as a highly versatile director who had melded images and sounds into a cinematic language that at its best was at once popular and modernist.

7 Pianos, Priests, and Popular Culture

Sirk, Lang, and the Legacy of American Populism

Robert Siodmak's triumph in Hollywood dovetailed with the boom of the American film industry during and shortly after World War II. Siodmak's film noirs of the mid-1940s indicated the extent to which the war had brought a host of new talents, a spirit of innovation, and relative progressivism to the classical studio system. As a B genre par excellence, film noir in the 1940s might have relied on the same kind of industry structures and moviegoing habits that had characterized American cinema since the arrival of synchronized sound in the late 1920s. It was designed for viewers who considered motion pictures an integral part of American cultural life and who went to the movies at least once a week on average. But on the other hand the rise of film noir in the early 1940s inaugurated a period in which various political, economic, social, and technological forces would deeply change dominant industry structures and audience expectations. Film noir demonstrated that the war experience had passed a new kind of maturity on to American audiences as much as to the film industry. Siodmak's success around 1945 in no small part relied on his ability to use studio filmmaking at the height of its productivity to communicate a pending sense of crisis and industrial transformation. His films espoused the entire range of modern experience and mass culture, yet at the same time they gratified newly emerging demands for greater product differentiation and cultural diversification.

Although American global power in the immediate postwar era was radically on the rise, the Hollywood film industry experienced a dramatic downturn in 1947. The late 1940s in fact became the most afflicted period of American filmmaking. The industry was plagued not only by drastically declining box office returns but also by labor struggles and runaway production costs, by censorship battles and anticommunist hysteria, by defiant exhibitors and antitrust rulings.[1] For many the 1948 Paramount Case—which outlawed the practice of vertical integration that had proven so profitable for the major studios and thus effectively terminated classical studio operations within less than a decade—signified the climax of Hollywood's postwar troubles. But the downfall of American filmmaking starting in the second half of the 1940s did not simply reflect the impact of unprecedented political interventions into studio structures, nor did it result solely from inner-industrial struggles or the escalating uncoupling of star and studio systems. Rather, it had much to do with postwar transformations of American society as a whole: "[P]ostwar changes in the average work week, leisure time, disposable income, and consumer interest disrupted the loyal partnership that had existed for more than twenty years between the motion picture industry and its audience."[2] Suburbanization moved audiences away from inner-city theaters. Instead of spending their money for movies, Americans in the immediate postwar period invested in homes, cars, house appliances, or bank accounts. After years of wartime shortages consumers suddenly yearned for new kinds of leisure activities that privileged participatory recreation over mass-produced entertainment. They wanted to engage in golfing or boating, camping or gardening, and found Hollywood particularly ill prepared to satisfy their demands for more diversified pastimes.

In spite of dwindling audience figures and growing political constraints, however, Hollywood features of the immediate postwar era showed some surprising signs of vitality and aesthetic experimentation. Films such as *The Best Years of Our Lives* (1946, William Wyler), *Crossfire* (1947, Edward Dmytryk), *Gentleman's Agreement* (1947, Elia Kazan), and *All the King's Men* (1949, Robert Rossen) infused American cinema with an innovative blend of realism and social awareness. They addressed burning issues of the day (veteran's reintegration, anti-Semitism, political corruption), brandished present hypocrisies from a liberal-left perspective, and upset dominant standards of illusionism and identification. By 1950, however, little was left of this spirit of departure. Troubled by both the HUAC inquiries and the dramatic decline of the market, studios such as MGM, Warner's, Paramount, and RKO eschewed whatever could be read as a trace of left-leaning liberalism. With the notable exception of Twentieth Century–Fox, Hollywood major studios turned openly conservative. They desisted from aesthetic innovation and social realism to appease anticommunist inquisitors as much as to recapture viewers who preferred to spend their leisure time amid the more alluring scenes of the outdoors and of suburban commodity consumption.

James Agee, in a 1948 column for *The Nation,* described the troubled position of postwar American cinema as follows:

> It is hard to believe that absolutely first-rate works of art can ever again be made in Hollywood, but it would be idiotic to assume that flatly. If they are to be made there, they will most probably develop along the directions worked out during the past year or two; they will be journalistic, semi-documentary, and "social-minded," or will start that way and transcend those levels. . . . It is now an absolute certainty that every most hopeful thing that has been stirring in Hollywood is petrified more grimly than ever before.[3]

Agee was certainly correct in pointing out that there was a major fault line separating American filmmaking around 1950 from its role during the war and prewar era. But he was wrong in predicting that Hollywood could and would reclaim lost territory by forgoing spectacle and illusionism in the name of some new realist aesthetic. As we will see in further detail in chapter 8, Hollywood's primary response to postwar declines was to invest in technology and spectacle. Although since the arrival of sound Hollywood studios had sensed no real need for new technologies to hold the interest of the moviegoing public, postwar transformations of American society caused the industry to develop a different kind of screen presentation and to rebuild the parameters of cinematic viewership through widescreen processes such as CinemaScope. Contrary to Agee's recommendation, the American film industry before long embarked on what must be understood as a veritable revolution. Deprived of the steady audiences of the 1930s and 1940s, Hollywood endorsed widescreen cinema in the 1950s so as to recuperate the erstwhile place of moviegoing in American cultural life. It designed a new kind of cinema of attraction and astonishment, a cinema of startlingly amplified sights and sounds that would refocus the viewer's attention on the extraordinary nature of the apparatus itself.

This chapter and the next will comment in a series of typological readings on the role of German émigré directors in the troubled last years of the classical Hollywood studio system. Although it would surely go too far to assign Hitler refugees a special position in what happened to Hollywood after Hitler, it is interesting to note that for some émigrés the disintegration of studio power resulted in new career opportunities. Fred Zinnemann and Otto Preminger did some of their most important directorial work after 1952; Billy Wilder was able to enhance his recognition as a bold producer-director throughout the 1950s and early 1960s; and Douglas Sirk's Universal melodramas clearly fitted well into the very culture of leisure and consumption that had caused audiences to abandon classical Hollywood features after the war. Furthermore, it is important to understand that in some films that were shot around 1950 at the margins of the tormented studio system, in independent or semi-independent production contexts, German émigré directors either addressed the burgeoning transformations of American mass culture head-on or provided striking allegories for the troubled position of Hollywood after 1946. As we will see in a moment, this self-thematization of modern industrial culture around 1950 was often expressed through a confrontation with the legacy of American populism, an ideological heritage with which Germans—recollecting the disastrous path of populism in Germany from 1914 to 1945 [4]—had and continue to have an ambivalent relationship, to say the least.

Two films are central to my discussion in this chapter, Douglas Sirk's *The First Legion* (1951) and Fritz Lang's *Rancho Notorious* (1952). Sirk's *The First Legion* undertakes a high cultural recuperation of the popular carried out to undercut the susceptibility of populism for commercialized mass culture. The film immerses the viewer in a quasi-heroic struggle against the consumption of sights and sounds in the present age; it suggests a Wagnerian overhaul of the popular's own reified Wagnerianism. Speaking from the entrenched position of American cinema circa 1950, *The First Legion* aspires to rejuvenate contemporary filmmaking by challenging popular culture over the right to inherit the legacy of the nineteenth century—its utopian dreams, sentimental affinities, and Wagnerian excesses. Lang's *Rancho Notorious,* by contrast, takes recourse to the most populist of all Hollywood film genres, the western, in order to engage the audience in a quasi-Brechtian reworking of the populist legacy. Lang's point is of course not to persuade his American audiences in any way to engage in communist political practice. Rather, by taking recourse to Brechtian strategies of distanciation and textual counterpoint, *Rancho Notorious* hopes to reinstate the heterogeneity of the popular and mobilize populism against its own petrification. Unlike Sirk, for whom the popular in *The First Legion* represents a site of manipulation, materialism, and vacuity, Lang insists on the relative autonomy of popular expressions from commodification and ideology. Whereas *The First Legion* denounces mass culture as a realm of spectacular seduction, Lang aims to reinvigorate the popular from within— by probing the viewer's relation to the single most popular genre of the studio era.

Their fundamental differences notwithstanding, both Sirk's Wagnerian recuperation of the popular and Lang's Brechtian overhaul of Hollywood populism must be understood as parts of an integral chapter of Berlin in

Hollywood. Both directors approach American realities around 1950 refracted through the prism of particular German cultural perspectives. Through the use of melos and music both films engage the viewer in their critical assessment of modern culture. For both Lang and Sirk sound becomes a valuable means of exploring modern culture as a heterogeneous space of contestation. Contrary to Nazi cinema's view of culture as homogeneous, Lang's and Sirk's films permit us to think of modern culture as multivocal: a vehicle of power and social homogenization as much as a mouthpiece of emancipation, nonidentity, and visions of a better life.

POPULISM AND ITS DISCONTENTS

Hollywood filmmaking during the studio era was deeply influenced by the legacy of the two major American reform movements around 1900, agrarian populism and urban progressivism.[5] Neither populism nor progressivism ever developed a fully coherent system of ideas, but both came to dominate American cultural life in the first half of the twentieth century because both addressed critical issues related to ongoing processes of social, economic, and technological modernization. In a country lacking any established vocabulary of socialism, both populism and progressivism challenged the rule of big government and business with the help of an amorphous array of ideas that revolved around the image of individual self-determination and "the people." At once utopian and activist, they offered unifying symbols to a widespread spectrum of wills and interests.

Populists opposed political and economic concentration, the rise of administrative centers, and the urban culture of intellectuals. They advocated the Edenic image of agrarian life, propagating the unhampered use of "land" as the primary vehicle of individual self-realization and communal integration. Unlike contemporary socialist movements in Europe, American populists mainly aspired to reform the current system by replacing corrupt and conspiratorial elites "with representatives of the truer, agricultural America."[6] Like turn-of-the-century populists, progressives believed that the roots of American democracy were originally formed on the farms and in small villages and that urbanization, industrialization, and mass immigration increasingly destroyed the kind of individualism and codes of conduct coupled with agrarian life. But rather than relying on traditional moral values alone, progressives hoped to find in the institutional framework of modern industrial America and in governmental policies the very means to correct the problems of the present. In contrast to populism, progressivism developed a more positive concept of the political. Politics' proper task was to reconstruct the possibility of individual self-expression and moral integrity, of economic self-determination and unrestricted communality. Its paramount, albeit paradoxical, mission was to make itself superfluous.

As a result of the Great Depression and New Deal politics, the 1930s witnessed a dramatic upswing of precisely the kind of phenomena that turn-of-the-century populists and progressives had loathed the most: industrial concentration, big government, and a more prominent role for intellectual elites in American cultural life. Hollywood's dream factories, however, in spite of their own drive toward bureaucratization and market control, continued to draw heavily on the rhetorical tropes of progressivism and populism, "blurring their differences and fusing them into a common ideological strand."[7] Classical Hollywood cinema upheld what historical developments seemed to negate. The populist and progressive myths of moral individualism and agency, of agrarian democracy and conspiratorial politics, helped define narrative conventions and character motivations throughout the studio era. These ideological tropes fundamentally influenced what became a cinema of active, goal-oriented protagonists.

Hitler refugees in the United States had an uneasy relationship with American populism, for populist sentiments had, of course, been key to National Socialist politics as well. Similar to American populists, Nazi politics relied on the integrative power of diffuse resentments and cultural prejudices. It disputed the rule of money and instrumental reason in modernity, translated discontent into celebrations of absolute difference, and privileged the local over the global. Unlike American populists, however, the Nazi movement channeled popular xenophobia into a full-fledged eliminationist program. It emphasized ethnic belonging rather than economic individualism as the principal path to national reawakening. Nazi discourse adulated the land as a mythic source of racial identity, not—like turn-of-the-century populists—as a means of economic self-realization. And in their efforts to renovate the body politic, Nazi populists had a much more ambivalent relationship to domestic traditions than did their American counterparts. Nazi ideologues embraced some political traditions, but they rejected many other traditions that were, for instance, coupled with eighteenth-century projects of enlightenment and emancipation.

Recalling the populist elements in Nazi politics, German exiles in Hollywood developed at least three distinct strategies to respond to the continued currency of populism in the United States. In all three strategies populist ideology often emerged as a screen of multiple misrecognitions, of cross-cultural displacements and projective anxieties. One response was to deny any affinity between German and American populism and to espouse the credo of economic individualism in the gesture of a fatherless child who embraces a new paternal authority. In this first model the populist defense of the local and unhampered self-realization was seen as a liberal-democratic bulwark against totalitarianism. The second possible reaction involved a quasi-Oedipal revolt against what was seen as direct correspondences between the affective agendas of American populists and the ultranationalism of Nazi politics. American populism in this view offered an allegory for Nazi realities, and vice versa. Both erased the normative substance and universalist reach of modern politics; both exchanged symmetrical communication and critical reason with prejudice, hysteria, and the glorification of authority. Finally, the third response—driven by a Marxist model of ideology critique—pointed at underlying complicities informing fascism, the rise of American populism, and the emergence of organized consumer capitalism in order to reveal their mutual implication in a self-destructive dialectic of modernization. Both American populism and Fordist capitalism, it was argued, want to speak in the name of the "common man." Both seek to provide something for everyone. But to do so, they obliterate personality, alterity, and nonidentity from above, duplicating the destruction of individuality and solidarity in German fascism.

Fritz Lang's and Douglas Sirk's role in the encounter of German film exiles with American populism is interesting not least of all because the success of both directors prior to Hollywood had rested in significant ways on their ability to cast populist sentiments into compelling cinematic expressions. Lang's *Metropolis* (1927) showcased images of cross-class mediation that referred to various populisms of the time,[8] and Sierck's German melodramas such as *To New Shores* and *La Habanera* supplied Nazi mass culture with populist visions of cultural synthesis. Furthermore, the Hollywood work of both directors evinces a recurring preoccupation with the vicissitudes of American populism. Often considered a film allegorizing Lang's experience of National Socialism, *Fury* (1936) explored the susceptibility of populism to mass hysteria and vigilantism; Sirk's Universal melodramas of the 1950s, by contrast, professed to be Balzacian panoramas of mainstream America, a cinematic folklore sampling popular values, ideas, and practices. *The First Legion* and *Rancho Notorious* may expose both directors as occupying opposite positions from their "accepted" ones: Lang as an emphatic populist, Sirk as an elitist critic of the popular. But the exceptional character of this material should not keep us from investigating it further. For, on the one hand, it is in the atypical that struggles over values and meanings often crystallize most intensely; and, on the other hand, it is not the individual biography that matters most for cultural studies but how the voices of individual actors participate in larger discourses of a given time, how the symbolic material at hand may confirm, nuance, or challenge these discourses in paradigmatic ways.[9]

TO OLD SHORES?

Married to a Jew, Detlef Sierck left Nazi Germany at the peak of his success at UFA in December 1937. He spent two years in Italy, Austria, and the Netherlands before Warner invited him to Hollywood in 1939 to shoot a remake of *To New Shores*, a project terminated in 1940. Sierck's first American film assignment was a 1941 documentary on winemaking in a monastery in Napa Valley. The film traveled to Catholic parishes all over the United States. Even though most filmographies fail to list this production, it in all likelihood remains Sierck's greatest popular success. Also in 1941 Detlef Sierck changed his name to Douglas Sirk. He dissociated his name from any German trace in order to accommodate Hollywood producers waging war against Hitler Germany and to appease the many German exiles who considered him a Nazi collaborator. In contrast to Max Ophüls, whose name experienced a series of dismemberments in exile (Ophuls, Opuls),[10] Sirk's cognominal redress signaled his eagerness to meet Hollywood more than halfway—to leave his past behind and excel in American culture on its own grounds.

"I was in love with America, and I often have a great nostalgia for it," Sirk recalled in 1971. "I think I was one of the few German émigrés who came to America with a certain background of reading about the country and a great interest in it—and I was about the only one who got around and about."[11] Sirk's move to Hollywood and change of name did not signify a radical rupture in his career. His preoccupation with America, as we have seen in chapter 3, had commenced long before his arrival in Hollywood. Films such as *To New Shores* and *La Habanera* had been deeply enmeshed in the ambivalent project of Nazi Americanism. Much of his Hollywood work, on the other hand, recalled and further developed the iconographic, thematic, and stylistic registers of his earlier films. It is in particular the use of organized religion as a sign for the popular (which, as I argued before, should not be automatically conflated with the category of industrial mass culture) that links Sirk's German and Hollywood periods. In *To New Shores* religious material elicited the viewer's desire for cultural synthesis. It conjured the vision of a new popular in which the divided tracks of modern culture— aesthetic refinement and commodified diversion—could reunify. Similarly, in the melodramas of the 1950s Sirk's references to organized religion are part of a persistent inquiry into the divisions and utopian potentials of modern American culture. They reveal the status of melodrama as a paradoxical source of transcendence in a postsacred world [12] but simultaneously express what Sirk considered the popular beliefs, meanings, and goals of American society.

Whereas films such as *The First Legion* (1951) or *Battle Hymn* (1956) directly address the delicate role of religious institutions in secularized America, other films are often literally framed by religious symbols. Church towers, for example, figure prominently in the opening shots of both *All I Desire* (1953) and *All That Heaven Allows* (1954). They set the stage on which small-town America regulates desire and molds conformity.[13] In *Imitation of Life* (1959), on the other hand, religious sights and sounds provide anchors to those lost in the storms of passion and excess. "I see religion as a very important part of bourgeois society," Sirk explained in an interview. "It is a pillar of this society, if a broken pillar. The marble is showing quite a bit of decay. If you want to make pictures about this society, I think it is an ingredient of a bygone charm—charm in the original sense of the word: sorcery."[14] Organized religion may have lost its hegemonic role in sanctifying norms and providing metaphysical securities, yet its symbols, according to Sirk, continue to speak to everyone. Sirk's melodramas resort to religious signs to bind images, sounds, and narratives into affective expressions. They reconstruct the sacred in order to recenter experience and smooth over the divisions of modern society. The priest's bygone sorcery thus reemerges as the magic of the film director who understands how to captivate the popular imagination and stir universal emotions. In the absence of a numinous center of things, melodrama reinscribes ethical imperatives that can operate as society's post-traditional glue. It reclaims through Manichean intensification and aesthetic stylization what religious belief systems no longer uniformly authorize.

Released through United Artists in 1951, *The First Legion* occupies an odd place within this melodramatic theology. The film surely pictures organized religion as a source of healing, of restoring body and spirit in a time of fragmentation. In contrast to *Battle Hymn* or *To New Shores*, however, the film eschews any eschatological vision of cultural synthesis and, instead, denounces the popular as the antithesis of authentic meaning and culture. The film reserves healing for those who are able to remove themselves from the pleasures and secular institutions of modern life. It may render religion as a utopian blueprint of spiritual renewal, but it does so by means of a stunningly elitist gesture—by radically separating religious from profane experience, theology from the popular. Like Wagner, for

whom the secluded Bayreuth festival was to counteract the commercialization of nineteenth-century art, Sirk challenges in *The First Legion* the pro-
fanity of modern culture from the vantage point of a sequestered monastery and its necessarily esoteric access to salvation.

Filmed entirely on location at Mission Inn, Riverside, California, *The
First Legion* was originally shot as an independent production in 1950. The
film confronts the viewer with a number of rather unlikely Jesuits—a former criminal attorney, an ex-concert pianist, an India traveler cum film director—who find themselves forced to revise their standards of belief after
experiencing first a makeshift and later a "real" miracle. On a formal level
The First Legion stages this concern with the issue of faith, redemption,
and the absurd by interrogating different regimes of vision and hearing.
Reminiscent of *To New Shores,* Sirk is at pains in this later production to
distinguish between authentic and inauthentic modes of sense perception.
Whereas the fake miracle and its initial mass popularity correspond to
forms of sentience skewered by the logic of the market, the true miracle in
the end represents the work of an introspective, contemplative form of audiovision that resists the spell of visual and auditory spectacle.

The Jesuit seminary is introduced as a space of expressive authenticity
and high cultural distinction. An enthusiast of classical music, Father Fulton (Wesley Addy) responds to the first miracle not with words of prayer
but by playing Edvard Grieg's Piano Sonata in A minor. In a curiously disembodied shot Sirk's camera shows us the labor of Fulton's hands on the
keyboard as if to underscore the work that is true art. Attracted to the alleged site of salvation, the masses outside the seminary, on the other hand,
hope to consume the miracle as distraction and cultural commodity—a
thing they can stick in their pockets and take home. Transformed into a media spectacle, the miracle here generates a delusory experience of social
harmony and charismatic wholeness. In the crowd's populist desire for individual redemption and community, repression and wish fulfillment, fantasy and symbolic containment join together in one mechanism.

Installed on the roof of the seminary, Father Fulton compares the people
outside the gate with the murmur of the crowd before a symphonic concert, the hum of a great orchestra, with the one exception that the boundaries between spectacle and audience have broken down and the crowd has
become its own object of delight. Looking at the masses and cameras looking at the seminary, Father Fulton welcomes the Jesuits' sudden media stardom as a sign of rejuvenation. Being looked at reinvigorates Fulton's faith
and mission; it overcomes the Jesuits' progressive isolation in a secularized
world. Father Arnoux (Charles Boyer), by way of contrast, otherwise con-

Figure 26. Theology reconsidered: Charles Boyer and Wesley Addy in Douglas Sirk's *The First Legion* (1951). Courtesy of Filmmuseum Berlin—Deutsche Kinemathek.

cerned with reconnecting the Jesuits to the timetables of the modern world, makes no secret of his disdain for the crowd outside. Fulton's hum, in Arnoux's perception, sounds more "like music that has swept you off your feet." Arnoux, in his controversial tractates, may argue for a liberalization of church doctrine, but his agenda is to bring the Jesuits to the world, not the world to the Jesuits. Media popularity, for Arnoux, bereaves the Jesuits of what is at the core of their mission. The spectacle disables communication and emotional authenticity. It blocks the resurrection of contemplative spaces in which true recognition and healing might be possible. For Arnoux, Fulton's populism effaces what transcends the given moment and thus diverts from the exertion necessary to achieve salvation (fig. 26).

"All right, I am out of joint like the rest of the world," Doctor Morrell, the forger of the first miracle, confesses in a climactic moment to Father Arnoux. "Nothing adds up to anything anymore." Like *To New Shores, The First Legion* offers an image of modern culture torn into hostile halves, halves that long to reconcile themselves within a higher organic totality. Whereas the crowd outside the seminary desires the priests' alleged bliss of charismatic experience, some of the fathers inside hope to reconnect their esoteric practice to the popular dimension. In contrast to the final images of Sirk's earlier film, however, *The First Legion* leaves little doubt that such a mutual integration of high and low will result in anything but a false unity, in delusion rather than insight or redemption. The division of modern culture is its truth, and the task of any authentic cultural practice is to work through, not to gloss over, the split that marks the modern condition. It is important to note in this context that the first—the fake—miracle happens precisely when the priests assemble in the seminary's meeting room to watch one of Father Quarterman's films shot during his travels in India. Holy people in India, Quarterman lectures, "capture the soul by capturing the imagination." And so does this film within the film, transforming the sacred into a direct effect of mechanical reproduction. Father Sierra appears suddenly from behind the space of projection, his presence on the staircase—his miraculous recovery of walking—coinciding with the image of an elephant strolling triumphantly across the screen. Captured by the cinematic image, the fathers' imagination eclipses their critical reason. Their desire to see and hear what cannot be perceived thus results in collective hypnosis. What they take as a charismatic intervention in fact constitutes a mere extension of screen reality.

Father Quarterman's cinema aspires to open the enclosed world of the seminary toward the popular. It induces the priests to reshape the real as an imaginary space of wish fulfillment and plenitude. At the same time, however, it replicates within the seminary itself the very separation that structures social relations at large. Transforming spiritual values into flat surfaces, Quarterman's projection literally cuts the meeting room in half.[15] It fragments the assembled group of priests and reintegrates them as audiovisual consumers into an imaginary community. Poaching the popular, Quarterman's cinema of attractions refracts traditional modes of integration and reconstructs the esoteric sphere of cultural refinement from the vantage point of public, commodified space. Thus, the spectacle onscreen and on the stairs, to use Guy Debord's phrase, "reunites the separate, but reunites it *as separate*."[16]

Propelled by instrumental reason, the priests—like the masses outside—sacrifice the bliss of salvation on the altar of commodified perception. Their very desire to behold redemption in the form of an image causes them to lose their vision. What they consider a miracle is a hoax: synthetic aura effected by modern technologies. Sirk's mise-en-scène and editing captures this loss of authentic vision as a loss of reciprocity. The film stages perception as disjointed; it relies on mismatched eyeline shots and diverging perspectives. The characters' gazes frequently wander offscreen as they fail to find a corresponding eye within the frame. Many shots picture awkward three-character constellations. Dispersed onto conflicting visual planes, the human triangles of these shots fail to establish any kind of meaningful, fulfilling exchange. Unlike *To New Shores,* which either reveled in well-orchestrated two-shots or froze the image of Zarah Leander into spectacular vignettes, the perceptual field of *The First Legion* thus remains incoherent and uncontained, as if to bespeak the logic of separation that resides under the popular's veneer of wholeness and salvation.

It is only in the film's final shots—picturing the real miracle in which Dr. Morrell's patient Terry Gilmartin learns how to use her legs again—that Sirk seems to renounce the film's underlying logic of skewered triangulation. The second miracle's place is neither the privatized public space of the street in front of the compound nor the publicized private sphere of the seminary's meeting room. Rather, it occurs in the enclosed space of the compound's chapel normally barred to any outside visitors. Sirk stages this second miracle as a drama of visuality resulting in the reassertion of authentic, noninstrumental perception. Once Terry has entered the chapel, Sirk intercuts between shots showing Terry looking intently at the altar, the altar itself, and Arnoux and Morrell silently looking at Terry looking, rising out of her wheelchair, and finally falling toward the altar.[17] Yet even though Sirk in this final sequence seems to revel in the restoration of true vision and corporeal unity, the film withholds any images that would rejoice in the foundation of a new, unified community. Rather than situating Terry, Arnoux, and Morrell in a congruous triangular constellation, the final montage splinters the group into separated individuals shown in isolating close-ups. Terry's miracle may thus overcome inauthentic images and reified perceptions. It may restore to vision the power of introspection and mimetic experience, the ability to yield to and become other. But in its failure to restore an operative community, this miracle also reminds the viewer of the very condition of separation that makes it possible in the first place. Contrary to the earlier mass spectacle, the representation of Terry's miracle elides any attempt to gloss over the divisions of modern culture. Instead of hypostatizing a world of unlimited universality, the second miracle presents the secluded realm of esoteric experience and refinement—the antipopular—as the only source of authentic salvation.

Commenting on one of his later Universal productions, Sirk remarked to Jon Halliday: "There is a very short distance between high art and trash, and trash that contains the element of craziness is by this very quality nearer to art."[18] Unlike the final images of *To New Shores,* which collapsed competing cultural practices into the vision of a unified, homogeneous culture, *The First Legion* insists on fundamental boundaries between high art and trash, aesthetic cultivation and mass culture. The film's final montage sequence valorizes authentic self-expression over mass-cultural kitsch. Curiously annulling melodrama's own origins in the popular, *The First Legion* in the end maps melodrama's aesthetics of polarization onto the topographies of modern culture itself, and it is this gesture of "craziness" that keeps the film from slipping into the domain of trash and kitsch. Unlike the ending of *To New Shores*, *The First Legion* disappoints any populist claim for social reconciliation and cultural synthesis. High and low remain locked in a melodramatic conflict between good and evil, light and dark.

This cultural Manicheanism of *The First Legion* shows Douglas Sirk in critical opposition to industrial culture and its strategies of collapsing diverse registers of expression into seamless unity. The film struggles with modern consumer culture over the right to inherit premodern meanings, values, and utopias, but in stark contrast to Sirk's earlier UFA films *The First Legion* elides any notion of cultural production that would try to appease the entire spectrum of society with standardized consumer goods. We should not think, however, that Sirk's rejection of popular culture in *The First Legion* allies him neatly with Horkheimer and Adorno and their assault on industrial culture in *Dialectic of Enlightenment*. Surely, similar to Sirk, Horkheimer and Adorno considered aesthetic autonomy as an enigmatic space of meaning and resistance to the homogenizing logic of cultural commodification. Unlike Sirk, however, Horkheimer and Adorno encouraged us to think of modern culture not in Manichean but in dialectical terms. They understood autonomous art and twentieth-century mass culture as opposite sides of the same coin, as cultural responses to the same process of social transformation. Neither modernism nor mass culture could do without the other. Commodified diversion was therefore not the radical other (as Sirk wants to have it) but the shadow of serious aesthetic practice. Seen in light of Adorno and Horkheimer's argument, Sirk's Manichean critique of modern culture in fact must be understood as being effected by the very kind of modernization and secularization that *The First Legion* intends to defy. Sirk's melodramatic segregation of high and low relies on reified forms of reason—a transposition of mediated relationships into categories of absolute difference and alterity—that in themselves are the outcome of a truncated process of Enlightenment.

Not Horkheimer and Adorno, for that reason, but Richard Wagner must be seen as the intellectual godfather of Sirk's melodramatic critique of modern culture in *The First Legion*. Read as an allegorical commentary, Sirk's

1951 film submits reforms to the troubled American film industry that recall Wagner's attempts to remake nineteenth-century culture with the help of the extraterrestrial Bayreuth festival. In his 1880 essay "Religion and Art" Wagner had suggested that modern culture should draw on the legacy of religion and myth not only to protect the aesthetic from commodification but also to reclaim semantic resources embedded in religious belief systems: "One might say that where Religion becomes artificial, it is reserved for Art to save the spirit of religion by recognizing the figurative value of the mythic symbols which the former would have us to believe in their literal sense, and revealing their deep and hidden truth through an ideal representation." [19] Inaugurated in 1882, the Bayreuth festival put this program into practice. Wagner designed Bayreuth as an autonomous framework in which Wagnerian music drama could revitalize the community-building symbols of the past and thus emancipate cultural expressions from the constraints of a competitive market society. Taking position in the wake of this project, Sirk in his 1951 film wants cinema to transfer older symbols to the present in order to employ them in current showdowns between authentic culture and popular diversion. Hollywood, for Sirk, should become a latter-day Bayreuth: *The First Legion* aspires to remove commercial imperatives from the production and distribution of film so as to redesign cinema as a sanctuary of communicative exchange, authentic expressiveness, and spiritual redemption. Sirk's use of diegetic and nondiegetic music underscores this Wagnerian figuration of Hollywood as an esoteric civil religion, and, as I will detail now, the film places pianos and organs at the threshold between the authentic and the popular.

BAYREUTH IN HOLLYWOOD

Grand pianos occupy prominent positions in many émigré films shot around 1950, even though this presence may at first seem counterintuitive. Founded by German immigrants in 1850, Steinway and Sons reported extraordinary losses in sales and profits in the late 1940s and early 1950s. Piano shipments, for instance, dropped from 163,807 in 1948 to 133,401 in 1949; in 1952 and 1953 the company's profits plummeted to the lowest figures since the Depression era.[20] In contrast to the years 1946–1948, when sales dramatically outpaced production, shifting American leisure activities, domestic arrangements, and investment preferences resulted in a fundamental restructuring of the piano industry during the late 1940s and early 1950s. Although clearly delivering quite different products, postwar American piano makers thus shared many of their woes with Hollywood filmmakers.

Arthur Loesser summarized the situation in 1955: "In the family, the piano competes manfully with the washing machine and the station wagon for the installment dollar, and rather more weakly with gardening, photography, and canasta for hobby time. As a source of passive musical enjoyment, it has been all but snuffed out by the phonograph, the radio, and the television set."[21]

Throughout the second half of the nineteenth century immigrant piano makers and pianists from Germany had often been mocked as missionaries colonizing American life with the bliss (and tribulation) of serious German music.[22] The most remarkable appearances of pianos in émigré films around 1950 give little reason to believe that German directors in Hollywood were eager to continue the cultural imperialism of nineteenth-century piano practitioners. In many cases, in fact, these appearances manifest the extent to which the piano was a child of nineteenth-century bourgeois society — its aesthetic preferences, its organization of domestic space, its definition of gender roles, and its vocabulary of social status and cultural distinction. Hollywood's grand pianos circa 1950 articulate precarious states of non-synchronicity. They signify voices of the past that fail to find a place in the present. Rather than inundate contemporary culture with the charm of highbrow refinement, grand pianos express critical disjunctions between then and now, high and low, "Europe" and "America." They bring discord and downfall instead of harmony and elevation. In many instances grand pianos not only help resound foreboding ruptures in modern American society but catalyze climactic fury and conflict. Death and destruction are near whenever grand pianos take center stage in émigré films of the immediate postwar period.

Father Fulton's piano in *The First Legion* adds in interesting ways to the figuration of keyboard instruments in postwar émigré films such as Curtis Bernhardt's *Possessed* (1947), Max Ophuls's *Letter from an Unknown Woman* (1948), Billy Wilder's *Sunset Boulevard* (1950), William Dieterle's *September Affair* (1950), and Irving Rapper's *Deception* (1946, a film not by an exile but about exile). Reminiscent of Bernhardt's *Possessed,* in which Schumann's piano concerto helps pit Joan Crawford's romantic sentimentalism against Van Heflin's disenchanted engineerdom, Fulton's piano at first seems to convey residues of expressive authenticity to a world governed by instrumental reason and impoverished affect. Likewise, on one's first viewing, one is tempted to compare Fulton's Grieg performance with the transom scene in *Letter from an Unknown Woman.* Analogous to Ophuls, Sirk seems to resort to diegetic piano music to set a vanished world of awe and introspection—the "happiest hour" of one's life, as Ophuls's Lisa (Joan Fontaine) puts it—against the exigencies of profane existence. Yet the function of keyboard instruments in *The First Legion* is much more complicated than merely orchestrating a confrontation between past and present. More is at stake than simply having passionate piano sounds signify a formulaic antagonism between emotion and scientific reason, between culture and civilization.

Let us backtrack for a moment: Father Fulton is introduced as a former pianist whose devotion to concert music diverts him from his teaching obligations at the seminary. In the opening sequence we witness Fulton rushing home by train and car to teach a course on Christian self-discipline. Fulton, we learn, had just attended a performance of Grieg's piano sonata. Yet although he had left the concert after the second movement, he will fail to appear for his lecture on time: passion and pleasure cut through the paths of methodical conduct and punctuality. Clocks, cars, and trains—the pacemakers of modern life—thus mark Fulton's entry into *The First Legion*. They show him as a haunted traveler between two worlds, a pilgrim oscillating between the existential possibilities of recluse and genius stardom, spiritual duty and sensual pleasure, ethics and aesthetics. Fulton's torment ends when Father Sierra recovers from his ailment. He hails the alleged miracle by playing parts of that very piano sonata that he had to abandon in the opening sequence. Sierra's convalescence thus seems to resolve the discord of Fulton's existence. The miracle, in Fulton's view, reconciles the diverging demands of music and prayer. It injects the cerebral world of the seminary with the bliss of corporeal experience and unfettered spontaneity.

Does it, though? And do plot and mise-en-scène endorse Fulton's utopian vision? The film's sound and image track indeed suggest something quite different. Otherwise fairly unnoticeable, Hans Sommer's musical score at the end of the first miracle sequence picks up Fulton's Grieg performance, carries selected motifs over to the nondiegetic level, and crescendos into a sappy carpet of sounds and emotions. The sonic switch from diegetic to nondiegetic coincides with a visual dissolve from Fulton's hands to the frenzied crowds outside the seminary's gate. Sound and editing thus reveal a curious complicity between Fulton's own recuperation and the crowd's sensationalism. Consolidating disparate spaces and temporalities, Sommer's sound bridge identifies Fulton as a populist whose quest for charismatic experience is driven by the very kind of strategic individualism that erodes charisma in the first place. Fulton's salvation is as fake as the first miracle itself. It connects to an other that in truth is a willful projection of the self. Contrary to our first impression, then, Fulton's grand piano is a harbinger not of expressive authenticity but of the popular's manipulation and commodification of desire. Grieg's piano sonata emerges as mass culture in the guise of high art, as popular materialism in the costume of aesthetic refinement, as instrumental reason in the attire of self-abnegating introspection.

Father Fulton literally drops out of the picture briefly after the first miracle sequence. He does not resurface until the film's last sequence, the second and "real" miracle. In contradistinction to his appearance in the opening sequence, however, Fulton now meets his ecclesiastical obligations—he plays the organ and coaches a choir in the seminary's chapel. Recalling Erich von Stroheim's mannered Bach recital in *Sunset Boulevard,* Fulton's organ performance is meant to offer a sign of some kind of radical alterity; it sets the stage for a miracle that shuns publicity, commodification, and rational explanation. It is important to note that in this final sequence sound and image track have reversed their earlier configuration: we first hear what could be nondiegetic music and only then learn about its diegetic source. The choice of music in this scene is equally momentous. Whereas earlier Grieg's neoromantic piano sonata underscored the phony nature of the first miracle, true redemption is authenticated by the devout sounds of the *Te Deum Laudamus.* Cured from his initial populism, Fulton, in playing Ignaz Franz's *Te Deum,* becomes an agent of simultaneous inclusion and exclusion. He launches a form of healing that purports to overcome self-interest and reification by radically turning away from ordinary social relations.

Sirk's eschatology in the end of *The First Legion* once again rings Wagnerian indeed. The film's final organ music appeals to preindustrial notions of popular culture and their embeddedness in religious belief systems so as to profess—like Wagner at Bayreuth—the absolute difference between commodified diversion and authentic culture in the present. It espouses an exoticized past and other in order to fortify authentic meaning against the materialism and vacuous populism of the day. Yet similar to Wagner's musical sanctuary at Bayreuth, Sirk's casting of hallowed organ music lays claim to forms of cultural autonomy that, in the final analysis, must remain delusionary. Both Wagner's and Sirk's Manichean quests for authenticity become cult because both stop short of recognizing that aesthetic autonomy owes its historical possibility to the very process that also initiated the emergence of commodified mass culture. At the end of *The First Legion* organs may displace pianos to evacuate popular kitsch and industrial mass culture, but, all things considered, Sirk's Wagnerian project of overhauling American culture and cinema cannot but fail when it tries to offer practical remedies to the troubled studio system of 1950, a system that, of course, was as far as ever from denying its commercial bases and that continued to extol the star commodity, not the vision of art as cult, as a modern proxy of sacred meaning.

CHUCK-A-LUCK RECONSIDERED

Fritz Lang's 1952 western *Rancho Notorious* also assigns a prominent role to a (baby) grand piano yet not in order to involve the viewer in a narrative about the place of individual expressiveness and salvation but rather to define a space that rules out symmetrical forms of intersubjectivity and unhampered communication. Lang's piano inhabits a space in which desire and vengeance erase the infrastructures of community, a space in which neither law nor morality sets limits to human conduct and in which, for that reason, secrets of the past consummate the present. Lang's fateful grand is located in a hideout for desperadoes operated by the ex-saloon singer Altar Keane (Marlene Dietrich). In its initial two appearances the grand provides the Dietrich character with a sonic background to feature her narcissistic desire for control and authority (fig. 27). First singing to piano accompaniment ("Get Away, Young Men"), and then playing the keyboard herself, Altar's musical sounds join attraction and rejection into an unpredictable aesthetics of coldness. Her music arrests her listeners in a masochistic desire for distanciation and deferral. It engrosses them in quasi-institutionalized games of waiting, in surprise gestures of tenderness and cruelty, in performative masquerades that delay consummation.[23] In its final appearance, by contrast, the piano remains mute. Its sheer physicality may dominate the space in which the climactic shootout takes place; it may protect Vern (Arthur Kennedy) and Frenchy (Mel Ferrer) from the bullets of their enemies; and it may set the scene for Altar's sacrificial death. But as a musical instrument the piano has nothing left to say. Desire and hate have obliterated all channels of human interaction, including masochist forms of bondage. The rest, it appears, is silence.

One of three westerns Lang shot during his career in Hollywood (*The Return of Frank James*, 1940; *Western Union*, 1941), *Rancho Notorious* was based on a screen story originally developed by Lang himself.[24] The film fitted well into postwar constellations, a period that witnessed not only a remarkable reemergence of the B western (westerns constituted 27 percent of all Hollywood feature films released from 1946 to 1949)[25] but also the rise of the so-called adult western, which pushed the genre beyond its classical naivety.[26] Narrated with the help of a series of rather unconventional flashbacks, *Rancho Notorious* tells the story of Vern, a Wyoming cowboy who sets out to avenge the rape and brutal murder of his fiancée. After many travels and travails Vern finally faces the murderer, Kinch, at Altar Keane's hideout ranch, a sanctuary run with profits accumulated from "Chuck-a-Luck" gambling. Altar is involved with the gunman Frenchy, but before long Vern, too, finds himself drawn to her magnetic persona. Passion displaces better judgment as unforeseen desire tends to override Vern's cold-blooded project of revenge. In the last sequence, however, Vern will unite with none other than Frenchy in order to confront Kinch and conclude his original mission. Altar saves Vern's life during the dramatic shootout by taking a bullet aimed at the avenger. She will die in Vern's and Frenchy's arms after they have killed Kinch and all of his sinister companions. In the film's final shot we see both cowboys riding off into the open landscape—two loners whose quest for punishing the crimes of the past ended up erasing the possibility of any meaningful present and future.

The enduring notoriety of *Rancho Notorious,* of course, stems neither from Lang's fatalism and signature focus on self-destructive agency nor from Dietrich's hyperbolic role as a singing cowgirl. Rather than the film's diegetic actions and sounds, it is Lang's intermittent recourse to a non-diegetic theme song that is usually considered the film's most palpable contribution to American film history. Composed by Ken Darby and sung by William Lee, this cowboy ballad owed its existence to an idea of screenwriter and Harvard Law School graduate Daniel Taradash. The song comes in three installments. It prepares the viewer for a "tale of hate, murder and revenge" during the opening credit sequence; it provides narrative cues during Vern's search for Altar's ranch; and it winds up the film with lyrics that strangely contradict what we see onscreen. Accompanied by guitar alone, the singer relies on melodic progressions and rhythmic patterns typical for nineteenth-century American folk music. The song echoes harmonic idioms regularly associated with the Hollywood western genre, yet Lee's expressive tempo changes and didactic crescendos echo a quite different musical legacy, namely that of Kurt Weill and the *Gebrauchsmusik* (utility music) that energized Weill's and Brecht's 1928 *Three Penny Opera.* Recalling Brecht's own work for Weimar cinema, his contribution to the making of *Kuhle Wampe* (1932), the theme song of *Rancho Notorious* forces the viewer, as some have argued, to become a quasi-Brechtian participant in the construction of the film's meaning. It shifts our attention away from the image track, presents sound as a stand-alone element, and encourages the viewer to oscillate between different and at times contradictory levels of narrative emplotment, between the diegetic and nondiegetic, between emotional identification and cognitive distanciation.

Figure 27.   The aesthetics of coldness: Marlene Dietrich in Fritz Lang's *Rancho Notorious* (1952). Courtesy of Filmmuseum Berlin—Deutsche Kinemathek.

Brecht in Hollywood? The studio system as an avant-garde laboratory of contrapuntal sound? A Brechtian reading of *Rancho Notorious*'s theme song, insinuated by none other than Lang himself, clearly calls for further examination. Brecht's position in Hollywood during his vexed years in American exile (1941–1947) was elusive, riddled with remarkable ambiguities and contradictions. Although he denounced Hollywood as an insufferable "showcase of easy going,"[27] Brecht hoped to find in Hollywood a conveyor belt for his political and aesthetic visions. Brecht's actual contribution to Hollywood filmmaking as a screenwriter remained limited to only one production—*Hangmen Also Die* (1943), by Fritz Lang. This is not the place to recall the controversies that marked Brecht's role in the making of this anti-Nazi film. What is important here, however, is that *Hangmen Also Die* indeed evinced traces of a Brechtian aesthetics of counterpoint and distanciation, thanks in particular to Hanns Eisler's score. Similar to Eisler's score for *Kuhle Wampe*,[28] *Hangmen Also Die* aspired to have nondiegetic music act not as a sensuous amplifier of the image track, of individual heroism and bourgeois subjectivity, but—in Eisler's words—"as the representative of the collectivity: not the collectivity drunk with its own power, but the oppressed invisible one, which does not figure in the scene."[29] The film's images of Heydrich's death, by way of contrast, were accompanied by dissonant piano figures and string pizzicatos. Cacophonous sounds here were meant to undercut any forms of sympathy that may result from rendering visible the oppressor's slain body.[30]

The general principles and possibilities of dialectical film sound were, of course, theorized most influentially by Eisler himself in his 1947 *Composing for the Films,* which he coauthored with Adorno during their exile years in Southern California. Polemically arguing against conventional practices of using film music as a subconscious trigger of emotional responses in the viewer, Eisler and Adorno called for a sonic aesthetics of interruption and affective distanciation that would concede to film music greater presence and autonomy, in fact would elevate it at certain points to the primary carrier of cinematic meaning. Echoing Eisenstein's theory of cinematic counterpoint,[31] Eisler and Adorno insisted,

> on the one hand, that standard cues for interpolating music—as for background effect, or in scenes of suspense or high emotion—should be avoided as far as possible and that music should no longer intervene automatically at certain moments as though obeying a cue. On the other hand, methods that take into account the relation between the two media should be developed, just as methods have been developed that take into account the modifications of photographic exposure and camera installation. Thanks to them, it would be possible to make music perceptible on different levels, more or less distant, as a figure or a background, overdistinct or quite vague.[32]

Subjected to the principles of dialectical montage, film music for Eisler and Adorno was meant to become an equal player in the composite art of filmmaking. It should complicate the viewer's relation to a particular film by pitting sound against image, encouraging viewers thereby to actively negotiate moments of tension, polyphony, ambiguity, and shock.

Produced only a few years after the initial publication of *Composing for the Films,* Fritz Lang's *Rancho Notorious* seems to put Eisler and Adorno's program into practice. The theme song, taking recourse to popular American folk traditions, promotes nondiegetic film music to an equal carrier of meaning. Certainly, at specific moments, Darby's cowboy ballad helps set the mood for the narrative, transport the viewer across time and space, and comment on narrative action; in this respect the song continues to adhere to the prioritization of image over sound scorned by Eisler and Adorno. At other points, however, Lang clearly allows the theme song to exceed such auxiliary functions so as to either have nondiegetic sounds assume control over the image track or to render film music a contrapuntal and hence quasi-autonomous medium of information and spectatorial attention. Witness an interesting passage halfway through the film when the ballad reports the cowboy's frenzied search for his fiancée's murderer while the image track offers a series of snapshots that present male faces in frontal perspective. The song here clearly pushes the visual beyond the conventional limits of the diegetic. Also witness the use of nondiegetic music in the final sequence, when Darby's lyrics contradict the ending imposed on *Rancho Notorious* by RKO producer Howard Welsch. While we watch Vern and Frenchy riding off into the open, the ballad tells the astonished viewer that both cowboys died "that day"—"with empty guns they fought and fell." Following Eisler and Adorno's suggestions, nondiegetic film music here assumes a right of its own, opening a space of ambiguity and spectatorial activity. The final stanza of the ballad offers alternative meanings that—according to each viewer's interpretation—either question, add to, or displace the images we behold at the same time.

It has become a commonplace to hail such instances of audiovisual dialectic and dissonance as a subversive deconstruction of dominant narrative conventions. Does *Rancho Notorious*, in espousing Eisler and Adorno's theory of dialectical sound, really live up to these expectations? Does the film offer a subversive model of popular culture in which formal aspects of cinematic representation—counterpoint, ambiguity, shock—empower the viewer to be an active maker of meaning? One possible answer to these questions, I suggest, can be found in the ballad itself as it is intoned during the film's opening credit sequence:

Oh listen, listen well,
Listen to the legend of Chuck-a-Luck, Chuck-a-Luck,
Listen to the song of the gambler's wheel,
A souvenir from a bygone year,
Spinning a tale of the old frontier,
And a man of skill and a passion that drew him on and on and on.

It began, they say, one summer day,
When the sun was blazing down.
It was back in the early seventies in a little Wyoming town.

So listen to the legend of Chuck-a-Luck, Chuck-a-Luck,
Listen to the wheel of fate,
As 'round and 'round, with a whispering sound,
It sings the old, old story of
Hate, murder, and revenge.

Oscillating between three different temporal planes, the ballad serves as a medium of narrative authentication. It speaks in the name of collective authorities rooted in the past ("the legend," "they say") in order to address the viewer of the present directly ("Oh listen, listen well"). Storytelling here is understood not simply as an attempt to cast the entropy of life into meaningful symbolic structures but rather to connect premodern and modern lifeworlds, the far and the near, the imaginary and the real. Speaking from a curiously unsettled location in between the narrated event, the original fables, and the present space of reception, the act of narration in fact aspires simultaneously to reveal what is new about the old and old about the new. Narrations only work, this first installment of the theme song suggests, if they succeed in intermeshing different horizons of lived experience and ship knowledge across space and time.

A popular, vertical version of roulette, "Chuck-a-Luck" gambling provides the central, although twofold, trope for this kind of narrative project. On the one hand, the song employs the game as a metonymy for the popular, for the hopes, excesses, and utopias that putatively structure the popular dimension at any given point in time. On the other hand, however, the gambling wheel also serves the ballad as a metaphoric substitution for the act of narration itself: the Chuck-a-Luck wheel spins out stories similar to the way storytellers spin their yarns. Significantly, however, the passage of the theme song quoted above by no means tries to keep these two different interpretations of Chuck-a-Luck gambling distinct. The text repeatedly blurs the lines between metaphoric and metonymic uses. The popular, as a result, becomes identified with practices of narrativity that link past and present; the telling of tales figures as the primary characteristic of popular culture. The signified slips underneath the signifier, stories displace events, and history emerges as a product of the invariable desires circulated in and through popular culture.

It is instructive to compare this slippage between the metaphoric and the metonymic, between narration and popular culture, with the model of cultural critique discussed earlier with regard to Sirk's *The First Legion.* Whereas for Sirk the popular constituted a site of vacuity and manipulation, for Lang it represents a crucible of desires and symbols that exceed political power and commercialization. Whereas Sirk conflated high cultural and religious practices intending to end the banality of modern secular society, Lang endorses the popular as a site at which archetypal human longings and depravities reveal themselves most graphically. Sirk's project is to explode the continuum of history; Lang's is to show how the past already contains the seeds of any future present. These differences notwithstanding, both Sirk and Lang of course share a view of history in which transcendental forces (Sirk's salvation, Lang's fate) in the final analysis categorically overwhelm individual self-determination and self-expression. In their respective attempts to remake contemporary culture from either above (Sirk) or below (Lang), both ironically deny autonomous forms of human agency. To put it differently, both the miracle play and the adult western offer antievolutionary and atrophic views of secular history. Both films suggest that modern history leads us away from the possibility of happiness or self-awareness. History extinguishes rather than enriches the cultural resources we may use in order to shape or understand our life as meaningful.

Lang's *Rancho Notorious*, then, confronts the viewer with a paradox. Whereas the very presence of the ballad calls for spectatorial activity and Brechtian distanciation, the lyrics of the song lay claim to the futility of shaping new meanings and becoming a Brechtian subject of history. People, according to the text of the theme song, may receive through popular culture semantic resources from the past, but there is little reason to believe that they can invent new symbols and meanings to change the course of history. Facing this paradox, Lang's viewers are left to draw their own conclusions—including the one that history makes them unfit for acts of choosing and concluding. How historical audiences in the early 1950s actually responded to this paradox must remain beyond what film historians are able to reconstruct, but Lang's vacillation between aesthetic innovation and premodern traditionalism, enlightenment and myth, should at least alert us to the fact that we cannot simply celebrate audiovisual counterpoint as subversive or avant-garde per se. Lang's *Rancho Notorious* is a telling example of the power of twentieth-century commercial culture simultaneously to incorporate certain avant-garde techniques and to disavow the avant-garde's hope for radical political change. Whereas the historical avant-garde hoped to close the gap between aesthetic modernism and vernacular experiences in order to achieve a profound reorganization of culture, postwar neo-avant-gardes and consumer cultures alike institutionalized the avant-garde as either art or commodity (or both at once) and thus negated genuinely avant-gardist intentions.[33] If *Rancho Notorious* teaches us a lesson, it is that our decisions about what is really subversive cannot simply be seen as a matter of textual interpretation and formal judgment. As Martin Jay has reminded us recently, the question of whether a text articulates true negativity and avant-gardism cannot be reduced to theory because "history has a way of subverting the logic we impute to it."[34]

It is in this sense that the use of sound in *Rancho Notorious* also urges us to reconsider the one-sided valorization of dialectical audiovision in the modernist work of Adorno, Brecht, Eisenstein, Eisler, and others. Dissonances between images and sounds may indeed, as I argued in chapter 6, complicate the viewer's relation to a particular film by multiplying possible meanings and channels of perception. But they do not necessarily do so. As an aesthetic formula dialectical sound has attained much of its currency because its advocates demonized as merely conventional any practice other than counterpoint. Neither Eisenstein nor Adorno, although authorities in dialectical reason, fully escaped the inclination to essentialize what in truth is an ideological product of historical processes. For even if classical codes sought to paper over their heterogeneous relationship, sound and image are in some fundamental ways always at odds with each other simply because both rely on different logics of expression, recording, and representation. There are, in other words, many more than merely two ways (dissonant vs. affirmative) to add sound and music to a given cinematic image. "Of this vast array of choices," as Michel Chion has warned scholars against overzealous political posturing, "some are wholly conventional. Others, without formally contradicting or 'negating' the image, carry the perception of the image to another level." [35] As long as we conceive of audiovisual dissonance as merely the inverse of convention, we remain caught in a binary logic that denies the many shades of gray characteristic for commercial filmmaking—a logic that blinds us to some of the basic principles according to which popular cinemas work.

HOME SWEET HOME?

For many German intellectuals and artists born during the 1940s and early 1950s, American mass culture offered welcome means by which to challenge the hegemonic valorization of high art over mass culture in postwar West Germany. Writers and filmmakers such as Herbert Achternbusch, Rolf Dieter Brinkmann, Peter Handke, Werner Herzog, Monika Treut, and Wim Wenders, in their often ambivalent appropriation of American popular culture, shared—as Gerd Gemünden has shown—"an anti-intellectual and antitheoretical sensibility that favor[ed] experience over meaning and sensuality over sense." [36] Haunted by the memory of war and Nazi genocide, German adult film audiences during the 1950s (that is, the parents of Achternbusch et al.) may have shown a similar hunger for sensual immediacy and nonconceptual delight, but they did not aspire, in spite of the spiraling "coca-colonization" of postwar West-Germany,[37] to find their primary sources of cultural renewal in Hollywood import products. Nor did their pleasures entail an antimetaphysical assault on sense and meaning in Gemünden's understanding. West German cinema of the 1950s, in fact, operated as a meaning machine. German homeland films, which by the early 1950s had pushed Hollywood releases almost completely from the annual top-ten list of box office hits,[38] endorsed traditional lifestyles and unquestioned normative arrangements. Domestic melodramas presented the patriarchal bourgeois household as a blueprint for the reconstruction of German national identity after Hitler and for preparing West German society for its new role in cold-war Europe.

It therefore should come as no surprise that émigré adult westerns such as Fritz Lang's *Rancho Notorious* found little resonance among West German audiences during the 1950s. American and homemade western films, as I argued in chapter 4, had been enormously popular in Germany during the entire interwar period. The genre's stress on physical immediacy and phallic reassertion had offered a projection screen for various ideological projects and utopian longings, but with their self-reflexive exploration of unfulfilled desire, repressed violence, and decadent morality, the Hollywood adult westerns of the 1950s raised considerably less enthusiasm in the moviegoing public of the Adenauer period than had their prewar predecessors. Lang's *Rancho Notorious,* in fact, was not released until 1960, a time at which dramatic changes in the international film market were underway, changes that would lead to the disintegration of former distribution circuits and the factual decline of West Germany's popular cinema of the 1950s. Lang's third western was distributed in Germany as *Die Gejagten* (The chased), a title that shifted the viewer's attention away from Vern's and Altar's predicaments and marketed the film as a conventional pursuit-of-justice tale. Eager to please domestic tastes and pieties, the German distributor also decided to rename the Dietrich character Cora-Kean. In a cultural atmosphere in which Christian church authorities continued to patrol popular entertainment closely, Dietrich's original "Altar Keane" must have rung all too blasphemous.[39] In spite of such firewalls and revisions, however, the reviewer of the Berlin *Abendzeitung,* for instance, still expressed outrage about Lang's exclusive focus on the "life of some outlaws on a ranch hermetically sealed off from the bourgeois world."[40] Lang's film, the reviewer implied, lacks any normative center and heroizes antibourgeois attitudes. Rather than uplifting the viewer with a narrative about the moral self-constitution of bourgeois society, Lang uses the western genre simply as a star vehicle for Dietrich and her "already rancid myth,"[41] thus offending in particular those German viewers who considered Dietrich's service for the U.S. Army during World War II an act of high treason.

In her study of postwar German film culture Heide Fehrenbach summarizes the often-ambivalent view of Hollywood feature films throughout the 1950s: "Critics feared that American cinema would facilitate social disintegration by seducing the German public (and particularly German women) with its slick production style, consumer values, and Hollywood brand of hedonism. Persuaded that film influenced social behavior, they suspected Hollywood of encouraging individual fulfillment and pleasure seeking over social responsibility to family and nation."[42] Although *Rancho Notorious* neither provided spectacular production values nor appealed to hedonistic modes of spectatorial identification, Fehrenbach's description explains both why *Rancho Notorious* received mostly negative responses on its German release and why Lang—similar to Robert Siodmak—was destined to disappoint critics and audiences alike when he returned to West Germany in the late 1950s to direct his last three feature films, *Der Tiger von Eschnapur* (The tiger of Bengal, 1959), *Das indische Grabmal* (The Indian tomb, 1959), and *Die tausend Augen des Dr. Mabuse* (The thousand eyes of Dr. Mabuse, 1960). Lang's cinema, Weimar and Hollywood, had always been driven by antibourgeois impulses. It had alternated between an aristocratic and a populist, a Nietzschean and a Rousseauean rejection of modern civil society and bourgeois morality. With its carefully crafted tales of perversion and excess, its self-reflexive concern with the dynamic of the cinematic medium, and its calculated exploitation of the viewers' desire for spectacle and voyeuristic identification, Lang's allegorical cinema was simply not fit for a German film public simultaneously unwilling to work through an unacceptable past and to face an increasingly international and decentered present.[43]

Fehrenbach's account of film spectatorship and criticism during the 1950s also helps explain why Sirk's *The First Legion,* by contrast, was able to draw ample praise on its original release on June 29, 1955, in West Germany. Many in Adenauer's Germany perceived American society as ungodly or sacrilegious, an iconoclastic harbinger of atheism, sectarianism, or misdirected faith. As L. L. Matthias put it in an influential 1953 treatise, "Christianity has lost the cross in America not only in a metaphorical but also in a literal sense."[44] Americans, he continued, consume rather than believe. Their Protestant work ethic blinds them to the affective symbolism and integrative power of organized religion, Catholicism in particular. Sirk's *The First Legion* was welcomed as a counterpoint to this absence of spirituality.

The film, according to critic Martin Ruppert, accomplished nothing less than "to heal a world infected with the virus of progress, and afflicted with delusions, hectic dreams and visions."[45] Critics such as Ruppert applauded *The First Legion* as a sophisticated art house feature, an "interesting dialogue film"[46] in which the community-building power of spiritual values prevailed over the materialist egotism of the time.

The success of *The First Legion* in Adenauer Germany is notable for at least three reasons. It tells us, in a symptomatic way, more about the often-contradictory predilections and phobias of West German film spectatorship during the 1950s than about the film itself. First, to create popular interest for Sirk's neo-Wagnerian tale of healing and redemption, the German distributor (Donau-Verleih) decided to release the film under the mismatched title *Die Beichte eines Arztes* (The confession of a doctor). The doctor genre was one of the most viable formulas of the 1950s aside from the homeland film genre. It inundated the viewer with repressive fantasies of social harmony and reconciliation, suggesting that any given pathology could be resolved within patriarchal domestic settings.[47] In placing Sirk's *The First Legion* in the genre of popular medical melodramas such as Rolf Hansen's *Sauerbruch: Das war mein Leben* (Sauerbruch: That was my life, 1954), Donau-Verleih wanted to amplify Sirk's emphasis on salvation so as to align the film with the escapist tendencies of 1950s German cinema. Second, most critics, defying these populist marketing strategies, downplayed the film's cinematic aspects in order to commend its theatrical, and hence highbrow, sources. The critics' hero of the moment was neither Sirk nor Dr. Morell but Emmet Lavery, the film's screenwriter and the author of the original 1934 theater play of the same title. Staged in Germany in the immediate postwar period, Lavery's theological dramas *The First Legion* and *Monsignore's Hour*, it was recalled, had helped "to eradicate the last sulfuric smoke of the anti-Christ's luciferous demonism, and to hold aloft again new banners in a new time in God's wind."[48] Thanks to Lavery's spiritual genius, Sirk's film thus served a double task in the eyes of the critics: it substantiated the reconstructive efforts of postwar German culture, and it warned domestic audiences not to seek salvation in an unmitigated embrace of American popular culture and Americanism. Third, and finally, neither the critics nor the distributor made any mention whatsoever of Sirk's professional past at UFA during the Nazi period and of his exile status in Hollywood after 1939. Once celebrated as a maestro of the melodrama, Detlef Sierck/Douglas Sirk for German critics around 1955 was simply "the director Sirk," for Sirk's name and identity, not his work, challenged the silent consensus of postwar German film culture in a double way. Any allusion to the director's past would have either broken the taboo on exile so characteristic for West German society until the 1960s or evoked in an all-too-explicit way the extent to which postwar German film relied on the directors, stars, and technicians of the Nazi period. A minefield of uncontrollable meanings and memories, "Sirk" was therefore veiled by German critics in a protective cloak of anonymity and statelessness.

The later revaluation of Douglas Sirk by filmmakers and psychoanalytic scholars during the 1970s is by now well documented. For Rainer Werner Fassbinder, Sirk's Universal melodramas of the 1950s provided a paradigmatic example of how to appropriate "the classical system to the point of rethinking not only what it meant to address audiences in what remained of the public space that was cinema, but what it meant to organize the field of vision that is the cinematic apparatus."[49] In films such as *Angst essen Seele auf* (Ali: Fear eats the soul, 1974) Fassbinder espoused the legacy of Sirk's American melodramas to unmask the hypocrisies of bourgeois morality and stress the artifice of cinematic representation. Douglas Sirk, by now retired in Lugano (Switzerland) and teaching occasional courses at the Munich Film School, thus became one of the elected fathers of the New German Cinema, even if it meant once again to render Detlef Sierck silent. Sirk's academic critics of the 1970s, on the other hand, celebrated films such as *Magnificent Obsession, Written on the Wind,* and *Imitation of Life* as exercises in subversion that articulated artistic authorship within the heart of standardized mass culture. Strangely enough, though, this scholarship, although proposing extremely sophisticated strategies of formal exegesis, often relied on highly conventional notions of cultural and national identity. Rather than understanding Sirk's work as a site of cultural syncretism, it valorized Sirk as a European art director who succeeded in smuggling aesthetic refinement into the camp of the enemy, as a secret agent who crossed borders yet did not unfix given identities. No longer rendering the continuities and ruptures between Sirk's German and his American work taboo, more recent scholarship has rightly questioned this image of Sirk as an undercover artist simply dismantling American culture and identity. In linking Sirk's extravagant mise-en-scène to the demands of 1950s consumer society, scholars such as Barbara Klinger read Sirk's style not in terms of subversion but of unbridled commodification: "[T]he production of films with lush visuals was strongly influenced by publicity considerations in the 1950s which sought to exploit the contemporary decor and fashions showcased in certain films as a means of advancing Hollywood's relation to consumer society. The rich mise-en-scène of family melodramas . . . did not result simply from directorial decision, but from socially influenced industry demands to render style *consumable.*"[50] Seen against the backdrop of industry dictates and other extratextual protocols, Sirk's melodramas of the 1950s—like *To New Shores*—catered directly to the audience's fantasies of consumption. Sirk's allegedly dissident style, according to this newer generation of critics, provided images of plentitude for a bourgeois society deeply submerged in hegemonic ideologies of domesticity and affluence.[51]

What is important to note in closing is that Sirk's American work after *The First Legion* continually replays as pastiche the earlier film's juxtaposition of high and low. Whatever their actual effects on historical spectators, even Sirk's most extravagant pageants made at Universal invoke his 1950 critique of aesthetic instrumentalization and commodification. In often paradoxical and self-contradictory ways Sirk's aesthetic resistance and cultural elitism thus became the stuff of popular entertainment itself. Nowhere does this become more evident than in Sirk's penultimate Hollywood film, *A Time to Love and a Time to Die* (1957). In one particular sequence Sirk leads the viewer into the villa of the Nazi official Oscar Binding. We see the villa's walls cluttered with confiscated artworks that are arranged like trophies. While a concentration camp officer plays Beethoven on the piano in the posture of a nineteenth-century genius artist, we view Binding and some prostitutes indulging in animalistic desires (fig. 28). In another important sequence, opposed to this scenario of aesthetic instrumentalization and coordination, we follow the protagonist, Ernst Graeber, as he wanders through the rubble of his hometown. Suddenly, his attention is drawn to the grotesque sound of atonal music, produced by a wire scraping over the strings of a broken piano. Heard against the decadent uses of Beethoven, the piano's dissonant, unauthored chords emerge as an idiom of authentic, noninstrumental articulation. They intone a language of suffering and negativity, a cryptogram of despair whose puzzling modernity lies in its mimetic relation to a world of material desolation. Authentic art not only has become literally homeless, but it also must eliminate the organizing power of the artist, the bourgeois genius so popular in the iconography of twentieth-century mass culture. As a mimesis of destruction, art challenges in this sequence the attempt to unify high and low in spectacles of false reconciliation. No longer defined as a work, it punctures the reshaping of modern culture as religion and cult of standardization. In their very negativity and dissonance, the piano's enigmatic sounds thus encrypt the utopian idea of aesthetic experience as a yielding to and becoming other. They recapture a sense of spontaneity that points beyond the scenes of cultural reification. Forsaking all magic, Sirk in this chilling sequence actualizes magic and plays it out against the sorcery of cultural leveling. He en-

Figure 28. Art, music, and Nazi perversion: Douglas Sirk's *A Time to Love and a Time to Die* (1958). Courtesy of Filmmuseum Berlin—Deutsche Kinemathek.

dorses a form of aesthetic experience and autonomy that, in Adorno's words, "renounces happiness for the sake of happiness, thus enabling desire to survive in art."[52]

Similar to many West German films shot during the Adenauer era, *A Time to Love and a Time to Die* presents Nazi warfare as a fiasco of operatic dimensions. It recasts the past as fate and natural disaster and suggests that modern art has no choice but to bear the scars of havoc and disruption. Art's esoteric task is to express the impossibility of expression. Its truth and authenticity lies in articulating that authentic experience has become untenable. For Sirk, as much as for Adorno, the role of modern art is thus that of a camera obscura belaboring the fact that nothing concerning art goes without saying anymore, including its own right to exist. Genuine art reflects the desolate landscapes of modern life, yet it does so only through acts of self-conscious negation, by radically separating itself from being and the logic of industrial culture. It is the remaining paradox, challenge, and scandal of Sirk's American work that it sought to examine these propositions with the means of industrial culture itself, that it aspired to amalgamate populist and antipopulist stances and elevate mass culture to a laboratory of aesthetic reflection. Sirk's later popularity among academics and filmmakers, in turn, resulted in no small measure from the extent to which Sirk himself—unlike Lang or Siodmak an ardent reader of contemporary film scholarship—was able and eager to couch such ambitions in sophisticated theoretical formulas. In many strange ways, indeed, Sirk's frequent self-interpretations not only provided film scholars of later periods with an opportune political aura, but they also distracted from the fact that the deconstructivist theory of textual resistance, in its zealous search for instances of subversion in mass culture, excised any further examination of the popular's historically specific institutions and practices of consumption.

8 Isolde Resurrected
Curtis Bernhardt's Interrupted Melody

Douglas Sirk's *The First Legion* pictured the American postwar period in terms of a melodramatic struggle between legitimate art and standardized consumption. Sirk understood modern culture as a Manichean confrontation between the incompatible codes of aesthetic experimentation and commodified diversion, even though the point might rather be to demonstrate that their "much heralded mutual exclusiveness is really a sign of their secret interdependence."[1] Sirk's praise of authentic art thus critically elided the fact that neither mass culture nor aesthetic modernism can do without the other, that one owes its emergence and continued existence to the other. Driven by his hope for noncommodified authenticity, Sirk's denigration of Fordist mass culture not only reinforced conventional binaries between high/low, true/false, and active/passive, but it also proved to be strangely out of synch with the historical developments of American society during the 1950s. For however one conceptualizes the location of industrial mass culture and its relation to legitimate art, it is difficult not to agree that 1950s American consumer capitalism ended up displacing many of the institutions, meanings, and modes of consumption that had structured the U.S. leisure market during previous decades. Often, and understandably, scolded as a period of suburban withdrawal and dull conservatism, the 1950s increasingly consumed the very categories according to which Sirk hoped to reform postwar culture.

A 1955 article in *Fortune* summarized this transformation: "The sharpest fact about the postwar leisure market is the growing preference for active fun rather than mere onlooking."[2] The 1950s saw the emergence of a new affluent middle class that did not hesitate to pursue traditional elite activities with a middle-class kind of zeal. The egalitarian populism of the

Depression era thus gave way, on the one hand, to a conception of culture as a sign of social differentiation and, on the other, to a redefinition of amusement as participatory event. Television now serviced what had drawn previous mass audiences to movie theaters, and America's new middle class demanded different and more diversified products from the film industry. "As the composition of the moviegoing audience shifted from an ill-defined and somewhat amorphous general audience to a more highly stratified, younger, better-educated, and more affluent middle-class audience,"[3] the motion picture industry developed new generic formulas that would cross former distinctions between elite and popular culture and thus liquefy some of the essential boundaries that had structured the era of the classical studio system.

The breakthrough of television after 1948 has often been seen as the primary cause for the decline of the studio system during the 1950s and for Hollywood's redemptive introduction of widescreen exhibition formats. Inaugurated in the early 1950s in various competing versions (Cinerama, CinemaScope, VistaVision, Todd-AO, Panavision), widescreen cinema, according to this argument, capitalized on what television was unable to grant. It was meant to lure people away from the minute images of early television sets by offering visual grandeur and exaltation. But to understand the advent of new exhibition standards during the early 1950s as merely an antidote to television clearly underestimates the extent to which widescreen cinema was both symptom and agent of larger cultural transformations. Unlike earlier attempts to establish wide-film formats during the 1920s, the widescreen revolution succeeded in the 1950s because American society was ready for it. Widescreen cinema, in other words, was not merely a result of the industry's endeavor to outshine television; rather, it actively participated in a remarkable diversification of American leisure-time activities, a crucial transformation of dominant paradigms of spectatorship, and a—however ideological—redefinition of mass consumption as participatory event.

Fredric Jameson has argued that every modern social formation must be viewed as a site at which nonsynchronous developments and temporal overlays are the order of the day.[4] Each historical moment and its forms of textualization, according to Jameson, are marked by older methods of production, but they will simultaneously articulate anticipatory practices and discourses. Jameson's theory of nonsynchronicity, I submit, elucidates the curious location of widescreen filmmaking in the 1950s in at least three respects. First, CinemaScope may have reemphasized the exhibitionist aspects of early silent film, the way in which preclassical filmmaking privileged visceral thrill and self-contained attraction over narrative integration and the illusion of a self-sufficient story world. At the same time, however, the introduction of widescreen cinema pointed toward a future of blockbuster productions eager to sacrifice stylistic coherence for the sake of spectatorial excitement and box office returns. Second, widescreen films of the 1950s, in heavily drawing on historic sources and epic narratives, may have sanctified the thick materiality of the past, but in recasting history as spectacular event they just as much anticipated the waning of historical depth frequently attributed to the postmodern condition.[5] And third, in trying to bestow mechanical reproduction with the bliss of cultural elevation, widescreen films may have perpetuated some of the ideological operations of Fordist mass culture; it falsely reconciled what Horkheimer and Adorno described as the antithesis between high art and the popular.[6] Yet, at the same time, the wide-film rage of the 1950s offered a foretaste of our own post-Fordist age—an age in which autonomous art has been so thoroughly incorporated into the global circuits of capital that Horkheimer and Adorno's notion of a great divide between aesthetic modernism and mass culture has lost its grasp.

It is the goal of this last chapter of *The Dark Mirror* to situate Curtis Bernhardt's 1955 *Interrupted Melody*, produced in CinemaScope for MGM, in the nonsynchronous force field of widescreen filmmaking. Shot by the same director whose 1933 *The Tunnel* had mobilized bodies and emotions for a new political cause, *Interrupted Melody* takes recourse to German cultural material—Wagnerian music drama—to tell a narrative of physical recovery and spiritual healing but also to reconstitute nineteenth-century opera as a source of audiovisual attractions for the new postwar middle class. A cinematic extravaganza of the first rank, Bernhardt's *Interrupted Melody* sheds light on basic continuities and ruptures in the makeup of postwar Hollywood filmmaking. More important, however, in its peculiar use of Wagnerian music drama *Interrupted Melody* adds another important chapter to the narrative of Berlin in Hollywood. A sumptuous Hollywood showcase of particularly German operatic sounds, Bernhardt's film offers an instructive negotiation of different cultural codes and temporalities. It mobilizes Wagner to close the gaps between modernism and mass culture, Europe and America, the auratic and the postauratic, art and money, and in so doing allows us better to understand the Wagnerian aspirations of both Hollywood and Nazi cinema in their respective historical contexts.

· · ·

THE WORLD'S FAVORITE MUSIC

"The world's favorite music / *Interrupted Melody* / in magnificent color / in the greatness of CinemaScope." The film's original theatrical trailer announced *Interrupted Melody* as a melodrama casting lavish sounds into majestic images. It praised the film as a story of courage and faith, a gripping narrative of tribulation and recovery. But it commended the coming release even more so for offering a panoply of self-contained operatic numbers and thus for bringing the blessings of legitimate culture to a wider audience: "Not since the great Caruso has any motion picture presented the world's most beautiful music as it was meant to be heard." Operatic music, according to the trailer's male voice-over, should be experienced with the ear and eye at once. And CinemaScope excels in offering this sense of synesthetic plentitude. The trailer, then, presents *Interrupted Melody* as performing a double mission. On a narrative level the film is meant to celebrate the greatness of nineteenth-century opera as a source of individual empowerment and recuperation. As a showcase of audiovisual attractions, however, *Interrupted Melody* is designed to prove the power of widescreen film—of the apparatus itself—to enable middle-class audiences to participate in traditional elite activities. Seeing opera as it was meant to be heard, the viewer of *Interrupted Melody* is promised a transcendence of former cultural distinctions and thereby an overcoming of the handicap of listening to opera merely in front of the radio or the record player.

Based on the autobiography of the Australian prima donna Marjorie Lawrence, *Interrupted Melody* tells the story of a farmer's daughter and her rise to international fame and recognition.[7] Lawrence (Eleanor Parker) receives her musical education in Paris. Her father's unexpected death forces Lawrence to take on an engagement at the Monte Carlo Opera, where she becomes enamored of Dr. Thomas King (Glenn Ford), a New York pediatrician ready to embark on a medical career. King returns to the United States to open his new clinic, whereas Lawrence moves on to Paris and then to the Metropolitan Opera in New York. Her debut as Brünnhilde in Wagner's *Die Götterdämmerung* is a great triumph, and so is her American reunion with Dr. King—they pick up their earlier romance and are married in spite of ominous frictions caused by their career paths. Shortly after the wedding Lawrence takes off for a six-month tour to South America, where her career will come to a dramatic halt as she contracts polio. Rehearsing the "Liebestod" scene from Wagner's *Tristan und Isolde*, Lawrence breaks down onstage, deprived of her ability to walk. King takes her home to New York, relocates them to Florida, and subjects Lawrence to a rigorous program

Figure 29.   Isolde resurrected: Eleanor Parker as Marjorie Lawrence as Isolde in Curtis Bernhardt's *Interrupted Melody* (1955). Courtesy of Filmmuseum Berlin— Deutsche Kinemathek.

of physical recovery. Lawrence falls into a state of depression and rejects King's therapy. Their fate takes a turn when King, threatened with bankruptcy, returns to New York to take up his job again, and Lawrence, left in Florida, is invited by an army doctor to entertain hospitalized veterans. At first reluctant to accept the offer, Lawrence visits the hospital in her wheelchair and sings "Over the Rainbow" to an audience of injured soldiers, some of them confined to wheelchairs themselves. Having thus recuperated her public voice, Lawrence is drafted by the army to entertain Allied troops abroad and to bolster combat morale. In the final sequence Lawrence returns to New York, King, and the Met to recommence her opera career with a dramatic performance of—*Tristan und Isolde*. Although still unable to walk, Lawrence, to the utter surprise of both King (backstage) and the audience, manages to stand up during the "Liebestod" aria before collapsing onto Tristan's dead body (fig. 29). The film's final image shows Lawrence onstage as she stands amid the set of *Tristan und Isolde* and listens to the frenetic applause of her audience: Isolde resurrected.

In *Interrupted Melody* music signifies motion and mobility, whereas physical stagnation corresponds to silence, to the loss of Lawrence's operatic voice. This linkage between melody and movement is best illustrated by Lawrence's various performances for the army. The recital of "Over the Rainbow" entrances Lawrence's afflicted listeners to such a degree that they fuse into a virtual ballet of wheelchairs. Likewise, Lawrence's later "Waltzing Mathilda" opens up a space in which melodic progression and physical movement provide allegories for each other, a space in which vocal music moves the mind and literally mobilizes the body. This association of sound and action not only typifies the protagonist, however; it also pertains to the film's formal organization in general. From the very beginning *Interrupted Melody* ushers the viewer through a whole series of different generic allusions.[8] What starts out in the Australian outback with references to the western and family-film genres quickly changes into a music film, an amorous romance, a conglomerate of doctor's, woman's, and social problem film, a musical-cum-war film, and finally a music film again. Driven by a notion of melodrama as a vessel of emotional turmoil and excess, the pace of the film's generic transformations directly correlates with the rhythms of Lawrence's career: when polio strikes the prima donna with immobility, *Interrupted Melody* decreases the speed of its genre switches as well.

Although the early 1950s can be considered MGM's musical golden age—*An American in Paris* (1951, Vincente Minnelli), *Show Boat* (1951, George Sidney), and *Singin' in the Rain* (1952, Gene Kelly) representing the most illustrious musical features of the period—MGM's decision to produce *Interrupted Melody* in CinemaScope might come as somewhat of a surprise. Based on an aspect ratio of 2.35:1, CinemaScope theater installations had soared dramatically throughout 1953 and 1954. One of the casualties of this rapid proliferation of the widescreen format, however, was the initial prospect of four-track stereo sound.[9] Hastily adopted as a shared industry standard, CinemaScope may have offered awe-inspiring images, but it reversed the various revolutions in sound recording and transmission that had distinguished the immediate postwar period.[10] Whereas the images became big indeed, sound technologies in the 1950s remained small—a discrepancy that clearly thwarted at least one purpose of films such as *Interrupted Melody*, namely to broadcast the world's favorite music as it could be heard in the opera house.

What should be less of a surprise is MGM's decision to engage Curtis Bernhardt as a director for *Interrupted Melody*. Like Siodmak and Sirk, Bernhardt left France in 1939 and immigrated directly to Southern California. Although Bernhardt's work prior to his arrival in Hollywood showed little evidence of topical, stylistic, or generic unity, he was able not only to secure a seven-year contract with Warner Brothers as early as 1940 but also to establish himself—unlike Siodmak and Sirk during the 1940s—as a director of lucrative A productions. Bernhardt quickly emerged as one of Warner's experts for directing the women's picture. In contrast to his earlier work most of Bernhardt's Warner productions of the 1940s revolved around strong female protagonists (played by stars such as Jane Wyman, Ida Lupino, Barbara Stanwyck, Bette Davis, and Joan Crawford) confronting repressed emotions and rectifying Oedipal dilemmas. After his contract with Warner expired, Bernhardt moved to MGM, where he directed five pictures with highly impressive production values during the 1950s *(The Merry Widow, Miss Sadie Thompson, Beau Brummell, Interrupted Melody, Gaby)*. Similar to the careers of other German émigré directors, Bernhardt's successes in the 1940s and 1950s resulted in great measure from his ability to meet Hollywood's professional standards. Contrary to Lang, Siodmak, and Sirk, however, Bernhardt's Hollywood work by and large lacked any urge for stylistic experimentation or cross-cultural mimicry.[11] Never seen or later theorized as an auteur, Bernhardt was reputed for his skill as an effective master at melodramatic material. His women's films of the 1940s and 1950s excelled in exteriorizing psychological conflict through acting, setting, decor, and music. They embraced Hollywood cinema as a crucible of dramatic gestures and theatrical effects and offered engrossing tableaus that handled feelings and ideas "virtually as plastic entities."[12]

Bernhardt's Hollywood work remains interesting not because it abounds with authorial signatures or subversive slippages but because it allows us to examine the vicissitudes of melodramatic filmmaking vis-à-vis shifting social, political, cultural, and industrial conditions. With its numerous generic crossovers, its deliberate stylistic bricolage, and its intense theatricality, *Interrupted Melody* was clearly in tune with Bernhardt's overall Hollywood track record. To be sure, it might be considered ironic that Bernhardt, when interviewed about the film in the 1970s, stressed the fact that prior to the making of *Interrupted Melody* he had been largely unfamiliar with the operatic works staged within the film.[13] Although a lover of classical music, he had to rely on various musical experts to carry out the film's stagings of Verdi's *Troubadour*, Puccini's *Madame Butterfly*, Bizet's *Carmen*, Saint-Saëns's *Samson et Delila,* and Wagner's *Götterdämmerung* and *Tristan und Isolde*. But seen in the larger context of this study, Bernhardt's professed operatic illiteracy once again attests to the curious dialectic between professional adaptation and performative repetition so typical of German émigré filmmakers in the Hollywood studio system since the late 1930s. A director known to accommodate commercial needs with competent solutions, Bernhardt attempted in *Interrupted Melody* to reference exoticized notions of European high art to satisfy new leisure-time demands and conse-crate a new technology with the astonishing power of melodramatic excess. This chapter addresses the question of how *Interrupted Melody* met these principal expectations and how the film enlisted the female voice and Wag-ner's music for the culture wars between cinema and television.

RECUPERATING THE FEMALE VOICE

The Hollywood cinema of the 1940s, according to feminist film scholarship, largely did not allow women to speak from outside the diegesis or to become autonomous agents of signification. In the opening sequence of Curtis Bern-hardt's 1947 *Possessed* an unconscious woman (Joan Crawford) is injected with a powerful drug designed to make her talk again. Drunk with his power to generate a woman's voice from a position of discursive mastery, the male doctor comments: "No matter how many times I do this, I still get the same thrill." Hollywood films of the 1940s sought to extract woman's speech from her body. They emphasized the grain and texture of her voice so as to re-fuse her access to discourse and meaningful communication and to emplace her even more firmly in the interiority of the diegesis.

The Hollywood cinema of the 1950s, in the critical perspective of Amy Lawrence, refined the mechanisms by which the previous decade had orches-trated the female voice. Examining the role of Rita Hayworth in Bernhardt's *Miss Sadie Thompson* (1953), Lawrence comes to the conclusion that "[t]he convulsive repressiveness we saw in response to women's efforts to speak in the films of the forties went underground in the fifties, camouflaged by spectacle on the one hand or transmuted into hysteria and melodrama."[14] The casting of Marjorie Lawrence's voice in *Interrupted Melody* seems to follow this formula closely. In what is perhaps the film's key sequence— Bernhardt considered it his favorite scene[15]—Dr. King subjects his wife to an uncompromising therapy that aims at restoring the prima donna's voice as much as her physical mobility. Against Lawrence's explicit will, King plays a record of Lawrence's performance in *Samson et Delila* to the paralyzed opera star. "Turn that off," Lawrence demands. "Turn it off yourself," King responds and leaves the room. Devastated by the sound of her former gran-deur, Lawrence manages to crawl across the floor and knocks over the turn-table. Delila's aria comes to a sudden halt, and King returns to the room, embraces Lawrence, and proclaims passionately: "Marjorie, you've done it! You've moved!" Lawrence in this scene takes the first step toward her res-urrection. She silences the echoes of the past to recuperate—under King's supervision—the spectacular presence of her voice and body.

The vocabularies of psychoanalytic and feminist film theory suggest the following reading of King's intervention. An individual who earlier in the film clearly struggled over the meaning of his own career in light of Lawrence's celebrity, the Glenn Ford character allows the viewer to project "male lack onto female characters in the guise of anatomical deficiency and discursive inadequacy."[16] The film in the above sequence obliges the female body and voice to display lack in order to protect the male subject from knowledge about his own fragmentation and castration anxiety. King may try to restore Lawrence's voice but only according to his own conditions. The phonograph in fact situates King in proximity to the cinematic apparatus. Like the doctor in *Possessed,* King assumes the role of the director's spokesman. King engineers the woman's voice as a sign that communicates her body as an object of male desire and control. He confers plenitude and coherence to the male subject so as to gloss over the lack he cannot tolerate in himself. Learning how to master the apparatus, King reconstitutes Lawrence as spectacle in order to camouflage his own role in the process. As King forces his wife to overcome Delila, the intrigant and femme fatale, and resurrect herself as Isolde, the film engages Richard Wagner in a project in which spectacularity expands from the woman's voice and body across to the cinematic apparatus itself.

This is not the place to probe the plausibility of this kind of reading. Suffice it to say that the film itself renders King's project transparent and that Lawrence's comeback clearly exceeds the terms of King's agenda, leaving the doctor in the end as powerless, marginalized, and "castrated" as he is in the film's beginning. I am more interested in the implications of the above argument for our understanding of Hollywood's appropriation during the 1950s of European cultural material in general and Wagner in particular. It is interesting to recall in this context that Saint-Saëns's *Samson et Delila,* in spite of the composer's efforts to fuse French operatic traditions with the Wagnerianism of his day, after its premiere in 1877 fared badly in both France and Germany. Whereas in France Saint-Saëns's opera was viewed as simply too German, in Germany Saint-Saëns was seen "merely as a virtuoso of the composer's trade, capable of assimilating any style because he possessed none of his own."[17] Prompting Lawrence to defeat the curious hybridity of *Samson et Delila* and to resurge as Wagner's Isolde, King's project of physical reeducation urges us to ask a number of questions that echo many of the issues addressed earlier in this study. Does Bernhardt's film, in simultaneously replacing the "false" Wagner Saint-Saëns with the real one, and the record player with the here-and-now of the female voice, engage the viewer in a cinema of German audiovisual attractions similar to the one that Nazi film theoreticians and practitioners—as we saw in part 1—had envisioned during the 1930s? Does the film's musical therapy, by at once producing and containing Lawrence's body and voice, secretly replay the methods of Nazi filmmaking, of folding desire and discipline into a single mechanism? Does Bernhardt's film, in fact, as it hails the power of sound as a conduit to corporeal self-assertion, recall the anaesthetic project of films such as *The Tunnel* and the way in which Bernhardt's earlier film obliterated the private body—whether male or female—as an autonomous site of desire and experience?

The following three sections will reject the suspicion expressed in these questions, not to disarm any feminist critique of *Interrupted Melody* but to challenge the parameters according to which many postwar intellectuals and filmmakers have flatly equated Hollywood filmmaking and the Nazi culture industry. Carrying out my argument in three consecutive steps, I suggest that neither a thematic nor a stylistic nor a culturalist reading of Bernhardt's film can substantiate the proposition that *Interrupted Melody* would resurrect Nazi cinema amid the shifting landscapes of classical studio filmmaking. As the film draws our attention to the historicity of different stylistic expressions and modes of spectatorship, it urges us to resist any facile leveling of differences and to recognize modern culture as necessarily multiple and contested.

POACHING ON WAGNER

Richard Wagner was celebrated by Hollywood practitioners during the 1930s as a dynamic film composer *avant la lettre,* yet his status in Hollywood underwent dramatic changes in the course of the 1940s. In Robert Siodmak's *Christmas Holiday* (1944) a performance of *Tristan und Isolde* sets the stage for a twisted tale of desire and murder. Jules Dassin's *Brute Force* (1947) presents an American penitentiary in likeness to a Nazi concentration camp and features Hume Cronyn in the role of a Hitler-like prison warden who listens to Wagner while tormenting his prisoners. Turning the essentializing tropes of Nazi Wagnerianism upside down, postwar Hollywood reified Wagner as an unmistakable symptom of sickness, death, and totalitarian control. Whoever listened to or was musically associated with Wagner had some affinity to Hitler's willing executioners. Wagnerian music drama, according to postwar Hollywood sound tracks, in fact expressed nothing less than the putative essence of the German soul and its innate penchant for romantic mysticism and authoritarian cynicism. Seen as deeply pathological, Hollywood's new Wagner epitomized what was seen as the eliminationist predicates of German culture, that which obstructs any progressive movement of bodies, emotions, goods, values, and meanings.

Bernhardt's *Interrupted Melody* simultaneously challenges the view of Wagner as essentially German and as essentially decadent. The film employs Wagnerian music as a metaphor for disease and stasis, but it also presents this music as a cure that allows Lawrence to recuperate her body and voice. *Interrupted Melody* suggests that there is no single way to understand the master's music, that it is neither the music nor the man but how one makes use of them that determines their relevant meanings. Accordingly, the film exposes Wagner's music to a creative process of reception in which present itineraries actively shape the understanding of the past just as much as past expressions can be used to change the present. Bernhardt's Wagner thus exists only in the plural. The meaning of his music depends on how people choose to piece together their "own" Wagner—even at the expense of textual integrity and hermeneutic interpretation. Rather than providing a canonical sense of essential beauty, Germanness, virility, or decadence, Bernhardt's Wagner demonstrates the productivity of reception and the negotiated character of cultural meaning. As the film fuses nineteenth-century expressions with twentieth-century practices, it creates a texture of symbolic references in which overlapping cultural codes potentially de-center naturalized conceptions of history, art, and identity.

Lawrence's performances as both Brünnhilde and Isolde neatly illustrate the film's emphasis on negotiated meaning. Of all possible operas that are part of the diva's repertoire, it is Wagner's *Götterdämmerung* that introduces Lawrence to the New York audience and lays the foundation for her American triumph. During the rehearsal Lawrence challenges the Met's conductor, Leopold Sachse (played by himself), over the staging of the *Ring's* final scene. Although willing to allow a horse onstage, Sachse wants Lawrence/Brünnhilde to *lead* her horse into the fire, whereas Lawrence— shown in the film's first sequence as a skillful equestrian—suggests she *ride* the horse. "This is *Götterdämmerung,* not a circus," Sachse insists in his thick Teutonic accent: the point is not to imitate jockeys, but to sing well. Lawrence, on the other hand, demands a more spectacle-oriented and in fact literal interpretation of Wagner's music drama, which indeed called for Brünnhilde to mount the horse and leap "with a single bound into the blazing pyre."[18] Sachse's highbrow view of opera as a cultivated presentation of song and music, not of bodily motions, prevails at the end of the rehearsal. But Lawrence violates the conductor's will in the actual performance and thus emancipates Wagner from his own historical transformation into an

icon of bourgeois respectability. At the end of a two-and-a-half-minute operatic interlude we witness Lawrence / Brünnhilde as she straddles her horse
and maneuvers it into the pyre while the famous Valkyre motifs thunder
through the auditorium. Similar to the ways in which literary modernism
once advocated a charismatic interruption of bourgeois culture,[19] Lawrence
challenges in this sequence the institutionalization of Wagner as a token of
bourgeois self-representation and detached contemplation. In contrast to
most representatives of aesthetic modernism, however, Lawrence's spectacular performance also aspires to blur the boundaries between modernism
and mass culture itself. Following Wagner's lead, which according to Adorno
assimilated high culture to popular taste, Lawrence wants to make art popular and sensual again. Pitting Wagner against his own history of reception,
Lawrence turns opera into what contemporary standards of respectability
denigrate as mere vaudeville, as inauthentic diversion.

Lawrence's electrifying performance in *Götterdämmerung* actualizes
Wagner's original design and, as we will see later, attunes the sensual spectacle of nineteenth-century opera to the perceptual novelties of the widescreen format. The two performances of *Tristan und Isolde,* by contrast,
clearly run counter to the ideas Wagner originally assigned to his music
drama. In both interludes Bernhardt in fact overwrites Wagner's text. The
film punctures the flow of Wagner's endless melody with gaps and silences,
infusing it with alternative interpretations. In the first staging, which leads
to Lawrence's dramatic breakdown onstage, we hear the diva intone the following passage from Isolde's last aria:

> Mild und leise
> wie er lächelt,
> wie das Auge
> hold er öffnet—
> seht ihr's, Freunde?
> Säht ihr's nicht?
> Immer lichter
> wie er leuchtet,
> Stern-umstrahlet
> hoch sich hebt?[20]
>
> [Mildly, gently,
> See him smiling,
> See his eyes
> Softly open.
> Ah behold him!
> See you not?

Ever brighter,
Brightly shining,
Borne in starlight
High above?]

In the face of Tristan's death Wagner's Isolde transfigures Tristan's corpse
and hails what she perceives as the lover's spiritual resurrection. For Bernhardt's Isolde, by contrast, Tristan's levitation triggers total collapse. Halfway through her lines Lawrence breaks down onstage, omits the crucial
passage of "leuchtet, / Stern-umstrahlet / hoch," and is struck with silence
after "sich hebt." Movement and transformation in Wagner thus become
stasis and muteness in Bernhardt. In a gesture of chiastic inversion the film
turns Wagner's text on its head.

The second staging of *Tristan und Isolde* confronts the viewer with a similar instance of textual recoding. The passage chosen to feature Lawrence's
triumphant New York comeback is taken from the same section that was
used earlier to dramatize the diva's sudden illness. Now, however, we hear
Lawrence sing not the first but the very last lines of Isolde's "Liebestod" aria:

Soll ich schlürfen,
untertauchen?
Süß in Düften
mich verhauchen?
In dem wogenden Schwall,
in dem tönenden Schall,
in des Welt-Atems
wehendem All,
ertrinken,
versinken,
unbewußt,
höchste Lust! [21]

[Shall I taste them,
Dive beneath them?
Drown in tide
Of melting sweetness?
In the rapturous swell,
In the turbulent spell,
In the welcoming wave,
Holding all.
I'm sinking,
I'm drowning,
Unaware,
Highest love!]

Although initially restrained to a sitting position, Lawrence, when singing these lines, slips out of her role and transposes Isolde's passing into a dramatic act of physical recovery. It is precisely when Wagner's libretto endorses death as a state of oceanic self-transcendence—"In dem wogenden Schwall . . ."—that Lawrence overcomes her paralysis. As she rises in front of a staggered audience, Lawrence thus actively remakes Wagner's original conception. Wagner, the reader might recall, conceived *Tristan und Isolde* as a tribute to Arthur Schopenhauer, whose philosophy he had admired ever since the early 1850s. Tristan's and Isolde's respective deaths, in the eyes of the composer, hallowed the redemptive power of individual self-abnegation; they articulated a triumphant victory of love over the agonies of will, desire, and subjectivity. The last sequence of Bernhardt's film, by way of contrast, recasts Wagner's opera as a quest for unencumbered willpower, sensuality, and self-presence. Prioritizing affirmative individuation over decadent self-denial, the film de- and reconstructs Wagner's text according to the perspective of none other than Wagner's most polemical critic—Friedrich Nietzsche. Like Nietzsche, who in retrospect regarded Wagner as "one of my sicknesses,"[22] *Interrupted Melody* employs *Tristan und Isolde* to revoke Wagner's desire for death and to embrace instead the exuberance of heightened subjectivity and sensual experience. In doing so the film renders Wagner's music drama not a container of immutable meanings but a source of conflicting interpretations and textual appropriations. Cultural meanings and pleasures here are realized not in the text itself but in selective acts of reception, in the open dialogue between text and interpreter, past and present.

The film's emphasis on the fundamental instability of the past and the dynamic relationship between textual production and reception clearly distinguishes Bernhardt's use of Wagner from the Wagnerian predilections of Nazi cinema as discussed in the first part of this study. Rather than enlisting Wagner in an attempt to represent history as nature, *Interrupted Melody* creates a sense of representation as an arena in which to negotiate conflicting notions of identity. Unlike Nazi Wagnerianism, which aspired to domesticate bodies and desires by means of an overabundant proliferation of signs and symbols, Bernhardt's Wagner illustrates that the individual body "itself—and not merely its representation—is involved in varying and shifting constructions of agency."[23] Echoing Chaplin's encounter with different Wagnerian legacies in *The Great Dictator*, Bernhardt's *Interrupted Melody* thus also challenges Hollywood's essentializing view of Wagner as the dystopian archetype of decadence and destructiveness. It draws our attention to the fact that in modern societies nothing concerning the meaning of cultural expressions goes without saying, that the symbolic orders of modern culture are not monolithic but internally diversified, and that each period has to create its values and meanings out of itself.

WAGNERSCOPE

After the 3-D extravaganza *Miss Sadie Thompson,* the CinemaScope production *Interrupted Melody* was Bernhardt's second attempt to cater to the changing exhibition standards of the 1950s. The film proved Bernhardt's ability to adapt effectively to the fluctuating demands of postwar Hollywood filmmaking. With its operatic tableaus and horizontal arrangement of actors across the visible space, with its prioritization of mise-en-scène over montage, *Interrupted Melody* in fact provided a kind of textbook example for how to align film style with the revolution in exhibition technology. Bernhardt was keenly aware of the fact that widescreen exhibition formats called for new staging and editing principles. When directing *Interrupted Melody,* Bernhardt was able to actualize his experience as a theater practitioner during the Weimar era in order to resolve some of the stylistic problems inherent in the use of anamorphic widescreen lenses and prestigious Technicolor film stock.

Although offering unprecedented possibilities of wide-angle coverage, the anamorphic lenses of the mid-1950s had a significantly longer focal length than their nonanamorphic counterparts. Amplified by the use of color film stock, which required more light than black-and-white material, the initial constraints of widescreen technologies precluded the simultaneous representation of sharp foregrounds and well-focused action in the background, as much as they ruled out smooth shot/countershot transitions. The majority of directors working with CinemaScope during the 1950s solved these technological problems by staging action laterally across the frame and generally reducing the frequency of cuts. The overwhelming panoplies of early CinemaScope productions (majestic landscapes, historical mass spectacles, theatrical performances) thus resulted from the industry's desire to establish a new cinema of astonishment just as much as from the need to circumvent crucial predicaments of anamorphic representation. To shoot films in CinemaScope, according to Elia Kazan, required an arrangement of figures or objects perpendicular to the spectator's look, "more like a stage—more 'across.'"[24] It called for horizontal displays instead of perspectival arrangements, diagrammatic spread instead of a multiplane depth of field. Whereas many directors and cinematographers considered the widescreen format a hapless return to the theater stage, others celebrated CinemaScope's emphasis on tableau and theatricality as the culmination of film's artistic possibilities. The principles of lateral staging and linear horizontal arrangement, as critics such as Jacques Rivette argued during the 1950s, "would finally make cinema an art of *mise en scène,* not only by minimizing cutting but also through achieving a classical, friezelike serenity."[25]

CinemaScope advanced the appeal of sweeping panoramic sights to one of the most marketable commodities of 1950s American cinema. Yet in rendering the cinematic image big in more than only one sense, the widescreen format also became, as Bernhardt himself claimed in unison with Rivette, a testing ground for directorial competence, choreographic artistry, and new modes of spectatorial activity. Interviewed about his experience with CinemaScope in 1977, Bernhardt recalled: "In my opinion, the saving for the average American director was the cut. Cuts saved a lot of lacks of continuity—today more than ever. But I didn't need the cut for safety, because I planned ahead. So my cuts were never arbitrary; they were always thought through. . . . [Y]ou have to use CinemaScope right. And CinemaScope allows you to avoid cuts and demonstrate a certain faith in the viewer's intelligence to pick things out himself."[26] Far from simply overwhelming the audience, the monumental images of the 1950s, in Bernhardt's view, produced new forms of spectatorial activity. CinemaScope required the individual viewer to scan the picture for nodes of visual information, to select whatever one deemed as relevant, and thus to assemble a highly personal film in one's own imagination. Lateral staging principles generated shots with more than just one center, and it was therefore left to the individual viewer to decide what was of greater and what of lesser importance.

One could no doubt raise many good arguments against Bernhardt's assessment of widescreen images as sources of spectatorial participation. What is interesting, however, is that *Interrupted Melody* at times indeed uses the lateral style of widescreen cinema to complicate the viewer's relation to what he or she sees and hears onscreen. In particular the extended operatic interludes of *Interrupted Melody* allow Bernhardt to stage horizontal arrangements in which the actors' gestural excess multiplies possible meanings *within the uncut image itself.* Consider Lawrence's performance of Puccini's *Madame Butterfly* in Monte Carlo, a three-and-a-half-minute musical number presenting the famous "Un bel di vedremo" aria of act 2 in front of a lavish orientalist set. Parker's/Lawrence's face remains austere and motionless throughout the entire interlude. All expressiveness has migrated into the work of her fingers. Rather than dwarfing the delicate movements of her hands, however, the widescreen format here places Lawrence's gesticulation into an extravagant spatial context. The horizontal staging and frontal representation of objects and actors draws the viewer's attention to the artificiality that marks not only the art of opera but also, and even more so, its filmic representation. CinemaScope thus enables the construction of a highly theatrical space of mimesis and masquerade, a space in which the seemingly authentic and original is constituted as effect and in which performative excess allows the audience to understand that melodramatic intensities themselves are nothing other than performances and gestures. As Norbert Grob has put it, "The clarity with which Parker plays her role on the opera stage proves to be a play within the play, whereas Parker otherwise presents rather than represents the role of Marjorie Lawrence. The exaggerated postures, the exaggerated gesticulations of the musical numbers imply the artificial gestus of opera. For opera lives not just from the world of great emotions, but also from gestus, from the fact that the world only exists as a world of great emotions."[27]

Bernhardt's CinemaScope, then, does not simply allow Hollywood to capture the masterpieces of European opera in their full visual grandeur; on the contrary, it recognizes the artifice of opera and its "pretension to lofty utterance"[28] as a guide to widescreen filmmaking. As the film positions CinemaScope and European opera as stylistic doppelgänger, it curiously inverts the parameters of earlier German controversies about the meaning of Americanism. As I have shown, throughout the first decades of the twentieth century German debates about the New World drew heavily from the representation of American society in newly developing mass media such as the cinema and the popular press. Many contributions to these debates in fact suggested that these media themselves were intrinsically American.[29] Bernhardt's *Interrupted Melody* reverses the logic of this argument: CinemaScope here not only disseminates the most extravagant expressions of European culture to American middle-class audiences, but it presents itself as a direct heir to nineteenth-century opera. CinemaScope is opera with other means. It redeems, rephrases, and popularizes the stylistic repertoire of European high art. The medium thus turns out to be the message. In resurrecting Wagner's Isolde in its final sequence, the film allegorizes its own cultural mission. It recuperates the stylistic idioms of European high art in order to consummate Wagner's desire to combine all art forms in a lofty presentation of audiovisual attractions.

Nothing would be more foolish, though, than to see Bernhardt's stylistic doubling of Wagner and CinemaScope as a return of Nazi cinema and its desire to redefine film as an ideologically effective total work of art. Surely, in projecting Wagner majestically onto the Hollywood screen Bernhardt's

Interrupted Melody seems to fulfill the most imperious ambitions of Nazi film ideologues: their hopes to capture gullible minds and markets with that most German of all arts—music. Similar to Nazi cinema, Bernhardt's use of the widescreen format privileges the human voice, restricts the possibility of disembodied sounds, and contains the body through ceaseless strategies of synchronization and diegeticization. But to describe Bernhardt's visual style in analogy to Nazi features as anaesthetic, as eager to neutralize sense perception and coordinate all possible effects within the text itself, is completely unacceptable. Bernhardt's use of CinemaScope might value lateral and often remarkably "unnatural" arrangements of actors within the frame, but it clearly does not replay the fundamental fears of corporeality so typical of Nazi staging principles and cinematography. Bernhardt's widescreen Wagnerianism might offer theatrical shots and frontal visions, but unlike Nazi cinema it does not privilege well-defined sets and horizontal stasis over shifting perspectives and alternating focal lengths. With its lateral staging of action Bernhardt's widescreen style in *Interrupted Melody* in fact revitalizes not Nazi film aesthetics but the staging principles of pre-1910 international film style, that is, early cinema's use of the long shot and its spreading of visual centers across the entire frame. Furthermore, as I will propose in the third step of my argument, rather than mimicking the Wagnerian project of Nazi film practitioners, Bernhardt's use of CinemaScope bears testimony to an increasing uncoupling of symbolic meanings, perceptual patterns, and ideological connotations from a film's specific formal organization. Prefiguring the historical transformation of Fordist mass culture into a more diversified, post-Fordist culture of participatory events, Bernhardt's CinemaScope spectacle decenters the methods by which modern industrial culture—Nazi or Hollywood style—organized the viewer's attention within the text itself.

AURATIC DISTRACTION/DISTRACTED AURA

As it projected expansive images that often overwhelmed a film's work of narrative integration, CinemaScope expanded the horizontal angle of vision in such a way that viewers would lose a proper sense for the actual boundaries of the screen image. Widescreen pictures were meant to lure suburban audiences and TV viewers back into the theaters by erasing the viewer's awareness of the frame. According to the industry advertisements of the mid-1950s, widescreen cinema extended an invitation to the viewer to enter the picture and explore the screen space like a virtual reality. CinemaScope pictures were thus intended simultaneously to center and decenter the spectator. They wanted to create awe for the sheer scale of cinematic representation, but at the same time they generated viewers unable to concentrate their attention on only one aspect of the image, viewers whose distracted gaze wandered across and "into" the screen and thus displaced the possibility of detached contemplation.

Theatrical trailers such as the one for *Interrupted Melody*—"The world's favorite music . . . in the greatness of CinemaScope"—presented this new relation between film and spectator as one that provided the viewer with visceral excitements and an intensified sense of self-presence. They focused the viewer's attention not on the narrative content of a particular film but on the extraordinary capacity of the apparatus to project monumental sights and sounds in the first place. At once devoid of any stable point of identification and folded into the largely expanded picture, the spectator was no longer constructed as a voyeuristic consumer but as an active participant in search of recreational attractions:

> Passive viewing became associated, in industry marketing discourse at least, with traditional narrow-screen motion pictures; widescreen cinema became identified with the notion of "audience participation," the experience of heightened physiological stimulation provided by wraparound widescreen image and multitrack stereotone. Although in both situations the spectator still remained immobile in a theater seat, the perceptible difference in audience-screen relationships between traditional cinema and the new widescreen formats was exaggerated in an attempt to foreground the spectator's new relationship with the screen, which was now, if nothing else, no longer invisible.[30]

Similar to the logic of early film exhibition around 1900, CinemaScope features such as *Interrupted Melody* underscored the act of display and hoped to capitalize on the viewer's conscious awareness of the act of watching a movie. Prioritizing exhibitionism over voyeurism, spectacle over narrative integration, widescreen films in the 1950s acknowledged their spectators and recognized their desire for instant sensual gratification. One should not, however, celebrate the widescreen format's disruption of classical narrative codes as a quasi-Brechtian instance of resistance or spectatorial empowerment. American widescreen cinema around 1955 intended to bond postwar desires for physical mobility and visceral self-presence to new institutions of consumption themselves. Shrewdly reckoning with the new middle class's thirst for more diversified products and cultural distinctions, widescreen technologies turned motion, activity, and expanded sensual perception into powerful ideologies and highly viable commodities.

Widescreen cinema nevertheless marked a crucial break with the history of modern industrial culture and its attempt to produce unified subjects of cultural consumption. CinemaScope, on the one hand, served as a training ground for what one might call with Michel de Certeau a post-Fordist society of cultural poachers.[31] The peripheral perspectives of widescreen presentations unfastened the viewer from the system of suture, that seductive dialectics of the seen and the unseen in classical cinema. Widescreen features encouraged the viewer to develop flexible tactics of cultural consumption through which they could ingest selective images and sounds and thus overcome their status as merely passive recipients. With its emphasis on display and visceral recreation, the widescreen format on the other hand foreshadowed the historical emergence of what sociologists such as Gerhard Schulze call our contemporary society of events and sensations (Erlebnisgesellschaft).[32] Not *what* one saw but *that* one saw—and that one was seen seeing—became the principal object of delight in the widescreen theaters of the 1950s. In conjunction with TV, for which it was meant to present a powerful alternative, widescreen filmmaking in this way launched a proliferation of sights and sounds that have made it increasingly impossible to say what certain images and codes actually do to people.[33] In an unwanted alliance indeed, television and widescreen cinema in fact inaugurated a process that before long was to displace all reliable codes of cinematic signification and—at least according to German director Volker Schlöndorff—undo what previous generations had ontologized as the common language of filmic expressions: "Whether we see a close-up or a long shot, whether the camera looks from below or above, whether it pulls toward or away from a face, no longer really matters. What we have is a total inflation of all effects. Even the use of the soundtrack has become void of any real expression, because it consumes all its means."[34]

Bernhardt's *Interrupted Melody* grants a preview of such coming postmodern attractions. Well before Leslie Fiedler defined the postmodern as a practice of art that would close "the gap between elite and mass culture,"[35] Bernhardt's widescreen spectacle made high art available for popular consumption. Similar to the "Three Tenor" events of our own era, *Interrupted Melody* de- and recontextualizes auratic art and pipes it through the commercial channels of postauratic culture. In thus blurring the modern boundaries between high and low, *Interrupted Melody* on the one hand foretells the extent to which aura today, as Jim Collins has argued, no longer designates a mode of textual address but rather is a matter of personal projection and appropriation that ironically cannot be realized *without* technological

Figure 30. Selling opera: Promotional material for Bernhardt's *Interrupted Melody*. Courtesy of Filmmuseum Berlin—Deutsche Kinemathek.

mediation. Contrary to Benjamin's expectation of 1936, *Interrupted Melody* suggests that "rather than being *eliminated* by ever more sophisticated forms of distribution and access, the production of 'aura' has only *proliferated* as it has been dispersed through the multiplication of information technologies and agents responsible for determining value."[36] Seen in a more general perspective, however, Bernhardt's film also signifies a historical moment at which some of the parameters that have guided this study of Nazi cinema and German Hollywood exile loosen their critical grip. In the face of Bernhardt's seamless incorporation of highbrow and mass culture neither Benjamin's juxtaposition of auratic art and mechanical reproduction nor Adorno's dialectics of mass culture and modernism offer critical points of reference anymore. History here starts to consume the very concepts that were once developed to theorize its course (fig. 30).

All this goes to show that Bernhardt's leveling of autonomous art and mass culture has little to do with the way the Nazi film industry aspired to harmonize the conflicting vectors of modern culture. As we saw in part 1, Goebbels's vision was that of a German culture industry whose streamlined products would simultaneously achieve artistic quality and satisfy popular demand. In spite of the inconsistencies of Nazi film politics, Goebbels emphasized the need to raise film above the language of mere commerce. Only state supervision and intervention, in the eyes of Goebbels, could ultimately warrant formal refinement and mass popularity; only the resolute nationalization of the film industry could guarantee that whatever people *wanted* to see was also what they were *supposed* to see.[37] Bernhardt's *Interrupted Melody,* by way of contrast, shows no real reservations about conflating the codes of art and business. Weighing future career options both before and after Lawrence's physical collapse, neither the prima donna nor her husband deny that commerce and culture have become inseparably intertwined. Contrary to Goebbels's desire to have artists and politicians rather than producers and markets decide the course of art and film, *Interrupted Melody* leaves little doubt about the fact that nineteenth-century notions of aesthetic genius and autonomy have succumbed to the historical process. The film sees Wagner and commodified diversion, aesthetic refinement and capital, as entirely compatible. No matter what one might think about this integration of culture and economics, the film's farewell to the autonomous romantic genius at least undercuts any totalitarian definition of political leadership in analogy to the genius's will to form and creativity.

BETWEEN CHAIRS

Many German intellectuals have viewed America throughout the twentieth century as nothing other than a genre film and simulacrum. Bernhardt's film returns this gaze at America. To the extent to which *Interrupted Melody* integrates autonomous art into postwar commodity consumption, it presents the appeal of European art and German music as a mere effect of the most advanced media technologies. Wagner's music dramas, one might

modify a 1913 line by Austrian writer Robert Müller,[38] no longer exist—
save as figments of Hollywood fantasy production. At the end of the great
divide between modernism and mass culture, New and Old World recognize
and penetrate each other, not as experiential realities but primarily in the
form of media constructs, as hybrid imaginaries that undo any stable notions of cultural specificity and difference, of the familiar and the other, of
home and displacement. As it closes the modern gap between high and low,
Bernhardt's *Interrupted Melody* thus also concludes the peculiar narrative
of German exile and assimilation in Hollywood that I have traced in this
and the preceding chapters of part 2.

Bernhardt's contemporary German audiences, however, were by no
means ready to give up their aesthetic hierarchies and notions of cultural
fixity. *Interrupted Melody* premiered in West Germany on October 28,
1955, only five months after its original American release. It received mixed
reviews from West German critics. Some praised the film's melodramatic
intensity; others lamented the "rather embarrassing" representation of
Lawrence's physical breakdown and her prolonged illness.[39] All reviewers
seemed to agree, however, that Bernhardt's film did not suit every viewer's
taste. Edmund Luft speculated in *Filmblätter,* for instance, that *Interrupted
Melody* would find its "most tearful and prodigal audience" among the female public,[40] whereas *Evangelischer Film-Beobachter* recommended the
film exclusively to "opera connoisseurs (older than 16)."[41] West German
film critics of the mid-1950s expected either cultivation or commerce. In
their opinion the commodification of European high art in *Interrupted Melody* simultaneously impaired the film's artistic quality and its popular appeal. Even weepy women or serious opera connoisseurs, according to contemporary West German reviews, could therefore draw only "fragmentary
pleasure" from this Hollywood feature.[42]

In 1947 director Wolfgang Staudte had argued that German filmmaking
after Hitler should start from scratch again: "We stand at the crossroads.
Will [German] film choose the laborious hike on the narrow path of art's
domain, bearing the burden of an inner accountability? [O]r will it carry a
light parcel of wretched irresponsibility on its merry march down the comfortable street of cheap effects in the empire of a mediocre entertainment
industry?"[43] By the mid-1950s Staudte's rhetorical question had lost little
of its urgency. Experiencing a brief postwar golden age, the West German
film industry offered light-entertainment products whose domestic appeal
relied heavily on the role of ex-UFA stars, directors, and genre conventions.
Middle-class cineastes, on the other hand, as they organized themselves in
the so-called *Filmklubbewegung* (film club movement), hoped to give Ger-

man film culture a new artistic spin. They promoted a resurgence of the older "Kulturfilm" genre to fortify West German film audiences against foreign influences, commercial imperatives, and illusionist desires.[44] It should thus come as no real surprise that *Interrupted Melody* failed to muster enthusiastic responses even within the different sectors of West German film culture. The film did not cater to those devoted to the *Heimatfilm* and its escapist privileging of ecology over economy, nor was it designed to satisfy the cineastes' call for autonomous culture instead of commerce. Although Bernhardt's staging of Wagner might have pleased rebounding German Wagnerians, the film's integration of elite culture and capital, the outback and the cityscape, clashed too drastically with the expectations of a German film public eager to see the rise of a new national cinema yet utterly divided about where to start and which legacies to endorse.

AN UNWILLING MODERNIST

In spite of this symptomatic failure of Bernhardt's film in postwar Germany Bernhardt decided to explore new avenues of directing films in Europe after completing a five-picture contract with MGM in 1956. In 1960 he shot *Stefanie in Rio,* a coproduction of Arthur Brauner's Central Cinema Comp.–Film (CCC–Film) and UFA; in 1962 he filmed *Damon and Pythias* in Italy, an MGM pageant loosely based on Friedrich Schiller's ballad "Die Bürgschaft." Yet like Robert Siodmak's and in particular Fritz Lang's experiences in West Germany during the late 1950s, Bernhardt's return to postwar Europe was remarkably unsuccessful and did not open up new creative possibilities. Representative of a largely "unknown cinema of emigration,"[45] Bernhardt was unable to find a place of his own within the altered landscapes of postwar European filmmaking. He quickly buried his hopes to patch the interrupted melodies of his career and returned to the United States. In 1963 Bernhardt was displaced again, back in Hollywood directing his last film, the comedy *Kisses for My President.*

The figure of displacement is often regarded as one of the most defining features of twentieth-century cultural history, whether or not we seek to divide this century into modernist and postmodernist eras respectively.[46] For Fredric Jameson modernism is predicated on the systematic displacement of unified traditions and identities; modernism produced ruptures between here and there, now and then, which subverted our ability to grasp any sense of meaningful totality.[47] Reconsidering Jameson's heroic narrative of modern displacement, Salman Rushdie in turn has emphasized the perspective of those involuntarily displaced by peculiarly modern constellations of power. He concludes that "those of us who have been forced by cultural displacement to accept the provisional nature of all truths, all certainties, have perhaps had modernism forced upon us."[48]

Curtis Bernhardt's extensive filmography conforms to Rushdie's notion of involuntary modernism. Bernhardt's cinema, from the very beginning of his career to its end in the early 1960s, was remarkably provisional and contingent. It traversed incongruous genres and styles, catered to completely different audiences and ideological demands, and repeatedly fused diverse elements into hybrid cinematic expressions. Not one but many truths surfaced in Bernhardt's cinema of uncertainty. Chameleon-like, Bernhardt captured the American fantasies of Goebbels's emerging culture industry as much as he proficiently used the most advanced technologies to poach on European culture and make postwar Hollywood entertainment more respectable. Bernhardt's career was that of a highly flexible professional displaced by tempestuous times into an ambivalent kind of modernism. It would clearly go too far to consider his work as that of an auteur. But his cinema nevertheless bore the signature of an uneasy modernist who yearned for more stability, certainty, and place yet who at the same time was capable of shaping the daydreams of an extremely unsettled, ever-shifting present.

Perhaps, too, it was because of his highly ambivalent modernism that Curtis Bernhardt showed little interest in the international emergence of young cinemas after the end of his active career as a Hollywood director. In stark contrast to Douglas Sirk, Bernhardt had no desire to have contact with the young German filmmakers who aspired to redefine German cinema in the wake of the 1962 Oberhausen manifesto. Many of these filmmakers, as John Davidson has argued recently, stylized themselves as colonized subjects marginalized by the double legacy of Nazism and Americanism. Eager to speak for an "other" Germany, these young filmmakers valorized narratives of national disidentification and images of displacement. Their self-promotion as colonized subjects in fact "developed into the primary international genre expectations about the new German national cinema."[49] The Hollywood retiree Curtis Bernhardt found nothing in this cinema of deterritorialization that echoed his own narrative of displacement. Bernhardt, whose emigrant cinema of mercurial emotions and provisional gestures was largely forgotten by then, looked with strong aversion on the work of younger German filmmakers. No longer obliged to masquerade as a modernist, Bernhardt commented four years before his death in 1981 on Werner Herzog's images of madness and nonidentity simply by saying, "I hate these new films from Germany. I think they are banal, conventional and pretentious."[50]

Epilogue:
"Talking about Germany"

The history of German cinema is filled with sudden departures and enforced demises. It is a history of disruptions and displacements, of competing memories and utopias. Radical industrial caesuras impacted the course of this cinema as much as did shifting political constellations and transnational alliances. How to group the many ambivalent moments of German film history into meaningful periods remains an unresolved issue. The continued debates over adequate models of periodization reveal only the highly unsettled nature of this cinema itself. Although more recent scholarship has often rightly emphasized the underlying continuities among Weimar, Nazi, and postwar German film culture, it is impossible to consider even seemingly coherent phases of German film history as homogeneous or unequivocal. German cinema may be seen at its most classical, popular, and German when it was organized under the direction of Joseph Goebbels. But the history of Nazi film does not simply entail the story of how German cinema tried to drive Hollywood out of Europe; it equally includes the disjointed narrative of Berlin in Hollywood, the emigration of German-Jewish film practitioners and their integration into the classical Hollywood studio system. Whether we write the history of German film from an industrial, political, stylistic, or audience-oriented perspective, whether we record the chronicle of its directors, stars, production codes, or genres, there is no way around understanding German national cinema as necessarily plural—as a differential cinema in which incongruous meanings and practices, fantasies and recollections, institutional frameworks and ideological mandates coexist in ways they don't necessarily in other national cinemas.

In eight paradigmatic readings *The Dark Mirror* has examined two interrelated chapters in the split narrative of German twentieth-century cinema.

Although clearly no longer persuaded by Horkheimer and Adorno's equation of the American culture industry and German National Socialism, the preceding analyses nevertheless have repeatedly revisited Adorno's work in particular in order to assess the positions of German cinema between Hitler and Hollywood. Adorno, I believe, remains a crucial figure in the effort to challenge some of the most intractable taboos and blind spots of German film history. His work proves helpful when exploring the ideological import of "apolitical" Nazi entertainment features, as well as when conceptualizing German exile filmmaking as part of a "minor" cinema, a cinema emphasizing that "wrong life cannot be lived rightly."[1] To be sure, contrary to Adorno's assumption, I have argued that Nazi feature films were by no means entirely readable in Hollywood terms, nor did Hollywood studio films necessarily echo the aesthetic designs and modes of spectatorial address typical for Nazi cinema. Throughout this book I have stressed the unique role of sound and music in the formation of German national cinema after 1930. The legacy of German national cinema, I have submitted, was never merely visual. Instead, this cinema sought to become national by rearticulating the centrality of sound and music to nineteenth-century definitions of German national identity. Whether situated in Berlin or Hollywood, the German film practitioners of this book were all engaged in recuperating or transforming the Wagnerian templates of modern German culture. Their work indicated competing projects of modernizing romantic idioms, of negotiating late romanticism and twentieth-century modernism within the realms of modern mass culture. In spite of his own equation of Hollywood and fascism, Adorno's work provided many valuable insights into the different uses of "German" sound on either side of the Atlantic. Itself part of the narrative of displacement told in these pages, Adorno's work—in spite of its many fallacies and overgeneralizations—remains relevant because it urges us to understand the structuring binaries of modern culture (for example, "modernism" vs. "mass culture," "legitimate art" vs. "the popular," "America" vs. "Germany") not as radical alterities but in their interconnectedness, hybridity, and historicity.

It is in this sense that the foregoing chapters evaluate how German-speaking directors, actors, and film composers between the early 1930s and the mid-1950s tried to negotiate conflicting cultural codes in their work, how some aspired to reify them into tokens of radical difference and how others set out to merge them into transient and mingled expressions. Both parts of this study depict German cinema as a cinema of imaginary or real voyages, of spurious or concrete displacements, a cinema of traveling and migrancy in which shared meanings were always in open or hidden competition with alternative sets of meaning. In all of the above readings we witnessed films testing out other images, sounds, and identities; wandering across imaginary land-, city-, and mindscapes; mimicking pasts that never existed or promising futures that would or could never materialize. In each scenario temporal overlays and historical nonsynchronicities went hand in hand with spatial and cultural border crossings. Whereas in most of the films examined in part 2, however, strategies of cross-cultural masquerade, assimilation, slippage, and doubling gave rise to more fluid and decentered notions of identity, the texts of part 1 primarily domesticated or erased the other in order to refix normative categories of nationality, class, gender, race, and cultural status. What simultaneously connects and separates the films of Nazi and exile cinema, then, is how they explore the innate capacity of cinematic machines to unsettle naturalized topographies and temporalities, how they either work through or ultimately disavow the utopian power of film to "burst this prison-world asunder by the dynamite of the tenth of a second, so that now, in the midst of its far-flung ruins and debris, we calmly and adventurously go traveling."[2]

The categories of traveling and exile enjoy great currency in the postcolonial discourses of our own times, discourses that often blur the coordinates of historical experience to elaborate a new, postmodern, unfixed notion of universal subjectivity.[3] Anticolonial criticism today, rightly challenging the binary tropes of colonial discourse, valorizes physical and symbolic voyages because they open up more complex realities of ongoing and potentially transgressive intermingling. But in often ontologizing nomadism, homelessness, and hybridity into quasi-automatic sites of resistance and subversion, the postcolonial project tends at the same time to normalize individual histories of involuntary displacement and thus to silence the suffering that speaks to us from the past. It can also reintroduce through the theoretical backdoor the very conceptual separation it hopes to debunk—just with inverted value signs.[4] Rather than celebrating difference and unfixity per se as signs of empowerment, rather than embracing exoticized notions of otherness or cross-cultural intermingling as new normative standards, the point then is to define operative frameworks according to which we can reasonably assess the concrete meaning of displacement and discriminate among different politics of symbolic transaction.

In his 1994 book, *Migrancy, Culture, Identity,* Iain Chambers proposed such a framework, offering a differential analysis of displacement, of traveling and migrancy, that also proves helpful in the evaluation of the various voyages and cultural transfers discussed in this book. "To travel," Chambers writes, implies movement between fixed positions, a site of departure, a point of arrival, the knowledge of an itinerary. It also intimates an eventual return, a potential homecoming. Migrancy, on the contrary, involves a movement in which neither the points of departure nor those of arrival are immutable or certain. It calls for a dwelling in language, in histories, in identities that are constantly subject to mutation. Always in transit, the promise of a homecoming—completing the story, domesticating the detour—becomes an impossibility.[5]

Chambers's distinction between traveling and migrancy is pertinent because it does not universalize difference; that is, it does not render crucial differences invisible. It allows us to recapitulate some of the pivotal contrasts between the Americanist passages of Nazi cinema and the referencing of German cultural material by German-speaking exiles in the Hollywood studio system. Nazi cinema was a cinema of imaginary voyages in which homecoming was preordained, a cinema in which fantasy could journey to distant places but remained unable to challenge the fixity of cultural boundaries and identities. Exile film practitioners in Hollywood, by contrast, had to dispose of the idea of dwelling in immutable images, sounds, narratives, and identities. At its best the exiles' work indexed imaginary traditions and cultural differences so as to show that no promise of homecoming, no completion of the voyage, was possible anymore, that detours and dissonances had become the order of the day. Nazi cinema was a cinema designed for symbolic travelers; it domesticated the other in order to fortify the home. Exile cinema, on the other hand, was a cinema of migrancy, a cinema in which neither the original point of departure nor the one of possible arrival were ever certain or stable.

It is in recognition of the exile's concrete experience of contingency and provisionalness that this study also insists on the differential use of yet another critical master trope of our times, namely that of masquerade. Similar to the notion of displacement, the concept of masquerade appreciates a nearly self-legitimizing force in contemporary discourse, connoting symbolic strategies of transgression, subversion, and resistance. For critics of deconstructive and poststructuralist provenance, cultural masquerades often seem to possess an almost natural ability to undo dominant codes of nationality, gender, or race and to expose the extent to which identity itself is a performance. *The Dark Mirror,* by contrast, having scrutinized a whole set of cross-cultural masquerades, shows that we ought not to overestimate the transformative force of symbolic negotiations and—in a crude misunderstanding of the project of cultural studies—reduce all social interactions and political dependencies to cultural matters. In the foregoing we witnessed German men cross-dressing as tough American engineers, Swedes slipping into exotic apparel to entertain German audiences, Tyroleans play-acting cowboys in California. We traced the paths of exile film composers draping American mass culture in German musical traditions, East Coast Victorians mimicking Nazi racists, émigré directors impersonating the role of expressionist auteurs and ambassadors of European high culture. We also observed how both Nazi and Hollywood exile cinema not only shredded film in older theatrical or operatic conventions but parroted early cinema and its emphasis on self-contained attractions. In none of these cases of cross-cultural appropriation, however, did assessment of the masquerade's full import prove adequate apart from analyzing how it interacted with larger political, social, technological, or industrial environments. In some instances the performative appropriation of other sounds, images, traditions, and symbols was successful in unfixing naturalized conceptions of history, agency, identity, and representation. It involved different cultures in a process of mutual interpretation and helped recognize the other as a potential source of emancipation. In other cases, however, the referencing of other cultures simply reinforced existing codes and cultural binaries. It blocked any experience of cultural difference as a springboard of self-critique and transformation. We therefore would do well to remember once more that acts of cultural redress and mimicry per se are neither subversive nor affirmative. Their meanings and effects depend on historically specific constellations. If cultural studies is to assess the politics of cultural cross-dressing, it cannot do so without analyzing the various institutional frameworks within which people negotiate different cultural codes. Nor can it ignore the question of how individual or collective agents seek to convert performative constructions of agency into institutional structures and political practices. I hope that the case studies in this book have provided some persuasive examples of how to carry out this kind of project.

HISTORY AND ITS DISCONTENTS

The narrative of German-American film relations after 1960—the end of the historical period covered by this book—has been told many times over. Although most of the tropes through which German filmmakers from the 1960s to the 1980s viewed American culture echoed the conventions of earlier decades, the cinematic topos "America" served less as a means of encoding hopes for or anxieties about one's own future than of catalyzing imaginary spaces in which to negotiate the German past. Not Richard Wagner's nineteenth-century utopianism but the "unmastered" Nazi period itself figured as the third point of reference in the triangulated relationships between Hollywood filmmaking and German national cinema after 1962. Curiously combining Americanist and anti-Americanist stances, the *Autoren* of the New German Cinema could simultaneously view Hollywood films as legitimate alternatives to German cinema and denounce them as harbingers of cultural imperialism. As in the case of Wim Wenders, American popular culture was endorsed as the "only thing [that] had nothing to do with fascism,"[6] yet at the same time it was seen as a ruthless instrument of cultural homogenization, as fascism with other means, as a leveler of differences that—according to the infamous line from *Kings of the Road* (1976)— has "colonized our subconscious." Germany's new national cinema was a cinema of self-proclaimed orphans and colonized subjects. In search of ersatz fathers and legitimate points of departure, celebrated filmmakers such as Herzog, Wenders, and Fassbinder took recourse to the work of Weimar expressionists (Murnau, Lang, Pabst) and/or projected images of rootlessness and disorientation. They rejected Germany's own popular cinema and/ or went to Hollywood in order to legitimate themselves. With the notable exception of Douglas Sirk's Universal melodramas (his career as Detlef Sierck was not considered), the war narrative and postwar narrative of Berlin in Hollywood, on the other hand, did not really play any formative role in the attempt to rebuild "a legitimate film culture in Germany again."[7] For the *Autoren* of the New German Cinema the classical Hollywood studio system and its industrial division of labor mostly signified a direct extension of Nazi coordination. With their critique of Fordist modes of film production they believed they were enacting a kind of antifascist resistance that their parents had failed to level against Hitler and Goebbels. Thanks to this negative view of studio filmmaking, the Hollywood work of German-Jewish directors such as, for instance, Robert Siodmak and Curtis Bernhardt experienced yet another history of displacement and misrecognition.

It is not without irony that the reputation of the New German Cinema largely rested on its favorable reception by American critics and cineastes. A national cinema without national audience, Germany's new "legitimate film culture" was in large measure a product of American demands for art house alternatives to mainstream Hollywood. The young filmmakers' attack on the colonization of authentic German culture through National Socialism and Hollywood imperialism resonated neatly with American highbrow expectations that Germans after Hitler would concern themselves exclusively with the atrocities of their history. For this reason it should come as no surprise that some of the most influential historiographies of the New German Cinema rely on psychoanalytical vocabularies to account for this cinema's complex relationship to America and Hollywood. The New German Cinema related to America as both father and mother, paternal authority and maternal nurturer. Eric Rentschler, for instance, argues that for the new German filmmakers of the 1970s the United States played "the role of an imaginary (in the Lacanian sense), a set of possibilities one contemplates and toys with, or put it another way, as a hall of mirrors one passes through while self-reflecting. Confused, inexperienced, and incomplete human subjects gain wisdom and insight in America."[8] Films such as Herzog's *Stroszek* (1977) and Wenders's *Alice in den Städten* (Alice in the cities, 1974) embraced America not as a tangible space but as a playground for the imagination where tormented subjects realized identity by experiencing themselves as others. The true point of these films, however, was the implied or depicted moment of homecoming when the German travelers believed they were exiting their American mirror stage and entering the German symbolic, thus achieving a seemingly autonomous standpoint of consciousness and self-expression.

Refocusing Rentschler's argument, Thomas Elsaesser separates New German Cinema's projective fantasies about America into three different scenarios.[9] In the perspective of one group of filmmakers postwar American cultural imperialism simply continued the Nazi destruction of authentic German culture. In a gesture of Oedipal revolt German cinema's task was seen to contest Germany's double colonization and, by directly or allegorically exploring the darkest chapters of German history, to find new forms of national authenticity (Syberberg, Herzog). Represented by directors such as Wenders or Fassbinder, the second strategy was that of a discriminating exploration of Hollywood cinema as a source of possible identifications. It entailed the orphan's search for alternative father figures (Ford, Ray, Sirk) who would not trigger neurotic dependencies: "Contact rather than conflict, identity lived and renewed by interchange rather than by territorial claims seems to be the goal, but it is a world that excludes women."[10] The third prototype, labeled by Elsaesser as the "no-contest paradigm," focused on the painful formation of German subjectivity, although with the conspicuous omission of any reference at all to American popular culture or Hollywood. Mother-daughter bonds in this paradigm became the primary trope of recalling the ruptures of twentieth-century German history and of recapturing a lost sense of expressive authenticity (Sanders-Brahms, Brückner).

Whether they employ a Lacanian or a Freudian matrix, both Rentschler's and Elsaesser's accounts of German-American film relations during the 1970s shed light on some crucial transformations in the role of American fantasies in twentieth-century German culture. As we saw in part 1 of this book, Nazi Americanism served as a vehicle to capture disparate longings and align conflicting temporal experiences, to even out unwanted discontinuities and project alternative futures. Integral to Goebbels's efforts to engineer fantasy through governmental interventions, the Americanist projections of Nazi cinema recalled eighteenth- and nineteenth-century visions of cultural homogeneity and provided mass audiences with a spurious sense of normalcy. In spite of many striking ideological inconsistencies they were meant to mold assent by unifying the national and the popular. The American topoi in the New German Cinema, on the other hand, were crucial in the younger directors' rejection of former notions of normalcy and mass consent. Rebelling against the fathers of the Nazi and the Adenauer period, the state-funded German cinema of the 1970s exploited "America" in order to expound the exceptionality of German history and subjectivity, their rudimentary ruptures and dissonances. The representation of nonidentity may have advanced to this cinema's new trademark and identity,[11] but with the exception of, arguably, Rainer Werner Fassbinder and Volker Schlöndorff the referencing of Hollywood and American popular culture now played a pivotal function in cutting through the linkage between the national and the popular.

Rentschler's and Elsaesser's models also prove helpful when mapping some of the striking transformations of German cinema since the second half of the 1980s. Recent German cinema, in particular that of the post-unification period, has developed into a self-confident genre cinema. It no longer shows exasperated subjects toying with the American imaginary, nor does it engage its viewers in Oedipal revolts against the specters of cultural imperialism, Nazi or Hollywood style. Surely, Hollywood continues to dominate the German market in almost all respects. Domestic feature productions earned as little as 9.5 percent of all German box office returns in 1998 and 14 percent in 1999.[12] But encouraged by the emergence of new domestic venues of film production and distribution, on the one hand, and by the increasing public historicization of the Nazi past, on the other, German cinema today has clearly broken away from the American dilemmas of earlier *Autorenfilme,* as well as from their hopes to rebuild the national through disidentification with the popular. The successful German comedies of the first half of the 1990s (*Abgeschminkt* [1993], *Der bewegte Mann* [1994], *Keiner liebt mich* [1995], *Männerpension* [1996]), in spite of the fact that their humor did not fare very well at all with American audiences, did by no means hesitate to imitate mainstream Hollywood models. Unlike many representatives of the previous generation of *Autorenfilmer,* younger directors such as Doris Dörrie, Katja von Garnier, and Sönke Wortmann are clearly guided by Hollywood paradigms of industrial filmmaking. As Gerd Gemünden argues: "With their fast editing, stylized interiors, witty dialogues, well-paced plot development, and a strong emphasis on entertainment rather than consciousness raising, these German comedies do indeed come very close to the Hollywood cinema they seek to emulate. Their surprising and enormous success with German audiences confirms that they speak a film language with which German viewers are very familiar."[13]

In the second half of the 1990s Hollywood formulas have also increasingly inspired the production of epic German melodramas that convert German twentieth-century history, including that of the Nazi period, into flamboyant spectacles of sight and sound. Films such as Joseph Vilsmaier's *Comedian Harmonists* (1997), Max Färberböck's *Aimée und Jaguar* (1998), Rolf Schübel's *Gloomy Sunday* (1999), Vilsmaier's *Marlene* (2000), and Xavier Koller's *Gripsholm* (2000) freely borrow from Hollywood conventions in order to appeal to post-Wall desires for historical memory. On the one hand, these films can be seen as part of the new European "heritage" cinema, a cinema of high production values and popular appeal that supplements, rather than really challenges, the role of Hollywood productions on the global market.[14] Devoid of the stylistic marks of European art authorship, heritage films represent issues of national history and myth with the help of classical narrative devices. As they explore residual pockets of exportability, these film productions indicate the extent to which globalized film culture at once homogenizes modes of expressions and effects new local structures of meaning and difference. On the other hand, the return of historical melodramas in the late 1990s clearly also participated in post-unification efforts to reorder German history and recuperate a sense of national normalcy.[15] As if trying to pass redemptive justice to those who gave their life to German history, these melodramas recuperate blocked national alternatives and extend revisionist images of Jewish-German symbiosis. *Aimée und Jaguar,* which tells the story of a Jewish-German lesbian couple during the last years of the war, not only pictures Nazi society as ruptured by fundamental inconsistencies between nationalist ideology and cosmopolitan everyday practice, but it also exploits these discrepancies in order to teach Germans a putatively Jewish lesson about how to overcome historical brooding and how to live life to the fullest. Vilsmaier's *Comedian Harmonists,* on the other hand, by following the path of the famous group of German a cappella singers from the late Weimar era into the Nazi period, suggests that, had it not been for the group's three Jewish members and the Nazis' anti-Semitism, twentieth-century Germany could have enjoyed powerful national *and* popular alternatives to American mass culture. The narrative of Hollywood in Berlin thus enters a stage in which German cinema reinvents the past as heritage so as to capitalize on present-day desires for undisturbed national identifications.

"A DESCARGAR LA CARRETA"?

Miramax Films marketed the American release of Vilsmaier's *Comedian Harmonists* in March 1999 with the catchphrase, "A true story that proves the voice is mightier than the sword." As much as it aspires to rewrite the German past, the film, indeed, returns to the familiar tradition of defining linguistic and musical properties as the central components of German national identity. Like almost all films discussed in this book, *Comedian Harmonists* is concerned with reassessing—and modernizing—the role of romantic traditions in the age of industrial mass culture. In the film's most intriguing sequences we witness the singers' efforts to make the most complex vocal arrangements sound natural and to integrate a multiplicity of voices into one higher unity. What is process must become product, and what relies on a Taylorist division of vocal labor must give the impression of organic harmony so that both national and popular success might ensue. Similar to the films discussed in part 1, Vilsmaier's melodrama renders the mellifluous texture of the German language as a trigger of overwhelming experiences of collectivity. The a cappella group's synchronized voices signify nothing less than the national community, a mythic voice silenced by the sword of Nazi politics yet powerful enough to reconstitute itself in the 1990s.[16]

Vilsmaier's reinscription of the German language as the principal conduit to national identity did not emerge in a vacuum. Instead, it cast the nationalist murmur of many German intellectuals after unification, their desire for self-confident expressions of national belonging, into a popular idiom.[17] In his 1991 lecture "Talking about Germany" filmmaker Wim Wenders helped inaugurate this renewed quest for a grounding of German identity in the fabric of the German language. Exasperated about the way Hollywood images flood the German market, Wenders returned to Genesis 1:1—the mythic creation of being through language—to overturn the intermingling of cultural codes in the present: "[O]ur balm in this land of lost souls, is our German language. It is differentiated, precise, subtle, endearing, accurate, and nurturing at the same time. It is a rich language. It is the only wealth that we have in a country that believes itself to be rich when it is not. The German language is everything that our country no longer is, what it is not yet, and what it may never be."[18] Wenders asks us to abandon the world of images in order to reclaim the word as a mythic predicate of national identity. Once thoroughly enthralled by the power of (American) sights to supersede the tainted legacies of German culture, he now endorses Kafka and Goethe as panaceas for the lack of integrative myths. Images can no longer produce identity in Germany, he claims. Authentic nationhood can only reemerge from the sonic spaces of language and storytelling.

In his earlier work Wenders used sound to great effect in order to interrupt voyeuristic modes of identification and to pit American popular culture against the authoritarian legacies of German history. Sound, in Wenders's work of the 1970s, created tensions between the diegetic and the nondiegetic and decentered the viewer's perception and pleasure. Wenders's films could thus be described as forays into cinematic polyphony and unsettled synesthesia. They explored the power of images to provide rhythm as much as the power of sound to stimulate the viewer's visual imagination. Wenders's 1991 project of linguistic self-assertion signaled a retreat from his previous exploration of sound as a means to emphasize the ambiguity and contingency of meaning. The sounds of the German language were now meant to fold the subject back into the mythic texture of the nation. Their task was to transpose history into *Heilsgeschichte* and bestow bliss to the ruptured scenes of German culture. By suggesting that a German intellectual's talk about Germany is a quintessential sign of Germanness, Wenders's utopia of sonic nationhood secretly aspired to the status of a self-fulfilling prophecy. The romantic vision of language as nation undercut alternative attempts to renegotiate the meaning of German identity in terms of Germany's unmasterable past as much as its many democratic, counter-hegemonic traditions.

It seems appropriate to conclude a book that followed the tracks of supplanted legacies and of selves identifying with imaginary others with yet another case of slippage and displacement. Whereas Vilsmaier's *Comedian Harmonists* converted Wenders's elitist vision of 1991 into a popular box office hit,[19] Wenders's cinema itself increasingly abandoned the project of sonic regrounding and national normalization. Surely, Wenders's sound tracks of the 1990s came to play an increasingly important role in the filmmaker's attempt to keep a check on the global proliferation of electronic images. Wenders's sounds are meant to slow down or countervail the ways in which digital reproduction reconfigures our eyes and decenters our identities.[20] But Wenders's work of the postunification period, unlike that of Vilsmaier, has been by and large not very determined to collect specifically German sounds and synchronize them into spectacles of national belonging.

Wenders's 1994 *Lisbon Story*, for instance, had a disillusioned sound engineer travel to Portugal to meet his film director. Recording all kinds of vernacular noises on the streets of the Portuguese capital, the German sound technician compiles a semiethnographic bricolage of Lisbon sounds to which the director in the end is meant to add appropriate images. In his more recent *Buena Vista Social Club* (1998), on the other hand, Wenders reconstructs and follows the paths of some forgotten Cuban musicians from a recording studio in Havana to concerts in Amsterdam and finally New York. Clandestinely, Wenders records the octo- and nonagenarians' enthusiasm about Manhattan, that locus classicus of Wenders's own Americanist fantasies. Rather than talking about Germany and increasing the gulf between self and other, Wenders's cinema now seems to record and actively participate in the intermingling of diverse cultures, visions, and sounds.

One of the songs in Wim Wenders's *Buena Vista Social Club* is called "El Carretero," a Cuban "blues" tune derived from Spanish traditions that are also very popular in West Africa:

> Por el camino del sitio mío
> Un carretero alegre pasó
> Con sus canciones que es muy sentida
> Y muy guajira alegre cantó
>
> Me voy al transbordador
> A descargar la carreta
> Me voy al transbordador
> A descargar la carreta
> Para cumplir con la meta
> De mi penosa labor.[21]
>
> [Along the track by my house
> A cart-driver passed
> With his sentimental songs
> The Guajiro sang:
>
> I'm going to the crossing
> To unburden my load
> I'm going to the crossing
> To unburden my load
> There I'll reach the end
> Of my crushing labor.]

"El Carretero" is a song of lament and imaginary redemption, of suffering and the bliss of aesthetic transformation. Both the observer's prelude and the cart driver's tune itself are sung by the same voice, a voice mimetically bridging the gap between different subject positions and bringing self and other into an open relationship. In the lyrics' binary oppositions of home and street, stasis and movement, vision and music, pain and deliverance, one pole thus at once reflects and produces its opposite. The other's difference is never as absolute as it may appear at first. Alterity here is recognized as also within the subject itself, and it can be appreciated and in fact even accessed performatively.

A delicate juncture of different sounds and voices, "El Carretero" sheds light on the location of German film today at the intersections of past and future, the popular and the national. Like the cart driver in "El Carretero," postunification cinema has imparted charming visions of individual redress and recovery. Even at its most epic, it has sought "a descargar la carreta"—to unload audiences from the burdens of a past that does not seem to go away. Contrary to "El Carretero," however, German cinema today rarely fuses grief and hope, lament and utopia, into dynamic relationships. As it reinvents historical traditions, reifies lost legends, or remakes yesterday in the image of the present, this cinema prefers to disavow the afflicted voices of the past, of the cart driver's distressed listener and onlooker. The majority of commercial German film productions of the post-Wall era want us to believe that in spite of the shadows of Goebbels and Auschwitz the codes of the popular and the nation have reattained the kind of normalcy they may enjoy somewhere else. Yet no adept master narrative, or any reference to the untroubled coexistence of Hollywood and German film today, can ever really succeed in reconciling the dissimilar legacies of Hollywood in Berlin and Berlin in Hollywood, of Nazi Americanism and German Hollywood exile. The marks left by the bifurcation of German cinema during the course of the 1930s remain indelible. Wrong history cannot be recalled rightly.

Notes

INTRODUCTION

1. See, e.g., the various contributions to Hamid Naficy, ed., *Home, Exile, Homeland: Film, Media, and the Politics of Place* (New York: Routledge, 1999); and Mette Hjort and Scott MacKenzie, eds., *Cinema and Nation* (London: Routledge, 2000).

2. See the various contributions to Randall Halle and Maggie McCarthy, eds., *Light Motives: German Popular Film in Perspective* (Detroit: Wayne State University Press, forthcoming); the recent work on Weimar and Nazi entertainment cinema (Karsten Witte, *Lachende Erben, Toller Tag: Filmkomödie im Dritten Reich* [Berlin: Vorwerk, 1995]; Eric Rentschler, *The Ministry of Illusion: Nazi Cinema and Its Afterlife* [Cambridge, Mass.: Harvard University Press, 1996]; Linda Schulte-Sasse, *Entertaining the Third Reich: Illusions of Wholeness in Nazi Cinema* [Durham, N.C.: Duke University Press, 1996]; Patrice Petro, "Nazi Cinema at the Intersection of the Classical and the Popular," *New German Critique* 74 [spring/fall 1998]: 41–56; and Thomas Elsaesser, *Weimar Cinema and After: Germany's Historical Imaginary* [London: Routledge, 2000]); on Hollywood exile (Christian Cargnelli and Michael Omasta, eds., *Schatten.Exil: Europäische Emigranten im Film noir* [Vienna: PVS Verleger, 1997]); on New German Cinema (John E. Davidson, *Deterritorializing the New German Cinema* [Minneapolis: University of Minnesota Press, 1999]); on issues of marginality and alterity in post-Wall German film (see the contributions to *Camera Obscura* 44 [spring 2001]); on queer cinema (Alice Kuzniar, *The Queer German Cinema* [Stanford: Stanford University Press, 2000]; and on the emergence of a Turkish-German minority cinema during the late 1990s (Deniz Göktürk, "Migration und Kino: Subnationale Mitleidskultur oder transnationale Rollenspiele?" *Einwanderung, Literatur, Kultur,* ed. Carmine Chiellino [Stuttgart: Metzler Verlag, forthcoming]). All this work has vastly complicated our sense of what may count as German national cinema in the first place. This new scholarship has made clear that we cannot talk about German national cinema without exploring its place within a much larger European and transatlantic

framework (see also Jörg Schöning, ed., *London Calling: Deutsche im britischen Film der dreißiger Jahre* [Munich: Text und Kritik, 1993]; Manfred Behn, ed., *Schwarzer Traum und weiße Sklavin: Deutsch-dänische Filmbeziehungen, 1910–1930* [Munich: Text und Kritik, 1994]; Jörg Schöning, ed., *Fantasies russes: Russische Filmemacher in Berlin und Paris, 1920–1930* [Munich: Text und Kritik, 1995]; and Sibylle M. Sturm, ed., *Hallo? Berlin? Ici Paris! Aspekte der französisch-deutschen Filmbeziehungen, 1918–1939* [Munich: Text und Kritik, 1996]).

3. For a prominent example see Edgar Reitz, *Bilder in Bewegung: Essays. Gespräche zum Kino* (Reinbek: Rowohlt, 1995).

4. Karsten Witte, "The Indivisible Legacy of Nazi Cinema," *New German Critique* 74 (spring/summer 1998): 29.

5. Gerd Gemünden, *Framed Visions: Popular Culture, Americanization, and the Contemporary German and Austrian Imagination* (Ann Arbor: University of Michigan Press, 1998), 20.

6. For extensive discussions of Syberberg's *Our Hitler* see Anton Kaes, *From Hitler to Heimat: The Return of History as Film* (Cambridge, Mass.: Harvard University Press, 1989), 37–72; and Eric L. Santner, *Stranded Objects: Mourning, Memory, and Film in Postwar Germany* (Ithaca, N.Y.: Cornell University Press, 1990), 103–149.

7. Thomas Elsaesser, *Fassbinder's Germany: History, Identity, Subject* (Amsterdam: Amsterdam University Press, 1996), 153–154.

8. Hans Jürgen Syberberg, *Hitler, ein Film aus Deutschland* (Reinbek: Rowohlt, 1978), 15.

9. Max Horkheimer and Theodor W. Adorno, *Dialectic of Enlightenment*, trans. John Cumming (New York: Continuum, 1995), 163. For one of the best readings of Adorno's exilic position in America see Nico Israel, "Adorno, Los Angeles, and the Dislocation of Culture," *Outlandish: Writing between Exile and Diaspora* (Stanford: Stanford University Press, 2000), 75–122.

10. Peter Uwe Hohendahl, *Prismatic Thought: Theodor W. Adorno* (Lincoln: University of Nebraska Press, 1995), 119.

11. For an extended discussion of this critique see Lutz Koepnick, *Walter Benjamin and the Aesthetics of Power* (Lincoln: University of Nebraska Press, 1999), 53–82.

12. Thomas Schatz, *The Genius of the System: Hollywood Filmmaking in the Studio Era* (New York: Pantheon Books, 1988), 12.

13. Max Pensky, "Minimal Adorno," *New German Critique* 75 (fall 1998): 190.

14. Theodor Adorno, *In Search of Wagner*, trans. Rodney Livingstone (London: New Left Books, 1981).

15. Hohendahl, *Prismatic Thought*, 141. See also Andreas Huyssen, "Adorno in Reverse: From Hollywood to Richard Wagner," in *After the Great Divide: Modernism, Mass Culture, Postmodernism*, by Andreas Huyssen (Bloomington: Indiana University Press, 1986), 16–43.

16. Jürgen Habermas, "Was ist ein Volk? Zum politischen Selbstverständnis der Geisteswissenschaften im Vormärz," in *Die postnationale Konstellation: Politische Essays* (Frankfurt / M.: Suhrkamp, 1998), 13–46.

17. Pamela M. Potter, *Most German of the Arts: Musicology and Society from the Weimar Republic to the End of Hitler's Reich* (New Haven, Conn.: Yale University Press, 1998), ix. See also David B. Dennis, *Beethoven in German Politics, 1870–1989* (New Haven, Conn.: Yale University Press, 1996), 1–31.

18. Qtd. in Felix Moeller, *Der Filmminister: Goebbels und der Film im Dritten Reich* (Berlin: Henschel, 1998), 60.

19. Horkheimer and Adorno, *Dialectic of Enlightenment,* 164.

20. According to Lotte Eisner, e.g., the figure of the doppelgänger encoded Weimar cinema's romantic attraction toward the obscure and undetermined. It transformed external history into meaningful inwardness, accidental forms into transcendental visions. According to Thomas Elsaesser, by contrast, the many doubles of the Weimar era displaced fundamental anxieties about social reality into the fantastic: Weimar film artists embraced the figure of the double so as to articulate what they considered a dramatic loss of control over the modes of mass cultural production and consumption. See Lotte H. Eisner, *The Haunted Screen: Expressionism in the German Cinema and the Influence of Max Reinhardt* (Berkeley: University of California Press, 1994); and Thomas Elsaesser, "Social Mobility and the Fantastic," *Wide Angle* 5, no. 2 (1982): 14–25.

21. Elsaesser, *Weimar Cinema and After,* 380.

22. Theodor W. Adorno, *Minima Moralia: Reflections from Damaged Life,* trans. E. F. N. Jephcott (London: New Left Books, 1951), 33.

23. Edward W. Said, *Representations of the Intellectual* (New York: Vintage Books, 1996), 49.

24. Gerd Gemünden, "Space Out of Joint: Ernst Lubitsch's *To Be or Not to Be,*" *New German Critique* (forthcoming).

25. David Bordwell, *The History of Film Style* (Cambridge, Mass.: Harvard University Press, 1997), 12–45.

26. Hannah Arendt, "The Nature of Totalitarianism," unpublished lecture, 1954, qtd. in Elisabeth Young-Bruehl, *Hannah Arendt: For Love of the World* (New Haven, Conn.: Yale University Press, 1982), 203.

27. Leslie Epstein, *Pandaemonium* (New York: St. Martin's Griffin, 1997), 98–99.

CHAPTER 1. SOUNDS OF SILENCE

1. Felix Moeller, *Der Filmminister: Goebbels und der Film im Dritten Reich* (Berlin: Henschel, 1998).

2. Russell A. Berman, foreword to *Reproductions of Banality: Fascism, Literature, and French Intellectual Life,* by Alice Yaeger Kaplan (Minneapolis: University of Minnesota Press, 1986), xi–xxiii.

3. Steve Neale, "*Triumph of the Will*: Notes on Documentary and Spec-

tacle," *Screen* 20, no. 1 (1979): 63–86; and Linda Schulte-Sasse, *Entertaining the Third Reich: Illusions of Wholeness in Nazi Cinema* (Durham, N.C.: Duke University Press, 1996).

4. Karsten Witte, "Politik als Nebenhandlung: Zu einer Theorie des faschistischen Films," *Politik und Kultur* 2, no. 9 (1982): 32–41.

5. Georg Seeßlen, *Tanz den Adolf Hitler: Faschismus in der populären Kultur* (Berlin: Edition Tiamat, 1994), 14–20.

6. Walter Murch, foreword to *Audio-Vision: Sound on Screen,* by Michel Chion, ed. and trans. Claudia Gorbman (New York: Columbia University Press, 1994), xi.

7. Erhard Schütz, "Das 'Dritte Reich' als Mediendiktatur. Medienpolitik und Modernisierung in Deutschland 1933 bis 1945," *Monatshefte* 87, no. 2 (summer 1995): 129–150; and Erhard Schütz, "Zur Modernität des 'Dritten Reiches,'" *Internationales Archiv für Sozialgeschichte der Literatur* 20, no. 1 (1995): 116–136.

8. Silent cinema, of course, had never been entirely silent either. On the uses of music and sound techniques in German theaters prior to the breakthrough of synchronized sound see the contributions by Richard Traubner, Horst Claus, and Michael Wedel to *MusikSpektakelFilm: Musiktheater und Tanzkultur im deutschen Film, 1922–1937,* ed. Hans-Michael Bock, Wolfgang Jacobsen, and Jörg Schöning (Munich: Edition Text und Kritik, 1998). See also Herbert Birett, *Stummfilm-Musik. Materialiensammlung* (Berlin: Deutsche Kinemathek, 1970); Walther Seidler, ed., *Stummfilmmusik gestern und heute* (Berlin: Spiess, 1979); and Hansjörg Pauli, *Filmmusik: Stummfilm* (Stuttgart: Klett-Cotta, 1981).

9. *The Singing Fool* was actually shown using the Vitaphone process, a sound-on-disk system already outmoded by 1929.

10. Tom Gunning, "An Aesthetic of Astonishment: Early Film and the (In)Credulous Spectator," in *Viewing Positions: Ways of Seeing Film,* ed. Linda Williams (New Brunswick, N.J.: Rutgers University Press, 1995), 114–133.

11. Fred Hildenbrandt, "Der Singende Narr," June 4, 1929, Archive of Stiftung Deutsche Kinemathek, Berlin. *The Singing Fool* premiered with two short sound films on the supporting bill. The choice was programmatic. The first short presented the performance of an American jazz band; the second showed tenor Benjamino Gigli intoning arias from Italian opera. "It is only a matter of time," rejoiced one reviewer, "and La Scala will play for only one Deutschmark in small provincial towns" (R. K. [author's initials], "Filmbesprechung: Der singende Narr," *Licht-Bild-Bühne,* June 4, 1929). According to this and other commentators, talking films redefined the role of the movie theater as a cultural institution. It promised a vernacular joining high art and popular culture, a synthesis that would appeal to audiences across the boundaries of class, status, and aesthetic preference.

12. See, e.g., Hans Wollenberg, "Filmbesprechung: 'Melodie des Herzens,'" *Licht-Bild-Bühne,* December 17, 1929.

13. Ernst Jäger, review of *Melodie des Herzens, Film-Kurier*, December 17, 1929.

14. For more on the market struggles between Hollywood and Weimar cinema see Thomas J. Saunders, *Hollywood in Berlin: American Cinema and Weimar Germany* (Berkeley: University of California Press, 1994).

15. Victoria de Grazia, "Mass Culture and Sovereignty: The American Challenge to European Cinemas, 1920–1960," *Journal of Modern History* 61 (March 1989): 68.

16. See, e.g., the speech delivered by Dr. James Birnholz, director of AEG, to industry representatives in December 1929, in *Film-Kurier*, December 16, 1929.

17. Guido Bagier, *Das tönende Licht* (Berlin: Gross, 1943), 398–399.

18. Anton Kaes, "Film in der Weimarer Republik: Motor der Moderne," in *Geschichte des deutschen Films*, ed. Wolfgang Jacobsen, Anton Kaes, and Hans Helmut Prinzler (Stuttgart: Metzler, 1993), 86.

19. Alan Williams, "Historical and Theoretical Issues in the Coming of Recorded Sound to the Cinema," in *Sound Theory, Sound Practice*, ed. Rick Altman (New York: Routledge, 1992), 128.

20. Miriam Hansen, *Babel and Babylon: Spectatorship in American Silent Film* (Cambridge, Mass.: Harvard University Press, 1991), 94.

21. Herbert Ihering, "Der akustische Film," *Berliner Börsen-Courier*, September 19, 1922.

22. Noël Carroll, "Lang, Pabst, and Sound," *Ciné-Tracts* 2, no. 1 (fall 1978): 15–23; Rick Altman, "Introduction," *Yale French Studies* 60 (1980): 3–15.

23. Emil Jannings, "Deutschland und der internationale Tonfilm," *Der Film*, June 3, 1929.

24. Qtd. in Gerd Rühle, *Das Dritte Reich: Dokumentarische Darstellung des Aufbaus der Nation. Das erste Jahr: 1933* (Berlin: Hummel, 1934), 82; also qtd. and trans. in Eric Rentschler, *The Ministry of Illusion: Nazi Cinema and Its Afterlife* (Cambridge, Mass.: Harvard University Press, 1996), 20.

25. Theodor W. Adorno, "On Popular Music," in *On Record: Rock, Pop, and the Written Word*, ed. Simon Frith and Andrew Goodwin (London: Routledge, 1990), 308.

26. Mary Ann Doane, "The Voice and the Cinema: The Articulation of Body and Space," in *Film Sound: Theory and Practice*, ed. Elisabeth Weis and John Belton (New York: Columbia University Press, 1985), 162.

27. Alan Williams, "Is Sound Recording Like a Language?" *Yale French Studies* 60 (1980): 51–66.

28. On Menzel's "star" status see Hans-Christoph Blumenberg, *Das Leben geht weiter: Der letzte Film des Dritten Reichs* (Berlin: Rowohlt, 1993), 68–71.

29. K. Zierold, "Bedeutung und Grenzen des Films als Erziehungsmittel," *Film und Bild*, April 10, 1935.

30. Gerd Eckert, "Filmtendenz und Tendenzfilm," *Wille und Macht. Führerorgan der nationalsozialistischen Jugend* 6, no. 4 (1938): 22.

31. Joseph Goebbels, "Rede anläßlich der Kriegstagung der Reichsfilm-

kammer am 15.2.1941 in Berlin," reprinted in Gerd Albrecht, *Nationalsozial-istische Filmpolitik* (Stuttgart: Enke, 1969), 469.

32. Karsten Witte, "Visual Pleasure Inhibited: Aspects of the German Re-vue Film," *New German Critique* 24/25 (fall/winter 1981/82): 238–263.

33. Rentschler, *Ministry of Illusion*, 216–217.

34. Heide Schlüpmann, "Faschistische Trugbilder weiblicher Autonomie," *Frauen und Film* 44/45 (1988): 59.

35. On the concept of the nonrepresentational sign see Richard Dyer, "En-tertainment and Utopia," *Genre: The Musical*, ed. Rick Altman (London: Rout-ledge and Kegan Paul, 1981), 177.

36. Film music, wrote Hermann Wanderscheck in 1942, "can compete with the soul of the image—the image remains silent, but music resounds, roars, paints, rings out in major and minor keys, spreading itself out like a rug over the image or flickering upward like a flame to provide the most powerful ex-pression of redemption and liberation." Spoken dialogue in many Nazi films, likewise, wants to roar, paint, and ring out in different keys in order to cue the spectator's dreaming. Hermann Wanderscheck, "Die Macht der Musik im Film," *Film-Kurier*, January 19, 1942; qtd. and trans. in Rentschler, *Ministry of Illusion*, 387.

37. A good case in point would be the 1937 UFA production *Patrioten* (Karl Ritter), which tells the story of a World War I ace stranded behind French en-emy lines. The film replays constellations typical for many much earlier Nazi feature films: the rewriting of World War I; the displaced German's quest for a return to his native soil; the desire to turn one's back on foreign cultures, im-ages, and sounds. Strangely enough, however, not only do the French in this film speak perfect high and regional German, but the narrative also systemat-ically omits any reference to the dilemma of a German forced to navigate for-eign linguistic territory. Although he pretends to be mute first, later we wit-ness the hero easily communicating with his enemies—as if no language barrier existed. *Patrioten* envisioned the many accents of the German language as a European lingua franca. It remade French culture in the name of regional Germanic linguistic properties.

38. Marc A. Weiner, *Richard Wagner and the Anti-Semitic Imagination* (Lincoln: University of Nebraska Press, 1995), 103–194.

39. Klaus Kreimeier, "Von Henny Porten zu Zarah Leander. Filmgenres und Genrefilm in der Weimarer Republik und im Nationalsozialismus," *mon-tage/av* 3, no. 2 (1994): 42.

40. Michel Chion, *Audio-Vision: Sound on Screen*, ed. and trans. Claudia Gorbman (New York: Columbia University Press), 131.

41. Filmmaking, Rósza claimed, "is a composite art, a Wagnerian *Gesamt-kunstwerk*, and film music should be written in that way" (qtd. in Caryl Flinn, *Strains of Utopia: Gender, Nostalgia, and Hollywood Film Music* [Princeton: Princeton University Press, 1992], 13); and Steiner did not hesitate to add, "If Wagner had lived in this century, he would have been the Number One film

composer" (qtd. in Tony Thomas, *Music for the Movies* [New York: Barnes, 1973], 122).

42. See Theodor Adorno and Hanns Eisler, *Composing for the Films* (London: Athlone Press, 1994), 135–157.

43. Flinn, *Strains of Utopia*, 34.

44. Helga Belach, ed., *Wir tanzen um die Welt: Deutsche Revuefilme, 1933–45* (Munich: Hanser, 1979).

45. Ursula Vossen, "Die große Attraktion: Opern- und Operettensänger im deutschsprachigen Tonfilm," in *MusikSpektakelFilm*, 105–122.

46. Adorno and Eisler, *Composing for the Films*, 114–133.

47. See *Die Musik* 28 (1936): 721.

48. Wolfgang Liebeneiner, "Die Harmonie von Bild, Wort und Musik im Film," *Film-Kurier*, March 13, 1939, 4–5. On Liebeneiner's considerable influence on Goebbels see Moeller, *Der Filmminister*, 144–148.

49. Liebeneiner, "Die Harmonie," 5.

50. Liebeneiner's argument in this respect clearly resonated with Béla Balázs's thoughts on sound film in his 1930 *Der Geist des Films*. Like Liebeneiner Balázs valorized the coloratura of language over its logic and meaning: "The human's sound in film is more interesting than what he has to say. Even in film dialogue, the acoustical-sensual impression is more important than the content." Unlike Liebeneiner and other Nazi film theorists, however, Balázs did not seek to ground the voice's sound in ethnic definition of national identity. Béla Balázs, *Schriften zum Film*, ed. Helmut H. Diederichs and Wolfgang Gersch (Munich: Hanser, 1984), 2:165; see also Jürgen Kasten, "Vom Visuellen zum Akustischen Sprechen: Das Drehbuch in der Übergangsphase vom Stumm- zum Tonfilm," *Sprache im Film*, ed. Gustav Ernst (Vienna: Wespennest, 1994), 41–56.

51. Liebeneiner, "Die Harmonie," 5.

52. Ibid.

53. Richard Wagner, "What Is German?" in *Prose Works*, trans. William Ashton Ellis (New York: Broude Brothers, 1895), 4:160.

54. It was only after 1939, as Pamela Potter has shown, that musicologists were able to solve many of their ideological dilemmas: "Territorial gains during World War II then inspired musicologists, in a sense, to 'annex' the musical achievements of subjugated countries and claim them as German" (Pamela M. Potter, *Most German of the Arts: Musicology and Society from the Weimar Republic to the End of Hitler's Reich* [New Haven, Conn.: Yale University Press, 1998], xvii, 200–234). See also Pamela M. Potter, "Did Himmler Really Like Gregorian Chant? The SS and Musicology," *Modernism/Modernity* 2, no. 3 (1995): 45–68.

55. Richard Traubner, "Operette als Stoff und Anregung: Entwicklungen im Musikfilm, 1907–1937," in *MusikSpektakelFilm*, 21.

56. Rentschler, *Ministry of Illusion*, 117.

57. See, e.g., Michael H. Kater, *Different Drummers: Jazz in the Culture of Nazi Germany* (Oxford: Oxford University Press, 1992); Wilfried Breyvogel,

Piraten, Swings, und Junge Garde: Jugendwiderstand im Nationalsozialismus (Bonn: Dietz, 1991); and Franz Ritter, ed., *Heinrich Himmler und die Liebe zum Swing: Erinnerungen und Dokumente* (Leipzig: Reclam, 1994). For more on jazz and swing in sound features of the late Weimar era see Marko Paysan, "' . . . Aus dem Geist des Boulevards'! Zur Physiognomie urbaner Tanzmusik- und Unterhaltungskultur in der Tonfilmoperette," in *MusikSpektakelFilm*, 46–66.

58. Kreuder was one of the most successful film music composers during the Third Reich in spite of his thinly veiled dedication to African American idioms. Trained in classical music, Kreuder founded his first jazz band in the 1920s in Hamburg and performed jazz throughout the 1930s. His hit songs were instrumental in establishing closer ties between the Nazi film and record industries. Because of Kreuder's predilection for jazz and swing, many of these hit songs bordered on the impermissible. Kreuder's continued success therefore relied on his talent in imaginative redress. Kreuder's musical number for the Nazi Western *Wasser für Canitoga* (1939), e.g., clearly emulated the rather "un-German" sound tracks of Hollywood pageants such as *San Francisco* (1936). But in order to release the film's popular ballad as a record, Kreuder changed its title from "Good bye, Jonny" to "Leb wohl, Peter" (Hans Christoph Worbs, *Der Schlager. Bestandsaufnahme, Analyse, Dokumentation* [Bremen: Schünemann, 1963], 62).

59. A quite different interpretation of the chicken dance has been proposed by Marie-Luise Bolte, "Vom Kabarett zum Film: Thesen zum Filmsong und vier Komponisten-Porträts," in *Als die Filme singen lernten: Innovation und Tradition im Musikfilm, 1928–1938*, ed. Hans-Michael Bock, Wolfgang Jacobsen, and Jörg Schöning (Munich: Edition Text und Kritik, 1999), 45.

60. Michael H. Kater, *The Twisted Muse: Musicians and Their Music in the Third Reich* (New York: Oxford University Press, 1997), 26.

61. Hermann Wanderscheck, "Sieben Fragen an zwölf Komponisten: Es geht um filmeigene Musik," *Film-Kurier*, December 31, 1938.

62. Konrad Vogelsang, *Filmmusik im Dritten Reich: Eine Dokumentation*, 2d ed. (Pfaffenweiler: Centaurus, 1993), 28. On the role of Beethoven in Nazi film scoring see Hans Rutz, "Beethoven und der Film: Querverbindungen zwischen Musik-Zitat und -Illustration," *Film-Kurier*, May 28, 1938; and David B. Dennis, *Beethoven in German Politics, 1870–1989* (New Haven, Conn.: Yale University Press, 1996), 158–159.

63. In 1936, e.g., Hans von Wolzogen defined Wagner's legacy to the Third Reich in terms of a comprehensive national project of spiritual and physical reeducation: "Germans! As nature lovers preserve and strengthen your bodies in strict discipline and healthy exercise, and search for and find your soul, like your Führer, in the magnificent art of the master of Bayreuth!" Hans Freiherr von Wolzogen, "Das politische Bayreuth," *Zeitschrift für Musik* (March 1936): 283–284.

64. Theodor Adorno, *In Search of Wagner*, trans. Rodney Livingstone (London: New Left Books, 1981), 31.

65. Simonetta Falasca-Zamponi, *Fascist Spectacle: The Aesthetics of Power in Mussolini's Italy* (Berkeley: University of California Press, 1997), 192.

66. Kristin Thompson, *Exporting Entertainment: America in the World Film Market, 1907–1934* (London: BFI, 1985), 148–170.

67. Reorganized under Goebbels, German cinema recaptured the major share of its own market from Hollywood by 1936. See Douglas Gomery, "Economic Struggle and Hollywood Imperialism: Europe Converts to Sound," in *Film Sound: Theory and Practice,* 30; see also Douglas Gomery, "The Coming of Sound to the German Cinema," in *Purdue Film Studies Annual, 1976* (West Lafayette, Ind.: Purdue University Press, 1976), 136–143.

68. Joseph Goebbels, "Der Film as Erzieher. Rede zur Eröffnung der Filmarbeit der HJ" [speech delivered in Berlin, October 12, 1941], in *Das eherne Herz: Reden und Aufsätze aus den Jahren 1941/42* (Munich: Fritz Eher, 1943), 44.

69. "The National Film Is the International Film," *Film-Kurier,* January 1, 1934 (written in English!).

70. Ernesto Laclau and Chantal Mouffe, *Hegemony and Socialist Strategy: Towards a Radical Democratic Politics* (London: Verso, 1985), 85.

71. Alexander Kluge, "On Film and the Public Sphere," *New German Critique* 24/25 (fall/winter 1981/82): 206–220; Miriam Hansen, "Alexander Kluge, Cinema, and the Public Sphere: The Construction Site of Counter History," *Discourse* 6 (1983): 53–74.

CHAPTER 2. INCORPORATING THE UNDERGROUND

1. Rudolf Arnheim, "A New Laocoön," in *Film as Art* (Berkeley: University of California Press, 1957), 199–230.

2. Claudia Gorbman, *Unheard Melodies: Narrative Film Music* (Bloomington: Indiana University Press, 1987), 51.

3. Rick Altman, "Introduction," *Yale French Studies* 60 (1980): 7.

4. See C. Hooper Trask, "On Berlin's Screens," *New York Times,* February 5, 1933; qtd. in Kristin Thompson, *Exporting Entertainment: America in the World Film Market, 1907–1934* (London: BFI, 1985), 163.

5. Rick Altman, "Moving Lips: Cinema as Ventriloquism," *Yale French Studies* 60 (1980): 67–79.

6. Nataša Ďurovičová, "Translating America: The Hollywood Multilinguals 1929–1933," in *Sound Theory, Sound Practice,* ed. Rick Altman (New York: Routledge, 1992), 139.

7. For a detailed discussion of Kellermann's novel and its first cinematic version of 1915 see Deniz Göktürk, *Künstler, Cowboys, Ingenieure . . . Kultur- und mediengeschichtliche Studien zu deutschen Amerika-Texten, 1912–1920* (Munich: Fink, 1998), 97–116.

8. In the French-language version, which premiered in November 1933 as well, the title role was played by Jean Gabin. Only Gustaf Gründgens, in the role of the banker, Woolf, remained from the original German cast. Thomas Elsaesser suggests that Bernhardt shot *The Tunnel* in France (Thomas Elsaesser,

"Moderne und Modernisierung: Der deutsche Film der dreißiger Jahre," *montage/av* 3, no. 2 [1994]: 35). Production records and trade magazine reports show, however, that both versions were produced at the Bavaria studios in Munich-Geiselgasteig. See "Filme im Werden: Im Bavaria-Tunnel," *Film-Kurier*, September 18, 1933.

9. For an insightful study of the few Nazi fantasy films see Kraft Wetzel and Peter Hagemann, *Liebe, Tod, und Technik: Kino des Phantastischen, 1933–1945* (Berlin: Spiess, 1977).

10. *Berliner Börsenzeitung*, November 4, 1933.

11. André Bazin, "The Virtues and Limitations of Montage," in *What Is Cinema?* trans. Hugh Gray (Berkeley: University of California Press, 1967), 1:41–52.

12. Vivian Carol Sobchack, *The Limits of Infinity: The American Science Fiction Film, 1950–1975* (South Brunswick, N.J.: A. S. Barnes, 1980), 141.

13. See, e.g., the review in *Kinematograph*, November 4, 1933.

14. Lothar Schwab, "Im Labyrinth der Männerängste. Kurt Bernhardts deutsche Filme (1924–1933)," in *Aufruhr der Gefühle: Die Kinowelt des Curtis Bernhardt*, ed. Helga Belach, Gero Gandert, and Hans Helmut Prinzler (Munich: Bucher, 1982), 48.

15. Christian Metz, "*Trucage* and the Film," *Critical Inquiry* 4 (summer 1977): 657–665.

16. Steve Neale, "'You've Got to Be Fucking Kidding!' Knowledge, Belief, and Judgement in Science Fiction," in *Alien Zone: Cultural Theory and Contemporary Science Fiction Cinema*, ed. Annette Kuhn (London: Verso, 1990), 164.

17. René Clair, "The Art of Sound," in *Film Sound: Theory and Practice*, ed. Elisabeth Weis and John Belton (New York: Columbia University Press, 1985), 92–95; Michel Chion, *Audio-Vision: Sound on Screen*, ed. and trans. Claudia Gorbman (New York: Columbia University Press, 1994), 179.

18. Miriam Hansen, "Early Silent Cinema: Whose Public Sphere?" *New German Critique* 29 (spring/summer 1983): 156.

19. Antonio Gramsci, *Selections from the Prison Notebooks*, trans. and ed. Quintin Hoare and Geoffrey Nowell Smith (New York: International Publishers, 1977), 195.

20. Linda Schulte-Sasse, *Entertaining the Third Reich: Illusions of Wholeness in Nazi Cinema* (Durham, N.C.: Duke University Press, 1996), 257.

21. Thomas Elsaesser, "Film History and Visual Pleasure: Weimar Cinema," *Cinema Histories, Cinema Practices*, ed. Patricia Mellencamp and Philip Rosen (Frederick, Md.: University Publications of America, 1984), 72.

22. Maurice Elvey's 1935 remake—entitled *Transatlantic Tunnel* and based on a screenplay by German exile Curt Siodmak—reverses the breakthrough sequence: Mac Allan's American crews greet the British workers first.

23. Hans Traub, "Der Film als politisches Machtmittel," qtd. in *Film und Gesellschaft in Deutschland: Dokumente und Materialien*, ed. Wilfried von Bredow and Rolf Zurek (Hamburg: Hoffmann und Campe, 1975), 171.

24. Giselher Wirsing, *Der maßlose Kontinent: Roosevelts Kampf um die Weltherrschaft* (Jena: Diederichs, 1942), 79.

25. David Bathrick, "Making a National Family with the Radio: The Nazi *Wunschkonzert*," *Modernism/Modernity* 4, no. 1 (January 1997): 120.

26. Qtd. in Wolfram Wessel, *Hörspiele im dritten Reich* (Bonn: Bouvier, 1985), 122; also qtd. and trans. in Bathrick, "Making a National Family," 116.

27. Hilmar Hoffmann, *The Triumph of Propaganda: Film and National Socialism, 1933–1945*, trans. John A. Broadwin and V. R. Berghahn (Providence: Berghahn, 1996), vii.

28. Rudolf Arnheim, *Radio* (London: Faber and Faber, 1936), 32.

29. Ibid., 72.

30. Ibid., 235.

31. Herbert Marcuse, "The Struggle against Liberalism in the Totalitarian View of the State," *Negations: Essays in Critical Theory*, trans. Jeremy J. Shapiro (Boston: Beacon, 1968), 3–42.

32. Traub, "Der Film als politisches Machtmittel," 171.

33. See Michael Ryan and Douglas Kellner, "Technophobia," in *Alien Zone*, 58–65.

34. See Mary Kiersch, *Curtis Bernhardt: A Directors Guild of America Oral History* (Metuchen, N.J.: Scarecrow Press, 1986), 58.

35. Jeffrey T. Schnapp, *Staging Fascism: 18 BL and the Theater of Masses for Masses* (Stanford: Stanford University Press, 1996), 90 (Schnapp's italics).

36. Ernst Jünger, *Der Arbeiter: Herrschaft und Gestalt. Sämtliche Werke: Zweite Abteilung* (Stuttgart: Klett-Cotta, 1981), 8:126.

37. Claudia Lenssen, "Durchlöcherte Finsternis: Das Melodramatische bei Curtis Bernhardt," in *Aufruhr der Gefühle*, 15–16.

38. Many of the film's first reviewers were clearly irritated by Mac Allan's clipped heroism in the end. The film, some argued, placed too much weight on an idea and too little on human drama. See *Film-Kurier*, January 17, September 18, and November 4, 1933, as well as the review in *Deutsche Filmzeitung*, November 19, 1933.

39. Ernst Bloch, "Die Angst des Ingenieurs," in *Gesamtausgabe* (Frankfurt/M.: Suhrkamp, 1965), 9:347–358.

40. Eric Rentschler, "The Elemental, the Ornamental, the Instrumental: *The Blue Light* and Nazi Film Aesthetics," in *The Other Perspective in Gender and Culture: Rewriting Women and the Symbolic*, ed. Juliet Flower MacCannell (New York: Columbia University Press, 1990), 175.

41. Klaus Theweleit, *Male Fantasies*, trans. Stephen Conway, 2 vols. (Minneapolis: University of Minnesota Press, 1987).

42. Marcia Klotz, "The Question of Fascist Erotics," *Faultline: Interdisciplinary Approaches to German Studies* 1 (1992): 69–82.

43. On the linkage of homosexuality and fascism see Andrew Hewitt, *Political Inversions: Homosexuality, Fascism, and the Modernist Imaginary* (Stanford: Stanford University Press, 1997).

44. For more on Bernhardt's cinema of male fantasies see Schwab, "Im

Labyrinth der Männerängste," 34–40; and Heinz-Gerd Rasner and Reinhard Wulf, "Sehnsucht, Schuld und Einsamkeit. Curtis Bernhardt in Hollywood," in *Aufruhr der Gefühle*, 76–80.

45. On the construction of the New York subway see Clifton Hood, *722 Miles: The Building of the Subways and How They Transformed New York* (New York: Simon and Schuster, 1993); and Benson Bobrick, *Labyrinths of Iron: A History of the World's Subways* (New York: Newsweek Books, 1982), 195–270.

46. Bobrick, *Labyrinths of Iron*, 258.

47. Heinrich Fischer, "Der Tunnel," *Die neue Weltbühne* 3, no. 1 (1934): 24.

48. Walter Benjamin, *Illuminations: Essays and Reflections*, trans. Harry Zohn (New York: Schocken, 1969), 241.

CHAPTER 3. ENGENDERING MASS CULTURE

1. Jeffrey Herf, *Reactionary Modernism: Technology, Culture, and Politics in Weimar and the Third Reich* (Cambridge: Cambridge University Press, 1984), 224.

2. See Hans Dieter Schäfer, *Das gespaltene Bewußtsein: Deutsche Kultur und Lebenswirklichkeit, 1933–1945* (Munich: Hanser, 1981); and Hans Dieter Schäfer, "Amerikanismus im Dritten Reich," in *Nationalsozialismus und Modernisierung*, ed. Michael Prinz and Rainer Zitelmann (Darmstadt: Wissenschaftliche Buchgesellschaft, 1991), 199–215.

3. Theodor W. Adorno, "On Popular Music," in *On Record: Rock, Pop, and the Written Word*, ed. Simon Frith and Andrew Goodwin (London: Routledge, 1990), 308.

4. Fredric Jameson, "Reification and Utopia in Mass Culture," in *Signatures of the Visible* (New York: Routledge, 1992), 34.

5. Francis Courtade and Pierre Cadars, *Geschichte des Films im Dritten Reich* (Munich: Heyne, 1975), 28–29.

6. Victoria de Grazia, "Mass Culture and Sovereignty: The American Challenge to European Cinemas, 1920–1960," *Journal of Modern History* 61 (March 1989): 78.

7. Thomas Elsaesser, "Moderne und Modernisierung: Der deutsche Film der dreißiger Jahre," *montage/av* 3, no. 2 (1994): 35.

8. David Bathrick, "Inscribing History, Prohibiting and Producing Desire: Fassbinder's *Lili Marleen*," *New German Critique* 63 (fall 1994): 48. On Nazi modernism and film culture see also Elsaesser's essays "Moderne und Modernisierung"; and "Hollywood Berlin," *Sight and Sound* 7, no. 11 (November 1997): 14–17; and Leonardo Quaresima, "Der Film im Dritten Reich: Moderne, Amerikanismus, Unterhaltungsfilm," *montage/av* 3, no. 2 (1994): 5–22.

9. See Hitler's speech to the Nazi Women Organization during the Party Congress in 1934, reprinted in Ute Benz, ed., *Frauen im Nationalsozialismus: Dokumente und Zeugnisse* (Munich: Beck, 1993), 41–45. On women's role

during the Third Reich see, e.g., Claudia Koonz, *Mothers in the Fatherland: Women, the Family, and Nazi Politics* (New York: St. Martin's, 1987).

10. Karsten Witte, "Visual Pleasure Inhibited: Aspects of the German Revue Film," *New German Critique* 24/25 (fall/winter 1981/82): 238–263.

11. Hans Christoph Worbs, *Der Schlager. Bestandsaufnahme, Analyse, Dokumentation* (Bremen: Schünemann, 1963), 64.

12. See, e.g., Fritz Hippler's comments on stars in his *Betrachtungen zum Filmschaffen* (Berlin: Hesse, 1942), 102–107; or the ranking of actors according to their achievements as "great artists and creative human beings," in *Film-Kurier*, April 25, 1936. On the uneasy but operative relationship between stars and Nazi film theorists see Andrea Winkler, "Starkult auf germanisch: Goebbels und Hippler hielten sich an die Rezepte Hollywoods," *Medium* 18, no. 3 (1988): 27–30; and Andrea Winkler, *Starkult als Propagandamittel? Studien zum Unterhaltungsfilm im Dritten Reich* (Munich: Ölschläger, 1992).

13. Georg Seeßlen, *Tanz den Adolf Hitler: Faschismus in der populären Kultur* (Berlin: Edition Tiamat, 1994), 56.

14. See Joseph Goebbels's "Sieben Film-Thesen" (1935; reprinted in *Film und Gesellschaft in Deutschland: Dokumente und Materialien*, ed. Wilfried von Bredow and Rolf Zurek [Hamburg: Hoffmann und Campe, 1975], 178–180).

15. Peter Adam, *Art of the Third Reich* (New York: Abrams, 1992), 89.

16. See, e.g., Paul Seiler, *Ein Mythos lebt: Zarah Leander. Eine Bildbiographie. Zum 10. Todestag* (Berlin: published by Paul Seiler, 1994), 28.

17. See Helma Sanders-Brahms, "Zarah," *Jahrbuch Film 81/82*, ed. Hans Günther Pflaum (Munich: Hanser, 1981), 165–172; and Rosa von Praunheim, "Die Baßamsel singt nicht mehr," *Der Spiegel* 27, June 19, 1981, 158.

18. For a timely reassessment of Leander's gay reception see Alice A. Kuzniar, "Zarah Leander and Transgender Specularity," *Film Criticism* 23, nos. 2–3 (winter/spring 1999): 74–93.

19. See, esp., Thomas Elsaesser, "Tales of Sound and Fury: Observations on the Family Melodrama," *Monogram* 4 (1972): 2–15; and Paul Willemen, "Distanciation and Douglas Sirk," *Screen* 13, no. 4 (1972/73): 128–134.

20. Jon Halliday, "Notes on Sirk's German Films," *Douglas Sirk*, ed. Laura Mulvey and Jon Halliday (Edinburgh: Edinburgh Film Festival, 1972), 22; Marc Silberman, *German Cinema: Texts in Contexts* (Detroit: Wayne State University Press, 1995), 51–65.

21. For a persuasive critique of this scholarship see Barbara Klinger, *Melodrama and Meaning: History, Culture, and the Films of Douglas Sirk* (Bloomington: Indiana University Press, 1994).

22. Mary Ann Doane, "The Economy of Desire: The Commodity Form in/of the Cinema," in *Movies and Mass Culture*, ed. John Belton (New Brunswick, N.J.: Rutgers University Press, 1996), 128.

23. Jameson, "Reification and Utopia," 11.

24. Eric Rentschler, *The Ministry of Illusion: Nazi Cinema and Its Afterlife* (Cambridge, Mass.: Harvard University Press, 1996), 139.

25. Theodor W. Adorno, "On the Fetish-Character in Music and the

Regression of Listening," *The Essential Frankfurt School Reader*, ed. Andrew Arato and Eike Gebhardt (New York: Urizen Books, 1978), 277.

26. *Der Film*, June 13, 1942.

27. Released only a month after *Die große Liebe*, the Universal production *Invisible Agent* (dir. Edwin L. Martin) already poked fun at this myth of a miracle weapon. Based on a screenplay by Curt Siodmak, the film tells the story of an invisible spy placed in Nazi Germany to obtain information about Nazi war plans. Jon Halls, in the role of the indeed mostly invisible agent, challenges the way in which Leander's dream of a miracle fuses images of mobilization with the sounds of a fantasmatic, self-present body.

28. For the most comprehensive discussion of Leander's star persona in English see Antje Ascheid, "A Sierckian Double Image: The Narration of Zarah Leander as a National Socialist Star," *Film Criticism* 23, nos. 2–3 (winter/spring 1999): 46–73.

29. Zarah Leander, *Es war so wunderbar! Mein Leben*, trans. Anna Liese Kornitzky (Hamburg: Hoffmann und Campe, 1973), 138.

30. Cornelia Zumkeller, *Zarah Leander: Ihre Filme—ihr Leben* (Munich: Heyne, 1988), 74.

31. *Filmwelt* 17 (1938).

32. Richard Dyer, *Heavenly Bodies: Film Stars and Society* (New York: St. Martin's, 1986), 10.

33. For an intriguing collection of historical comments on Leander's voice see Paul Seiler, *Zarah Leander: Ich bin eine Stimme* (Berlin: Ullstein, 1997), 133–156.

34. *Berliner Lokalanzeiger*, September 2, 1937.

35. Charles Eckert, "The Carole Lombard in Macy's Window," in *Movies and Mass Culture*, 116.

36. See, e.g., Georg Herzberg, "La Habanera," *Film-Kurier*, December 20, 1937.

37. Ernst von der Decken, "Zarah Leander wurde gefeiert," *Berliner Zeitung*, December 21, 1937.

38. Ulrike Sanders, *Zarah Leander—Kann denn Schlager Sünde sein?* (Cologne: Pahl-Rugenstein, 1988), 36.

39. Heide Schlüpmann, "Faschistische Trugbilder weiblicher Autonomie," *Frauen und Film* 44/45 (1988): 60.

40. For more see Stanley Sadie, ed., *The New Grove Dictionary of Music and Musicians* (London: Macmillan, 1980), 8:8.

41. Katie Trumpener, "Puerto Rico Fever: Douglas Sirk, *La Habanera* (1937), and the Epistemology of Exoticism," in *'Neue Welt'/'Dritte Welt': Interkulturelle Beziehungen Deutschlands zu Lateinamerika und der Karibik*, ed. Sigrid Bauschinger and Susan L. Cocalis (Tübingen: Francke, 1994), 115–140. Leander's American critics, it should be noted, were rather dismayed by Sierck's cinematic construction of Puerto Rico. After the U.S. release in July 1938, the *New York Times* showed little enthusiasm about this "burlesque" of Puerto Rico: "Zarah Leander, the Swedish actress who has become

rather popular on the Teutonic screen during the last year or so, has to contend with what American audiences (without exaggerated patriotism) are bound to consider an impossible story" (*New York Times,* July 9, 1939).

42. Rentschler shows in detail that the film's narrative, although at pains to establish borders between the home and the other, between the familiar and the foreign, presents the spaces of Astrée's Aryan homeland and exotic Puerto Rico as not so distant: Puerto Rico simultaneously conceals and speaks the truth about Germany. "*La Habanera* emanated from a nation threatened with international quarantine and dramatized the fate of an island faced with a similar predicament. . . . Puerto Rico appears as a 'wild' state, a country, like Germany, that operates outside international legality. . . . Seen in this light, this German film about Puerto Rico embodies what it depicts: the 'primitive' island becomes both the Aryan state's structured opposite and its displaced double" (*Ministry of Illusion,* 134).

43. Stefana Sabin, *Frauen am Klavier: Skizze einer Kulturgeschichte* (Frankfurt / M.: Insel, 1998).

44. See, e.g., the previews and reviews in *Film-Kurier,* November 23, December 20, 1937; and *Berliner Zeitung,* December 21, 1937.

45. "Habanera gegen Weihnachtslied: Filmdramatik aus natürlichen Gegebenheiten," *Film-Kurier,* December 10, 1937.

46. "Filme, die wir vor und nach Weihnachten sehen werden," *Der Film,* December 18, 1937.

47. Klaus Kreimeier, *Die UFA-Story: Geschichte eines Filmkonzerns* (Munich: Hanser, 1992), 338.

48. Max Horkheimer and Theodor W. Adorno, *Dialectic of Enlightenment,* trans. John Cumming (New York: Continuum, 1995), 142.

49. Georg Seeßlen, "Zarah Leander," *CineGraph: Lexikon zum deutschsprachigen Film,* ed. Hans-Michael Bock (Munich: Edition Text und Kritik, 1984–), E3.

50. John Fiske, *Understanding Popular Culture* (London: Routledge, 1989), 143.

51. Miriam Hansen, *Babel and Babylon: Spectatorship in American Silent Film* (Cambridge, Mass.: Harvard University Press, 1991), 246.

52. Hugo Zehder, "Autor und Regisseur," *Filmtechnik,* August 3, 1929, 319.

53. Jon Halliday, *Sirk on Sirk: Conversations with Jon Halliday,* rev. ed. (London: Faber and Faber, 1997), 45.

54. *Film-Kurier,* September 1, 1937.

55. Peter Brooks, *The Melodramatic Imagination: Balzac, Henry James, Melodrama, and the Mode of Excess,* 2d ed. (New Haven, Conn.: Yale University Press, 1995), 21–22.

56. Gertrud Koch, "Von Detlef Sierck zu Douglas Sirk," *Frauen und Film* 44/45 (1988): 109–129.

57. Ibid., 116.

58. Horkheimer and Adorno, *Dialectic of Enlightenment,* 123.

59. Ibid., 135.

60. Peter Uwe Hohendahl, *Prismatic Thought: Theodor W. Adorno* (Lincoln: University of Nebraska Press, 1995), 146–147.

61. Rentschler, *Ministry of Illusion*, 144.

62. For a recent version of this argument see Linda Schulte-Sasse, "Douglas Sirk's *Schlussakkord* and the Question of Aesthetic Resistance," *Germanic Review* 73, no. 1 (1998): 2–31.

63. Walter Benjamin, *Illuminations: Essays and Reflections*, trans. Harry Zohn (New York: Schocken, 1969), 241–242.

64. Patrice Petro, *Joyless Streets: Women and Melodramatic Representation in Weimar Germany* (Princeton: Princeton University Press, 1989).

65. Ibid., 67.

66. Umberto Eco, "Ur-Fascism," *New York Review of Books*, June 22, 1995, 13.

67. *Der Film*, September 4, 1937.

68. *Wirtschaftspost*, December 21, 1937.

CHAPTER 4. SIEGFRIED RIDES AGAIN

1. Klaus Kreimeier, "Von Henny Porten zu Zarah Leander. Filmgenres und Genrefilm in der Weimarer Republik und im Nationalsozialismus," *montage/av* 3, no. 2 (1994): 45.

2. For landmark texts on the theory and practice of film genres see Barry K. Grant, ed., *Film Genre Reader II* (Austin: University of Texas Press, 1995); Stephen Neale, *Genre* (London: BFI, 1980); Thomas Schatz, *Hollywood Genres: Formulas, Filmmaking, and the Studio System* (New York: McGraw-Hill, 1981); and Rick Altman, *Film/Genre* (London: BFI, 1999).

3. John Fiske, *Understanding Popular Culture* (London: Routledge, 1989), 23.

4. Eric Rentschler, *The Ministry of Illusion: Nazi Cinema and Its Afterlife* (Cambridge, Mass.: Harvard University Press, 1996), 19.

5. Christopher Frayling, *Spaghetti Westerns: Cowboys and Europeans from Karl May to Sergio Leone* (London: Routledge and Kegan Paul, 1981), 105.

6. A. J. P. Taylor, *Observer*, June 12, 1977; cited in Frayling, *Spaghetti Westerns*, 105.

7. Klaus Mann, "Cowboy Mentor of the Führer," *Living Age*, November 1940, 217.

8. Ibid., 218.

9. On the early history of western films in Germany see Deniz Göktürk, *Künstler, Cowboys, Ingenieure . . . Kultur- und mediengeschichtliche Studien zu deutschen Amerika-Texten, 1912–1920* (Munich: Fink, 1998), 157–204.

10. For a critical examination of the concept of "Heimat" see Celia Applegate, *A Nation of Provincials: The German Idea of Heimat* (Berkeley: University of California Press, 1990).

11. Joshua Taylor, *America as Art* (Washington, D.C.: Smithsonian Institution Press, 1976), 171.

12. Ray Allen Billington, *Land of Savagery/Land of Promise: The European Image of the American Frontier in the Nineteenth Century* (New York: Norton, 1981), 35.

13. On Karl May and his cultural politics see the respective articles in Helmut Schmiedt, ed., *Karl May* (Frankfurt/M.: Suhrkamp, 1983); Heinz Ludwig Arnold, ed., *Karl May. Sonderband Text und Kritik* (Munich: Edition Text und Kritik, 1987); and Dieter Sudhoff and Hartmut Vollmer, eds., *Karl Mays "Winnetou": Studien zu einem Mythos* (Frankfurt/M.: Suhrkamp, 1989).

14. Jochen Schulte-Sasse, "Karl Mays Amerika-Exotik. Zur sozialpsychologischen Funktion von Trivialliteratur im wilhelminischen Deutschland," in *Karl May*, ed. Helmut Schmiedt, 120.

15. Peter Uwe Hohendahl, "Von der Rothaut zum Edelmenschen: Karl Mays Amerikaromane," in *Karl Mays "Winnetou,"* 214–238.

16. Edward Said, *Culture and Imperialism* (New York: Knopf, 1993), 3–61.

17. Eric L. Santner, *Stranded Objects: Mourning, Memory, and Film in Postwar Germany* (Ithaca, N.Y.: Cornell University Press, 1990), 119–120.

18. Deniz Göktürk, "Neckar-Western statt Donau-Walzer: Der Geschmack von Freiheit und Abenteuer im frühen Kino," *Kintop: Jahrbuch zur Erforschung des frühen Films* 2 (1993): 117–142; and Deniz Göktürk, "Moving Images of America in Early German Cinema," in *A Second Life: German Cinema's First Decades*, ed. Thomas Elsaesser (Amsterdam: Amsterdam University Press, 1996), 93–100.

19. Beeke Sell Tower, *Envisioning America: Prints, Drawings, and Photographs by George Grosz and His Contemporaries, 1915–1933* (Cambridge, Mass.: Busch-Reisinger Museum, 1990), 22–24.

20. Rudolf Schlichter, *Die tönernen Füße* (Berlin: Rowohlt, 1933), 26; qtd. in Tower, *Envisioning America*, 22.

21. On the mountain film genre see Eric Rentschler, "Mountains and Modernity: Relocating the *Bergfilm*," *New German Critique* 51 (fall 1990): 137–161; Eric Rentschler, "Fatal Attractions: Leni Riefenstahl's *The Blue Light*," *October* 48 (spring 1989): 46–68; Beate Bechtold-Comforty et al., "Zwanziger Jahre und Nationalsozialismus: Vom Bergfilm zum Bauernmythos," in *Der deutsche Heimatfilm: Bildwelten und Weltbilder*, ed. Wolfgang Kaschuba et al. (Tübingen: Tübinger Verein für Volkskunde, 1989), 33–67; and Christian Rapp, *Höhenrausch: Der deutsche Bergfilm* (Vienna: Sonderzahl, 1997).

22. André Bazin, "The Western, or the American Film par Excellence," in *What Is Cinema?* (Berkeley: University of California Press, 1971), 2:140–148.

23. Jane Tompkins, *West of Everything: The Inner Life of Westerns* (New York: Oxford University Press, 1992), 44.

24. *New York Times*, May 8, 1937.

25. *Licht-Bild-Bühne*, January 27, 1939; see also *Deutsche Filmzeitung*, January 1, 1939.

26. See, e.g., William K. Everson's article "Luis Trenker," *Films in Review* (May 1984): 275–278.

27. *Film-Kurier*, July 22, 1936.

28. Karsten Witte, "Hans Albers: Athlet in Halbseide," *Die Unsterblichen des Kinos. Band 2: Glanz und Mythos der Stars der 40er und 50er Jahre*, ed. Adolf Heinzlmeier et al. (Frankfurt/M.: Fischer, 1980), 35.

29. George Fenin and William Everson, e.g., single out "pointed sequences and 'blue' dialogue" in Albers's western performances, an ingredient they consider utterly foreign to the genre. George N. Fenin and William K. Everson, *The Western: From Silents to the Seventies: A New and Expanded Edition* (New York: Grossman, 1973), 327.

30. Tompkins, *West of Everything*, 50.

31. Joseph Goebbels, "Rede bei der ersten Jahrestagung der Reichsfilmkammer am 5.3.1937 in der Krolloper, Berlin," reprinted in Gerd Albrecht, *Nationalsozialistische Filmpolitik* (Stuttgart: Enke, 1969), 457.

32. Roman Jakobson, "Linguistics and Poetics," in *Language in Literature*, ed. Krystyna Pomorska and Stephen Rudy (Cambridge, Mass.: Harvard University Press, 1987), 66.

33. Ibid., 68.

34. Everson, "Luis Trenker," 271.

35. Rapp, *Höhenrausch*, 238–242.

36. "Filme im Werden: Senator—General—Bettler: Massenszenen bei Trenkers 'Kaiser von Kalifornien,'" *Film-Kurier*, February 15, 1936.

37. David Spurr, *The Rhetoric of Empire: Colonial Discourse in Journalism, Travel Writing, and Imperial Administration* (Durham, N.C.: Duke University Press, 1993), 16.

38. Mary Louise Pratt, *Imperial Eyes: Travel Writing and Transculturation* (London: Routledge, 1992), 201–227.

39. On the treatment of the Napoleonic period in Nazi cinema see Irmbert Schenk, "Geschichte im NS-Film. Kritische Anmerkungen zur filmwissenschaftlichen Suggestion der Identität von Propaganda und Wirkung," *montage/av* 3, no. 2 (1994): 73–98.

40. Adolf Halfeld, *Amerika und der Amerikanismus: Kritische Betrachtungen eines Deutschen und Europäers* (Jena: Diederichs, 1928), 19; see also Halfeld's sequel, *USA greift ein* (Hamburg: Broscheck, 1941).

41. "Sutter, the German immigrant, the hereditary landowner, the symbol of industriousness and patriotism, embodies the spiritual indivisibility of what Nazi ideology called blood and soil. Driven from his homeland, from the *Heimat* of the soul, Sutter creates a new one by cultivating the land" (Jan-Christopher Horak, "Luis Trenker's *The Kaiser of California*: How the West was Won, Nazi Style," *Historical Journal of Film, Radio, and Television* 6, no. 2 [1986]: 186).

42. Frayling, *Spaghetti Westerns*, 20–21.

43. See Rentschler, "Mountains and Modernity," 141–153.

44. Ibid., 146.

45. Leo Lowenthal, *Literature and the Image of Man: Sociological Studies of the European Drama and Novel, 1600–1900* (Boston: Beacon, 1957), 202.

46. Simonetta Falasca-Zamponi, *Fascist Spectacle: The Aesthetics of Power in Mussolini's Italy* (Berkeley: University of California Press, 1997), 12.

47. Rudolf Borchardt, "Villa," in *Gesammelte Werke in Einzelbänden: Prosa III*, ed. Marie Luise Borchardt (Stuttgart: Klett, 1962), 38–70.

48. Russell A. Berman, *Modern Culture and Critical Theory: Art, Politics, and the Legacy of the Frankfurt School* (Madison: University of Wisconsin Press, 1989), 29.

49. Clouds are ubiquitous in Trenker's film. They set moods, define rhythms, and interpret human drama as fate and destiny; they dwarf the viewer and evoke a sense of natural sublimity. In the history of European art, clouds—according to Hubert Damisch (*Théorie du nuage: Pour une historie de la peinture* [Paris: Éditions du Seuil, 1972]—have been an important ingredient not simply to conjure sensations of monumentality but to codify the process of exhibition itself. As Steve Neale has put it in a different context, "In offering to the spectator's gaze a set of forms which mask and fill an otherwise empty and potentially infinite space (the sky) while simultaneously signifying the very emptiness and infinity they mask, clouds have come to function, in a sense, to signify spectacle itself" (*"Triumph of the Will:* Notes on Documentary and Spectacle," *Screen* 20, no. 1 [1979]: 67). Placeholders of infinity, Trenker's clouds likewise define cinema as a spectacle of the first order. They allegorize the motion of film itself, the unreeling of images that overwhelm the viewer with a surplus of representation.

50. "Deutscher Triumph auf der Biennale," *Film-Kurier*, September 2, 1936.

51. Luis Trenker, *Alles gut gegangen: Geschichten aus meinem Leben* (Munich: Bertelsmann, 1972), 345. On Hitler's and Goebbels's actual views of Trenker see Felix Moeller, *Der Filmminister: Goebbels und der Film im Dritten Reich* (Berlin: Henschel, 1998), 419–420.

52. Schneider, "*Der Kaiser von Kalifornien,*" *Licht-Bild-Bühne*, July 22, 1936.

53. Linda Schulte-Sasse, *Entertaining the Third Reich: Illusions of Wholeness in Nazi Cinema* (Durham, N.C.: Duke University Press, 1996), 248.

54. *Der Film*, July 25, 1936.

55. For more biographical details see the entry "Giuseppe Becce," *Cine-Graph: Lexikon zum deutschsprachigen Film*, ed. Hans-Michael Bock (Munich: Edition Text und Kritik, 1984–), B1–B5.

56. Ennio Simeon, "Giuseppe Becce and *Richard Wagner:* Paradoxes of the First German Film Score," in *A Second Life*, 221.

57. For more on German film music of the silent era see Herbert Birett, *Stummfilm-Musik. Materialiensammlung* (Berlin: Deutsche Kinemathek, 1970); Hansjörg Pauli, *Filmmusik: Stummfilm* (Stuttgart: Klett-Cotta, 1981); Ulrich Rügner, *Filmmusik in Deutschland zwischen 1924 und 1934* (Hildesheim: Olms, 1988); and Ulrich Eberhard Siebert, *Filmmusik in Theorie und Praxis. Eine Untersuchung der 20er und frühen 30er Jahre anhand des Werkes von Hans Erdmann* (Frankfurt / M.: Lang, 1990).

58. Giuseppe Becce, *Kinothek*, 6 vols. (Berlin: Schlesinger'sche Buch- und Musikhandlung Robert Lienau, 1919–1929). Goebbels continued Becce's archival project in the early 1940s. To make the production of newsreel shows more effective, he called for a systematic storage of musical sound tracks "so that in the future the endless search for effective background music could be limited to a minimum" (qtd. in Moeller, *Der Filmminister*, 378).

59. Giuseppe Becce and Hans Erdmann, *Allgemeines Handbuch der Film-Musik* (Berlin: Schlesinger'sche Buch- und Musikhandlung Robert Lienau, 1927), 45.

60. On Herbert Windt and his reception during the Nazi period see "Herbert Windt: Der Komponist heroischer Filme," *Film-Kurier*, November 19, 1937; and "Musikalische Pionierleistungen im Olympiafilm," *Film-Kurier*, April 11, 1938.

61. See Becce's self-description, qtd. in Hermann Wanderscheck, "Es geht um filmeigene Musik," *Film-Kurier*, December 31, 1938.

62. Theodor Adorno, *In Search of Wagner*, trans. Rodney Livingstone (London: New Left Books, 1981), 42.

63. Theodor Adorno and Hanns Eisler, *Composing for the Films* (London: Athlone Press, 1994), 55.

64. About fascism as a manipulative mimesis of mimesis see Max Horkheimer and Theodor W. Adorno, *Dialectic of Enlightenment*, trans. John Cumming (New York: Continuum, 1995), 184–185.

65. Hans-Walther Betz, "Der neue Albers-Film—ganz groß: 'Wasser für Canitoga,'" *Der Film*, March 18, 1939.

66. Wolfgang Schivelbusch, *Das Paradies, der Geschmack und die Vernunft: Eine Geschichte der Genußmittel* (Frankfurt / M.: Fischer, 1990), 25–95.

67. Georg Seeßlen and Claudius Weil, *Western-Kino: Geschichte und Mythologie des Western-Films* (Reinbek: Rowohlt, 1979), 24.

68. Hasso Spode, *Die Macht der Trunkenheit: Kultur- und Sozialgeschichte des Alkohols in Deutschland* (Leverkusen: Leske und Budrich, 1993), 203–268.

69. Jeffrey Herf, *Reactionary Modernism: Technology, Culture, and Politics in Weimar and the Third Reich* (Cambridge: Cambridge University Press, 1984), 152–216.

70. Ibid., 188.

71. Alice Yaeger Kaplan, *Reproductions of Banality: Fascism, Literature, and French Intellectual Life* (Minneapolis: University of Minnesota Press, 1986), 30.

72. Oskar Kalbus, *Vom Werden deutscher Filmkunst* (Altona-Bahrenfeld: Cigaretten-Bilderdienst, 1935), 2:110.

73. The song, composed by Peter Kreuder, was a "rhythmically explosive American-style hit song," according to *Deutsche Filmzeitung*, March 19, 1939. It became enormously successful as a separate record.

74. Peter Schwenger has analyzed the role of tough, masculine talk in great detail in *Phallic Critiques: Masculinity and Twentieth-Century Literature* (London: Routledge and Kegan Paul, 1984).

75. "Bummel durch die Main-Street einer Kolonisten-Stadt: Kanada ob der Isar," *Der Film*, December 17, 1938.

76. Joseph Goebbels, "Rede zur Eröffnung der Automobilaustellung, Berlin, Februar 1939," qtd. in Leonardo Quaresima, "Der Film im Dritten Reich: Moderne, Amerikanismus, Unterhaltungsfilm," *montage/av* 3, no. 2 (1994): 10.

77. For critical examinations of Nazi experiments with television see Heiko Zeutschner, *Die braune Mattscheibe: Fernsehen im Nationalsozialismus* (Hamburg: Rotbuch, 1995), 91; Erwin Reiss, *'Wir senden Frohsinn': Fernsehen unterm Faschismus* (Berlin: Elefanten, 1979); Siegfried Zielinski, *Audiovisionen: Kino und Fernsehen als Zwischenspiele in der Geschichte* (Reinbek: Rowohlt, 1989), 98–174; and William Uricchio, ed., *Die Anfänge des deutschen Fernsehens: Kritische Annäherungen an die Entwicklung bis 1945* (Tübingen: Niemeyer, 1991).

78. "'Wasser für Canitoga' im Fernsehsender," *Licht-Bild-Bühne*, March 17, 1939.

79. "Hans Albers über seine kommenden Filme," *Film-Kurier*, December 15, 1938.

80. See, esp., Giselher Wirsing, *Der maßlose Kontinent: Roosevelts Kampf um die Weltherrschaft* (Jena: Diederichs, 1942), 30–49.

81. David A. Cook, *A History of Narrative Film* (New York: Norton, 1981), 264.

82. On the postwar history of western fantasies in Germany see Gerd Gemünden, *Framed Visions: Popular Culture, Americanization, and the Contemporary German and Austrian Imagination* (Ann Arbor: University of Michigan Press, 1998), 108–132; and Katrin Sieg, "Ethnic Drag and National Identity: Multicultural Crises, Crossings, and Interventions," in *The Imperialist Imagination: German Colonialism and Its Legacy*, ed. Sara Friedrichsmeyer, Sara Lennox, and Susanne Zantop (Ann Arbor: University of Michigan Press, 1998), 295–320.

83. Michael Geyer, "The State in National Socialist Germany," *Statemaking and Social Movements: Essays in History and Theory*, ed. Charles Bright and Susan Harding (Ann Arbor: University of Michigan Press, 1984), 210.

84. Ian Kershaw, *The "Hitler Myth": Image and Reality in the Third Reich* (Oxford: Oxford University Press, 1987).

85. See Joseph Goebbels, "Rede vor den Filmschaffenden am 28.2.1942 in Berlin," reprinted in Albrecht, *Nationalsozialistische Filmpolitik*, 493.

86. Ibid., 488.

87. Jan-Christopher Horak, *Anti-Nazi-Filme der deutschsprachigen Emigration von Hollywood, 1939–1945*, 2d ed. (Münster: MAkS Publikationen, 1985), 54.

CHAPTER 5. WAGNER AT WARNER'S

1. Qtd. in Margaret Farrand Thorp, *America at the Movies* (New Haven, Conn.: Yale University Press, 1939), 274.

2. David Cook, *A History of Narrative Film* (New York: Norton, 1981), 308.

3. "The Production Code," reprinted in *Movies and Mass Culture*, ed. John Belton (New Brunswick, N.J.: Rutgers University Press, 1996), 141.

4. Ibid.

5. See Jan-Christopher Horak, *Anti-Nazi-Filme der deutschsprachigen Emigration von Hollywood, 1939–1945*, 2d. ed. (Münster: MAkS Publikationen, 1985); Jan-Christopher Horak, *Fluchtpunkt Hollywood: Eine Dokumentation zur Filmemigration nach 1933* (Münster: MAkS Publikationen, 1985); Jan-Christopher Horak, "Exilfilm, 1933–1945: In der Fremde," *Geschichte des deutschen Films*, ed. Wolfgang Jacobsen, Anton Kaes, and Hans Helmut Prinzler (Stuttgart: Metzler, 1993), 101–118. See also Clayton R. Koppes and Gregory D. Black, *Hollywood Goes to War: How Politics, Profits, and Propaganda Shaped World War II Movies* (New York: Free Press, 1987); and Thomas Doherty, *Projections of War: Hollywood, American Culture, and World War II* (New York: Columbia University Press, 1993).

6. "The classical Hollywood film," writes David Bordwell, "presents psychologically defined individuals who struggle to solve a clear-cut problem or to attain specific goals. In the course of this struggle, the characters enter into conflict with others or with external circumstances. The story ends with a decisive victory or defeat. . . . The principal causal agency is thus the character, a distinctive individual endowed with an evident, consistent batch of traits, qualities, and behaviors" (David Bordwell, "Classical Hollywood Cinema: Narrational Principles and Procedures," in *Narrative, Apparatus, Ideology*, ed. Philip Rosen [New York: Columbia University Press, 1986], 18).

7. On the *Sonderweg* thesis see David Blackbourn and Geoff Eley, *The Peculiarities of German History: Bourgeois Society and Politics in Nineteenth-Century Germany* (Oxford: Oxford University Press, 1984).

8. Umberto Eco, "Ur-Fascism," *New York Review of Books*, June 22, 1995, 12–15.

9. Andreas Huyssen, "Adorno in Reverse: From Hollywood to Richard Wagner," in *After the Great Divide: Modernism, Mass Culture, Postmodernism*, by Andreas Huyssen (Bloomington: Indiana University Press, 1986), 34–42.

10. Walter Benjamin, *Gesammelte Schriften*, ed. Rolf Tiedemann and Hermann Schweppenhäuser (Frankfurt/M.: Suhrkamp, 1985), 6:103.

11. Warren Susman, *Culture as History: The Transformation of American Society in the Twentieth Century* (New York: Pantheon Books, 1984), 159.

12. Giuliana Muscio, *Hollywood's New Deal* (Philadelphia: Temple University Press, 1996), 74.

13. Thomas Cripps, *Hollywood's High Noon: Moviemaking and Society before Television* (Baltimore: Johns Hopkins University Press, 1997), 112.

14. Horak, *Anti-Nazi-Filme*, 35–36.

15. Anthony Heilbut, *Exiled in Paradise: German Refugee Artists and Intellectuals in America, from the 1930s to the Present* (New York: Viking Press, 1983), 71.

16. Qtd. in Horak, *Anti-Nazi-Filme,* xiii.

17. Hans Kafka, "Hollywood Calling," *Der Aufbau,* September 3, 1943, 15.

18. Patrick McGilligan, *Fritz Lang: The Nature of the Beast* (New York: St. Martin's, 1997), 296–298.

19. On Brecht's involvement in the making of *Hangmen Also Die* see also the well-researched novel by Jürgen Alberts, *Hitler in Hollywood oder: Die Suche nach dem Idealscript* (Göttingen: Steidl, 1997).

20. Bertolt Brecht, *Arbeitsjournal,* ed. Werner Hecht (Frankfurt / M.: Suhrkamp, 1973), 2:530.

21. Gruber, however, is of course the film's most interesting character, as Tom Gunning has pointed out in *The Films of Fritz Lang: Allegories of Vision and Modernity* (London: BFI, 2000), 294.

22. Edward W. Said, *Representations of the Intellectual* (New York: Vintage Books, 1996), 49.

23. Heilbut, *Exiled in Paradise,* 59.

24. Important theoretical studies and textbook accounts of classical Hollywood film music include Mark Evans, *Soundtrack: The Music of the Movies* (New York: Hopkinson and Blake, 1975); Claudia Gorbman, *Unheard Melodies: Narrative Film Music* (Bloomington: Indiana University Press, 1987); Caryl Flinn, *Strains of Utopia: Gender, Nostalgia, and Hollywood Film Music* (Princeton: Princeton University Press, 1992); Kathryn Kalinak, *Settling the Score: Music and the Classical Hollywood Film* (Madison: University of Wisconsin Press, 1992); Roy Prendergast, *Film Music: A Neglected Art* (New York: Norton, 1992); Royal S. Brown, *Overtones and Undertones: Reading Film Music* (Berkeley: University of California Press, 1994); George Burt, *The Art of Film Music* (Boston: Northeastern University Press, 1994). On what superseded the dominant paradigm in the course of the 1950s see Jeff Smith, *The Sounds of Commerce: Marketing Popular Music* (New York: Columbia University Press, 1998).

25. Gorbman, *Unheard Melodies,* 58.

26. Flinn, *Strains of Utopia,* 88.

27. W. Stephen Bush, "Giving Musical Expression to the Drama," *Moving Picture World,* August 12, 1911, 354; qtd. in Flinn, *Strains of Utopia,* 15.

28. Flinn, *Strains of Utopia,* 14.

29. Michael Chanan, *Musica Practica: The Social Practice of Western Music from Gregorian Chant to Postmodernism* (London: Verso, 1994), 251.

30. Flinn, *Strains of Utopia,* 20–23.

31. For more on Korngold's pre-Hollywood career see Brenda Carroll, *The Last Prodigy: A Biography of Erich Wolfgang Korngold* (Portland, Ore.: Amadeus Press, 1997); Jessica Duchen, *Erich Wolfgang Korngold* (London: Phaidon Press, 1996); Rudolph Stephan Hoffmann, *Erich Wolfgang Korngold* (Vienna: Stephenson, 1922); and Julius Korngold, *Die Korngolds in Wien: Der Musikkritiker und das Wunderkind—Aufzeichungen von Julius Korngold* (Zurich: M. und T. Verlag, 1991).

32. Duchen, *Korngold,* 181.

33. "It's on the Sound Track," *Overture* (November 1946); qtd. in Duchen, *Korngold*, 180.

34. Thomas Schatz, *The Genius of the System: Hollywood Filmmaking in the Studio Era* (New York: Pantheon Books, 1988).

35. Theodor Adorno and Hanns Eisler, *Composing for the Films* (London: Athlone Press, 1994), 61.

36. Ibid., lii.

37. Lewis Jacobs, *The Rise of American Film*, new ed. (New York: Teachers College Press, 1967), 296.

38. Max Weber, *The Protestant Ethic and the Spirit of Capitalism*, trans. Talcott Parsons (New York: Scribner's Sons, 1958), 182.

39. Richard B. Jewell, "How Howard Hawks Brought *Baby* Up: An *Apologia* for the Studio System," in *The Studio System*, ed. Janet Staiger (New Brunswick, N.J.: Rutgers University Press, 1995), 40.

40. Schatz, *Genius of the System*, 8–9.

41. Thomas Schatz, *Boom and Bust: The American Cinema in the 1940s* (New York: Scribner's Sons, 1997), 83.

42. Thomas Elsaesser, "Das Vermächtnis des Dr. Caligari: Film noir und deutscher Einfluß," in *Schatten.Exil: Europäische Emigranten im Film noir*, ed. Christian Cargnelli and Michael Omasta (Vienna: PVS Verleger, 1997), 44.

43. George Wilson, *Narration in Light* (Baltimore: Johns Hopkins University Press, 1986), 135.

44. David Bordwell, "The Bounds of Difference," in *The Classical Hollywood Cinema: Film Style and Mode of Production to 1960*, by David Bordwell, Janet Staiger, and Kristin Thompson (New York: Columbia University Press, 1985), 77–78.

45. David Bordwell, "Art-Cinema Narration," in *Narration in the Fiction Film* (Madison: University of Wisconsin Press, 1985), 205–233.

46. Alison Landsberg, "Prosthetic Memory: The Logics and Politics of Memory in Modern American Culture," Ph.D. diss., University of Chicago, 1996.

47. Robert Burgoyne, *Film Nation: Hollywood Looks at U.S. History* (Minneapolis: University of Minnesota Press, 1997), 11.

48. Theodor W. Adorno, *Minima Moralia: Reflections from Damaged Life*, trans. E. F. N. Jephcott (London: New Left Books, 1951), 38–39.

CHAPTER 6. BERLIN NOIR

1. Thomas Schatz, *Boom and Bust: The American Cinema in the 1940s* (New York: Scribner's Sons, 1997), 1.

2. Dana Polan, *Power and Paranoia: History, Narrative, and the American Cinema, 1940–1950* (New York: Columbia University Press, 1986), 75.

3. Ibid., 289.

4. Michel Foucault, "Of Other Spaces," trans. Jay Miskowiec, *Diacritics* (spring 1986): 22–27.

5. Ibid., 24.

6. Paul Jensen, "The Return of Dr. Caligari: Paranoia in Hollywood," *Film Comment* 7, no. 4 (winter 1971/72): 36–45.

7. Foster Hirsch, *The Dark Side of the Screen: Film Noir* (New York: Da Capo Press, 1983), 115.

8. Thomas Elsaesser, "Das Vermächtnis des Dr. Caligari: Film noir und deutscher Einfluß," in *Schatten.Exil: Europäische Emigranten im Film noir*, ed. Christian Cargnelli and Michael Omasta (Vienna: PVS Verleger, 1997), 44–50.

9. Thomas Elsaesser, *Weimar Cinema and After: Germany's Historical Imaginary* (London: Routledge, 2000), 420–444.

10. Marc Vernet, "*Film Noir* on the Edge of Doom," *Shades of Noir: A Reader*, ed. Joan Copjec (London: Verso, 1993), 1–32.

11. Fredric Jameson, *The Political Unconscious: Narrative as a Socially Symbolic Act* (Ithaca, N.Y.: Cornell University Press, 1981), 35–43.

12. Ibid., 35 (Jameson's italics).

13. Robert Siodmak, *Zwischen Berlin und Hollywood: Erinnerungen eines großen Filmregisseurs*, ed. Hans C. Blumenberg (Munich: Herbig, 1980).

14. Cited in Wolfgang Jacobsen, "'Kann ich mal das Salz haben?'" in *Siodmak Bros.: Berlin—Paris—London—Hollywood*, ed. Wolfgang Jacobsen and Hans Helmut Prinzler (Berlin: Stiftung Deutsche Kinemathek/Argon, 1998), 28. Siodmak's skill in overcoming cultural binaries and distinctions was praised already in an American review of his very first film, the groundbreaking *Menschen am Sonntag* (People on a Sunday, 1929). *People on a Sunday*, according to the reviewer of the *New York Times*, offered "a satisfactory compromise between what the few and what almost everybody likes" ("Herr Siodmak," *New York Times*, March 16, 1931).

15. Robert Siodmak, "Das bewegte Bild und der Ton," *8 Uhr-Abendblatt*, August 18, 1930.

16. Karl Prümm, "Universeller Erzähler: Realist des Unmittelbaren," in *Siodmak Bros.: Berlin—Paris—London—Hollywood*, ed. Wolfgang Jacobsen and Hans Helmut Prinzler (Berlin: Stiftung Deutsche Kinemathek/Argon, 1998), 91.

17. On the sound track as "acoustical panorama" see Martina Müller, "Vom Souffleurkasten über das Mikro auf die Leinwand: Max Ophüls," *Frauen und Film* 42 (August 1987): 60–71. See also Gertrud Koch, "Die masochistische Lust am Verkennen—Zur Rolle der Hörwelt in *Letter from an Unknown Woman*," in *"Was ich erbeute, sind Bilder": Zum Diskurs der Geschlechter im Film* (Basel: Stroemfeld/Roter Stern, 1989), 77–82; and Susan M. White, *The Cinema of Max Ophuls: Magisterial Vision and the Figure of Woman* (New York: Columbia University Press, 1995), 129–224.

18. In the original novel on which Siodmak's film was based, Cornell Woolrich describes the jamming session as a marijuana-induced spectacle of surreal qualities:

> The next two hours were a sort of Dante-esque Inferno. She knew as soon as it was over she wouldn't believe it had actually been real at all. It wasn't the music, the music was good. It was the phantasmagoria of their shad-

ows, looming black, wavering ceiling-high on the walls. It was the actuality of their faces, possessed, demonic, peering out here and there on sudden notes, then seeming to recede again. It was the gin and the marihuana cigarettes, filling the air with haze and flux. It was the wildness that got into them, that at times made her cower into a far corner or climb up on a packing-case with both feet. (Cornell Woolrich [writing as William Irish], *Phantom Lady* [New York: Ace Books, 1942], 142–143)

Although Siodmak's mise-en-scène clearly borrows from Woolrich's hallucinatory description, any reference to drugs in the film was, of course, excluded by the Hays Office.

19. For more on Kansas see Tony Williams, "*Phantom Lady,* Cornell Woolrich, and the Masochistic Aesthetic," in *Film Noir Reader,* ed. Alain Silver and James Ursini, 5th ed. (New York: Limelight Editions, 1999), 129–144.

20. David Bordwell, Janet Staiger, and Kristin Thompson, *The Classical Hollywood Cinema* (New York: Columbia University Press, 1985), 301.

21. Michel Chion, *Audio-Vision: Sound on Screen,* ed. and trans. Claudia Gorbman (New York: Columbia University Press, 1994), 93–94.

22. Goebbels, "Rede bei der ersten Jahrestagung der Reichsfilmkammer am 5.3.1937 in der Krolloper, Berlin," reprinted in Gerd Albrecht, *Nationalsozialistische Filmpolitik* (Stuttgart: Enke, 1969), 461. Goebbels's Krolloper speech recycled crucial sections of Goebbels's 1929 expressionist novel *Michael,* in which the relation of politics and art is defined as follows:

Art is an expression of feeling. The artist differs from the non-artist in his ability to express what he feels. In some form or other. One artist does it in painting, another in clay, a third in words, and a fourth in marble— or even in historical forms. The statesman is also an artist. For him, the nation is exactly what the stone is for the sculptor. Führer and masses, that is as little of a problem as, say, painter and color. (Joseph Goebbels, *Michael: A Novel,* trans. Joachim Neugroschel [New York: Amok Press, 1987], 14)

23. Alain Silver and Elizabeth Ward, eds., *Film Noir* (London: Secker and Warburg, 1980), 226.

24. Walt. [pseudo.], "Phantom Lady," *Variety,* January 26, 1944. *Phantom Lady*—not least of all thanks to its acoustical qualities—was broadcast as a radio play on March 27, 1944, in the series *Radio Lux Theatre.*

25. Walter Benjamin, *Illuminations: Essays and Reflections,* trans. Harry Zohn (New York: Schocken, 1969), 223.

26. Heide Schlüpmann, "Faschistische Trugbilder weiblicher Autonomie," *Frauen und Film* 44/45 (1988): 58.

27. Ernst Krieck, *Volk im Werden* (Oldenburg: Stalling, 1932), 53.

28. Ibid., 54.

29. Chion, *Audio-Vision,* 76.

30. "There is always something uncanny about a voice which emanates from

a source outside the frame" (Mary Ann Doane, "The Voice and the Cinema: The Articulation of Body and Space," in *Film Sound: Theory and Practice,* ed. Elisabeth Weis and John Belton [New York: Columbia University Press, 1985], 167).

31. Kaja Silverman, *The Acoustic Mirror: The Female Voice in Psychoanalysis and Cinema* (Bloomington: Indiana University Press, 1988), 52.

32. Walter Ong, *Orality and Literacy: The Technologizing of the Word* (London: Routledge, 1982), 78–138.

33. Amy Lawrence, *Echo and Narcissus: Women's Voices in Classical Hollywood Cinema* (Berkeley: University of California Press, 1991), 132.

34. Silverman, *The Acoustic Mirror,* 53.

35. Ibid., 39.

36. Lawrence, *Echo and Narcissus,* 115–116.

37. T. M. P., "At the Palace: *The Spiral Staircase,*" *New York Times,* February 7, 1946.

38. Prümm, "Universeller Erzähler," 169.

39. Michel de Certeau, *The Practice of Everyday Life,* trans. Steven Rendall (Berkeley: University of California Press, 1984), 117.

40. Mary Ann Doane, *The Desire to Desire: The Woman's Film of the 1940s* (Bloomington: Indiana University Press, 1987).

41. Ethel Lina White, *Some Must Watch* (New York: Harper, 1941), 11.

42. Patrice Petro, *Joyless Streets: Women and Melodramatic Representation in Weimar Germany* (Princeton: Princeton University Press, 1989), 8.

43. Silverman, *The Acoustic Mirror,* 24.

44. "The New Pictures," *Time,* February 4, 1946.

45. "Die Wendeltreppe: Kriminalfilm in den Kronenlichtspielen," *Die Welt,* January 6, 1948.

46. "Oma auf der Wendeltreppe," *Der Abend,* January 6, 1948; "Die Wendeltreppe," *Der Tagesspiegel,* January 7, 1948.

47. "Die Wendeltreppe," *Filmdienst der Jugend,* May 18, 1948.

48. "Die Wendeltreppe," *Evangelischer Film-Beobachter,* May 2, 1949.

49. Hans Ulrich Eylau, "Filmexport und Kunstgeschäft: Gedanken anläßlich der 'Wendeltreppe,'" *Tägliche Rundschau Berlin,* January 15, 1948.

50. Prümm, "Universeller Erzähler," 63.

51. Ursula Hardt, *From Caligari to California: Erich Pommer's Life in the International Film Wars* (Providence: Berghahn, 1996).

52. Hellmuth Karasek, *Billy Wilder: Eine Nahaufnahme,* 3d ed. (Munich: Heyne, 1995), 303–323.

53. In 1946 the American trade paper *Film Daily* aptly described the multiple functions of postwar U.S. media policy as a concerted effort to "integrate the German and Austrian film industries, . . . purge both pro-Nazi and pro-Communist personnel, . . . build strong pro-American sentiment . . . and open up the German market, potentially Europe's greatest, to American products" ("Pommer to Integrate German, Austrian Pix Trade," *Film Daily,* September 6,

1946; qtd. in Heide Fehrenbach, *Cinema in Democratizing Germany: Reconstructing National Identity after Hitler* [Chapel Hill: University of North Carolina Press, 1995], 65).

54. Fehrenbach, *Cinema in Democratizing Germany*, 62.

55. Thomas Elsaesser, "German Postwar Cinema and Hollywood," in *Hollywood in Europe: Experiences of a Cultural Hegemony*, ed. David W. Ellwood and Rob Kroes (Amsterdam: VU University Press, 1994), 285–286.

56. See Fehrenbach, *Cinema in Democratizing Germany*, 92–117; and Uta G. Poiger, "Rebels with a Cause? American Popular Culture, the 1956 Youth Riots, and the New Conception of Masculinity in East and West Germany," in *The American Impact on Postwar Germany*, ed. Reiner Pommerin (Providence: Berghahn, 1995), 93–124.

57. Eric Rentschler, "Germany: The Past That Would Not Go Away," in *World Cinema since 1945*, ed. William Luhr (New York: Ungar, 1987), 215. See also Gerhard Bliersbach, *So grün war die Heide . . . Die gar nicht so heile Welt im Nachkriegsfilm* (Weinheim: Beltz, 1989).

58. Franziska Violet, "Nachts, wenn der Teufel kam," *Süddeutsche Zeitung*, September 24, 1957.

59. Prümm, "Universeller Erzähler," 173.

60. Kr., ". . . und schon geht uns ein Licht auf: Robert Siodmak spaziert mit uns in den Sonntag zwischen Gedächtniskirche und Halensee," *Der Abend*, October 27, 1952.

61. Hans Borgelt, "Der 'Markenwert des Namens': Kleines Filmporträt Robert Siodmak," *Der neue Film*, August 4, 1955.

62. E. P., "Die Wendeltreppe (The Spiral Staircase)," *Filmkritik* 6 (June 1959), reprinted in *Siodmak Bros.: Berlin—Paris—London—Hollywood*, ed. Wolfgang Jacobsen and Hans Helmut Prinzler (Berlin: Stiftung Deutsche Kinemathek/Argon, 1998), 58.

63. "The Oberhausen Manifesto," in *West German Filmmakers on Film: Visions and Voices*, ed. Eric Rentschler (New York: Holmes and Meier, 1988), 2.

CHAPTER 7. PIANOS, PRIESTS, AND POPULAR CULTURE

1. Thomas Schatz, *Boom and Bust: The American Cinema in the 1940s* (New York: Scribner's Sons, 1997), 285–352.

2. John Belton, *Widescreen Cinema* (Cambridge, Mass.: Harvard University Press, 1992), 70.

3. James Agee, *Agee on Film* (New York: McDowell, Obolensky, 1958), 289–290; also qtd. in Schatz, *Boom and Bust*, 382.

4. See Peter Fritzsche, *Germans into Nazis* (Cambridge, Mass.: Harvard University Press, 1998).

5. John Belton, introduction to *Movies and Mass Culture*, ed. John Belton (New Brunswick, N.J.: Rutgers University Press, 1996), 1–22; and Brian Neve, *Film and Politics in America: A Social Tradition* (London: Routledge, 1992), 28–55.

6. Neve, *Film and Politics in America*, 29. For a comprehensive analysis of the populist legacy see also Richard Hofstadter, *The Age of Reform: From Bryan to F. D. R.* (New York: Knopf, 1956).

7. Belton, *Movies and Mass Culture*, 7.

8. R. L. Rutsky, "The Mediation of Technology and Gender: *Metropolis*, Nazism, Modernism," in *New German Critique* 60 (fall 1993): 3–32.

9. See Russell A. Berman, *Enlightenment or Empire: Colonial Discourse in German Culture* (Lincoln: University of Nebraska Press, 1998), 66, 104.

10. Susan M. White, *The Cinema of Max Ophuls: Magisterial Vision and the Figure of Woman* (New York: Columbia University Press, 1995), 11.

11. Jon Halliday, *Sirk on Sirk: Conversations with Jon Halliday*, rev. ed. (London: Faber and Faber, 1997), 69–70.

12. Peter Brooks, *The Melodramatic Imagination: Balzac, Henry James, Melodrama, and the Mode of Excess*, 2d ed. (New Haven, Conn.: Yale University Press, 1995).

13. For more on churches in Sirk's films see Jan-Christopher Horak, "Sirk's Early Exile Films: *Boeffie* and *Hitler's Madman*," *Film Criticism* 23, nos. 2–3 (winter/spring 1999): 122–135.

14. Halliday, *Sirk on Sirk*, 95.

15. Dave Grosz, "*The First Legion:* Vision and Perception in Sirk," *Screen* 12, no. 2 (summer 1971): 108–109.

16. Guy Debord, *Society of the Spectacle* (Detroit: Black and Red, 1983), 29 (Debord's italics).

17. For a very detailed sequence description see Grosz, "*The First Legion*," 115.

18. Halliday, *Sirk on Sirk*, 110.

19. Richard Wagner, "Religion and Art," in *Prose Works*, trans. William Ashton Ellis (1897; reprint, New York: Broude Brothers, 1966), 6:213.

20. Richard K. Lieberman, *Steinway and Sons* (New Haven, Conn.: Yale University Press, 1995), 241–242.

21. Arthur Loesser, *Men, Women, and Pianos: A Social History* (London: Gollancz, 1955), 613.

22. "In every sizable American city the mid-century German musicians persisted in their missionary work and soon converted many an exceptional American of the older stock to the enjoyment of the greater instrumental literature, to the gospel according to the Saints Beethoven and Mozart and Saints Schumann, Chopin, and Mendelssohn" (Loesser, *Men, Women, and Pianos*, 537).

23. On Dietrich's masochist screen personae see Gaylyn Studlar, *In the Realm of Pleasure: Von Sternberg, Dietrich, and the Masochistic Aesthetic* (New York: Columbia University Press, 1988).

24. Lang's preoccupation with the western reached back to his tenure at UFA in the 1920s. In the second part of *The Nibelungen* (1924–1925) Lang for instance pictured Attila's Huns as if borrowed directly from Hollywood frontier features: their tents look like Indian tepees; their hairdos and makeup resemble those conventionally reserved for Native Americans. Lang's personal

library, as Patrick McGilligan details, included a great number of well-thumbed western novels by Max Brand, Eugene Cunningham, Zane Grey, and Ernest Haycox. See Patrick McGilligan, *Fritz Lang: The Nature of the Beast* (New York: St. Martin's, 1997), 383.

25. Schatz, *Boom and Bust*, 371.

26. Produced by Fidelity Pictures, a subdivision of Howard Hughes's RKO, the final cut of *Rancho Notorious* clearly diverged from Lang's original designs. Irritated by Lang's personal and professional agendas, producer Howard Welsch banned his director from the editing room and recut the film according to more conventional expectations. Welsch slimmed down the film from 105 to 89 minutes, reconfigured the ending, and changed the project title from "Chuck-a-Luck" to *Rancho Notorious*.

27. Bertolt Brecht, *Arbeitsjournal*, ed. Werner Hecht (Frankfurt / M.: Suhrkamp, 1973), 1:291.

28. For more on the polyphonic texture of *Kuhle Wampe* see Bruce A. Murray, *Film and the German Left in the Weimar Republic: From "Caligari" to "Kuhle Wampe"* (Austin: University of Texas Press, 1990); and Marc Silberman, *German Cinema: Texts in Contexts* (Detroit: Wayne State University Press, 1995), 34–48.

29. Theodor Adorno and Hanns Eisler, *Composing for the Films* (London: Athlone Press, 1994), 25.

30. For more on the politics of corporeality and representation in *Hangmen Also Die*, see Jean Louis Comolli and Francois Géré, "Two Fictions Concerning Hate," *Fritz Lang: The Image and the Look*, ed. Stephen Jenkins (London: BFI, 1981) 125–146.

31. Sergei Eisenstein, *Film Form: Essays in Film Theory*, ed. and trans. Jay Leyda (San Diego: Harcourt Brace Jovanovich, 1977), 257–260.

32. Adorno and Eisler, *Composing for the Films*, 78–79.

33. See Peter Bürger, *Theory of the Avant-Garde*, trans. Michael Shaw (Minneapolis: University of Minnesota Press, 1984). For a critique of Bürger's model see Russell A. Berman, *Modern Culture and Critical Theory: Art, Politics, and the Legacy of the Frankfurt School* (Madison: University of Wisconsin Press, 1989), 42–53; Franz Dröge and Michael Müller, *Die Macht der Schönheit: Avantgarde und Faschismus oder Die Geburt der Massenkultur* (Hamburg: Europäische Verlagsanstalt, 1995); and Lutz Koepnick, *Walter Benjamin and the Aesthetics of Power* (Lincoln: University of Nebraska Press, 1999), 1–26.

34. Martin Jay, *Cultural Semantics: Keywords of Our Time* (Amherst: University of Massachusetts Press, 1998), 93.

35. Michel Chion, *Audio-Vision: Sound on Screen*, ed. and trans. Claudia Gorbman (New York: Columbia University Press, 1994), 38.

36. Gerd Gemünden, *Framed Visions: Popular Culture, Americanization, and the Contemporary German and Austrian Imagination* (Ann Arbor: University of Michigan Press, 1998), 14. For more on the figure of America in German literature see Sigrid Bauschinger, Horst Denkler, and Wilfried Malsch,

eds., *Amerika in der deutschen Literatur: Neue Welt—Nordamerika—USA* (Stuttgart: Reclam, 1975); Manfred Durzak, *Das Amerikabild in der deutschen Gegenwartsliteratur* (Stuttgart: Kohlhammer, 1979); Heinz D. Osterle, ed., *Amerika! New Images in German Literature* (New York: Lang, 1989); and Dan Diner, *America in the Eyes of the Germans: An Essay on Anti-Americanism*, trans. Allison Brown (Princeton: Markus Wiener Publishers, 1996).

37. Reinhold Wagnleiter, *Coca-Colonization and the Cold War: The Cultural Mission of the United States in Austria after the Second World War*, trans. Diana M. Wolf (Chapel Hill: University of North Carolina Press, 1994). See also Ralph Willet, *The Americanization of Germany, 1945–1949* (London: Routledge, 1989); and Reiner Pommerin, ed., *The American Impact on Postwar Germany* (Providence: Berghahn, 1995).

38. Joseph Garncarz, "Hollywood in Germany: The Role of American Films in Germany, 1925–1990," in *Hollywood in Europe: Experiences of a Cultural Hegemony*, ed. David W. Ellwood and Rob Kroes (Amsterdam: VU University Press, 1994), 124–125.

39. For more on "Altar" see Steven Bach, *Marlene Dietrich: Life and Legend* (New York: Morrow, 1992), 354.

40. Wolf, "Die Gejagten," *Abendzeitung*, October 6, 1960.

41. Ibid.

42. Heide Fehrenbach, *Cinema in Democratizing Germany: Reconstructing National Identity after Hitler* (Chapel Hill: University of North Carolina Press, 1995), 255.

43. On Lang's use of allegory see Tom Gunning, *The Films of Fritz Lang: Allegories of Vision and Modernity* (London: BFI, 2000), 1–11.

44. L. L. Matthias, *Die Entdeckung Amerikas Anno 1953, oder Das geordnete Chaos* (Hamburg: Rowohlt, 1953), 120–121.

45. Martin Ruppert, "Die erste Legion," *Frankfurter Allgemeine Zeitung*, January 14, 1956.

46. Jeanette Meith, "Neuer Film: 'Die Beichte eines Arztes,'" *Abendpost*, January 17, 1956.

47. Gerhard Bliersbach, *So grün war die Heide . . . Die gar nicht so heile Welt im Nachkriegsfilm* (Weinheim: Beltz, 1989), 111–140.

48. Ruppert, "Die erste Legion."

49. Thomas Elsaesser, *Fassbinder's Germany: History, Identity, Subject* (Amsterdam: Amsterdam University Press, 1996), 58. For Sirk's influence on Fassbinder see Judith Mayne, "Fassbinder and Spectatorship," in *New German Critique* 12 (fall 1977): 61–74; Andrew Sarris, "Fassbinder and Sirk: The Ties That Unbind," *Village Voice*, September 3, 1980; Eric Rentschler, *West German Film in the Course of Time* (Bedford Hills: Redgrave, 1984), 191–202; Timothy Corrigan, *New German Film: The Displaced Image*, rev. ed. (Bloomington: Indiana University Press, 1994), 33–54; Gemünden, *Framed Visions*, 89–107; and, of course, Rainer Werner Fassbinder, "Six Films by Douglas Sirk," in *Douglas Sirk*, ed. Laura Mulvey and Jon Halliday (Edinburgh: Edinburgh Film Festival, 1972), 95–107.

50. Barbara Klinger, *Melodrama and Meaning: History, Culture, and the Films of Douglas Sirk* (Bloomington: Indiana University Press, 1994), 66–67.

51. For a more recent version of this argument see Amy Lawrence, "Trapped in a Tomb of Their Own Making: Max Ophuls's *The Reckless Moment* and Douglas Sirk's *There's Always Tomorrow*," *Film Criticism* 23, nos. 2–3 (winter/ spring 1999): 150–166.

52. Theodor W. Adorno, *Aesthetic Theory*, trans. C. Lenhard (London: Routledge and Kegan Paul, 1984), 18.

CHAPTER 8. ISOLDE RESURRECTED

1. Andreas Huyssen, *After the Great Divide: Modernism, Mass Culture, Postmodernism* (Bloomington: Indiana University Press, 1986), 16.

2. "$30 Billion for Fun," *The Changing American Market* (New York: Fortune, 1955); qtd. in John Belton, *Widescreen Cinema* (Cambridge, Mass.: Harvard University Press, 1992), 77.

3. Belton, *Widescreen Cinema*, 84.

4. Fredric Jameson, *The Political Unconscious: Narrative as a Socially Symbolic Act* (Ithaca, N.Y.: Cornell University Press, 1981), 218.

5. Fredric Jameson, *Postmodernism, or, The Cultural Logic of Late Capitalism* (Durham, N.C.: Duke University Press, 1991).

6. Max Horkheimer and Theodor W. Adorno, *Dialectic of Enlightenment*, trans. John Cumming (New York: Continuum, 1995), 135.

7. See Marjorie Lawrence, *Interrupted Melody* (New York: Appleton, 1949).

8. Norbert Grob, "Interrupted Melody," in *Aufruhr der Gefühle: Die Kinowelt des Curtis Bernhardt*, ed. Helga Belach, Gero Gandert, and Hans Helmut Prinzler (Munich: Bucher, 1982), 215.

9. Belton, *Widescreen Cinema*, 137.

10. On the impact of tape editing and multiple-track recording on postwar music production see Michael Chanan, *Musica Practica: The Social Practice of Western Music from Gregorian Chant to Postmodernism* (London: Verso, 1994), 250–289.

11. "I was a perfect symbol for the two cultures," Bernhardt recalled in 1977, "of two differing sensibilities" (Mary Kiersch, *Curtis Bernhardt: A Directors Guild of America Oral History* [Metuchen, N.J.: Scarecrow Press, 1986], 78).

12. Peter Brooks, *The Melodramatic Imagination: Balzac, Henry James, Melodrama, and the Mode of Excess*, 2d ed. (New Haven, Conn.: Yale University Press, 1995), 41.

13. Kiersch, *Curtis Bernhardt*, 172.

14. Amy Lawrence, *Echo and Narcissus: Women's Voices in Classical Hollywood Cinema* (Berkeley: University of California Press, 1991), 154.

15. Kiersch, *Curtis Bernhardt*, 173.

16. Kaja Silverman, *The Acoustic Mirror: The Female Voice in Psychoanalysis and Cinema* (Bloomington: Indiana University Press, 1988), 1.

17. Carl Dahlhaus, *Nineteenth-Century Music*, trans. Bradford Robinson (Berkeley: University of California Press, 1989), 289.

18. Richard Wagner, *Twilight of the Gods. Götterdämmerung*, trans. Andrew Porter (London: Calder, 1985), 124.

19. Russell A. Berman, *The Rise of the Modern German Novel: Crisis and Charisma* (Cambridge, Mass.: Harvard University Press, 1986).

20. Richard Wagner, *Die Musikdramen* (Munich: Deutscher Taschenbuch Verlag, 1978), 383. The English translation that follows in the text is from Andrew Porter, trans., *Tristan and Isolde*, by Richard Wagner (London: Calder, 1981), 91–92.

21. Wagner, *Die Musikdramen*, 384; translation is from Porter, *Tristan and Isolde*, 92.

22. Friedrich Nietzsche, *The Birth of Tragedy and the Case of Wagner*, trans. Walter Kaufmann (New York: Vintage, 1967), 155.

23. Leslie A. Adelson, *Making Bodies, Making History: Feminism and German Identity* (Lincoln: University of Nebraska Press, 1993), 22.

24. Michel Ciment, ed., *Kazan on Kazan* (New York: Viking, 1974), 122–123; qtd. in David Bordwell, *On the History of Film Style* (Cambridge, Mass.: Harvard University Press, 1997), 239.

25. Bordwell, *History of Film Style*, 239.

26. Kiersch, *Curtis Bernhardt*, 169.

27. Grob, "Interrupted Melody," 215.

28. Herbert Lindenberger, *Opera: The Extravagant Art* (Ithaca, N.Y.: Cornell University Press, 1984), 17.

29. Deniz Göktürk, *Künstler, Cowboys, Ingenieure . . . Kultur- und mediengeschichtliche Studien zu deutschen Amerika-Texten, 1912–1920* (Munich: Fink, 1998), 11–16.

30. Belton, *Widescreen Cinema*, 187.

31. Michel de Certeau, *The Practice of Everyday Life*, trans. Steven Rendall (Berkeley: University of California Press, 1984), 165–177.

32. Gerhard Schulze, *Die Erlebnisgesellschaft: Kultursoziologie der Gegenwart* (Frankfurt / M.: Campus, 1992).

33. Theodor W. Adorno, "Prolog zum Fernsehen," in *Eingriffe: Neun kritische Modelle* (Frankfurt / M.: Suhrkamp, 1963), 69–80.

34. Edgar Reitz, *Bilder in Bewegung: Essays. Gespräche zum Kino* (Reinbek: Rowohlt, 1995), 135.

35. Leslie Fiedler, "Cross the Border—Close the Gap," in *The Collected Essays of Leslie Fiedler* (New York: Stein and Day, 1971), 2:468.

36. Jim Collins, *Architectures of Excess: Cultural Life in the Information Age* (New York: Routledge, 1995), 25 (Collins's italics).

37. Volker Schlöndorff, "Vorwort," in Felix Moeller, *Der Filmminister: Goebbels und der Film im Dritten Reich* (Berlin: Henschel, 1998), 11.

38. Robert Müller, "Der Roman des Amerikanismus," *Saturn* 3, no. 9 (September 1913): 253–258; qtd. in Göktürk, *Künstler, Cowboys, Ingenieure*, 211.

39. "Unterbrochene Melodie," *Katholischer Film-Dienst*, March 1, 1956.

40. Edmund Luft, "Lebenswille: 'Unterbrochene Melodie,'" *Filmblätter*, November 11, 1955.

41. Fr., "'Unterbrochene Melodie,'" *Evangelischer Film-Beobachter*, November 17, 1955.

42. Ibid.

43. Wolfgang Staudte, "Eine Antwort: Auf die Frage, Deutscher Film—wohin?" *Staudte*, ed. Eva Orbanz and Hans Helmut Prinzler (Berlin: Spiess, 1991), 158; qtd. in Heide Fehrenbach, *Cinema in Democratizing Germany: Reconstructing National Identity after Hitler* (Chapel Hill: University of North Carolina Press, 1995), 209.

44. On the history and mission of German film clubs during the 1950s see Fehrenbach, *Cinema in Democratizing Germany*, 169–210.

45. Volker Baer, "Unbekanntes Emigrationskino," *Der Tagesspiegel*, February 14, 1982.

46. Angelika Bammer, introduction to *Displacements: Cultural Identities in Question*, ed. Angelika Bammer (Bloomington: Indiana University Press, 1994), xi–xx.

47. Fredric Jameson, "Modernism and Imperialism," in *Nationalism, Colonialism, and Literature*, ed. Terry Eagleton, Fredric Jameson, and Edward Said (Minneapolis: University of Minnesota Press, 1990), 43–66.

48. Salman Rushdie, *Imaginary Homelands: Essays and Criticism, 1981–1991* (New York: Viking, 1991), 13; qtd. in Bammer, *Displacements*, xii.

49. John E. Davidson, *Deterritorializing the New German Cinema* (Minneapolis: University of Minnesota Press, 1999), 52.

50. Kiersch, *Curtis Bernhardt*, 123.

EPILOGUE

1. Theodor W. Adorno, *Minima Moralia: Reflections from Damaged Life*, trans. E. F. N. Jephcott (London: New Left Books, 1951), 38–39.

2. Walter Benjamin, *Illuminations: Essays and Reflections*, trans. Harry Zohn (New York: Schocken, 1969), 236.

3. Angelika Bammer, introduction to *Displacements: Cultural Identities in Question*, ed. Angelika Bammer (Bloomington: Indiana University Press, 1994), xiii.

4. Russell A. Berman, *Enlightenment or Empire: Colonial Discourse in German Culture* (Lincoln: University of Nebraska Press, 1998), 219.

5. Iain Chambers, *Migrancy, Culture, Identity* (London: Routledge, 1994), 50; qtd. in Anton Kaes, "Leaving Home: Film, Migration, and the Urban Experience," *New German Critique* 74 (spring/summer 1998): 191.

6. Jan Dawson, *Wim Wenders*, trans. Carla Wartenberg (New York: Zoetrope, 1976), 12.

7. Werner Herzog, "Tribute to Lotte Eisner (1982)," in *West German Filmmakers on Film: Visions and Voices*, ed. Eric Rentschler (New York: Holmes and Meier, 1988), 117.

8. Eric Rentschler, "How American Is It? The U.S. as Image and Imaginary in German Film," *Persistence of Vision* 2 (1985): 13.

9. Thomas Elsaesser, "German Postwar Cinema and Hollywood," in *Hollywood in Europe: Experiences of a Cultural Hegemony*, ed. David W. Ellwood and Rob Kroes (Amsterdam: VU University Press, 1994), 283–302; see also Thomas Elsaesser, *New German Cinema: A History* (New Brunswick, N.J.: Rutgers University Press, 1989).

10. Elsaesser, "German Postwar Cinema and Hollywood," 297.

11. John E. Davidson, *Deterritorializing the New German Cinema* (Minneapolis: University of Minnesota Press, 1999), 35–64.

12. "Das Kinojahr 1998," *FFA Intern*, February 10, 1999, 7; "Das Kinojahr 1999," *FFA Intern*, February 10, 2000, 9.

13. Gerd Gemünden, *Framed Visions: Popular Culture, Americanization, and the Contemporary German and Austrian Imagination* (Ann Arbor: University of Michigan Press, 1998), 212–213.

14. On the heritage film see Andrew Higson, "Re-presenting the National Past: Nostalgia and Pastiche in the Heritage Film," in *Fires Were Started: British Cinema and Thatcherism*, ed. Lester Friedman (Minneapolis: University of Minnesota Press, 1993), 109–129; and Ginette Vincendeau, "Issues in European Cinema," in *The Oxford Guide to Film Studies*, ed. John Hill and Pamela Church Gibson (Oxford: Oxford University Press, 1998), 440–448.

15. Jürgen Habermas, *Die Normalität einer Berliner Republik* (Frankfurt/M.: Suhrkamp, 1995).

16. For a more thorough reading of *Comedian Harmonists* and its ideological project see Lutz Koepnick, "'Honor Your German Masters': History, Memory, and National Identity in Joseph Vilsmaier's *Comedian Harmonists*," in *Light Motives: German Popular Film in Perspective*, ed. Maggie McCarthy and Randall Halle (Detroit: Wayne State University Press, forthcoming).

17. See, e.g., the various contributions to *Die selbstbewußte Nation: "Anschwellender Bocksgesang" und weitere Beiträge zu einer deutschen Debatte*, ed. Heimo Schwilk and Ulrich Schacht (Berlin: Ullstein, 1995).

18. Wim Wenders, "Talking about Germany," in *The Cinema of Wim Wenders: Image, Narrative, and the Postmodern Condition*, ed. Roger F. Cook and Gerd Gemünden (Detroit: Wayne State University Press, 1996), 59.

19. Released on December 25, 1997, *Comedian Harmonists* attracted a total of 2.8 million viewers to German cinemas. It was by far the most successful domestic production at German box offices in 1998. "Das Kinojahr 1998," *FFA Intern*, February 10, 1999, 8.

20. William J. Mitchell, *The Reconfigured Eye: Visual Truth in the Post-Photographic Era* (Cambridge, Mass.: MIT Press, 1994). On Wenders's response to the visual revolutions of the 1990s see Nora M. Alter, "Documentary as Simulacrum: *Tokyo-Ga*," in *The Cinema of Wim Wenders: Image, Narrative, and the Postmodern Condition*, ed. Roger F. Cook and Gerd Gemünden (Detroit: Wayne State University Press, 1996), 136–162.

21. Ry Cooder, *Buena Vista Social Club*, Nonesuch Records 79478–2, 1997.

Index

Page numbers in *italic* type indicate illustrations.

Compositor: G & S Typesetters, Inc.
Text: 10/13 Aldus
Display: Aldus
Printer and binder: Malloy Lithographing, Inc.